For Alexandra

THE WELFARE STATE QUIZ

Most people think they know a lot about the welfare state. After all, they live in it. But try this quiz to discover how good your knowledge really is. Answers and your rating at the end.

1. When did the state first make education compulsory?
a) 1870 b) 1930 c) 1944 d) 1948

2. In the mid-nineteenth century – before state schooling was introduced – how many children had five to seven years' education?
a) 5% b) 12% c) 32% d) 95%

3. When was the law passed making free elementary education available for all?
a) 1918 b) 1925 c) 1944 d) 1948

4. David Lloyd George was brought up in modest circumstances in a remote part of Wales in the nineteenth century and went to a charity-based school. When he left, aged 14, was he...
a) unable to read or write b) able to read, but not to write c) able to read and write but otherwise uneducated d) literate and widely read?

5. After many decades of state education, what is now the rate of 'functional illiteracy' among adults?
a) 1% b) 3% c) 10% d) 25%

6. When was national health insurance started?
a) 1911 b) 1924 c) 1942 d) 1948

7. Which minister founded the NHS?
a) R. A. Butler b) Ernest Bevin c) Aneurin Bevan d) Harold Wilson

8. Penicillin was probably Britain's greatest contribution to world medicine in the twentieth century. Who funded the research which led to it?

First published in Great Britain 2004
This paperback edition published 2006 by
Politico's Publishing, an imprint of
Methuen Publishing Limited
11–12 Buckingham Gate
London
SW1E 6LB

Reprinted with corrections 2006

3 5 7 9 10 8 6 4 2

Copyright © James Bartholomew 2004

James Bartholomew has asserted his rights under the Copyright, Design & Patents Act, 1988, to be identified as the author of this work.

A CIP catalogue record for this book is available from the British Library.

ISBN-10: 1 84275 161 1
ISBN-13: 978-1-84275-161-9

Printed and bound in Great Britain by St. Edmundsbury Press, Bury St. Edmunds, Suffolk.

a) the NHS b) a special fund set up in 1942 by the wartime coalition government   c) the Medical Research Council   d) mainly charitable donors

9. How many of London's famous teaching hospitals were created by the NHS?
a) none b) one c) two d) four

10. Who founded St Bartholomew's Hospital?
a) the NHS b) London County Council c) the Greater London Council d) a twelfth-century friar

11. According to Professor Karol Sikora, how many people a year die in Britain because the NHS's treatment of cancer is inferior to the average of other advanced European countries?
a) 100 b) 1,000 c) 3,000 d) 10,000

12. According to the OECD, which country has the lowest number of doctors per thousand population in the advanced world?
a) Spain b) Switzerland c) Britain d) Finland

13. When the did the British government first pass a law compelling the rich to hand over money for the benefit of the poor?
a) 1563 b) 1870 c) 1911 d) 1948

14. How many of the seven million men working in industry in 1892 were members of a friendly society?
a) 500,000 b) one million c) three million d) six million

15. Who said: 'The minister who will apply to this country the successful experiences of Germany in social organisation ... will ... have left a memorial which time will not deface.'?
a) Otto von Bismarck   b) David Lloyd George
c) Winston Churchill d) Clement Attlee

16. Which minister created the first national unemployment insurance scheme in the world?
a) Martin von Stockhausen in Germany in 1881 b) Winston Churchill

in 1911 c) Leon Trotsky in the Soviet Union in 1921 d) Aneurin Bevan in 1946

17. By how much did per capita Gross Domestic Product increase between 1950 and 2000?
a) 33%   b) 62%   c) 95%   d) 165%

18. Bearing in mind the rise in prosperity, how did the proportion of people in receipt of welfare benefits change between 1950 and 2001?
a) down from 25% to 5.3%   b) down from 25% to 15%   c) unchanged at 17%   d) up from 3.4% to 24%

19. Who said: 'I want to achieve what in fifty years of the welfare state has never been achieved: the end of the means test for our elderly people.'?
a) Barbara Castle in 1975   b) Peter Lilley in 1993   c) Gordon Brown in 1993   d) Frank Field in 1997

20. What proportion of pensioners were estimated to be entitled to means-tested benefits in 2003?
a) 5%   b) 11%   c) 32%   d) 57%

21. What happened to three ten-storey council blocks of flats in Birkenhead in 1979?
a) they were given the Queen's Award for design   b) the lifts stopped working   c) they were deemed a health hazard   d) they were blown up

22. How many violent crimes took place in 2002/3 compared to 1898?
a) 40% fewer   b) 5% fewer   c) 200% more   d) 12,800% more

23. In 1938/9 3.8 million people paid income tax. How many paid it in 2003/4?
a) 5.2 million   b) 9.3 million   c) 23.2 million   d) 30.7 million

24. In 1913, Britain was fourth in an international league table of economic output per capita. Where did it come in 1999?
a) 4th   b) 8th   c) 12th   d) 17th

25. Who said: 'In a totalitarian state or in a field already made into a state monopoly, those dissatisfied with the institutions that they find can seek a remedy only by seeking to change the government of the country. In a free society and a free field they have a different remedy: discontented individuals with new ideas can make a new institution to meet their needs.'?

a) Friederich von Hayek b) Milton Friedman c) Margaret Thatcher d) Lord Beveridge

26. Which famous writer said: 'An imaginary foreign observer would certainly be struck by our gentleness; by the orderly behaviour of English crowds, the lack of pushing and quarrelling ... And except for certain well-defined areas in half-a-dozen big towns, there is very little crime or violence.'?
a) George Orwell in 1944 b) Evelyn Waugh in 1965 c) Kingsley Amis in 1980 d) Harold Pinter in 2002

Answers: 1 a; 2 d; 3 a; 4 d; 5 d; 6 a; 7 c; 8 d (they included the Rockefeller Foundation and those who had donated money to St Mary's Hospital and Oxford University); 9 a; 10 d (see the NHS chapter for the remarkable story); 11 d; 12 c; 13 a; 14 d; 15 c (writing to Asquith in 1909); 16 b; 17 d; 18 d; 19 c; 20 d; 21 d; 22 d;[1] 23 d (before the welfare state mushroomed in cost, only the rich paid income tax. Now the poor pay – see the chapter on tax and economic growth); 24 d; 25 d (Lord Beveridge is generally treated as though he created the modern welfare state. But as this quotation shows, he never wanted the welfare state to be monopolistic, which is what happened); 26 a.

Score one point for every correct answer.
Ratings: 1–8 You may live in the welfare state but there are important gaps in your knowledge about it – good reason for you to read this book. 8–18 You have real interest in and knowledge about the welfare state. But you could improve your understanding further by reading this book. 19–26 Your knowledge is impressive. But do you know who Sir John Cowperthwaite is, what Martin Luther said about social security and what Cary Grant has got to do with the NHS? If not, there may still be things of interest in this book, even to you.

THE WELFARE STATE – SOME OF THE MAJOR DATES

1536–47 The monasteries – major benefactors of the poor – are expropriated by Henry VIII.

1563 Queen Elizabeth's government compels the rich to give money for the benefit of the poor.

1601 The Poor Laws become settled (after many previous changes).

1795 Meeting in Speenhamland – leading to means-tested welfare benefits based on 'needs' and paid outside the workhouse.

1834 Royal Commission on Poor Laws leads to reduction of benefits outside the workhouse.

1870 Education is made compulsory.

1908 State pension is created.

1911 State health insurance begins (but is intended to run alongside private insurance).

1911 State unemployment insurance is created for 2.4 million people (but is intended not to damage the friendly societies).

1942 Beveridge Report published and all leading parties endorse it.

1944 R. A. Butler's Education Act leads to state control over most church schools and increases the years of compulsory education.

1945 Government embarks on building five million houses in 'quick time'.

1946 Unemployment insurance is extended to all workers. State pensions are combined with the scheme.

1948 The state takes over hospitals to create the National Health Service.

1967 Rate rebates are introduced. Government encourages local authorities to give council rent rebates.

1972 Rent rebates are made mandatory nationwide. Rent allowances are created for private tenancies. (These later become housing benefit.)

1970–72 Invalidity benefit developed.

PREFACE
Growing up with the welfare state

I was brought up with the welfare state. When I was about eight, I was suddenly taken ill with suspected appendicitis. An ambulance rushed to our home in Belsize Park, London, its bell ringing, and I was loaded into it on a stretcher, to be taken to the Royal Free Hospital.

There was no room in the children's ward, so I was put in a men's ward. I still remember it. The grown men and myself – the one boy – lay in beds in two long rows. The ward had plenty of windows, so it was bright and airy. The beds had crisp white sheets, made up by a small army of smartly dressed nurses. The men flirted with the nurses. I don't think I had ever witnessed such a thing before, so I was fascinated. As for the hospital, there seemed no question but that it was efficiently run and all was well with the welfare state world.

Only gradually, over many years, did I begin to have doubts about the welfare state. Many events, people and books chipped away at my early assumption that the welfare state was a 'good thing'. My times in Hong Kong and then travelling through its economic opposite – the Soviet Union – had their influence.

Jumping ahead to the early 1990s, I was a leader-writer at the *Daily Mail*. The normal practice, at least in those days, was for the leader-writer of the day to attend the morning news conference. One day I sat down, as usual, with my A4 pad of paper on which I had jotted down a few ideas for editorials. I cannot remember the details, but the news editor's list that day was particularly grim. The normal diet of vileness that reaches a newspaper office is always richer than the public knows. There is so much unpleasantness that editors filter it out. If they printed all the horrors, people would change to another paper offering less depressing fare. Paul Dacre, the editor of the *Daily Mail*, used to demand of his news editor, 'Get me something light!'

But on this particular day, the diet of murders, rapes, senseless violence, incivility, unmarried parenting, poor educational standards and hospital waiting lists was particularly heavy. Among the stories there was, I think, the rape and murder of a very old woman. A few pounds had been stolen from her. It was depressing.

When the conference finished, the news team left, leaving Paul Dacre, his number three, Peter Wright (now editor of the *Mail on Sunday*) and myself. Normally the editor would stay behind his ample desk to discuss the leaders. This time he came around to join us. He slumped down on a sofa, put his face in his hands for a moment, then sat back with a despairing sigh. Instead of discussing leaders, he exclaimed: 'What has happened to this country? It wasn't like this when we were growing up, was it? It isn't that we just have a rosy view of the past, is it? It is so depressing! What's happened?'

We did not need to ask what he meant.

I had been writing repeatedly about all these things and more as a leader-writer. Many correspondents specialise in crime or health or something else. But a leader-writer for the *Daily Mail* has to consider everything – from foreign wars to soccer hooliganism. When Paul Dacre asked 'what happened?', although the idea was only half formed, I hesitantly replied: 'The welfare state'.

There was a silence in the room for a while. It seemed almost a sacrilege to suggest such a thing. All three of us, I suspect, had been brought up to think the welfare state was Britain's crowning peacetime achievement. Surely this was the thing which had brought peace of mind and security to millions of people? It had brought education to all. It had brought healthcare 'free at the point of delivery'. Even a drunk whose life was in tatters would be looked after by the welfare state. It was decent and kind. Could this well-loved institution possibly be the cause of the unwelcome changes in Britain?

I do not know how far Paul Dacre was persuaded. He did, though, commission me to write an article – under Peter Wright's careful supervision. Even modest criticisms were considered at the time as sensitive. The article certainly did not appear as an editorial, indicating that it was the view of the newspaper, but only under my own name, which meant it could be dismissed as the wild view of a maverick.

That first article went in the paper on 30 March 1993 with the headline: 'Is the Welfare State destroying Britain?'. It was followed by half a dozen more on related subjects. Of course I was not the first to suggest that the welfare state had damaged society. Others had gone before and far further – in America and in various think tank studies in Britain. But this was at, or near, the beginning of the time when such thoughts were expressed in the British popular press.

I have since thought a great deal about the reply I gave that day in

1993. Was it justified? Could such terrible things as the murder and rape of an old woman really be linked with such an idealistic thing as the welfare state? By what route could the connection be made? Did it stand up to examination?

And what would there be to look after the poor and the weak without the welfare state? Had there been anything there before the welfare state existed? I would not want to condemn people to Dickensian misery. I would not want to make a 'better' society if it meant people being left uneducated, untreated in illness, hungry and without shelter.

The first issue, though, was to establish whether the premise was true. Has Britain really changed a great deal since the 1950s and before? Is it so much worse? Idealising the 1950s as a 'golden age' is likely to get an immediate, scornful response. We think of rationing and rather strait-laced people leading drab lives. No one would want to go back to that. How has Britain really changed since the mid-century and before? Is there more crime? Are people less decent? Has Britain genuinely suffered some sort of fall from grace?

Preface to the paperback edition

When this book was first published, reaction varied from scornful condemnation to enthusiastic praise. One reaction, though, was notable for its rarity: only occasionally did anyone maintain that the welfare state has been a great success.

State welfare is like a religion in which belief is weakening. This religion is still respected. People go to its churches. They bow their heads and sing the hymns. They are shocked if anyone behaves disrespectfully. But in their hearts, they no longer believe it is marvellous or that it has succeeded in what it was meant to do.

Evidence of low educational standards, inferior healthcare and social breakdown keeps on building up. Few now express the passion of certain founders of the welfare state such as Nye Bevan and Clement Attlee. Attlee's talk of a 'New Jerusalem' has gone. Instead, the best that most people can manage is: 'With one more heave here, a bit of reform there and, of course, more cash, it should be all right.'

It is a reflection of changed attitudes that I was allowed to present my case on BBC Radio 4 for forty-five 'prime time' minutes at the end of 2005. Ten years before, BBC executives would have thought the arguments in this book too far beyond the pale to be allowed on air. Now these views are only considered 'controversial'. Maybe one day they will be conventional wisdom.

As with religion, there are probably many people who hush their doubts because they want to believe. They find it comforting. Supporting the welfare state makes some people feel that they have demonstrated that they care about the poor and needy – even though this system is one which, in fact, is particularly damaging to those very people. There is also a fear of not believing. People are uncertain about what could take the place of large-scale state welfare. They are not sure how it could be 'downsized' without hurting people.

So we are in a transitional phase – a period in which belief has been dented but people don't like to admit it and don't like to look at the evidence. Politicians still think – and with reason – that they can achieve power only by continuing to bow to the altar of the welfare state. They continue to do so even when, as with Tony Blair, it is clear that they have actually given up on the old, wholly state-run model, at least.

Things will therefore have to get worse before they get better – before radical reform takes place. Democracies are susceptible to the superficial appeal of state welfare. That is not to say that reform within democracies is impossible or that people are not capable of seeing through that surface appeal. The United States launched a radical programme of welfare benefits reform in 1996. This helped to bring the national benefits caseload down 60 per cent by June 2002. Sweden, which is traditionally thought of as having the most thoroughgoing of welfare states, has introduced education vouchers and, as described in Chapter 3, has allowed a large element of commercial enterprise in healthcare in Stockholm.

So far, though, the British public and body politic have not shown the will to go anything like as far. Britain arguably had its chance when Blair was first elected in a surge of popularity, but the country – or, perhaps, he – did not take it.

For the time being, therefore, the moral and cultural decline of Britain is likely to continue. Our healthcare will continue to lag behind the standards of other advanced countries. Crime will continue to rise. Drinking and drug-taking will continue to increase. The streets will continue to become less safe. Taxes will remain high or go even higher – damaging our economic performance. Along with much of the rest of Europe, we will continue to decline economically compared to other parts of the world.

As long as Britain remains a nation in denial about the true nature of its welfare state, the troubling question is how bad things need to get before the electorate is ready for change. If, in ten, twenty or thirty years, the streets become really dangerous, incivility is everywhere evident and poor educational levels are inescapably obvious, what will happen then? Will the voters finally accept radical steps? I hope there will be a change of heart before such a dire situation is reached.

There is no need for us to get to that stage. But to avoid it, the country needs to face the reality described in this book. And then move decisively.

Contents

1. From Stanley Matthews to Vinnie Jones   1

Has the character of the British people changed? What did Orwell make of us in the 1940s? And what do the number of red cards issued in football matches tell us about attitudes today? How Willie was treated compared to Vinnie.

2. Social security: Catherine's four dead boys and Frank's bingo blow-out   25

What did Catherine of Aragon have to do with the origins of the welfare state? The reason Frank Stent spent his windfall instead of saving. What *The Full Monty* tells us about living without a job. Do welfare benefits cause unemployment?

3. The NHS: like a train crash every day   87

Healthcare before the NHS. Did the poor get any? Aneurin Bevan, rebel with a cause, who created the NHS on Marxist principles. Does the NHS do what was promised? In which advanced country do you not want to be ill? The cost of the NHS in lives lost.

4. Education: eleven years at school and still illiterate   151

Did the poor get any education before the state took over? The unlikely man who began the state monopoly and who had nothing like that in mind. Has state education given better chances to the less well off? How state education contributes to incivility and crime.

The website, www.thewelfarestatewerein.com, has supplementary material, photographs, links, debate and the opportunity to e-mail the author.

CHAPTER 1
From Stanley Matthews to Vinnie Jones

There have certainly been changes for the better in the past fifty, sixty years and more.

Our average wealth has much increased. This new wealth gives us freedom to drive where we like, go on holiday abroad and take longer holidays. Fifty years ago, even senior management worked on Saturday mornings and most people had holidays of two weeks or less. Now nine out of ten people have a holiday entitlement of four weeks or more.[1] There are more and better restaurants. The contraceptive pill has helped to make sex between unmarried people commonplace, suggesting increased physical pleasure, whatever the emotional and other effects may be. People are less constricted. These can all be held out as improvements in the quality of our lives.

But what else has changed? What are British people like now and how does that compare with how they used to be? It is the most profound question you can ask about a country and one of the most difficult to answer.

I will offer some objective ways of gauging how we have changed later on. But first, here are some images of the British, past and present.

Were the British really like that?

Professor Geoffrey Gorer, a psychologist and anthropologist, wrote about all sorts: the inhabitants of a Himalayan village, the Americans and the Russians. Finally, in the early 1950s, he turned his attention to his own people. His research was sponsored by the *People*, which had an estimated readership of twelve million at the time, and appeared in his book *Exploring English Character*.[2]

As a psychologist Gorer was puzzled. He took it for granted that aggression was part of human nature. What he found intriguing about the English was that their natural aggression was so successfully controlled.

In public life today, the English are certainly among the most peaceful, gentle, courteous and orderly populations that the civilised world has ever seen ... You hardly ever see a fight in a bar (a not uncommon spectacle in most of the rest of Europe or the USA) ... Football crowds are as orderly as church meetings. ... This orderliness and gentleness, this absence of overt aggression calls for an explanation.

The crowd at a Bristol Rovers versus Bristol City match in 1935. 'Football crowds are as orderly as church meetings,' observed Professor Gorer.

He was puzzled all the more because the English had not always been this way. In the seventeenth and eighteenth centuries they had been pugnacious and violent. But somehow, during the nineteenth century, violence and pleasure in fighting had almost completely disappeared and England produced, instead, institutions of care and philanthropy such as the Royal Society for the Prevention of Cruelty to Animals.

George Orwell, from a very different standpoint, came to a similar conclusion. He wrote in 1944: 'An imaginary foreign observer would certainly be struck by our gentleness; by the orderly behaviour of English crowds, the lack of pushing and quarrelling ... and except for certain well-defined areas in half-a-dozen big towns, there is very little crime or violence.'[3]

George Santayana, the leading American philosopher, lived the latter part of his life in various parts of Europe, including Britain. In 1922 he wrote:

The Englishman ... is disciplined, skilful, and calm – in eating, in sport, in public gatherings, in hardship. ... He is the ideal comrade in a tight place; he knows how to be ... well-dressed without show, and pleasure-loving without loudness. ... What ferocious Anglophobe ... is not immensely flattered if you pretend to have mistaken him for an Englishman?[4]

And again: 'The Englishman's heart is seldom designing or mean. There are nations where people are always ... cheating in small matters, to get out of some predicament, or secure some advantage ... Such is not the Englishman's way.' The praise of the British up to at least 1960 is so fulsome it may surprise younger people.

Where did the good behaviour come from?

It seems the ideal of good behaviour became prevalent during the nineteenth century. The words varied. Among the working classes, it was considered important to be 'respectable' and of 'good character'.[5] The word 'character' had an extra meaning. It could be a written testimony by an employer about a man's qualities – his honesty, industriousness, sobriety and punctuality.

A working-class man could be 'respectable' even if less well off than another worker who was 'rough'. Even children shared in a sense of family and individual self-respect. Working-class memoirs reveal that children thought it natural that they should help in the house and then, as they got older, earn small sums by running errands or doing chores for neighbours. Finally they would get a regular job. As Gertrude Himmelfarb, who has specialised in nineteenth-century culture, put it:

Part of the ethos of work was the pride of growing up, assuming the mantle of adulthood, and with it of work. But part of it was also a sense of responsibility to the family and, beyond this, a sense that work itself was something to be proud of, a source of self-respect and the respect of others.

Among the middle class, the terms were different but the meaning was similar. The terms 'gentleman' and 'lady' denoted moral qualities almost as much as social status. Hippolyte Taine, writing just after the middle of the century, contrasted the French *gentilhomme* with the British gentleman. The former was elegant, stylish and chivalrous. The latter was a 'disinterested man of integrity' capable of 'sacrificing himself for those he leads' and a man 'of honour'. A 'gentleman' in the latter half of the nineteenth century was honest, gracious and considerate to others. This concept remained part of British culture right up to fifty years ago at least.

The culture of decency was reflected and perpetuated in children's books that

> **REMEMBER DUTY?**
> The concept of personal duty was so strong in the nineteenth century that William Wordsworth, usually thought of a member of the Romantic movement, wrote an ode to it. It begins:
> *Stern Daughter of the Voice of God!*
> *O Duty! if that name thou love,*
> *Who art a light to guide, a rod*
> *To check the erring and reprove;*
> *Thou, who are victory and law*
> *When empty terrors overawe;*
> *From vain temptations dost set free;*
> *And calm'st the weary strife of frail humanity!*

were widely read in the 1950s. In *Little Women*, Christian kindness permeates the pages. Consideration for others was a moral duty which, early in the story, means the children, who are not rich, give up their special Christmas breakfast and take it round to people more seriously poor than themselves. In *Children of the New Forest*, honour, bravery, self-reliance and loyalty are implicitly the characteristics that are most valued.

Each of the short stories in *Tales after Tea* by Enid Blyton has a firm moral. An Alsatian dog bullies and frightens other animals. It gets its comeuppance. A boy is rude and aggressive to other children who have been building a sandcastle. He takes over and insists on getting on top.

He ends up surrounded by sea and in fear for his life. He is saved, but gets a powerful lesson in modesty and consideration. The children to whom these stories were read were being taught a moral system.

> 'The girls didn't come to Malory Towers only to learn lessons in class – they came to learn other things too – to be just and fair, generous, brave, kind. Perhaps those things were even more important than the lessons.'[6]
>
> Enid Blyton, *Third Year at Malory Towers,* **1948**

And what about now? What are the modern British like?

The travel company Expedia contacted tourist offices in seventeen countries and asked how they regarded their visitors. From the answers, Expedia created a league table.

Germany easily came out best. Tourists from Japan and the USA were also repeatedly mentioned as being well behaved. The worst-behaved tourists were the British. They were rated the worst or second worst by more than half the tourist offices polled.

The British take their crime with them on holiday. In Rhodes, the police said in 2003 that British tourists had created a crime wave. The resort of Faliraki was particularly hard hit. Out of 105 people who were arrested, ninety-nine were British.[8]

Even the British themselves no longer think they are polite and considerate. Birmingham Midshires Building Society asked people whether they thought that most Britons gave up bus or train seats for women and the elderly. Seven out of ten said 'no'. In a Gallup poll, four out of five people who expressed an opinion believed that British society today is less moral than fifty years ago.[9] A large majority felt that we leave it too much to individuals to develop their own moral code. We do not have an agreed set of moral standards.

Where do the best- and worst-behaved tourists come from?

Germany	+20
Japan	+9
USA	+7
Norway	+3
Spain	+3
China	+2
Italy	+2
France	+1
Sweden	0
Poland	-1
Denmark	-1
Russia	-3
Ireland	-3
Israel	-6
Britain	-11

A positive number denotes the best behaved, a negative the worst behaved.

Source: www.expedia.co.uk[7]

Swearing is now so commonplace that it appears regularly on television and even people who know they are being filmed have been known to swear obscenely. In a Channel 4 series called *Wife Swap*, Justin Wells lived for a while with Kellie Ansell, a vegan. She removed his cola drinks from the fridge, which provoked him into a tirade in front of his son Dre, two, and his stepdaughters Antonella, twelve, and Amy, nine.

'There was nothing said about f***ing fizzy drinks. I'll have whatever I f***ing want. That's all b******s. I'll wipe my f***ing a*** with that,' he said.

One of his children said he wasn't allowed to swear in front of them. He replied, 'F***, f***, f***. There you go.'

Children reading *The Wizard* in 1948. Children and teenagers in the 1940s and 1950s wore uniforms, shoes (polished) and perhaps flat caps.

Youths today often wear hoods which obsure their faces or baseball caps, back to front. A significant minority walks in an intimidating way – hunched over, as if absorbed in anger or depression.

An affair that never took place

Two ordinary middle-class people are in the tea room of a suburban train station. A cinder from a steam engine gets into the eye of one of them, Laura Jesson. Alec Harvey, a doctor, comes to her aid and gets it out with the end of a handkerchief. This is the beginning of the classic film *Brief Encounter*, released in 1945. Laura, played by Celia Johnson,

'In the first half of this year [2003], the "F" word was used more than 1,400 times in films shown on terrestrial television ... The corruption of language in public culture is just one aspect of the general coarsening of life ... There are many of us today on the Left who can see that something precious, possibly unrecoverable, is being destroyed.'[10]

Yasmin Alibhai-Brown, columnist for the *Independent*

rushes off immediately to catch her train and thinks no more about it. But they accidentally meet again since they both travel by train into town each Thursday. Both are happily married but, as they get to know each other better, they fall in love. Alec, played by Trevor Howard, becomes increasingly ardent and Laura is powerfully attracted to him – he is dashing and handsome whereas her husband is neither.

Towards the end of the film, Alec wants to consummate their passion and start life afresh with her. Laura is tempted but summons up her courage and, instead, stops the relationship entirely. She goes back to her stolid husband. At the end of the film, she is seated in her suburban home with him. It is a strange tale by modern standards – about an affair that does not happen. Laura is powerfully attracted to Alec but quells her excitement. Why?

Trevor Howard and Celia Johnson in *Brief Encounter*, 1945. The story is about a woman who decides *not* to be unfaithful to her husband.

Implicitly because she thinks it right. She loves and is committed to her children. If she embarked on an affair or divorce, it could hurt them. As for her husband, although she no longer loves him passionately, she sees him as a decent person to whom she has made a commitment. She sees no justification for breaking it. He has done his best. The struggle within her is between her desires and her moral sense. Her sense of honour, or duty, is an integral part of the way she makes decisions.

Forty-four years later came another British film about a woman tempted to be unfaithful to her husband. The eponymous heroine in *Shirley Valentine* – played by Pauline Collins – is bored with her life and feels her husband has lost the sparkle which first attracted her to him. Egged on by a girlfriend, she flies off to a Greek island. There she is attracted to a Greek man, played by Tom Conti, who seems excitingly romantic. They go to bed on their first date. The event is portrayed not as a grave decision but as a moment of liberation.

Her husband, Joe, follows her to Greece. Implicitly it is all his fault that she went off at all and he is the one who ought to be ashamed. He has been boorish and mundane. The film-maker does not suggest she had any responsibility to keep her marriage vows to him. Her responsibility is not to others – not even her husband. Only to herself.

Of course not everyone was faithful to their husbands in the 1940s and 1950s. But *Brief Encounter* suggests the culture at the time had a strong sense that married people ought to be faithful.

Another change in morality is revealed in the 1953 film *Genevieve*. Two old friends race their veteran cars against each other on the annual London-to-Brighton rally. Alan, the family man – played by John Gregson – is sure his car will beat that of Ambrose, played by

Pauline Collins and Tom Conti in *Shirley Valentine*, 1989. The story is about a woman who has no hesitation in being unfaithful to her husband.

Kenneth More. They bet £100 on it.

First one gets the advantage, then the other. Ambrose sabotages Alan's car. Alan is arrested for speeding. They call the race off because it is getting out of hand. Then it is on again. Finally the winning point on Westminster Bridge is only a few hundred yards away. Alan is in the lead and about to win when he has to stop at a red traffic light. An elderly gentleman comes up to him and exclaims what a wonderful car Alan has. He talks about the time he used to have one like it himself. The traffic lights turn green. Alan is desperate to get away and win the race. He struggles with his conscience ... and his conscience wins. He politely hears the gentleman out and invites him to come to have a spin in the car when he likes. Ambrose swoops past. The lights turn red again. Alan has let victory slip his grasp – at least, so it seems. The ethos of the film is that being a good, kind person is more important than winning.

> 'At the end of the annual Oxford/Cambridge boat race on the Thames, crews in the 1950s and 1960s gave each other three cheers and approached each other to shake hands across the water.
>
> In April 2000, the Oxford crew won. The victors made catcalls and rude gestures at the Cambridge crew.'[11]

The red card index

Much of the above is open to argument. It is possible, for example, to find 1950s British films in which people behave very badly – although in such cases the bad behaviour is generally treated as such by the director. What about some objective measure – one that has been recorded year after year for a century or more? There are not many such measures, but fortunately there is one, at least: in football.

Bad behaviour in football has always taken place. A match between Scotland and Austria in 1951 got so nasty that the journalist who saw it said it came to resemble a battlefield. But has the amount of bad behaviour on the football field always stayed about the same? We can try to get an idea by looking at the number of people sent off each season.

In 1946/7 – the first season after the war – ten men were sent off in league football. The next year was a bit better. There were only eight. The next season was worse – fifteen got their marching orders. Jumping forward to 1954/5, seven players were dismissed. The figures for every year are not readily available, but Tony Brown, the sendings-off expert, estimates that from the 1891/2 season up to 1961/2, there was a 'steady state' of about a dozen sendings-off per season.

It was then, in the early 1960s, that things began distinctly to change. The figures suddenly took off. By 1979/80, the number of sendings off had reached 115. Over a mere two decades, the number of sendings off had jumped eight-fold.

The football authorities tried to clamp down on the growing violence and cheating in 1982. Referees were instructed to enforce the laws more rigorously. It is important to understand that the tougher regime was a response to the growing lawlessness, not some strange, arbitrary decision that football should not be physical any more. It was hoped that a sudden assertion of authority would bring order back to the game.

It didn't work. The sendings off rose higher still. In 1990/91, they reached two hundred in a single season for the first time – nearly double the level of eleven years before. They quickly rose higher again, passing three hundred in 1994/5. In the latest year for which figures are available, the total number of sendings off was 451 – that makes a total rise of 3,658 per cent compared to the years between 1891/2 and 1961/2.

Send him off, ref!

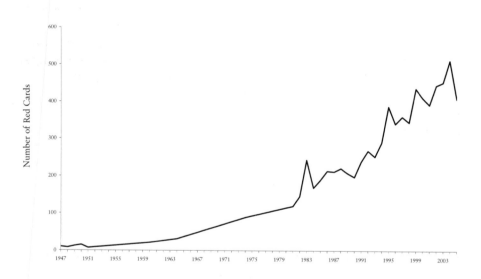

Sendings off in first-class football matches: English, Welsh and Scottish league games and cup competitions.[12] The figures from 1959/60 to 1973/4 are less reliable, being based on samples. Source: Tony Brown.[13]

Some football fans may still want to believe that the rise has all been due to the referees being more pernickety. But surely the enormous scale of the rise and its persistence under various footballing authorities will persuade most people. We might ask the opinion of those who were there at the time and professionally involved.

Sir Tom Finney was a star of the post-war years, a winger playing for Preston and England. He later recalled:

Throughout my playing career with Preston North End, I can only recall two sendings off. This was not because referees were more lenient but because standards of conduct were much higher. Yes, we played hard, but we were also fair ... To be sent off was a cause for shame. You had let your team, the manager and the spectators down.[14]

It is noticeable that he thought there was shame attached to being sent off. There is not much shame now.

Mervyn Griffiths was the referee of the 'Matthews final'– the celebrated FA Cup final in 1953 in which Stanley Matthews, the most admired forward of his time, sensationally turned a 3-1 deficit for Bolton into a 4-3 victory in the final twenty minutes. When Griffiths later wrote about the game as it was in those days, he said, 'Players were better behaved. There was more sportsmanship than gamesmanship in those days and it showed in so many ways.'[16] He remembered a match in the early postwar days in which a Millwall player questioned one of his decisions. The Millwall manager, Benny Fenton, angrily shouted at his player, 'You don't question decisions by that ref!' Griffiths said, 'Players had a much better spirit towards referees ... There were no big arguments and demonstrations when I had the whistle. It makes my hair stand on end when I see players today surrounding a referee, hurling abuse and even laying hands on him. Such a thing was unheard of.'

John Charles was a big man who played for Wales. Griffiths remarked of him, 'As big as he was, he never used his weight unfairly.' So those who knew the game up close in the 1950s and 1960s certainly think there has been a big change.

> **'There was nothing malicious about the tackling.'**[15]
> **Sir Tom Finney, writing about his days at the top of English football in the 1950s**

Never mind the violence, feel the success

It is revealing how the authorities and others reacted to bad behaviour.
Another leading player of the early post-war years was Willie Wood-

Willie Woodburn, playing for Scotland, pokes the ball away from England's Tommy
Lawton. After five serious fouls in his career, Woodburn was banned for life in 1954.

burn, a Scottish international. He appeared before the Scottish FA Referees Committee for misbehaviour four times. Then, on 28 August 1954, he played for Rangers against Stirling Albion and fouled someone again – the method is not described.[17] He went before the Referees Committee for a fifth time. The committee suspended him from the game *sine die* – that is, indefinitely. His footballing career was finished. Over. He was asked to comment but only said 'It is too bad to talk about.' Bad behaviour was punished severely.

In more recent times, there was another player with a bad record. Vinnie Jones was – and still is – a big man, like John Charles. But he was not admired, in his relatively recent footballing career, for using his size fairly – as Charles had been.

Jones was sent off twelve times in his career. He was not called in, though, after five major infringements, like Woodburn, and told that he would never play professional football again. He was never permanently banned. Instead of his career being finished, it thrived. A video was made of his most unpleasant attacks on other players. He was invited onto television chat shows such as *The Mrs Merton Show*. He was used as a model by Charles Tyrwhitt, a mail-order shirt-seller. He became well enough known to be cast as a tough-guy villain in the film *Lock, Stock and Two Smoking Barrels*. What would have earned him disgrace in the late 1940s and 1950s won him fame and fortune.

In 1998, Jones was tried for assault.[18] He had called on a neighbour, Mr

Timothy Gear, late at night. He wanted to know why Mr Gear had removed a stile near his smallholding. According to Mr Gear's evidence, Jones banged on the door of his mobile home and smashed a window. Mr Gear claimed that when he opened the door, Jones bit him on top of the head, punched, kicked and then stamped on him. Jones gave a different version of events. But the magistrates found Jones guilty of assault causing actual bodily harm and criminal damage. Jones thus became a convicted criminal. How did the press cover the incident? It concentrated on how the months since his assault on his neighbour had been 'terrible' for Jones.[19] His feelings of stress were given more prominence than his violent, criminal behaviour. Four years later, Vinnie Jones was even made 'the new face of Burton', the men's clothes store, for the company's centenary year.[20] The marketing director said Jones was chosen to launch the campaign because 'he is a gutsy, modern British character . . . He represents the modern version of a British icon.'

Despite being sent off twelve times Vinnie Jones was never banned. His reputation for violence helped him become a celebrity.

In June 2003, the 'icon' flew with Virgin Atlantic to Tokyo in Upper Class.[21] He left his seat to drink at the Airbus bar and began talking to three men and a woman. The woman felt that Jones had become boorish and returned to her seat. Jones went over to her where she was sitting. He put a plate of food on her lap and told her to go to the bar. One of the men went to Jones and told him to stop pestering the woman. Jones slapped the man around the face and pushed his head into a window of the plane. He was aggressive and abusive. At one point, when air crew were trying to pacify him, he screamed at them, 'Go and pour the f****** coffee like you are paid to. I can get you murdered. I can get the whole crew murdered for £3,000.' He was later convicted of assault and threatening behaviour.[22]

Vinnie Jones might be regarded as a one-off. Actually – in football, at least – he was more like a path-finder. What seemed exceptional in his early days has now become mainstream.

Acceptance of malicious violence has reached the heart of the game.

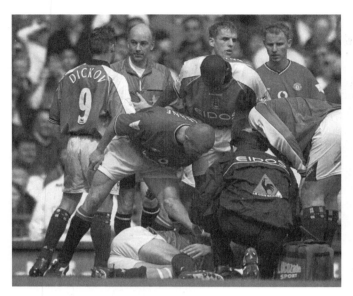

Roy Keane shouts abuse at Alfie Haaland after deliberately hurting him in a Manchester United versus Manchester City match, in April 2001. 'I f****** hit him hard,' he wrote later.

Roy Keane was captain of Manchester United in 2001 when United – the most successful British team at the time – was playing Manchester City. He had a grudge against one of the City players, Alfie Haaland. Keane set out to hurt him. According to his own autobiography, 'I f****** hit him hard. Take that you c***.' The attack caused knee ligament damage. Following it, Haaland only played four substitute appearances in the next sixteen months.[23]

In August 2002, Keane was sent off for the tenth time in his career. What did his manager, Sir Alex Ferguson, say about his repeated acts of violence? Did he say, as Barry Fenton, the Millwall manager, had shouted to his player, 'Don't question decisions by that ref!'? At an annual general meeting in November 2002, Ferguson said, 'There are moments when he gets those flashes of temper but that is because he is a winner.'[24] The ethic Ferguson revealed was simple: it does not matter if a player cheats and injures people as long as he wins games. It seems a long way from *Genevieve*.

> 'The game was always played hard in my day and I had the bruises to prove it. But there is a difference between being a hard man and a thug . . . Shuffling up from behind, not giving his opponent a chance to defend himself and BANG! That is not the action of a hard man – it was pathetic.'[25]
>
> **Jimmy Greaves, leading England forward in the 1960s, writing after one of Keane's fouls**

The unreported crime wave

Is there another kind of behaviour which provides a fairly objective measure of behaviour, year after year? Yes. And it happens to concern one of the most crucial kinds of human behaviour: crime.

The figures are even more dramatic than those for sendings off in football. In 1898 there were 4,221 violent crimes in England and Wales. Just over a century later, in 1998/9, there were 331,843. The number of violent crimes had increased seventy-seven times over. Of course the population had risen but even after adjusting the figures for that they still show a 47-fold rise in violent crime.[26] The rise began in the 1920s and 1930s and continued remorselessly thereafter.

Violent crimes

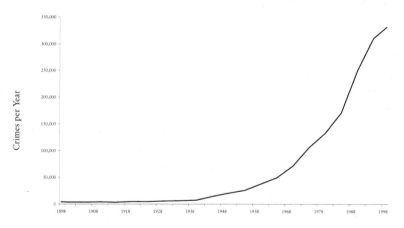

Later figures have not been compiled on a comparable basis. They show the trend continuing – 605,797 for 1998/9 on the new basis; 733,374 for 2000/1; 813,271 for 2001/2; 991,603 for 2002/3; 1,109,016 for 2003/4; 1,184,702 for 2004/5. Recorded crime, England and Wales. Source: Home Office.[27]

Once again, there are some who will argue that the figures give a false impression.[28] It is said that reporting of crime has increased. It is far from clear that this is true, let alone to the extent which would explain away such a massive change. In fact the very opposite may be true. According to Professor Jose Harris:

A very high proportion of Edwardian convicts were in prison for offences that would have been much more lightly treated or wholly disregarded by law enforcers in the late twentieth century. In 1912–13, for example, one quarter of males aged 16 to 21 who were imprisoned in the metropolitan area of London were serving seven-day sentences for offences which included drunkenness, 'playing games in the street', riding a bicycle without lights, gaming, obscene language and sleeping rough. If late twentieth century standards of policing and sentencing had been applied in Edwardian Britain, the prisons would have been virtually empty; conversely, if Edwardian standards were applied in the 1990s then most of the youth of Britain would be in gaol.[29]

Where is crime most common?

England and Wales	58
Australia	58
Netherlands	51
Sweden	46
Scotland	43
United States	43
Canada	42
Belgium	37
France	36
Portugal	27
Switzerland	24
Japan	22

Source: UN Crime and Justice Research Institute. All crime, number of crimes per 100 people

Further evidence of the massive increase in crime comes from international comparisons. The United Nations ignored official national figures and asked random samples of 2,000 people in different countries about their experiences.[31] England and Wales had the highest crime rate of all – equal to that of Australia but well above rates in the United States, France, Switzerland and Japan.

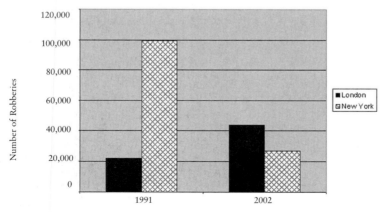

Robberies in London and New York

Source: *The Failure of Britain's Police*

In the crime epidemic, children have been particularly badly hit – often literally. The figures have soared even over quite short periods. Prosecutions for cruelty to or neglect of children rose from 228 in 1988 to 839 in 1999.[32] Abuse of children has increased dramatically too. 'Gross indecency with a child' was three times more frequent in 2000 than in 1983.[33]

Babies: the most commonly killed people in modern Britain

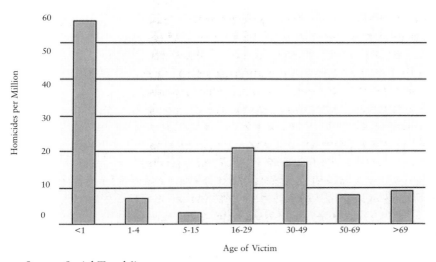

Source: Social Trends[34]

Just one crime may bring home some of the reality behind the figures. A ten-year-old boy was brought by his loving mother from Nigeria to Britain in 2000. The family had saved £5,000 over two years to have his sister treated for severe epilepsy at King's College Hospital. The mother had lived in Britain before and was able to get a flat in Peckham, south London. The boy attended Oliver Goldsmith primary school while his sister was being treated. He was a bright, keen boy. But after only a few months in London, his mother discovered that boys at school were swearing at him and calling him names. The mother told his teachers of the taunts and abuse but, according to her, they did not take her seriously.

After four months, one Friday, he told his mother that some boys had beaten him at school. His mother asked, 'Did you fight with them?' He replied, 'No, Mummy, I did not fight with them.' The next Monday, he walked to the

> In 1931 there were three crimes a year for every police officer. In 2001 there were 44.[30]

'I can't believe how much Britain has changed since we left.'[36]

Mrs Gloria Taylor, mother of Damilola, who left Britain in the early 1980s and returned in 2000

library after school for an extra computer class. He left the library at 4.25 p.m. to go home. When he was in Blakes Road, he was stabbed. He started bleeding heavily. He staggered one hundred yards before collapsing and dying. His murder was one of the small minority of crimes which, for a variety of reasons, make it into the newspapers and – even more difficult – onto national television. The name of the boy was Damilola Taylor. [35]

The reason for choosing the death of Damilola Taylor out of all the thousands of crimes in recent years is that it resulted in newspaper coverage of a sort rarely seen. Journalists left their comfortable offices and went to Peckham. Their stories often had two bylines – the journalists were sent in pairs for safety. One of these pairs talked to two black sisters who were discussing teenagers on the estate – children really – who regularly threatened them. One explained, 'They smashed my car with an iron bar. That's why I park two miles away.'

At that moment, a boy, estimated by the reporters to be about twelve, loped past, his face and head hidden in the hood of his sweatshirt. One of the women shrieked, 'Him, ask him, he's one of them!' This terrified her sister who clamped her hand over her mouth, whispering, 'Shut up, shut up.' The two women hurried away, frightened of what the twelve-year-old boy – or perhaps his fellow gang members – might do to them. This boy – a child – swaggered over to the two journalists. He said his mother had told him to tell journalists to 'f*** off'. He slowly pulled down his hood and stared. The journalists interpreted this to mean, 'You walk away, not me. This is my patch.'

What is it like to live an area like that? A couple of women were interviewed about the daily fear of muggings and stabbings, the no-go areas, the syringes littering the stairwells, the drunken parties and blaring music thudding through their walls from dusk to dawn.[37] They said gangs of kids would roam the streets searching for other

In a poll conducted by the Youth Justice Board, more than a quarter of all schoolchildren confessed to having committed a crime in the past twelve months.[38]

Homerton Hospital in Hackney, east London, treats fifty-five knife or gunshot wounds a month.[40]

kids to rob or mug. Even in daylight you weren't safe. One old lady was attacked on her way to buy a newspaper. When they found out she had only 40p on her, they ripped off her wedding ring and knocked her to the ground.

Connie opened her door reluctantly even to journalists, keeping closed an outer steel mesh which protected her.[39] 'I talk to nobody,' she said. 'That way I don't get involved. I know nothing. No one who has any sense round here knows nothing.' She had three menacing Alsatian dogs behind her. The dogs snarled. She slammed the door. What horrifying fear and nastiness can Connie have lived through to end up behaving this way?

Britain has been through a crime epidemic. It reflects the changed character of a significant minority of people. And for every one of them actually convicted of a crime, there are surely many others who have been aggressive and anti-social.

Move over, Keats, it's Johnny Rotten

What else has changed? What about the intellectual and cultural life of British people?

English and German football fans clashing in Munich in 2001. The frequency of violent crime has increased 47 times since 1898.

In 2002, a television cable channel conducted a survey in which people were asked what they considered the most significant event in British history over the previous hundred years out of a choice of ten.[41] What event did the British choose? The most popular choice – selected by nearly of quarter of those questioned – was the death of Princess Diana. That was, of course, a tragic event. But was it an historical event to compare with the start of the Second World War or the end of the First, both of which were ranked lower?

In another survey, secondary-school pupils were asked who the English were fighting in the Battle of Hastings.[42] One in three did not know. They were asked when the First World War took place. Two out of three did not know. Nearly a quarter could not even place it in the right century. Half had no idea that Oliver Cromwell was a key figure in the English Civil War.

The BBC asked a very large sample of people – thirty-three thousand – to draw up a list of one hundred people who could be candidates for the title of the 'Greatest Briton' of all time. They did not select John Milton, William Wordsworth, John Keats, Samuel Johnson or Rudyard Kipling for the top 100.[43] John Locke, Thomas Hobbes and David Hume – some of Britain's most celebrated philosophers – did not make it either. Nor did Britain's most famous painters, John Constable and William Turner. Was this because the competition was so strong? Well, the hundred did include people you might expect, such as William Shakespeare and Winston Churchill. But also among their number were Cliff Richard, David Beckham, radio presenter John Peel, Julie Andrews, Michael Crawford and Johnny Rotten. These individuals have certainly each had their achievements. But did they truly deserve to push out people of the stature of Kipling and Constable? The easiest explanation for this is that most Britons nowadays know little or nothing about many of the greatest British people to have lived.

How well do people follow current events? *Whitaker's Almanack* questioned over a thousand people, asking them to name members of the British Cabinet.[44] More than two out of five could not name one. Slightly under a quarter were able

> **'It was pretty disheartening. They were given pretty basic numeracy and literacy tests and the majority couldn't do them.'[45]**
>
> Sir Dominic Cadbury, when revealing that only thirty out of two hundred young applicants were good enough for production line jobs at his company's factory in Birmingham

to name the Chancellor of the Exchequer. In contrast, 63 per cent could name a character from the television soap opera *East-Enders*. A remarkable 46 per cent could name five of the characters. *EastEnders* personalities are better known than members of the government – by far.

Children's language skills are getting worse, according to Alan Wells, director of the Basic Skills Agency. He revealed that an estimated 50 per cent of children in Wales were not ready to start primary school at five because of their limited ability to talk.[46]

University academics were asked how students coming from schools compared with those in the past.[47] An overwhelming 70 per cent said they were less well prepared. Three-quarters said they had been forced to adapt their teaching techniques to the increasingly 'diverse' mix of students – 'diverse' being the euphemistic way of saying that they included seriously weak students.

> **The number of boys taking maths at A-level halved between 1980 and 2000.[48] Maths is considered a relatively difficult subject.**

We are beginning to build up a picture of intellectual and cultural deterioration (which is investigated more fully in the education chapter).

A Faustian pact?

It is not going too far to say that there seems to have been a revolution in the culture and character of the British people in the last sixty years. The evidence is overwhelming that they are less polite and more violent. We live in a far more crime-ridden society. Though educated for longer, the effectiveness of the education appears poor. We will see evidence in later chapters of other kinds of deterioration in healthcare, parenting, unemployment and benefits dependency. And though we have indeed enjoyed a rise in wealth, we will see it has been less dramatic than that in various countries which were once far poorer than ourselves. Taxes, of course, are vastly higher than a century ago.

A picture emerges of a country that has become brutish and even degenerate compared to how it was. On the surface, it is as if it had made a Faustian pact: greater wealth in exchange for moral decline. But there was no pact. Even greater prosperity could have been achieved without the moral decline. A country which had a remarkable history and character appears to have just thrown it away.

SPOT THE DIFFERENCE
Cartoon by Ron McTrusty, *Evening Standard*, 15 August 2002. This was at the time of the controversy over Roy Keane's fouls and a court case about a fight at a London nightclub involving other prominent footballers.

This happy breed?

There could be one last kind of defence. Are the British happy? If, at least, we are happier, perhaps we need not care about the rest. It is an idea that can be tested.

No single study covers the whole period but two studies over shorter, overlapping time-frames provide telling evidence. Psychologist Glyn Lewis sought to compare the mental state of people in 1985 to a similar sample in 1977. Even over this relatively short period he discovered a big change. He looked at the proportion suffering from 'psychiatric morbidity' – that is psychiatric illness or distress.[49] The sort of symptoms included were panic attacks, phobias and depression. In the earlier sample, 22 per cent were suffering mentally in one way or another. In the later sample, the percentage had increased to 31 per cent – almost one-third of the population.

Another study examined the changing state of British minds a little later. It was based on two major, well-known surveys: one of children born in a single week in 1958 and another of children born in 1970. Both groups were looked at when they reached the age of twenty-six – i.e. in 1984 and 1996 respectively. The proportion of those born in the 1950s who said they were depressed was 7 per cent. The second group, a dozen years later, was richer and had been educated, on average, for longer. Were they happier? Not at all. The proportion reporting that they were depressed had doubled, to 14 per cent.

> **HAPPY DAYS?**
> '**Compared with 1950, there is an epidemic of irritability and aggression, of depression and paranoia, of obsessions, panics, addictions, compulsions [and] relationships that are not working.'**[52]
>
> **Oliver James, psychologist**

Why should the British be less happy? They are wealthier and have had lengthier educations. What is causing the unhappiness?

Oliver James, the psychologist and author, suggests, among other things, 'We are increasingly likely to live alone, the care of children has become increasingly erratic and the elderly are left to fend for themselves in unnaturally lonely, estranged circumstances.'[50] He mentions, too, the 'divorce epidemic' which damages first the adults, who become far more likely to suffer depression, and then the children. Among women, rates of smoking and drinking – 'signs of distress' – indicate their unhappiness is rocketing.

James's remarks about drinking are supported by a Datamonitor survey from 2003, which found that young British women drink more alcohol than those of any of the other European countries studied. They drink more than three times as much as young Italian women.[51]

Drug-taking, like heavy drinking, may well be a symptom of 'psychological distress'. The European Union con-

Teenagers on cannabis

England and Wales	41%
Ireland	37%
Netherlands	31%
Spain	24%
Belgium	24%
France	23%
Italy	19%
Greece	10%
Austria	9%
Sweden	7%

Percentage of 15- and 16-year-olds who have tried cannabis, 1999.

Source: EU[53]

ducted a study of fifteen- and sixteen-year-olds to see how many had tried cannabis. In England and Wales more than four out of ten had tried it – again, a higher figure than for any other country in the European Union.

The great rise in wealth over the past sixty years has been a marvellous thing, bringing many benefits, but the story has been marred by an equally astonishing decline in the way British people are. And we are not even happier. Quite the reverse. We have indeed suffered a fall from grace. The vital question remains, why? And can it really be something to do with the welfare state?

CHAPTER 2

Social Security: Catherine's four dead boys and Frank's bingo blow-out

Where did the welfare state come from? How did it start?

People think they know, but the majority have got it wrong. The story is a revelation. In some ways it is humbling. It is a story rich in lessons that have been forgotten – lessons which would have been useful if only people had recalled them in recent times. People cannot hope to reach a proper understanding of the welfare state we're in if they have completely misunderstood what happened before. The story sets the stage for the rest of the book.

The popular view of the origin of the welfare state goes something like this: after the Second World War, the Labour Party won the general election by a landslide. The new government was led by a studious-looking man called Clement Attlee and other men with confusingly similar names like Bevan and Bevin. They created the welfare state, which was a great achievement showing the humanity of the British people. Before then things were extremely harsh and if you stumbled in life you could easily end up in the gutter.

That concise version is not entirely wrong. But it is wrong in its most important respects. The idea that either Attlee, in 1945, or William Beveridge, writing his famous report in 1942, represented 'zero hour' for the welfare state is wrong. If people think that, they are many miles away from understanding welfare. True, Attlee and his colleagues gave a major boost to the role of the state in welfare. But they did not create the welfare state and they certainly did not create social security – its core. If we want to understand welfare, we need to go back to its real beginning – to a married couple called Catherine and Henry, who were having a difficult time producing children.

The problem was not one of conception. Catherine conceived often. She gave birth frequently, too, bringing to term seven children in all. The trouble was that most of them did not live long. Mary, one of the three girls brought to term, managed to live to adulthood. But girls were only second best for the parents. Henry and Catherine desperately wanted a

Catherine of Aragon desperately wanted a boy.

boy. Catherine did give birth to four boys but they all died. That meant there was a crisis – not just for the father but for the country. The Henry in question was King Henry VIII.

He was determined to have a son to succeed him on the throne. As Catherine of Aragon, his wife, had not produced one, he set about getting the marriage annulled. Cardinal Wolsey assured Henry that he could persuade the Pope to cooperate. But, after long negotiations, annulment was refused. This encouraged Henry to break with the Papacy. He asserted that he was the head of the Church and therefore his marriage could be annulled in an English court without appeal to Rome. Henry married his mistress, Anne Boleyn, hoping that this, at last, would result in the son he desperately wanted.

This familiar story lies at the origin of the welfare state because of one of its knock-on effects. Henry's break with Rome put him into a much better position to grab the wealth of the monasteries.

Being vain and self-indulgent, he was spending lavishly and fighting wars unnecessarily. He therefore became in desperate need of money. The monasteries had been building up their wealth over centuries. They received donations year after year from the wealthy and the not so wealthy. Giving money to religious institutions was part of most people's way of life. People saw it as their duty and as a way of increasing their chances of going to heaven. The wealth accumulated by the monasteries reached fabulous levels. In modern times, the rich own shares and have cash in the bank. In the sixteenth century, being rich meant owning land. Land was let to farmers, who paid rent. It produced a continuing income. The monasteries were said to own up to one-third of the land in England.

Henry VIII's expropriation of the monasteries led to the beginnings of the welfare state.

Henry expropriated the monasteries on the pretext that they were misusing the money which had been given to them.[1] Inspectors were sent round with the clear understanding that they were to find corruption, prostitution or anything else which could possibly justify shutting them down. Henry started by expropriating the smaller monasteries in 1536. Lead was stripped from the roofs, bells were taken from the towers, the crops and the houses were sold. Then Henry moved onto the large monasteries, killing those who got in his way. In 1538, the Abbot of Woburn and the Prior of Lenton were executed. Next, the Abbots of Glastonbury, Colchester and Reading were all hanged. It must have taken great courage to oppose the King. Between 1539 and the end of his reign in 1547, he extracted nearly three-quarters of a million pounds from the sale of monastery land – a fabulous fortune in those days.

Henry had got what he wanted regardless of other people. But who suffered? Many monks, nuns, secular residents and others were compensated. But there was one quite large group of people who received no compensation: the poverty-stricken, the old and the infirm.

Approaching 10 per cent of the income of the monasteries was spent on charitable work of one sort or another.[2] That may not sound much. But it was 10 per cent of an awful lot.

As one authority on the subject has put it, 'considerable quantities of the basic foodstuffs must have filtered down to the poor of the neighbourhood.' The journal of Prior More shows that he gave money or 'alms', as they were then called, to friars and to 'victims of calamity'. The monasteries made gifts of used clothing. They looked after children and educated them – in some cases because of their fine singing voices, in others because they were in poverty, perhaps orphans. Monasteries sometimes provided hospitals and almshouses, as did the one in Durham. In those days, a hospital was typically a place of rest for the old and infirm rather than one where medicine, let alone surgery, was carried out.

> **'the real if unspectacular service of the monasteries in providing free education must not be forgotten'[3]**
>
> **David Knowles, *Bare Ruined Choirs***

Monasteries also provided a kind of medieval nursing-home plan. If you lived – rather unusually – to a good old age, you could pay a sum to the monastery, which would then look after you until you died. The people who took out these plans were called 'corridans'.

Those who could not work because of illness or disability would sometimes find sanctuary in monasteries. The monasteries certainly did not pretend to cover the whole population. Families were expected to look after their own. They were the first line of defence. But monasteries offered some kind of longstop. They picked up some, at least, of the desperate and friendless. What Henry was destroying, therefore, when he expropriated the monasteries, was a welfare system based on religion – a 'welfare church' that existed long before the welfare state. The destruction of this welfare church – which led to the creation of the welfare state – owed a surprisingly large amount to the sad deaths of Catherine's four boys.

The ruins of Llanthony Priory, one of the religious institutions expropriated by Henry VIII. Monasteries and priories had provided welfare to the poor.

What happened next, after the welfare longstop had been removed? Among other things, you might guess that towns and villages around the country would find they had more beggars on their hands. That is certainly what seems to have occurred. You might think that there would be more people in desperate straits suffering illness and incapacity with no one to care for them. And you might even think that there would be legislation to try to deal with these problems.

New laws did indeed come thick and fast. Their multiplicity and the way they changed tack several times surely reflects a society trying to get to grips with a sudden increase in the problems of begging and incapacity.

The first reaction was generous. Henry, in the very same year as he was expropriating the small monasteries, issued a law requiring local mayors, governors and head officers to obtain charitable donations to help the 'impotent' (those incapable of work) and the 'lame' and also to assist the able-bodied to get a job. Those welfare measures should sound familiar. They are not far off what social security systems try to do now.

What came next also revealed the pattern of things to come. That relatively generous-sounding law was abruptly reversed. We may reasonably suppose – on the basis of the later ups and downs in legislation – that parishes and towns found the cost of looking after all of those who made claims alarming. The charitable giving was not sufficient to cover it. So, suddenly in 1547, the earlier law was replaced by something much harsher. It was decreed that 'idlers' and 'wanderers' should have a V branded on their chests and be enslaved for two years. If they ran away during the two years and were caught again, they should be branded with an S on their foreheads or cheeks and enslaved forever.

After this law – possibly the ultimate in anti-scrounger legislation – came a swing back again. The authorities in the parishes were unwilling to go quite so far. One can imagine them shying away from taking a branding iron to people whom they might have known for years. Two years later, the 1541 law was repealed.

Thus began a cycle in the story of welfare that has continued from the sixteenth century right up to now. Laws are made generous. This causes unforeseen problems. Then they are made more stringent. This then seems too harsh. Then they are made more generous again. And so on and on. There is a cycle in the story of welfare. There has not been a simple, continuous increase in provision.

When was the precise moment the welfare state began?

Once the harsh 'branding' law of 1541 was repealed, the problem once again became that of cost – the expense of looking after all those people who presented themselves as needing help. It was more than could be raised in charitable donations. Elizabeth I's first shot at the problem was to give power to the local authorities to put pressure on reluctant charity-givers. Reluctant donors could be made to appear in front of the bishop, like naughty schoolchildren.

Evidently a lecture from a bishop was still not enough to get money out of some of them, however. Because, in 1563, Elizabeth enacted that those people who were reluctant to give money could be forced to do so. They would be assessed for an appropriate amount and, if they refused to pay it, they could be imprisoned. It was at this moment in 1563 that all the elements of a welfare state fell into place. The parishes were legally obliged to look after the poor and the people of the parish were legally obliged to pay the cost. The welfare state had been created – at least in embryo.

During the rest of Elizabeth's reign, the law was refined by many amendments. But in 1601, the laws affecting the poor became settled for sixty years without any further revision. They became known as the Elizabethan Poor Laws and were the basis of state social security for the next three centuries. The fact that they lasted so long might suggest that they had something going for them. So what was their character?

They were parish-based. The communities which paid for the poor lived close to them and knew them. The way in which the law was administered varied a great deal from one locality to another. Those who were able to work were required to do so and the parish was obliged to help them find work. The idea was simple and clear. Apart from the antique language that was used, it is exactly the sort of thing a modern reformer might say today. It was intended that work should be found for the able-bodied so that young people 'may be accustomed and brought up in labour and work, and then not like to be idle rogues'. Work was to be made available so that those 'such as be already grown up in idleness ... may not have any just excuse in saying that they cannot get any service or work'. It is exactly the reasoning for modern 'workfare' programmes.

The final part of the Elizabethan system was the power given to churchwardens and overseers (administrators of the new laws) to erect 'convenient houses of habitation' for the 'impotent poor' (those incapable of earning a living).

Martin Luther and the welfare state

The leading intellectuals of the day debated the best way to look after the poor. Thomas More (King Henry's Lord Chancellor) was one. So were Hugh Latimer (Bishop of Worcester and adviser to the King) and Nicholas Ridley (Chaplain to the King, who contributed to the first revision of the prayer book in 1548).[4] Best known of the Continental intellectuals was Martin Luther.

Luther came up with a model plan in 1523. Citizens would pay money to a 'Common Chest' and the cash would be used for three purposes: to pay church officials, to pay schoolmasters and to assist the poor. He was keen that 'every town and village should know their own paupers ... and assist them. But as to ... strange beggars [from outside the area] they ought not be born with' because many were cheats.[5] The debate in Tudor and other times in the past was often at a much higher level of intelligence, knowledge and – above all – honesty than in recent times.

Although the Poor Laws remained largely in place for three centuries, there were some significant variations. The biggest change started in 1698 when the first workhouses were created in Bristol. The idea was to give work to people who claimed they could not get any.

Once again, this was something that went through a cycle. The regime was relatively benign to begin with. Then it was toughened up and made so beastly that no one but the most desperate would resort to a workhouse. Then the beastliness was considered so dreadful that the whole idea fell into disrepute.

But let us skip forward now to the nineteenth century to find one of the most important moments in the story. This is a part which should comprehensively remove any assumption that we are in some brand new welfare world and that we have nothing to learn from the past.

The first of February 1832 was a dry, cold day. The weather was so grim that several Continental ports were unusable. The water in them had frozen. In Scotland, a cholera epidemic had already killed 1,026 people, though there was reason to hope that it was starting to dissipate. In Ireland, an archdeacon had been murdered in a rash of protests about the tithe – the tax raised by the Anglican Church. The stock market was modestly up. In the House of Commons, at about noon, the Chancellor of the Exchequer and Leader of the House, Viscount Althorp, took questions.

Althorp – eccentrically pronounced 'Altrup' – was a shy, rather tongue-tied man. His real love in life was hunting. He used to gallop through the night after a sitting in the House in order to be able to ride to hounds with his beloved Pytchley hunt the next day. Three years later he would inherit the title Third Earl Spencer. He was an ancestor of Diana Spencer, later Diana, Princess of Wales. She grew up in Althorp House knowing the same furniture, pictures and – most important to the third Earl – the same ample stables.

The first question for the Viscount Althorp of 1832 came from Sir Robert Peel – creator of the 'bobbies', the first modern police force – who asked about improvements in municipal policing. After him came a much less well-known figure, a Mr Weyland. He asked a seemingly innocuous question about whether the government would propose some measure to improve the Poor Laws. But in reply, Viscount Althorp made one of the most significant announcements in the story of welfare. He said the subject had been under serious consideration. Commissioners were 'in course of being appointed' for the purpose of 'ascertaining how the different systems worked in different parishes'. It was implicit, in his reply, that major problems had emerged. These problems had to be understood and sorted out.

The commissioners were led by Edwin Chadwick, a dynamic, decisive man who was a leading campaigner for better sanitation and public health. Questionnaires were sent out across the country to those who administered the Poor Laws – 'overseers' and others. Assistant commissioners were despatched to go to allotted areas and investigate. The report they produced was the largest social investigation ever to have been made. It was a revelation.

In 1833, John Stuart Mill, the leading philosopher, wrote to Thomas Carlyle, one of Britain's most celebrated historians, when the preliminary report on the evidence was published: 'Have you seen the book published by the Poor Law Commissioners? If you have not, let me send it to you. Often you have complained how little of a state of a people is to be learned from books; much is to be learned from that book.' The report, issued in full in 1834, was as influential in its time as the Beveridge Report in 1942. Both reports were led by men who suffered no lack of self-confidence – or intelligence either. One difference, though, is that the 1834 report was based on information from the ground.

Edwin Chadwick led the Royal Commission which wrote an unprecedented, sensational report.

It was a sensation. The commissioners condemned the operation of the Poor Law in a variety of ways, nearly all of which correspond to failings that have been claimed about the modern welfare state. Virtually everything one can think of that has been said about the failings of modern social security was said 170 years ago.

The report asserted that the welfare system damaged the character of those who received benefits. A Mr Cowell was quoted saying that when he started his investigations he thought the major problem with the Poor Law was the financial burden on the rate-payers. But 'the experience of a very few weeks served to convince me that this evil, however great, sinks into insignificance when compared with the dreadful effects which the system produces on the morals and happiness of the lower orders.' To understand how bad it is, he continued, one must 'hear the pauper threaten to abandon his wife and family unless more money is allowed him – threaten to abandon an aged bed-ridden mother, to turn her out of his house and lay her down at the overseer's door, unless he is paid for giving her shelter'.[6]

The report included a direct and unflinching contrast between those on benefits and those who – though also poor – provided for themselves. A Dr Brushfield reported from Spitalfields:

In the pauper's habitation [a 'pauper' is a welfare dependant] ...
the children are dirty, and appear to be under no control; the
clothes of both parents and children, in nine cases out of ten,
are ragged, but evidently are so for the lack of the least attempt
to make them otherwise; for I have very rarely found the clothes
of a pauper with a patch put or a seam made upon them since
new.

In contrast,

In the habitation of the labouring man who receives no parish
relief, you will find (I have done so), even in the poorest, an
appearance of comfort: the articles of furniture, few and humble
as they might be, have their best side seen ... The children
appear under parental control, are sent to school ... their clothes
you will find patched and taken care of, so as to make them wear
as long a time as possible; there is a sense of moral feeling and
dignity easily discerned.[7]

Mr Okeden, for the Commission, reports: 'Moral character is annihi-
lated, and the poor man of twenty years ago, who tried to earn his
money, and was thankful for it, is now converted into an insolent, discontented, surly, thoughtless pauper, who talks of "right and income".'[8]

The welfare system, it was argued, created a self-perpetuating
dependency. A heart-rending story was told of a family named Wintle
which had tried to avoid this fate. The family got into great financial
difficulties and had resorted to selling the furniture. The mother, father
and two of the five children had become very ill. A Mr Booker, on
behalf of the parish, offered them money. They refused, keen to maintain their self-respect and independence. He went again with the churchwarden, telling them of 'the necessity' of accepting money. They again refused.
He and the churchwarden then sent them four shillings in a parcel, asking
them to apply for more. At last they finally succumbed.

> **PSYCHOLOGY OF THE WELFARE DEPENDANT**
>
> *'He need not bestir himself to seek work; he need not study to please his master; he need not put any restraint upon his temper; he need not ask relief as a favour.'*[9]
>
> **Royal Commission on the Poor Laws, 1834**

And once they started taking parish money, they did not stop.

Mr Booker blamed himself.

> *We effectively spoiled the habits acquired by their previous industry; and I have no hesitation in saying that, in nine cases out of ten, such is the constant effect of having once tasted of parish bounty ... If once a young lad gets a pair of shoes given him by the parish, he never afterwards lays by sufficient to buy a pair.*[10]

The report saw a link between welfare dependency and crime. In the parish of Mancetter in Warwickshire, the magistrates insisted that those on benefit should not work on three days a week so that they could seek work. But the men used the spare time 'thieving and poaching', with the result that no one wanted to employ them afterwards anyway.

The report suggested that tax-payers' money was wasted by both claimants and their employers. In some parishes, the wages of the lower paid were made up to a minimum level with benefits. This has come to be known as the Speenhamland system because a scale of subsistence needs was drawn up in an inn there[11] in 1795 and spread through England. It is the same idea as the more recent family credit and working families' tax credit. The purpose is to enable people to have a 'decent' standard of living or else to make it worthwhile working rather than staying on benefits and being idle. But whatever the motivation, they system was abused by both the employers and the labourers. An artificially low wage would be paid in the knowledge that it would be made up by the parish. The employer saved money. The employee got the wage he expected anyway. Only the tax-payers suffered. Exactly the same would be said about family credit 160 years later.

> 'At Burnash, in East Sussex, in the year 1822, the surplus labourers were put up to auction, and hired as low as 2d and 3d per day; the rest of their maintenance [income] being made up by the parish. The consequence was, that the farmers turned off their regular hands, in order to hire them by auction when they wanted them.'[12]
>
> **Royal Commission on the Poor Law**

Landlords and tenants abused the old equivalent of housing benefit in the same way. In many cases, landlords knew that the parishes would pay the rents of those on benefits, so they charged more: 'an overseer of Dolgelly stated that there were many apartments and small houses in the town not worth to let £1 a year, for which, in consequence of parochial interference with rents, from £1 14 shillings to £2 was paid.' Exactly the same has been said about modern housing benefit. Moreover, the welfare system caused bad housing to be built. Only inferior housing was exempted from rates. So people demanded housing with the defects that would gain the exemption.[13]

The welfare system discouraged saving, too. Employers in some parishes were required to take on a number of people on benefits. So being on benefit became a way to get a job. But you couldn't be on benefits if you had savings, therefore it became unwise to save.

The parallels with modern welfare problems are so many that it seems positively uncanny. The welfare system gave rise to fraud. James Peaton, in Southwark, was receiving relief from six different parishes. 'He made it his entire business to live on parish pensions, and he received one week's pension every day.'[15]

Of course the administrators tried to stop the fraud but it was difficult. George Huish, an assistant overseer in the parish of St George, Southwark, explained the problem:

> 'If an industrious man [from a poor family] was known to have laid by any part of his wages, and thus to have accumulated any considerable sum, there are some parishes in which he would be refused work till savings were gone; and the knowledge that this would be the case, acts as a preventive against saving.'[14]
>
> **Report from Mr Courthope, Ticehurst, East Sussex**

Suppose you go to a man's house as a visitor; you ask, where is Smith (the pauper)? You see his wife or his children, who say they do not know where he is, but that they believe he is gone in search of work. How are you to tell, in such a case, whether he is at work or not? It could only be by following him in the morning; and you must do that every day, because he may be in work one day, and not another.

A modern-day inspector working for the Department of Work and Pensions might well say the same.

'Suppose you have a shoemaker,' wrote Huish again, 'who demands relief [money from the parish] of you and you give it to him on his declaring that he is out of work. You visit his place, and you find him in work; you say to him, as I have said to one of our own paupers, "Why, Edwards, I thought you said you had no work?" And he will answer, "Neither had I any: and I have only got a little job for the day."'

The report makes the more subtle point that the welfare system was tempting previously honest people into fraud. 'It is an aphorism amongst the active parish officers that "cases [claims] which are good to-day are bad to-morrow, unless they are incessantly watched",' says the report. 'A person obtains relief on the grounds of sickness; when he has become capable of returning to moderate work, he is tempted, by the enjoyment of subsistence without labour, to conceal his convalescence, and fraudulently extend the period of relief.'

The report is full of things which bring us straight back to the problems of the modern welfare state. It is as if we had been here before without realising it. Most striking of the parallels are the reports on how the welfare system encouraged unmarried motherhood.

Unmarried women would get money for each of their children, in many parishes. There was only one condition: that she should name the father. It is reminiscent of the modern Child Support Agency. The guarantee of money – whether married or not – encouraged unmarried mothering, according to the report.

> We have many illegitimate children; and we think that the numbers
> have increased of late years. If a young woman has two or three
> bastard children, and receives 2s. 6d. a week for each, it is a little
> fortune to them. As soon as the children can run about, they can
> be taken into infant schools for 2d. a week, and kept from nine in
> the morning till five in the evening; so that the mothers can get
> their living by work, or waste their time in idleness.

That was a report from Battersea. Similar reports came from all over the country.

According to a report by a Mr Maclean, several clergymen had told him the women in the parish of Cranley were frequently about to give birth at the time of their marriage. They attributed this 'want of chastity' to 'the law of bastardy, which secures to the woman either a husband or a weekly allowance for the support of the child'.[16]

But perhaps the most spectacular example came from Norfolk, where 'a woman of Swaffham was reproached by the magistrate, Mr Young, with the burdens she had brought upon the parish, upon the occasion of her appearing before him to present the parish with her seventh bastard. She replied, "I am not going to be disappointed in my company with men to save the parish.""[17]

> 'Parish aid has a tendency to remove all shame.'
>
> **Royal Commission Report, 1834**

As long ago as 1834, it was asserted that morals were being changed by the welfare system. The attempt to get fathers to pay up often failed, again bringing to mind the problems faced by the Child Support Agency. Many ran away to a different part of the country. In Cornwall 'it was a matter of general notoriety' that poor men would be paid something by the natural parents to agree to be named as the father. The idea was the real natural father would get off scot free. Meanwhile the man named in his place would be too poor for the parish to be able to get any money off him. 'So general is the system . . . that it was the opinion of the most experienced parochial officers, that, . . . nine bastards in ten are falsely sworn.'

The Commission concludes that illegitimacy has not been discouraged by trying to get money off the men. Why? For a reason that might possibly be as good today: because 'the guidance of nature has been neglected, the task of resistance has been thrown upon the man instead of the woman.'[18]

A final observation of the 1834 report is that the welfare system was getting too costly. The cost of 'relief' (welfare payments) had jumped to a level five and a half times higher in 1832 than it had been in 1760 whereas the population had only doubled.[19]

So the stage was set. The commissioners had clearly decided that the welfare state of 1834 was causing massive social, moral and financial problems. What would they recommend should be done? Would the government take any notice? Would it actually do something effective?

The commissioners noted that many people agreed that the way the Poor Law operated was bad but 'many who acknowledge the evil seem to expect the cure of an inveterate disease, without exposing the patient to any suffering or even discomfort.'[20] The commissioners were not going to be guilty of any such irresolution. They had been impressed by what had been achieved in certain parishes to get people off welfare dependency. The Rev. Robert Lowe in the parish of Bingham, in Nottinghamshire, had refused to give welfare benefits outside the poorhouse – a very uncompromising regime. But the results had been dramatic. After a few months, the numbers in the workhouse had dropped from forty-five to twelve, 'who were all either old, idiots, or infirm and to whom a workhouse is really a place of comfort'.

The commissioners commented:

> *When the relief, though adequate, has been rendered ineligible* [i.e. unattractive] – *new life, new energy is infused into the constitution of the pauper; he is aroused like one from sleep, his relation with all his neighbours, high and low, is changed; he surveys his former employers with new eyes. He begs a job – he will not take a denial – he discovers that everyone wants something to be done. He desires to make up this man's hedges, to clear out another man's ditches, to grub stumps out of the hedgerows for a third; nothing can escape his eye, and he is ready to turn his hand to anything.*[21]

Accordingly, the commissioners proposed a solution so radical that it may astonish a modern audience. They proposed that virtually all welfare benefits paid to people outside the poorhouse should be abolished. More draconian still, they proposed that the regime of the poorhouses should be made tougher.

In the most famous words of this remarkable report, it was said that the life of a person on benefits should 'not be made really or apparently more eligible as the situation of the independent labourer of the lowest class'.

The logic was impeccable. If living on benefits was *more* attractive than work for a low-paid worker, why should that man or woman bother to work?

The commissioners convinced the country – or at least Parliament – that their ideas were correct. The report was signed on 20 February 1834. A law embodying it was introduced and enacted within the year. The government response to the report was staggeringly fast by modern standards. The principle of 'less eligibility' dominated treatment of the poor for the next seventy-five years.

What happened to Britain in the wake of the 1834 report?

Was it a coincidence that Chadwick's reforms were followed a period in which virtue, duty and work came to be highly esteemed?

Samuel Smiles wrote *Self-Help* in 1859, an extended tribute to independence and self-sufficiency. The book told the inspirational stories of people who had made good, often despite very difficult circumstances at the beginning. It was very influential, selling quarter of a million copies by the end of the century.

What we now call the Victorian virtues flourished. Of course there were criminals and violence, but in so far as it is possible to tell, this was a period of time in which there was more sense of decency and purpose than in most other times. It is surely possible, to put it modestly, that the change in economic and moral behaviour in Victorian times was, at least partly, due to the changes made as a result of the Royal Commission. And all from the announcement made in Parliament on that cold, dry winter's day in 1832 by Viscount Althorp.

On the economic side, growth in the following seventy years was dramatic. Industrial production at the end of the century was 5.4 times what it had been in 1834.[22] There was a major rise in the wealth of the average Briton despite a vast increase in the population – something which would normally keep down the rise in individual wealth. Average wages, after adjusting for inflation, rose 50 per cent between 1880 and the end of the century.[23]

> **'The spirit of self-help is the root of all genuine growth in the individual ... Help from without is often enfeebling.'**
>
> **Samuel Smiles, *Self-Help***

According to another authority, the rate of growth per head was faster between 1855 and 1884 than at any time since.[24]

The following years also brought forth something that even Chadwick did not forecast. It is also something about which most British commentators about politics and society know absolutely nothing. It is a lost part of British history.

The winter of 1860–61 was extremely cold. There were heavy, long-lasting frosts. Snowfall was prolonged. Many outdoor industries such as house-building were forced to stop with the result that people could not get work. So people who had never previously applied for money from the parish did so.

In many cases, no doubt, they got it. But many parishes – not all – were trying to enforce the tough law instituted in 1834. In such cases, the applicant was told that he would get no money unless he entered the workhouse. People who were by no means 'work shy' had major financial problems. In the face of this, many, many new charities were established. Some newspapers invited readers to send in money for relief of the poor. People even sent money direct to the magistrates who

> 'In spite of the deficiencies of data,
> however, and the erratic path of U.K.
> growth in the twentieth century it
> seems clear that long term rates of
> growth have been substantially lower
> than those prevailing at the end of the
> nineteenth century'
>
> **Phyllis Deane and W. A. Cole,**
> **British Economic Growth 1688–1959**

decided on whether applicants for funds should be given any.

Then, a few years later, came a crisis affecting the cotton industry. Again, many people wanted to help those affected with charitable gifts.

Finally there came a third blow. A slump, in 1866, threw people out of work and, again, this stimulated the many charities.

Of course charity existed on a major scale before the 1860s. But in that decade it grew to an unprecedented size. Charitable work undoubtedly increased in response to the toughening up of the state's welfare in 1834. A climate of opinion was created among the middle and upper classes which was totally different from that of today. Charitable giving and charitable work had been going on for centuries before, but in the Victorian age they reached a new peak.

It is hard for us to imagine now how large charity loomed in people's lives during the late nineteenth century. *The Times* in 1885 reported that the combined incomes of London charities came to more than the revenues of several European governments. Ten years later, a survey reported that the average middle-class household spent 10 per cent of its income on charities. It spent more on charity than on housing or on clothing – more, in fact, than on anything else with the exception of food. If one thinks of people in modern times spending more on charity than on, say, their clothes, the expenditure would be enormous.

Charity was not confined to the middle classes, either. A survey of working-class and artisan families found that half of them made weekly subscriptions to charities. About a quarter also donated money to a church or chapel. It is quite a contrast with modern Britain, where only a small minority gives money of any substance. The BBC makes appeals for Children in Need and congratulates viewers and listeners on their 'magnificent generosity'. But the charitable giving of modern Britain is a pinprick compared to that of the Victorians. Modern Britons give away only a small fraction of the what the Victorians gave. Charitable giving in Britain has collapsed. The Victorians gave up to 10 per cent of their incomes. Modern Britons give less than 1 per cent.

You name it and a charity was created to look after it. William Beveridge, best known for his 1942 report, wrote *Voluntary Action*, a book on charities and other voluntary activities. He listed leading charities under seventeen categories. Let's take just one: provision for the homeless. He named the SOS Society, the Fellowship of St Christopher, the Society for the Relief of the Houseless Poor, Rowton Houses Ltd, Cecil Houses, Homes for Working Boys in London, Embankment Fellowship Centre, the Morning Post Embankment Home and the Wayfarers Benevolent Association. These were only the leading charities in this sphere, remember. There were plenty more working in the same sphere.

Beveridge also had a chapter on the 'pioneers' of charitable work – people he evidently regarded as heroes. The majority were Victorians. They created many of the best-known of modern charities such as the National Institute for the Blind (created by a Thomas Armitage, who himself became blind), the NSPCC (created by Benjamin Waugh) and Dr Barnardo's Homes.

The massive effort being devoted to charities of various sorts even caused some problems. Different charities for the poor could be operating in the same area trying to do the same sort of thing. They could even be giving money to the same people. As a vicar observed, 'a hundred different agencies for the relief of distress are at work over the same ground, without concert or co-operation, or the slightest information as to each other's exertions.' The result, he said, was unparalleled

'Are there no workhouses?' said Scrooge. He was being asked to contribute to a charity just before Christmas. This was the most famous sentence in a tirade against giving. Modern audiences may be tempted to take it as an example of Victorian meanness and money-grubbing. In fact, we should note that the two well-to-do gentlemen who had come round to ask for money were astonished and incredulous at his refusal. As the Victorian readers would have known, it was highly unusual for a wealthy man not to give to charity.

growth in begging and 'shameless pauperism'. This word 'pauperism' was generally used in the nineteenth century to mean what we would call welfare dependency. But here it seems to mean something more like 'professional welfare dependency'. He is suggesting that some of the poor arranged as well as they could to receive a collection of hand-outs from as many different charities as possible.

The rise and fall of charity

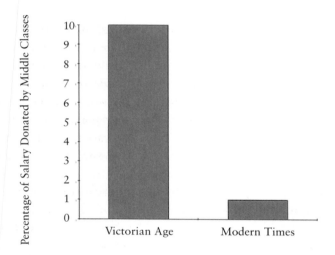

Sources: *The Times* survey of middle-class donations in late nineteenth century; the NCVO and *Social Trends* for modern times[25]

Just as the state's attempts at being kind had come unstuck in the scandals and distortions at the beginning of the nineteenth century, so, soon after the middle of the century, the charities seemed to be getting into great difficulty, too. In response, the Charity Organisation Society was created. The idea was that any charity which wanted to find out about a person, before giving him or her money, could ask the Charitable Organisation Society. The organisation would therefore prevent two, three or more charities giving to the same person. The fact that this was a serious problem gives an idea of just how big the business of charity had become.

The Charity Organisation Society, like others, adopted the philosophy of Thomas Chalmers. Chalmers was one of several people who worked with the poor in the nineteenth century and whose views became highly influential. He, like the others, knew and thought about welfare far more than the vast majority of commentators on the subject today. He should, perhaps, be better known.

Who was this man? Why was he so influential?

He came from a big, middle-class Scottish family.[26] From early on, his exceptional ability was obvious. He entered St Andrews University at the age of eleven and enrolled as a student of divinity aged fifteen. He was only twenty-two when he became an assistant in the subject at the same university.

His lectures at St Andrews were more lively than those of his superiors. They did not like this, so he was sacked at the end of the term. In the summer he was ordained as minister of the parish of Kilmany, not far from St Andrews. He was therefore able to visit the town despite having lost his job at the university. He offered classes independently. Pupils had to pay to attend and the university was against him, but his lectures were so popular that he was soon conducting three classes in mathematics and one in chemistry. In the end, his special ability was admitted by the university and he was taken back.

He added astronomy and political economy to the subjects on which he lectured. Then came the major turning point in his life. He became severely ill. His life was in grave danger. When he recovered he thanked God and resolved, aged twenty-nine, to change his life. From that moment on, he gave his all to 'pastoral visitation' – visiting the people of his parish to help and comfort them – and to preaching.

He had noticed something when he was working with the poor in his twenties. He had worked in two parishes. The first, in Roxburghshire, had adopted the Poor Laws from England. The second, Kilmany, relied entirely on private charity.

He noted the difference in behaviour between the people of the two parishes. In the former 'I saw as much poverty and more depravity of character than I hope I shall ever witness in these northern climes.' Although the population of the two parishes was similar, the expenditure on the poor was six times greater in the one with the Poor Laws

Thomas Chalmers noticed a contrast between the effect of state benefits and that of private charity.

than in that where only private charity was available. He saw a connection between liberal state hand-outs and poor behaviour.

But as his ideas about looking after the poor developed, he went further. He began to oppose large, centrally run charities as much as state welfare. The reason was that he had come to believe that – with encouragement and advice – most people could get through a bad patch and continue to be self-reliant. He thought that any cash payment should be temporary and accompanied by a great deal of personal contact. This is the very opposite of what a modern welfare state does. Modern social security systems typically offer a great deal of cash and hardly any personal contact.

His comment about the effect of money from overlarge charities could be applied just as well to state social security. He said 'the imagination of a mighty and inexhaustible fund' was sure to 'excite the appetite and so to relax the frugal and providential habits of its receivers'.

Quite contrary to the Royal Commissioners, he was against centrally run welfare in any form. He argued, 'There is a charm in locality most powerfully felt by every man who tries it ... who has personally attached himself to a manageable portion of the civic territory.' Those who have been governors of a single school or constables with a defined beat may readily understand what he meant.

His emphasis on local work, done within local limits, set Chalmers apart from the drift of nearly all policy-making in the past two centuries. But it was quite in tune with social security as it had evolved under Henry VIII and Elizabeth I. That had always been parish-based and a parish could well consist of 1,000 people or fewer.

Thomas Chalmers' chance to put his ideas into action came when his considerable fame as a preacher saw him appointed to the newly created parish of St John in Glasgow. Before agreeing to take it on, he insisted that he should be given full control over assistance to the poor.

The parish was a big one, with more than 8,000 residents. That was too big for his idea of the benefits of 'locality'. So he divided it into twenty-five districts and appointed deacons to be responsible for administering charity within them. He instructed the deacons to offer advice, civility and goodwill but at the same time – if it seemed that money might be paid over – to enquire very closely into the circumstances of the family. This is the opposite of a modern welfare state. In modern times, a claimant will answer questions in a form but will not be questioned 'very closely'. He or she may be treated with 'civility' but would be lucky to receive 'goodwill'.

Chalmers told the deacons to go through stages before offering money. First, they were to see if there was any kind of work that would enable the poor person to avoid becoming dependent on charity at all. Second, they were to ask whether the person's relatives and friends could help. Third, they were to check whether there was any charity the person was receiving from any other church.

If, after this, the deacon felt that money should be given to the person, then he might give a temporary amount. If the deacon felt that a regular allowance should be made, he would call in another deacon to look at the case in even more detail, enquiring into the rent paid, any earnings received and so on. Chalmers' view was, 'in proportion to the care with which you investigate will be the rarity of the applications that are made to you'. This kind of 'tough love' charitable work was new at the time. It has its echo in modern America, where some charitable organisations now befriend people in difficulty.[27]

And how did Chalmers' charitable work turn out? During the four years he was running it, only twenty new applications were accepted from the population of 8,000 – a rate far below that elsewhere. So much money was saved that the parish was able to contribute to the endowment of a school.

Chalmers' work and his writings influenced charity work during the whole of the rest of the century and his ideas spread across the world. Only as the twentieth century progressed did the memory of his ideas diminish.

But it would be quite wrong to get an image of nineteenth-century Britain simply as a place where most of the people were giving to charity and the rest were receiving it. Something else happened that was even more important. It was utterly different, very positive, and even inspirational.

Henry Brady was a teacher at Ackworth School near Ponte-fract in Yorkshire. He was married, with children. This was a time when lives could easily be cut short by diseases such as tuberculosis and

> 'There is a far greater sufficiency among the lower classes of society than is generally imagined; and our first impressions of their want and wretchedness are generally by much too aggravated: nor do we know a more effectual method of reducing these impressions than to cultivate a closer acquaintance with their resources, and their habit, and their whole domestic economy.'
>
> **Thomas Chalmers**

typhoid. Cholera had begun to take lives, too. One of those who died from it was Brady. Unfortunately he was not old enough to have saved much, so his wife and children were suddenly in serious difficulties without his income. The family were Quakers and may well have received some support from their community. But it was far from ideal.

The next year, 1829, when Ackworth School had its usual annual reunion, Samuel Tuke and Joseph Rowntree were among the former students who attended. They heard of Brady's death and the unfortunate circumstances of his wife and children. They wondered whether there was something that could be done which would stop people getting into that kind of difficulty in future. Was there a way in which families could protect themselves against such disasters?

They came up with some ideas. Two years later, in 1831, they went to another of the annual reunions and put forward a suggestion. They proposed a 'friendly society'. The object would be to offer ways in which members could counter the major risks of life. A variety of policies would be offered but the central one, at first, would be a 'whole life' policy. People would be able to pay in a regular sum. If they died, a large lump sum would be paid to their surviving families. Most people who took out such policies would not die young, of course. So the money they subscribed would look after the minority of families which did suffer a calamity. It was a simple idea.

The society they started was called Friends Provident Institution. That same friendly society has since grown. As laws have changed it has had to change its legal status so it is now called Friends Provident plc. It has become a vast company with £29 billion of investments. Its roots, though, lie in the death of that one teacher, Henry Brady, in 1828.

Friends Provident was just one of thousands of friendly societies created in the nineteenth century. Once the Poor Laws had been tightened up in 1834 and again later, people had every reason to protect themselves against all manner of things: old age, illness and unemployment.

The Manchester Oddfellows friendly society was, according to tradition, set up by a group of friends meeting in a pub. Plenty of other friendly societies were first established in a similar way. Others were based on religious communities, like Friends Provident. Others still were based on professions such as medicine or on a particular place.

Wherever you lived, you were likely to have a choice. In Cottenham, Cambridgeshire, nine different friendly societies were active in the early 1870s although there were only 500 members of friendly societies there in all.[28] You could choose a society that fitted your needs and tastes. It was a strength compared to state welfare that William Beveridge himself recognised and admired. He said that in a totalitarian state, the only thing you could do if you did not like the institutions was to change the government. But in 'a free society' anyone unhappy with the institutions could make a new one. 'The field is open to experiment and success or failure ... The new one may fail or remain limited. It may grow according to the life that is in it, and growing may change the world.'[29]

That is what the friendly societies did. They grew up spontaneously and changed the world. They transformed Britain along with other mutual and cooperative societies. They spread to America, Australia, Canada and elsewhere.

The growth of friendly societies was an astonishing phenomenon. Between 1803 and 1877, the membership more than tripled to 2.7 million people. In the next decade nearly another million were added. In the decade after that, more than a million were added, and in the thirteen years after that, nearly two million more (see table). The numbers were not just going up. They were galloping – much faster than the population at large. And these were only the registered friendly societies. There were also unregistered ones, which were thought to have just as many members.

In 1892, the total membership of the registered societies came to 3.8 million, which represents around three million people, allowing for those who were members of more than one society. Adding another three million for members of the unregistered societies brings the total to six million out of an industrial male population of seven million.[30] That is without counting 873,000 members of trade unions, some of which offered benefits similar to those of friendly societies.

The chief registrar of friendly societies at the time, Sir Edward Brabrook, estimated that there was only 'a kind of residuum' of people going without some kind of insurance against the risks of life.

Membership of registered friendly societies

	Members
1803	704,350
1877	2,750,000
1887	3,600,000
1897	4,800,000
1910	6,600,000

Source: Green, David, *Reinventing Civil Society* (Institute of Economic Affairs, London, 1993)

The friendly societies offered security. But they offered something else as well. New members of many friendly societies had to go to lectures to understand what they could expect of the society and what the society would expect of them. New members at the Ancient Order of Foresters were told that they should be 'affectionate and trustful' as husbands, 'regardful of the moral and material well-being of your children and dependants' as fathers, 'dutiful and exemplary' as sons and, as friends, 'steadfast and true'.

A judge or a baron of commerce could easily be junior to a dock worker within a friendly society. A poor manual worker could become chairman of his local lodge. In the lodges of the Manchester Unity, the chairman would have two 'supporters' who would sit on each side of him at a meeting.[31] Traditionally the chairman would choose a personal friend and someone who was experienced in the rules and practices of the society. The office of chairman was rotated so that, over time, almost everyone would hold the post. It gave an experience of give and take, of community action and of voluntarily holding and responding to authority which few people now enjoy.

Commercial insurance companies started offering insurance against illness, too. But they were forced to give it up because of the high level of fraud. Friendly societies were able to go on offering sickness benefits because they suffered much less fraud. Members felt a sense of commitment to the community they had entered which they did not feel towards a remote commercial company.

Most people who write about the friendly societies do so – as I have here – with barely repressed enthusiasm and admiration. Doubtless the societies had their faults. At the very least, one can readily imagine, as in a golf club, some leading members getting carried away with their sense of self-importance. But it is hard not to believe that they helped many people become better than they otherwise might have been, as well as offering security against many of life's dangers.

Their great flowering, however, was about to undermined. They were to be dealt two blows. The first wounded. The second was mortal. Because of these two blows, there is only a rump of friendly societies today and few people have even heard of them. Who destroyed the friendly societies and why?

A trip to Germany

David Lloyd George went for his summer holiday in 1908 to Germany. It was a rather unusual affair. This rising political star found someone else to pick up the bill. A Mr Henry, a rich and, apparently, pompous MP, also in the Liberal Party, paid the expenses and came along.

According to the gossip, he generously provided something else, too: his wife. The sleeping arrangements are not recorded, but the trip provided the perfect cover for a liaison.

Making up the party in a junior role was Harold Spender – a journalist who wrote for the relatively down-market *Daily Chronicle*. He was taken along, no doubt, to ensure the trip was reported in the British press in the way Lloyd George would want.

They took a train to Amiens in France, where they were met by their 'motor'.[32] As a result of a 'happy miscalculation' they spent the first night at a clean little *auberge* just within France, high up in the Vosges mountains. The next day they drove down to Strasbourg and happened to be there on the day when Count Zeppelin was starting his new airship on a voyage. The local crowd patriotically sang *Deutschland über alles* and the airship rose, but then burst into flames and crashed. Lloyd George's party arrived just after this terrible moment and was confronted by the crowd fleeing in alarm.

The supposed purpose of this bizarre holiday was for Lloyd George to study German social policy. For a while, he seemed more interested in making pronouncements on foreign affairs but eventually he devoted three days of serious study to the subject.[33] He went to the Imperial Insurance Offices on one of these days to learn about German health and old-age insurance policies. The officials flatteringly told him that they had never met such a 'quick-witted man' who had achieved an 'extraordinary grasp' of the issues, placing him 'on a level with the most perfectly equipped specialists'. Mind you, this account comes from Harold Spender, the journalist taken on the trip to report things the right way.

Lloyd George gave an interview – to the *Daily Chronicle* of course – on his arrival back at Southampton docks. He announced that government insurance for sickness and invalidity was 'one of the most magnificent pieces of social organisation that the world at present possesses'. It was 'wonderful'. It was 'gigantic'.

Lloyd George was building up to introducing something similar in Britain. Why was he so keen to find a 'wonderful' answer? What was the problem which was in need of a solution? Had Britain suddenly developed a new problem with sickness and invalidity which it had never experienced before? No. Something else had changed. The politics had changed.

In 1883, the Fabian Society was founded. In 1884, the franchise had been extended from three million to about five million voters. James Keir Hardie, a former miner, became a member of Parliament as an

Independent in 1892 and was the first leader of the Independent Labour Party in the House of Commons. The ideas of Marx and Engels were spreading within and outside the Labour Party. The working classes were being encouraged to see themselves as victims of the capitalist economic system. Between 1886 and 1903, Charles Booth issued a series of reports suggesting that one-third of the population was on or below the poverty line. R. Seebohm Rowntree issued a report in 1901 arguing that 27.84 per cent of the population was in poverty.

These changes in working-class perceptions and political power changed everything. They even changed the language. The word 'unemployed' was first found in a dictionary in 1888. Before that time, unemployment had existed, of course. But it was previously something that happened because of a downturn in a particular industry or because someone was between jobs or because someone was work-shy or incapable. Now theories began to be developed as to how it was a systemic failing of capitalism. It therefore had to be given a new title.

Two years previously, in February 1886, came a major wake-up call for the bourgeoisie nervously watching such developments. There was a riot in the prosperous West End of London. It was a nothing compared to what the Continent had experienced over the last century, but it helped convince many of the richer people that something had to be done to palliate the irate workers.

In 1906, the Liberals overwhelmingly won the election. But Labour got thirty seats – a great leap from the two it had before. Labour then started winning by-elections. The threat to the Liberals was obvious. By 1908, the Liberal government was struggling for direction and some way to head off the threat of socialism, at which moment Lloyd George made his trip to Germany. That is why a great scheme supposedly for the benefit of the working class was something that this canny politician was keen to embrace. Lloyd George was not an expert in social policies. The action he took was that of a politician trying to save his party's – and thus his own – skin.

Lloyd George brought forward his Bill in 1911 for insurance against sickness and invalidity. The contributions were fixed, as were the benefits, so everyone still had every reason to save and be thrifty with their money. There were no reductions in payments if you had savings.

This Bill was not intended to damage the friendly societies. Lloyd George, like most people, greatly admired them. The last thing he wanted to do was hurt them. The administration of this insurance was even to be in the hands of the friendly societies, such was the respect in which they were held. But this was the first blow they suffered. The voluntary membership which the friendly societies had was beginning to be replaced by a compulsory, state system.

The new law went well beyond the German model in one very significant way. The second part of the bill, introduced by the young Winston Churchill (then also a Liberal), introduced national insurance against unemployment. This was the first compulsory national insurance scheme introduced anywhere in the world. Churchill thought he could make a name for himself. He wrote to the Prime Minister, Herbert Asquith: 'The Minister who will apply to this country the successful experiences of Germany in Social Organisation ... will ... have left a memorial which time will not deface.'

Typically, Churchill made it sound all very grand. But the fact remains that the vast majority of people were already

Lloyd George and Churchill, the originators of the modern welfare state.

covered. About ten million out of the twelve million who came to be covered by national insurance in 1911 were already insured though their friendly society or trade union.

This was, perhaps, the moment when the *modern* welfare state began. Most people think it was 1942 or 1945 but 1911 is when the core was put in place. And it was not long until it began significantly to affect British society. The interwar years were the first to feel its impact – and they did so in a way that is completely unknown to most people. We are now coming to the first of three main charges against the social security aspect of the modern welfare state.

The first charge

For fifteen years or so after the National Insurance Act was introduced by Lloyd George and Churchill, it was extended and liberalised far

beyond the original conception. Insurance for the unemployed originally only covered 2.25 million people. But in 1916 it was extended to
cover four million. In 1920 it was made to cover two-thirds of the
employed workforce.[34] The conditions and amounts of the benefits
grew as politicians vied to show how generous they could be. In 1918,
former soldiers who were unemployed were given benefits quite beyond
anything that could genuinely be called 'insurance'. Soon after, the rule
that people had to pay contributions for a certain length of time before
getting benefits was bent. In no time, the state stopped being an insurer
in a real sense and became a benefactor instead. The state was heading
fast towards high spending on the unemployed and the ill.

Many educated people reckon they have a pretty good idea what happened in the following interwar years. First there was the 'Roaring
Twenties'. Then there was the Wall Street Crash, which came down
hard on Britain as well as America. Things were made worse than they
need have been because Britain clung to the gold standard, which was
harshly deflationary at precisely the wrong time. So we then got the
Great Depression. The King and many politicians were appalled at the
conditions of the long-term unemployed. Then along came the war,
which increased demand and belatedly saved the day. After the war, the
welfare state was created to make sure nothing so awful as the depression could hurt Britain ever again.

I used to believe this account. It has been taught in schools and universities and replayed, in whole or in part, in countless books, radio
interviews and television documentaries. But there is a problem. It does
not fit the facts.

There was actually significant economic growth during the interwar
years. The average rate of growth between 1921 and 1938 was two per
cent, not very different from the growth rate just before the First World
War.[35] There was no long-term shortage of demand.

Unemployment was not predominantly long-term either. A Royal
Commission on Unemployment Insurance in 1930 found that claimants
had on average experienced 7.3 separate periods of unemployment in
that single year. The taking of many short bursts of unemployment was
extremely commonplace. This was made possible by the conditions of
unemployment benefit. So the idea of persistent low demand and long-
term unemployment is not accurate.

Also, large-scale unemployment did not take place only after the
Wall Street Crash. There were high levels throughout the 1920s and
1930s. The average rate was 14 per cent and the figure never fell below

9.5 per cent. The usual story about the interwar years does not account for why unemployment should have stayed so high for so long. It does not explain why unemployment in those years was consistently higher than in the pre-war years too. In only two years between 1855 and 1920 was unemployment as high as it was in every year from 1921 to 1938. Though the economy grew for six straight years from 1932 to 1938, unemployment still did not fall below 9.5 per cent. After six years of growth, unemployment was still three times higher than the prewar rate. It is true that the stock market crash and adherence to the gold standard caused a major economic problem. But was something else contributing to the unprecedented level of unemployment?

One big thing that had changed compared to previous decades was the national insurance for the unemployed introduced by Churchill. Could that have had anything to do with it?

By 1931, weekly benefit exceeded half average weekly earnings. The benefit could be drawn by someone who had made thirty weekly insurance contributions at any time in his life. He could draw the unemployment benefit for an unlimited period. It sounds dry and technical.

But the potentially powerful effect of these terms becomes clearer when you imagine someone who had below-average earnings; let us say, 30 to 50 per cent below average. That person received between 80 and 100 per cent of the money he could earn from working by getting unemployment benefits instead. Such a person would not have been as desperate to get a job. Such a person certainly would not have accepted a new job paying less than the benefit. Benefits were increased in 1936 and 1938 to the point where they were nearly 60 per cent of average wages.

What about the frequent short-term unemployment reported by the government in 1931? Could it have had anything to do with the terms of the benefits?

It was easily possible, under the terms which existed then, to work for three days in the week and be unemployed on benefits for the other three. The system was so well known, there was even a catchphrase for it. It was called 'three on the book, three on the hook'. Workers could also rotate their jobs in what came to be called the 'OXO' system. Each day you worked was an O and each day you took benefit instead was an X. The employee would get the benefit of plenty of days off with little, if any, reduction of income. Meanwhile the employer could keep available to him a bigger workforce to cover any upturn in demand for his product.

William Beveridge was among those who observed this. He remarked that some industries, such as cotton, were tending to practise short-time working 'continually' and 'to keep an excessive labour force together at the cost of the unemployment fund'.[36] So while the Wall Street Crash and the effort to adhere to the gold standard certainly contributed to severe unemployment in the short term, the high level of continuing unemployment may have been caused by the benefits.

The welfare state – at least as far as social security was concerned – was much bigger and more 'generous' before the Second World War than most people realise. It is hard to resist the conclusion that it contributed to The Great Depression.

We now get to the moment where most accounts of the welfare state begin. But even here, there are major misunderstandings. People think it worked pretty well to begin with, but then unemployment became a persistent problem. However, they have no real explanation of why it worked pretty well to begin with and why unemployment then spoiled the picture. It may be possible to explain both.

The true nature of William Beveridge – the most famous man in British welfare – provides part of the answer. He was not the man people think him to be. And his report was not what most people think it was.

Born in 1879, Beveridge was the son of a British judge working in India.[38] He was an upper-class Victorian. The home in which he was brought up had twenty-six servants. He went to public school – at Charterhouse – and then to Balliol College, Oxford. He was undoubtedly extremely clever, if rather pompous and self-regarding.

> 'It is significant that after every public holiday – Christmas, Easter, Whitsuntide – there is a very large addition to the unemployment total, which falls off again a few weeks later.'[37]
>
> **Winston Churchill, 1930**

At Balliol he was influenced by the Master, Edward Caird, who used to urge undergraduates to 'go and discover why, with so much wealth in Britain, there continues to be so much poverty and how poverty can be cured.' Following that instruction, Beveridge, at twenty-four, went to Toynbee Hall, the university foundation for the poor in the East End of London. In 1905, on Caird's recommendation, he became a leader-writer for the Tory-supporting *Morning Post*, which was later merged with the *Daily Telegraph*.[39] In 1907 he visited Germany to study the social insurance system, a year before Lloyd George did the same. His writing on social insurance issues brought him to the attention of Churchill, who recruited him to work as a civil servant. Over the next three years, Beveridge created a national network of labour exchanges for

Churchill. He was the first director of them. Beveridge was part of the Lloyd George–Churchill team which kicked off the modern welfare state. And like Lloyd George and Churchill, his hopes and ambitions were miles away from what the welfare state has become. He wanted people to remain self-reliant. He wanted self-sufficiency and mutual support through friendly societies to continue. He never had it in mind to destroy the welfare system that already existed before the welfare state.

He carried with him the idea – powerfully expressed by Edwin Chadwick in 1834 – that benefits should never be so high as to deter a low-paid worker from taking a job. He knew the risks of benefits. But he thought that the problem of poverty could be overcome if everyone was compelled to take out insurance against the risks of life. It was a 'third way' which avoided the problems both of excess harshness and dangerous generosity. There would be no hardship because everybody would be insured. End of problem.

One of the curiosities of Beveridge and his report is that he did not want to write it. He regarded himself as a leading figure who should have a vital job. After working for Churchill, he had been Director of the London School of Economics and Master of University College, Oxford. He had been at the top for decades. He had known Sidney and Beatrice Webb, the prominent welfare reformers, and Churchill, of course. He was in touch with the leading economist John Maynard Keynes. He wanted to organise the workforce for the war effort.

But Ernest Bevin, for whom Beveridge was working at the time, did not much like this pompous, pushy man, so he asked him to write the report as a way of 'getting rid of someone whom he had come to see as a pain in the neck'.[40] The report Beveridge was meant to write sounded tedious in the extreme. He was to 'undertake, with special reference to the inter-relation of the schemes, a survey of the existing national schemes of social insurance and allied services, including workmen's compensation, and to make recommendations'. It was a mere tidying-up operation. Famously tears 'started to his eyes' because he was so disappointed. He sulked for a few months, completing other work.

An extraordinary article which was turned up during the research for this book appeared in *Picture Post* in March 1942. It was obviously written with Beveridge's cooperation. It said he was a brilliant person 'presiding over an investigation into social insurance'. 'But is this job worthy of him?' the writer asked. Beveridge himself was quoted saying, 'It's very interesting. But it's post-war. I could only be satisfied with it if I thought you young fellows could win the war alone.' The final words of the article were 'can we afford to waste such talents?'.

This was part of Beveridge's sulk. But once he had reconciled himself to the task, Beveridge set about turning this 'waste' of his talents into a triumph. He went miles beyond his original brief. He adopted the language of a grand, new plan for making a better Britain. He made it appear that he was recommending something brand new and extraordinary.

Beveridge himself started the continuing myth about his report – that it was radically generous. He made his plan seem bold and comprehensive. He depicted a future Britain that was nothing to do with his remit. He talked of a national health service. He 'assumed' full employment, being a believer that Keynes's theory of 'aggregate demand' had solved the problem of unemployment. He wrote grandiloquently of defeating the 'five giants': want, ignorance, disease, squalor and idleness. By throwing in 'ignorance' he barged into the field of education for good measure.

The apparent over-arching ambition of his plan, couched in language that made it appear thoroughly logical and achievable, answered a kind of longing in the British public. Homes were being destroyed and lives lost. People wanted to believe that at the end of it all, they were making sacrifices for a better tomorrow.

Beveridge's report was to be published on the first day of December 1942. The night before, a queue formed outside His Majesty's Stationery Office in London. The report flew off the shelves as quickly as a novel by Dickens or the next volume in the story of Harry Potter. Sales topped a hundred thousand in the first month. Copies were circulated to the troops. In addition to the full report, a cut-down summary was available for threepence (1-1/4p). The two versions together sold six hundred thousand copies.

William Beveridge himself started the myth about his report.

In a survey at the time, nineteen out of twenty people had heard of the report and almost all were in favour of it.[41] Virtually all politicians felt they must endorse it – Churchill among them. In March the next year, he made a broadcast which reflected and increased the enthusiasm. He declared: 'You must rank me and my colleagues as strong partisans of national compulsory insurance for all classes, for all purposes, from the cradle to the grave.' Most people who talk about a welfare state offering care 'from the cradle to the grave' have no idea it was Churchill – who by then had long since changed from a Liberal to a Conservative – who created the phrase.

So what did Beveridge propose? It was very simple. Everyone would make flat-rate contributions to a national insurance scheme. Those who fell ill, became unemployed or reached retirement age would, in return, receive flat-rate payments. That is it. The rest was detail.

The attractions of his plan were many. No one would fall through the net because everyone would, compulsorily, be covered. The same scheme would apply to everyone, rich and poor. That appealed to the wartime sense that 'we are all in the same boat.'

But beneath these populist appeals, there was gritty Victorian reasoning that many people did not notice at the time and have not recognised or understood since. He asserted that the benefits should be at a 'subsistence' level. Subsistence! The word is barely noticed by most who write about the report. Subsistence level means 'a standard of living barely adequate to support life'.[42] The person credited with launching a new period of generosity in welfare only recommended a bare minimum. The benefits should only be basic, he argued, otherwise they would discourage voluntary insurance and savings. Beveridge was a great admirer of the friendly societies and indeed of charities and other voluntary organisations. His was meanness with a purpose – to preserve self-reliance while at the same time eliminating poverty – real poverty.

This is not the Beveridge of folklore. This is the real, Victorian Beveridge – someone who wanted to interfere in people's lives as little as possible and to leave them with maximum responsibility and freedom. He wanted anyone on benefit to be required to go to a work or training centre. The unemployed would not be allowed to stay that way long term.

Beveridge thought that there would be little need for the means-tested benefit of national assistance because nearly everyone would be covered by his insurance plan. But anyone who did claim such a benefit was to have his 'means' (income and assets) examined and would be subject to unnamed conditions about his or her behaviour.

Beveridge rejected, on balance, a separate housing benefit based on the cost of someone's rent. Housing needs should be wrapped up in the weekly benefit, he said. Everyone should get the same amount. He thought it would be unfair to give someone living in a large house more

SEVEN QUOTATIONS FROM THE BEVERIDGE REPORT

'Flat rate of subsistence benefit; flat rate of contribution.' (s17)

'The state in organising security should not stifle incentive, opportunity, responsibility.' (s9)

'Unemployment benefit will ... normally be subject to a condition of attendance at a work or training centre after a certain period.' (s19vii)

'National assistance [means-tested benefit] is an essential subsidiary method in the whole plan ... The scope of assistance will be narrowed from the beginning and will diminish.' (s23)

'Assistance ... must be felt to be something less desirable than insurance benefit; otherwise the insured persons get nothing for their contributions. Assistance therefore will be given always subject to proof of needs and examination of means; it will be subject also to any conditions as to behaviour which may seem likely to hasten restoration of earning capacity.' (s369)

On the idea of a housing benefit: 'The proposal to adjust benefit according to the rent actually paid by individuals should, provisionally, be rejected.' (s215)

'Complete idleness even on an income demoralises.' (s440)

benefit than someone in a small one. He worried that the administration would be more complicated if it were made to cover precisely each rent paid. Under the Beveridge plan, anyone who became unemployed while living in a large or expensively located home might have to give it up and move somewhere more modest.

People who looked at the detail and actually read his words understood that the old Victorian was not proposing the bonanza which many assumed then and continue to believe. Keynes advised Beveridge on his costings and said, 'The Chancellor of the Exchequer should thank his stars that he has got off so cheap.' Members of the economic section of the Treasury believed that the Beveridge plan was actually cheaper than the provision which existed previously.[43]

They had every reason. Beveridge recommended unemployment benefit for a single man after the war of £1.20 a week.[44] But on the basis of his own calculations and expectations, this £1.20 would only have been worth 96p in pre-war money because of high inflation during the war. The benefit would have been only 13 per cent above the 1938 level of 85p – a modest rise indeed over the period of seven years between 1938 and the end of the war.

But alongside even this relatively modest increase, he recommended that, after six months, work or training would be 'required'. This was surely intended to end some of the prewar abuses of the welfare state. So the idea that Beveridge introduced an era of open-handed liberality does not fit his actual proposals.

Of course, Beveridge could only recommend what the rates should be and guess how wartime inflation would eventually turn out. But inflation continued so that, by 1946, prices had risen 65 per cent since 1938. The result was that the basic benefit was only worth 72.5p in 1938 money – a major drop. But a bigger fall was coming. The benefit was only increased occasionally, so its real value was undermined by inflation. By 1947, its real value had slumped to only 67.5p. And in 1950 – after all the hullabaloo about the Beveridge Plan and all the excitement over a new Labour government bent on providing generous social security – the benefit reached a new low of only 65.2p in real terms. It was a real decline of 23 per cent since 1938.

Weekly unemployment benefit adjusted for inflation

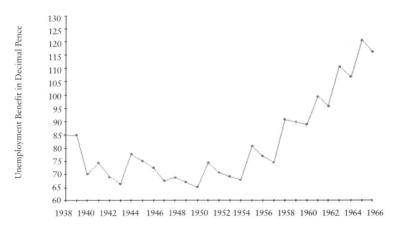

Sources: Benefit rates from Institute for Fiscal Studies website from 1948 and from Charles Clarke, *Social Insurance in Britain* from 1938.[45] Inflation statistics from House of Commons Library research paper, 1999

So Beveridge, combined with inflation and the government's parlous condition at the end of the war, significantly cut benefits during this period – the very opposite of what most people think. Beveridge also made the conditions under which benefits were given rather tougher and less easy to manipulate than they had been before the war.

These facts may make it easier to understand what might otherwise be one of the great puzzles about the welfare state. Why was unemployment low to begin with? And why did it keep rising afterwards?

In 1946, the unemployment rate was a mere 2.5 per cent. It fell to the 1.6–1.8 per cent range soon after and kept returning to that level right until 1966. But from then until the early 1980s, every new peak in unemployment was higher than the previous one. And even when the jobless total fell back during the short periods of growth, it never fell as low as it had done on the previous occasion. The long-term trend in joblessness was up, up, up. It reached 3.3 million in 1986, whereas it had been as low as 216,000 in 1954. Why?

The postwar puzzle of rising unemployment

Unemployment rate. Source: Labour Market Trends special feature January 1996

People do not always look at the numbers when studying welfare. But sometimes the numbers matter a great deal.

In July 1948, unemployment benefit for a single adult – at £1.30 a week – was 19 per cent lower than it had been ten years before. And what was the level of unemployment? Only 1.3 per cent of the workforce. The benefit was low and unemployment, similarly, was low. In 1951, the benefit was raised by a quarter, which must have seemed a big jump. But inflation since 1948 had reduced the value of money by more than that. So benefits stayed low in real terms. Unemployment stayed low, too.[46]

Registered unemployment before and after the real-term cuts in benefit effected after the Beveridge Report by the Attlee government

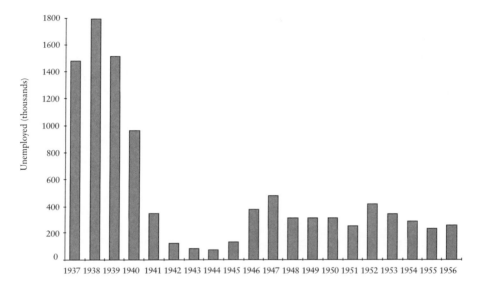

Note: after July 1940, men at Government Training Centres were no longer recorded as unemployed.
Source: Mitchell, B. R. and Deane, Phyllis, *Abstract of British Historical Statistics* (Cambridge University Press, Cambridge, 1962)

In 1955, things began to change a little. In May that year, after Sir Anthony Eden had taken over as Prime Minister from Sir Winston Churchill, benefits were dramatically increased. The rate for a single person leapt by 23.1 per cent whereas inflation in the previous three years had only amounted to 6.5 per cent. For the first time since 1938, the real income of the unemployed was significantly increased and the rise was sustained. But of course wages had risen quite a bit over the previous seventeen years, so the benefit was still lower than it had been compared to average wages. In 1958, when Harold Macmillan, another Conservative, was Prime Minister, the government did it again. It was a jump of a quarter in the benefit to £2.50 even though inflation between the two dates had amounted to only half that. Further jumps in benefit rate well above inflation came in 1961 and 1963. It was as if the Conservatives felt they had to show how generous they were. Not to be

outdone, when Labour finally regained power in 1965 under Harold
Wilson, it boosted the benefit by another 18.5 per cent to £4 a week.

In the decade beginning in April 1955, the increase in unemployment
benefit soared 72 per cent above inflation. The gap between what
someone could earn by working and what he or she could receive on
benefit was dramatically narrowed. Even after adjusting for inflation
and wages, the benefit was now at a new high.

If benefit levels were going to affect unemployment, you would
expect them to take time. People would not give up their jobs just to go
on benefits. But if they lost their job, they might not pursue a new one
so energetically if they found benefits were high. One would therefore
expect the higher benefit rates to impact only after some two to six
years. Bearing this in mind, was there a rise in unemployment after the
major rise in benefits between 1955 and 1965? Yes, it mushroomed.
After 1967, unemployment never went below 2 per cent again.

Weekly unemployment benefit adjusted for wage rises

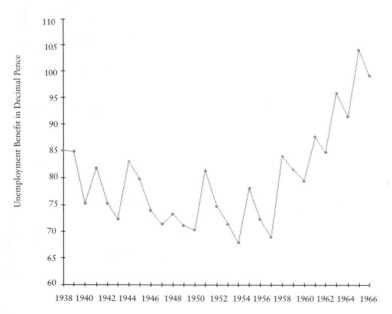

Sources: Benefit rates Institute for Fiscal Studies and Clarke, *Social Insurance in Britain*.
Basic weekly wage rates (June each year) from Office for National Statistics.

Over the next nine years, the rate of unemployment benefit continued
rising in real terms. The real value reached a new peak in July 1974 after

Harold Wilson gave the benefit one last boost, having won the election in March that year.

What happened to unemployment? Two years after the 1974 hike, it had risen to 5.7 per cent. Benefits stayed high through the 1970s, only declining a little under Labour. So what happened to the jobless rate? Soon after the end of that decade, in 1981, it stood at the unheard-of rate of 11.4 per cent. The peak would occur in the next year, when it reached 13 per cent of the workforce.

As the real value of unemployment benefit rose, so – after a lag – did unemployment.

The connection between benefit levels and unemployment appears all the stronger when we consider what happened next.

The real value of unemployment benefit reached a peak of £54.95 (at 2001 prices) in 1985. Ever since then, the value of the benefit in real terms has been similar or lower. By April 2001 it was down to £53.05. Meanwhile, of course, average earnings have continued to rise. The result is that it has gradually become worthwhile for more people to work again. For a married couple, unemployment benefit as a percentage of average earnings has fallen from 32.3 per cent in 1977 to only 19.8 per cent in 2001. To compound this, income tax payable on average earnings has been reduced too, widening further still the gap between earning and living on benefit. And what has happened? Unemployment has fallen. Reduced benefits have been followed by fewer people out of work.

SEVEN WAYS BEVERIDGE'S IDEAS WERE SUBSEQUENTLY IGNORED.

1. Benefits were raised above 'subsistence'.
2. Specific housing benefit was introduced.
3. National insurance benefits became worth little more than the means-tested benefits and sometimes less.
4. Means-tested benefits changed from being a mopping up for the minority into being the main form of welfare payment.
5. Flat-rate national insurance contributions were made variable.
6. Flat-rate benefits were made variable.
7. Conditions of benefit were relaxed. For example, the requirement on those who had been unemployed for six months to seek training was dropped.

The theory that high unemployment benefits lead to high unemployment is comprehensible in theory and is backed by the evidence.

The theory fits the low level of unemployment after the war, the rise from the late 1960s to the early 1980s and then the subsequent decline. On this basis, I conclude that the welfare state had the major role in causing post-war unemployment – unemployment which was on a scale never known before in British history. That is the first charge against social security and the welfare state.

Some may object that countries such as Sweden have managed high rates of benefit without causing unemployment at such a high level. This points to something else, apart from the value of benefits, which affects the impact.

Sweden has offered high benefits. The highest rate amounts to over £52 per working day at the time of writing.[47] But the conditionality of the benefits has been tough. That highest benefit is related to earnings. It is only available to those who have made earnings-related contributions to a voluntary insurance scheme. Those who have not contributed get less than half as much. Those contributing to the voluntary scheme get the benefit only if they have been a member of one of the forty schemes over the previous year. During that time they must have been employed for at least six months. The benefit is available for only three hundred days. In the words of the Swedish government, the scheme makes 'heavy demands' on the unemployed person to 'find a job quickly'. The individual 'must accept an offer of work even outside his or her previous occupational sphere, must accept a change of pay or must be prepared to relocate'.

These sorts of condition are almost as tough as those which would apply to a private scheme and it is not surprising that the Swedish system has its origins in private employment insurance. It is still divided into forty semi-independent schemes based on different kinds of work. But in Britain during the 1960s, 1970s and 1980s, it was regarded as far too harsh to expect a jobless person to change occupation, take a drop in pay or move to a different town.

Though the level of unemployment is well down on that of the 1980s, there were still a million people officially unemployed in 2003. That number of jobless people was regarded as scandalous in the early 1970s and perhaps it should still be regarded as scandalous.

But actually, the real numbers of unemployed may be far higher than one million.

For in addition to the official unemployed there may be a much bigger number of hidden unemployed. Here are some of the reasons to suspect it.

There was a remarkable rise in the number of people incapacitated by illness during the 1980s and early 1990s. People claiming invalidity benefit – now renamed 'incapacity benefit' – jumped from six hundred thousand in 1979 to 1.5 million in 1995.

There were a few curious things about this massive increase in incapacity that swept the country. One was the very particular nature of the kinds of long-term diseases and disabilities from which people suffered. Out of the 2.4 million people claiming incapacity benefit in May 2002, by far the biggest categories were the 819,000 people apparently suffering 'mental and behavioural disorders', a category which includes 'stress', and 523,000 people afflicted with 'diseases of the musculo-skeletal system and connective tissue', which includes backache. These two conditions have something in common. It is virtually impossible to prove whether people have them or not. The two categories account for over 56 per cent of all diseases causing incapacity. Meanwhile those suffering with readily verifiable conditions came in much smaller numbers. Those with diseases of the ear, for example, amount to only 9,800.

A second curious characteristic about this wave of incapacity was that it predominantly affected people in areas with high unemployment. Backache appeared to be something people particularly got if wages were low in relation to invalidity benefit.

A third point worth noting is that the conditions attached to invalidity benefit were different from those relating to unemployment benefit. The benefit was paid indefinitely, not for a fixed term. This made it more desirable.

But the most notable thing about this sudden attack of disability was the timing. It took place after the invalidity benefit rates were increased. When Bev-

Who is unwell?

1	Merthyr Tydfil	26.9%
2	Easington	26.2%
3	Glasgow	20.7%
4	Blaenau Gwent	19.8%
5	Liverpool	18.9%

Percentage of men aged 16–64 claiming sickness benefits: the top five districts for high incidence.

Source: Sheffield Hallam University[48]

eridge designed his plan, he recommended that everyone should get the same whether they were unemployed or incapacitated. This recommendation was followed until 1973 but then Edward Heath's government broke away from this principle and paid five per cent extra to the incapacitated. The incoming Labour government under Harold Wilson went a great deal further so that by, November 1978, invalidity benefit was worth 22.4 per cent more than unemployment benefit. It has kept and slightly increased its premium over unemployment benefit ever since.

France	2%
Spain	3%
Germany	4%
UK	7%

Percentage of working-age population on incapacity or other sickness benefits.[49]

It is hard to imagine that many of the 900,000 extra people who were claiming benefits in 1995 compared to sixteen years earlier were truly incapable of work. Dr Alan Paterson, a government occupational therapist, estimated in 1997 that 80 per cent of claimants were able to work and described the benefit as 'the biggest scam in the country'.

The Labour Party in the 1980s shouted from the rooftops that the Conservatives were hiding unemployment in invalidity benefit. It was right, although the great rise in numbers was a result of the actions of Heath and Wilson rather than Margaret Thatcher.

In 2002, researchers at Sheffield Hallam University estimated that half of those on sickness benefits should be described as 'hidden unemployed'. So with 1.5 million on incapacity benefit in 2003, 750,000 were really unemployed.

But have any more unemployed people been tucked away outside the official statistics for unemployment?

> **'For too long it [incapacity benefit] has been used as a support for early retirement.'**
>
> **Tony Blair, 1999**

The core benefit of the modern welfare state is income support. It is the main means-tested benefit. Among the recipients, 2.2 million are of working age.

The numbers of people on income support who are registered as 'disabled' has rocketed to a million. Assuming that half of these are like those on incapacity benefit and are really unemployed adds another 500,000. Add in another 260,000 people on income support who are of working age and neither disabled nor lone parents and it brings us to a grand total of 2.3 million unemployed. This is without counting any of the 861,000 lone mothers on income support. If the lone parents were included, the total would be 3.1 million.

Income support, in itself, would probably not discourage work too heavily in many cases. But often it is combined with housing benefit. The individual would lose both and other 'passport benefits' on taking a job.

In 1985, largely as a result of housing benefit, 1.87 million people were working who got little financial advantage out of it.[50] They would have received more than 70 per cent of their earning by just loafing around. That is why unemployment – both open and hidden – was particularly high in the 1980s. It is still high today, even after attempts to 'make work pay' such as the working families' tax credit.

Sheffield Hallam University, using a different approach, estimated that there were 2.8 million unemployed people as at January 2002.[51] That represented an unemployment rate of 9.5 per cent.

So when people assume that unemployment is a solved problem, they are taking an overly sanguine view. It is certainly less bad than in the mid-1980s. But there is still a massive army of unemployed. There has been such an army now for two decades and more. Long-term mass unemployment has become a persistent feature of British life.

Some may suggest that it does not really matter. More may feel, 'Yes, of course it matters.' Those in the first camp need an answer. But even those in the second may be surprised by why and how 'it matters.'

The unemployed have not starved. They have generally kept their homes. Most of them have been financially worse off but not by a very great deal in those cases where the parent or parents have been low paid and there have been children.

But joblessness can be profoundly damaging in ways that are not immediately obvious. Being out of the job market means not gaining experience and then promotion to higher-paid work. There is also the effect on other people. The unemployed, instead of contributing through tax to services like the police, take from the pot instead. This increases the tax and national insurance contributions others have to pay. Higher taxes have acted as a discouragement to enterprise and work, leading to a less prosperous economy altogether.

A possible way of measuring real unemployment

Claimants of jobseeker's allowance	800,000
Half the claimants of incapacity benefit	750,000
Half the claimants on income support registered as disabled	535,000
Other working-age claimants of income support excluding all lone parents	263,000
Total	2,348,000

Based on: Department of Work and Pensions income support statistics for August 2002, published November 2002. Jobseeker's allowance and incapacity benefit figures from DWP statistical summary published 16 January 2003

What about the effect on the feelings of the unemployed and the way they lead their lives? Does unemployment make people unhappy? Most people might think, 'Yes, I suppose it might make people somewhat unhappy. But it is probably manageable. The main problem would be the loss of income.'

This may not be true.

In the British hit film *The Full Monty*, the leading characters are all unemployed. The story is of how they put on a male strip show to raise some money. But before this triumph over adversity, the film suggests that unemployment has done far more to them than make them poor.

Gaz, or 'Gary the lad' – the leading character played by Robert Carlyle – is cocky and better able to take knocks than most. He has been made redundant from the local steel works. 'Miserable at his financial castration and unable to cope with being a househusband', he starts to drink too much and not long afterwards he begins 'fooling around'.[52] Mandy, his wife, leaves him, taking their son. Gary adores his son and is miserable at being allowed access to him only two days a week. Then his wife applies for Gary to have no further access to their son at all.

Dave Horsfall is Gaz's best friend and accomplice. Since being laid off, his self-esteem has gradually been chipped away. He has put on weight. Dave has succumbed to 'the hopelessness that enveloped many

Men do a triumphant strip show towards the end of *The Full Monty*, but the whole basis of the film is that unemployment causes depression.

of the unemployed'. His worsening depression is beginning to drag his wife Jean down with him. Jean tells a friend, 'It's like he's given up. Work ... me ... everything.' He does not even have sex with his wife.

'Lomper' is no friend of theirs but he, too, has been made redundant. He has a temporary job as a security guard but that will soon end. Gaz and Dave come across him as he is attempting to commit suicide by gassing himself in a car.

The whole basis for *The Full Monty* is the idea that unemployment is devastating to people not because of the money but because of the emotional effect.

For many years, the European Union has been asking people how they feel in the Eurobarometer survey. This survey includes the question: 'On the whole, are you very satisfied, fairly satisfied, not very satisfied, or not at all satisfied with the life you lead?'

Among people with jobs, only 12 per cent said they were 'not very satisfied' or 'not at all satisfied'. Among the unemployed, those on the unhappy side of the divide amounted to 41 per cent. The unemployed are more than three times as likely to be unhappy.

Those who are familiar with social science may immediately object: 'Yes, but this could be misleading. Unemployed people are poorer than average. Perhaps more of them are divorced or separated, too. It could be poverty or loneliness making them unhappy rather than the lack of a job.' But the unemployed are more unhappy than those in the lowest quartile of income or those who are divorced.

Two academics, Professor David Blanchflower of Dartmouth College in the USA and Professor Andrew Oswald of Warwick University have taken the raw figures from the Eurobarometer surveys between 1975 and 1998 and separated out the identifiable factors which could affect

Percentage saying they are 'not at all satisfied' with the life they lead

Unemployed	15%
Divorced	10%
Separated	10%
Bottom-quartile income	7%
Second-quartile income	7%
Widowed	5%
Retired	4%
Keeping house	4%
Single	4%
Living as married	4%
Married	3%
Third-quartile income	3%
Employed	3%
Top-quartile income	2%
Students	1%

Source: Eurobarometer surveys 1975–98

happiness.[53] In the jargon of social science, they 'controlled' for other factors. They calculated that the effect on happiness of being unemployed, excluding other depressing circumstances, is minus 1.18 – the largest influence, positive or negative – identified in their whole study. Being jobless, according to their analysis of the Eurobarometer figures, is an outstandingly powerful depressant.

Men are hit particularly hard. They are, on average, twice as depressed by unemployment as women.

The following figures are not 'controlled'. But in the light of the analysis by Blanchflower and Oswald, we have reason to think they largely reflect the impact of being unemployed more than anything else:

How satisfaction with life is affected by ...	
being unemployed	-1.180
being separated	-0.570
being divorced	-0.559
being widowed	-0.268
being male	-0.141
keeping house	-0.118
being retired	-0.018
being a student	-0.018
having second-quartile income	+0.099
living as married	+0.116
having third-quartile income	+0.156
having top-quartile income	+0.322
being married	+0.400

Minus figures represent lower satisfaction with life, plus figures represent greater satisfaction. Coefficient effects on satisfaction derived from Eurobarometer surveys, 1975–98 Source: Blanchflower, David and Oswald, Andrew, *Well-being over Time in Britain and the USA,* University of Warwick, revised June 2002.

• The unemployed are more than twice as likely to have symptoms of neurosis. A quarter of the unemployed suffer from such symptoms.

• Half of all unemployed men smoke whereas only 29 per cent of those who are employed do.

• Almost a third of unemployed men have taken drugs in the past year, compared with only one in ten of those in work.

• Unemployed women are 50 per cent more likely than those in work to be admitted to hospital. Jobless men are 60 per cent more likely to need hospitalisation.

• The unemployed are 81 per cent more likely to die than those who are employed.

Why do so many die? Generally they die of the same things as everybody else. But they suffer one cause of death far more than people in work: suicide. Attempted suicide is ten times more common among the jobless than those in work.[54] Unemployment clearly does cause very serious unhappiness. It is part of the knock-on damage caused by social security.

Digging a little deeper still, why does joblessness have such a terrible impact?

Sigmund Freud suggested that work was mankind's strongest tie to reality. Without it, we are likely to be psychologically damaged. Professor Marie Jahoda, a specialist in the study of unemployment, has suggested[55] that psychological needs are satisfied by employment through structured time, social experience in areas less emotionally charged than the family, participation in a collective effort, regular activity, status and a sense of identity. These needs may come, perhaps, from our long evolutionary history. For hundreds of thousands of years, human beings have acted in groups and may have come to feel it is important to participate in a group and to have a status in it.

John Burnett has collected together comments made by the unemployed.[56] Here are a few:

I miss the people at work.

By the end of the first month you're bored stiff.

You felt you were playing a part in the community [when working]: *it was right for someone to go to work from nine till six and bring a certain amount home ... You weren't on the scrap-heap, rendered useless ... You might as well be dead.*

Burnett comments, 'Men in their middle years with family responsibilities ... feel their role as a breadwinner diminished and their status in the household and society "demeaned" – a word often used.'

Unemployment may also change the way people behave towards the rest of the world. Here we may be getting towards a connection between the welfare state and the change in the behaviour of the British. Here are a few more quotations assembled by Burnett:

I was out one Tuesday night and was very bored, because I didn't have a job. I decided to go joy-riding ... I then walked down to Temple Meads and took a Morris Oxford ... I stripped the car of radio/cassette player, speakers and battery.

I gang into town every day now. I go shoplifting. Me mam says, 'Get a job.' I say, 'I've got one.'

*If you want things, you have to go roguing ... It gets you all
excited while you're doing it, then afterwards you feel relaxed, it
feels good. You feel you've achieved something.*

*I used to be a really good-tempered and friendly chap, but while
on the dole someone just says something I don't like and I'll
have a good go to give them a fat lip.*

Burnett comments, 'Such symptoms of rejection and alienation from
family and society seem to be shared quite widely by the young jobless.'

A picture emerges from Burnett's testimonies of older people who
become depressed and younger people whose depression alternates
with outbursts of anger.

In one experiment, unemployed school-leavers were interviewed
three times in Birmingham over a period of twenty-four weeks.[57] At the
beginning they were despairing and pessimistic. Later they became
resigned and apathetic. But one psychological response remained the
same throughout: 'a diffused hostility against the community'.

Do the unemployed commit crimes more than other people, then?
Academic studies have varying views but the majority conclude that
unemployment does indeed contribute to the likelihood of someone
committing a crime. It is not the only factor but it is a significant one.

A study was made of sixteen- to eighteen-year-old offenders in
Northern Ireland.[58] It found they were twice as likely to commit crimes
when not in work, education or training. In Germany, 560 juvenile
delinquents were investigated.[59] It turned out that 27 per cent of them
were unemployed. Delinquency was shown to be far more common
among the unemployed than among those in work. These figures are
not 'controlled'. But the evidence, put together, points to a simple conclusion. Unemployment helps to cause crime.

It also surely causes what you could call 'incivility' – anti-social
behaviour which does not amount to crime. The 'diffused hostility'
reported in the Birmingham study means a man is more likely to start
swearing and threatening others, a youth is more likely to paint graffiti
on a wall, a woman in a train is less likely to stand up to allow a pregnant woman to take her place.

The unemployed themselves suffer most from unemployment. But
the rest of us are affected too. We pay for the benefits, the hospitalisation of those who become unwell, the policing. We may become victims
of the crimes and we receive the everyday incivility.

Oh no! Not welfare fraud!

Now for the second main charge against the social security aspect of the welfare state. There is one kind of crime – apart from suicide – particularly associated with the unemployed and others on benefit. It is fraud.

The subject makes people very angry. In the 1980s, some newspapers and the Conservative government suggested that there was a great deal of fraud going on in the benefits system. This was greeted with fury by most of the Labour Party and certain other newspapers. They argued that only a tiny minority of people made false claims and that talking about fraud was just a mean pretext for cutting benefits and oppressing those who were already 'socially excluded'. What is the truth of the matter?

In 1998, I went with officials from the Benefits Agency – which hands out the money – on a fraudster hunt. We were in and around Chislehurst, amid leafy suburban streets in south London and on the edge of Kent. We started at a large building site. We visited the canteen and found a woman who was working there part time. The officials pressed a button on a mobile phone which automatically dialled their central office in Leeds. Within twenty seconds they discovered that the woman was claiming benefits and not declaring the income from her part-time work.

Later the same day, we went to a 'road stop'. It was something I had never seen or heard of before. A range of officials of different sorts were gathered together. There were immigration officials together with people from the Contributions Agency (which then collected national insurance), from the Inland Revenue, from Customs and Excise (which levies duties on petrol, alcohol and cigarettes) and from the DVLA (Driver and Vehicle Licensing Agency – which taxes those who want to drive). The officials were accompanied by police officers, the only ones allowed to stop people. Every now and then, the police would pull over a car or van. The occupants would be interviewed by any of the agencies which thought they might find some law being broken.

A large, white, hired van was pulled over. Richard, one of the officials I was with, started his routine dialogue. The driver's name was Irish; let's call him O'Rourke. He had light brown hair and was in working clothes. He stood awkwardly with his hand against the side of his head.

After calling up the Leeds central office, Richard said, 'You are claiming jobseeker's allowance, aren't you, sir?'

'But I haven't signed on for ages,' Mr O'Rourke protested.

Richard did not contradict him. 'It may be that the details from your local office have not yet reached the central computer,' he politely suggested. 'How long have you now been in work?'

Mr O'Rourke seemed to have difficulty remembering. He suggested it might have been since the end of February or so. Richard said that he would write down mid-February. Mr O'Rourke did not disagree.

Richard was completing a form which he offered to Mr O'Rourke. 'If I could ask you to sign this to get the claim closed down so it is not left outstanding,' he said. Mr O'Rourke readily signed the form, which stated that he was working and that he no longer qualified for welfare benefits.

'Thank you for your time,' said Richard. 'You can go now.' Off Mr O'Rourke went, looking rather relieved.

You might be surprised at how respectfully Mr O'Rourke was treated, considering that he was, to put it bluntly, stealing. But it was all very decorous – as if the official were directing Lord Eminent to his seat at the opera.

In another instance, a minibus was stopped which was found to contain eleven Nepalese women accompanied by two Nepalese men. The interviews were difficult because they did not speak much English – or at least, appeared not to. Richard told me they were probably working in the rag trade. Four of the women were taken by immigration officials because they appeared to be illegal immigrants. They would not be paying tax, of course. Two were claiming benefits to which they were not entitled. Not many were paying the national insurance contributions due.

In the end, the work of Richard and the other Benefits Agency officials was cut short. So many people had been arrested on suspicion of being illegal immigrants that there were no police left to stop the cars and vans. Nevertheless, in a few hours the Benefits Agency had detected six people claiming benefits to which they were not entitled. The saving to the taxpayer of stopping these benefits was estimated to be £18,000.

It is the essence of things that we cannot know exactly how much fraud there is – especially organised fraud. But in 1997, the Benefits Agency completed an experiment.[60] It zoomed in on four thousand of those claiming the major means-tested benefit, income support. Every one of them was interviewed in depth about their circumstances. Of course, even this process could not be guaranteed to find every case of fraud. But the results were astonishing nonetheless. Even among pensioners nearly one in twenty was definitely or possibly committing a fraud. Among the disabled and 'others', the figure was 11.7 per cent. But the incidence of fraud became worse still among two of the biggest categories of people claiming income support: the unemployed and lone parents. For the unemployed 23.3 per cent were definitely or possibly committing fraud. Among the lone parents, the figure reached an horrific 26.7 per cent. In other words nearly a quarter of the unemployed on income support were definitely or possibly claiming benefits fraudulently and more than a quarter of lone parents were doing so too.

The scale of the fraud went unreported in many newspapers, perhaps because it did not fit in with their agendas. But this report, by the Benefits Agency itself, showed that fraud is extraordinarily commonplace. It is routine. It is normal.

Incidence of fraud among people claiming income support

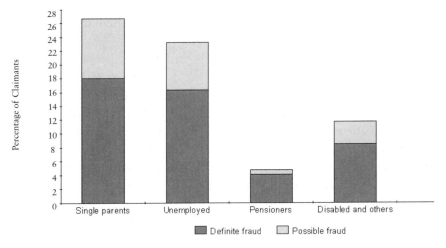

Source: Department of Social Security[61]

In what way were the lone parents cheating the system? By far the most common way, accounting for nearly half the fraudulent cases, was claiming to be living alone while in fact living with a partner. The next most common way of cheating was falsely claiming to be not working at all or earning only a little.

How common is housing benefit fraud? Lambeth Borough Council did a large study of fraud by private-sector landlords receiving the benefit directly. It found that 18 per cent of the claims were fraudulent.

There are a variety of benefits available to the ill and disabled. In 1998, the government estimated that two out of seven people claiming disability living allowance were entitled to none of that benefit at all.[62]

Putting it all together, there are 850,000 or so claiming incapacity benefit fraudulently, 200,000 to 250,000 lone parents claiming income support to which they are not entitled, other substantial numbers of unemployed fraudulently claiming income support, many people also claiming illness and disability benefits such as disability living allowance and there is fraud committed by some of those on jobseeker's allowance. And this is just the fraud that is officially acknowledged.

Large-scale welfare fraud does not consist generally of determined crooks who occasionally appear in the newspapers if they are caught. It consists instead of well over a million people who are committing relatively small-scale crimes – ones which, individually, are not considered important enough for a great expenditure of time and money by the authorities. These crimes are so commonplace that you only have to walk onto a building site or stop twenty or thirty cars to find people committing them. This is a nation with a large proportion of welfare cheats. Walk down the street and you are passing them all the time.

Unfortunately – for those interested in the truth – governments have usually been slow to admit how bad the situation is. It reflects too much on their own performance. In 2002, when the government more than doubled its estimate of the cost of fraud and mistakes in two of the major benefits – income support and jobseeker's allowance – from £1.32 billion to £3 billion, the news was quietly revealed in a parliamentary written answer.[63]

The creation of new benefits permits new fraud – sometimes on a spectacular scale. Disability living allowance, defrauded by at least two claimants out of every seven, was only invented in 1992. But the outstanding case was that of individual learning accounts. New Labour created them amidst much fanfare to subsidise education and training for adults. They became so renowned for being defrauded that the government had to close the whole scheme down in 2001. Frank Field MP, the former social security minister, has said, 'Fraud is so serious that no minister would dare to tell the public its true scale.'

Official fraud estimates by government are highly variable and influenced by the politics of the day. They are simply untrustworthy. If 50 per cent of those on sickness and invalidity benefits are in fact capable of work, as indicated by Sheffield Hallam University, and more than 20 per cent of lone parents and those registered as unemployed are fraudsters too, as indicated by a government survey in 1997, then the cost of fraud is extremely high. An average 15 per cent fraud rate across all benefits would mean a total bill of approximately £15 billion.

One of the key problems is that governments, while boasting of their 'zero tolerance' of fraud and occasionally instituting another 'unprecedented' crackdown on fraud, never before seen on earth, actually spend relatively little effort on it. There were 160,000 cases of fraud in housing and council tax benefit in 1999. There were only 800 successful prosecutions.

What is the price of welfare fraud? Does the price consist of money taken from tax-payers? Yes, that is part of it. If the total fraud bill is in the region of £15 billion, that is 5p in the pound for everyone paying the standard rate of income tax. And the tax does not just come from the rich. It comes from everybody else. A poor widow aged seventy pays income tax on any income over £6,100.[64] She pays VAT when she goes to the shops. Poor people are made to pay for the fraud. That is part of the price.

Another part is the impact on the way people think. If you imagine yourself as a typical welfare cheat, you are accepting benefits even though you are breaking the law and cheating other people. Human nature being what it is, you do not think of it as shameful. You think, 'I would be short of money if I didn't keep on taking the money. Anyway, everyone's doing it.' You might even feel, 'I'd be a mug not to do it.' That kind of thinking is a massive change from the kind which would have been normal fifty years ago. The huge temptation to fall into welfare fraud has damaged people's morality.

Benefit fraud has also undermined respect for the law. So, of course, has tax fraud, the other side of the same coin. Tax fraud is like benefit fraud in that it is caused by strong temptation and the ease of getting away with it. It is not unreasonable to think that honest returns would be more numerous if the tax rate (including national insurance) fell to 18 per cent. It easily could go down to this level, if it were not for the cost of social security.

We have got accustomed to lies which we avoid calling 'lies'. But if we lie as a matter of routine to the government, do we expect to tell the truth to other people? Do we expect other people to tell the truth to us? On BBC Radio 5 Live in December 2002, one of the presenters remarked that the then Leader of the Opposition, Iain Duncan Smith, had misled people in his curriculum vitae. She added that Tony Blair, the Prime Minister, had done the same. Then she joked that she and other presenters would not have got their jobs if they had not made things up too. It was all a joke.

It is a tremendous change from Victorian times and the first half of the twentieth century. The telling of a lie then was a matter of great shame. It would blacken a gentleman's name to be caught out in one.

In June 1963, when John Profumo was exposed as having lied to the House of Commons, he resigned immediately and his career as an MP was finished. Yet ministers more recently have failed to tell the truth and stayed in – or returned – to office. Peter Mandelson told an untruth in a form applying for a mortgage. He failed to mention to the Britannia Building Society a loan of £373,000 which he had received from his friend and colleague Geoffrey Robinson. In so doing he 'breached the code of conduct for Members of Parliament', according to the parliamentary-standards watchdog, Elizabeth Filkin. He also failed to inform the House of Commons of this loan. But the House of Commons Standards and Privileges Committee interviewed him using first-name terms and was keen to take into account any possibly excuse including that he was busy with the Labour Party conference at the time. In the ensuing scandal, he did lose his job. But ten months later, in October 1999, he was made Northern Ireland secretary. We now make excuses. Fifty years ago, there were no excuses.

Who cares about means-testing?

So the welfare state is charged with creating mass unemployment that continues to this day, resulting in misery for those directly affected and making a significant proportion of them less civil or even criminal. It is also charged with creating widespread fraud which, in turn, is likely to have damaged morality and respect for the law. But there may be another kind of damage that is more subtle and rarely recognised. This is the third main charge against social security in our welfare state.

Means-tested benefits have become dominant as the years have gone by. They have often been favoured by the Treasury because they have the apparent advantage of 'putting money where it is most needed'. But there is a major problem with means-tested benefits, as anyone who has looked at this from society's point of view – rather than the Treasury's – has realised. Every major figure in the history of welfare has seen it. Edwin Chadwick saw it, so did the Webbs, Churchill, Lloyd George, Beveridge and, most recently, the Labour Party specialist in welfare policy, Frank Field. Only those who know little of social security do not know it.

The problem with means-tested benefits is that they send out three bad messages – 'the three don'ts':

1. DON'T save
2. DON'T earn
3. DON'T tell the truth.

Those on means-tested benefits get the message 'Don't save' because if they do, they can lose their entitlement to any means-tested benefit. Income support, for example, is only available in full to people with less than £3,000 of savings. It is not available at all to anyone who admits to savings of £8,000 or more. These limits, in early 2003, have not been changed since at least 1995.

The least well-off get the message 'Don't earn' because means-tested benefits are reduced as their earnings rise and tax can start on incomes below £5,000.[65] For much of the existence of the modern welfare state, working for the low paid has been barely worthwhile. In 1994, for example, a couple with two children earning £120 for a sixteen-hour week would take home £188 net income including benefits. If they worked twenty-eight hours a week instead, it would bring in only an extra £2 a week. Who would be so saintly or mad as to work an extra twelve hours for a mere £2?

> **'Most low-income workers will not be able to save anywhere near enough to make themselves better off than if they simply spent every penny now and relied on the Minimum Income Guarantee in retirement.'**
>
> **Frank Field**

Those on means-tested benefits also get the message 'Don't tell the truth' because they can get benefits if they lie about their assets or income. Lying – or 'forgetting to tell the truth' – is very often the difference between money coming in or not.

Means-testing also encourages 'the five dos':

1. DO fill in long forms
2. DO lose your benefits if you are too old, proud, busy or ill edu-

Weekly net income for a couple with two children

Hours	Wage	Income benefits	Housing benefits	Other benefits	Tax	Net income
0	0	113	53	12	0	178
8	60	59	53	12	1	183
16	120	59	16	4	12	188
28	210	18	4	0	43	190
40	300	18	0	0	74	244

Source: *Liverpool Quarterly Economic Bulletin*, October 1994. The net income may not exactly equal wage plus benefits minus tax owing to the rounding of figures

THE THREE 'DON'TS' IN ACTION

'DON'T SAVE' A kindly godmother wished to give £3,000 to her eight-year old goddaughter for her education expenses when she grew older. But the godmother learnt that if she gave the money to her goddaughter, the mother would lose some of her benefits entitlement.[66]

'DON'T EARN' The Citizens Advice Bureau in Stroud, Gloucestershire was advising some people on benefits in 1997 that they were better off on the dole. Caroline Pymm, who ran the bureau, said, 'We frequently tell people that by the time they take child care and travelling costs into account, they are better off without a job.'

'DON'T TELL THE TRUTH' Social security inspectors visited a company which distributed magazines. The employees included Count Dracula, Ronald Mac-Donald and Jack O'Nory. Twelve people were prosecuted. The workers were going under assumed names because if they worked under their real names, they could lose their welfare benefits.[67]

cated to fill in the forms. Almost six hundred thousand pensioners were not getting the means-tested 'minimum income guarantee' in 2001.[68]

3. DO give up your privacy. Every little change in your personal circumstances must be revealed to strangers.

4. DO agree a scam. Your employer may suggest he pay you a low wage but that you won't suffer because your income will be made up by means-tested benefits.

5. DO put your job in danger. The Citizens Advice Bureau announced in February 2001 that a small number of people had been sacked because they wanted their employer to claim working families' tax credit on their behalf. The employers found the WFTC forms, instruction leaflets and procedures too complicated and onerous. The Citizens Advice Bureau said that 'many people' had agreed not to claim the WFTC because of the associated hassle.

In recent times, Gordon Brown has significantly increased the amount of means-testing in Britain. It is now estimated that 38 per cent of households are on one means-tested benefit or another. Nine out of ten families are able to claim the children's tax credit – which involves filling in a fifty-six-question form accompanied by forty-seven pages of advisory notes.[69] Brown has been keen to ensure that it is always financially advantageous to work, which is sensible in itself. But he has only been able to make work moderately worthwhile. And to achieve even this, he has put more people are on benefits. That means more people suffer the damaging effects of means-tested benefits.

Britain is wealthier, but more benefit dependent

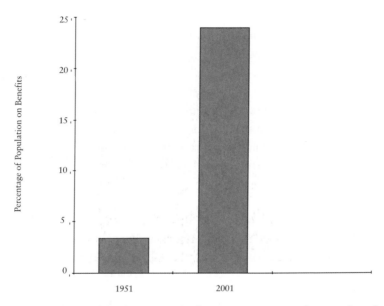

The 1951 figure is the percentage on national assistance or unemployment benefit. The 2001 figure is the percentage of households relying on means-tested benefits. It excludes those just on the state pension.
Source: David Green, Civitas

The means-tested 'pension credit' now means that it is not worthwhile for low-paid people to save unless they can amass a very considerable pension fund (see Chapter 7). The result is that most low-paid people don't save.

The charge sheet against modern social security has become longer and more appalling as the story has unfolded. Mass unemployment has been made a permanent feature of life, whereas previously it was cyclical and nearly always at a much lower level. It has made many people – especially the lowest-earning third – less well off than they need have been. The lowest third gets caught in the benefits trap. They are discouraged from being prudent in their expenditure and from saving. They are the ones most affected financially and – perhaps more important – mentally.

WHY FRANK STENT 'BLEW THIRTY GRAND'

Frank Stent won a £31,000 bingo jackpot in 1994. It was a fabulous win for a 25p stake. He certainly needed the money. He had been unemployed for nine years. His wife had cerebral palsy. They were poor.

But when he got his big bingo win, he deliberately went out and 'blew it' in only seven weeks.

He bought an antique gold medallion for £750. He spent £6,000 on holidays and splashed out £500 on children's games. Judging by the photo of him in the *Daily Star*, he spent quite a bit on gold chains and bracelets, which seem to have been an alternative form of saving for him. Why did he behave so strangely?

'Ideally, I would have bought £20,000 of bonds and banked the rest,' he told the *Daily Star*. 'I would have liked a nest-egg for my old age.' But he understood that if he kept the £31,000, he would lose most of his welfare benefits. He feared that the £180 a week payments he received would be cut to only £70 because they were means-tested. The state encouraged him to throw away money, despite the fact that he was poor.

Frank Stent illustrates that means-tested benefits discourage saving, prudence and self-reliance. They also show one reason why 'poverty' figures should not be trusted. The poor in Britain have strong reasons to dump their financial assets – either spending them or exchanging them for physical assets.

There was, sadly for Frank Stent, a sting in the tail of this story. He was getting disability and attendance allowances. His particular benefits were not means-tested. He could have kept the money. When the *Daily Star* told him, his wife Kim shouted, 'What? Oh no, I don't believe it!'

WHAT FRANK BLEW IT ON

F-reg Renault £4,300
Second-hand Scooter wheelchair for his wife Kim £1,900
3-piece Chesterfield suite £1,440
Pram, car seat, bath high chair and other baby goodies £1,000
Car insurance for daughter Nickie £975
TVs and video recorders £875
Antique gold medallion £5 coin £750
Carpets £700
Freezer-load of food £700
Six new beds £535
Children's games £500
Presents for children and grandchild £500
Stereo and CD-players £450
Various bills £400
Curtains and nets £350
Seven new duvets £280
Back garden fence £200
Video films £200
Second-hand space-invader arcade machine £180
Second-hand microwave £170
Keyboard £127
Second-hand chest freezer £100
Coffee table £49
And one week for eight in a holiday camp (including spending money) £3,000

Mass unemployment has caused widespread unhappiness even to the point of increasing the number of suicides. Much of the population has been 'pauperised' – to use the Victorian word. That is to say people have been made dependent on hand-outs. In the process they have lost the sense of proud independence which was once normal. They have lost the self-respect that comes from self-provision.

They demand their benefits whereas, once, people of similar means in the late nineteenth century took pride in making weekly contributions to charity. Where previous generations thought of their duty and their honour, they think of their 'rights'. They have become so accustomed to lying they do not see it in such moral terms. They do not experience the civilising experience of being a member of a friendly society. Their income depends on how much the government gives them – or rather how much the government takes from other people in order to give to them. The process is humiliating and causes alienation, depression and incivility.

> '[The problem of the expense of the Poor Laws] sinks into insignificance when compared with the dreadful effects which the system produces on the morals and happiness of the lower orders.'
>
> **Royal Commission, 1834**

We have experienced a re-run of the same problems of government welfare described in the 1834 Royal Commission on the Poor Laws. Unemployment has been created, as then. Morality and decency have been damaged, as then. Prudence and self-reliance have been reduced. Social security has been even more disastrous in the past eighty years than in the early nineteenth century. But our response has been feeble compared to that of 1834. Modern social security has been a disaster which has been barely admitted, let alone reacted to. In the sixteenth century, thinkers like Martin Luther recognised that money should not be given to the poor too freely. In the nineteenth century, Thomas Chalmers was among those who became well known for warning about the harm that could be done if money were too readily handed over. Edwin Chadwick and the Royal Commission saw where the state had been going wrong and what damage was being done. Lloyd George, Churchill and Beveridge – the three men at the origin of the modern welfare state – all admired self-provision in welfare through friendly soci-

> '**Complete idleness even on an income demoralises.**'
>
> **Beveridge report, 1942**

eties. All were aware of the dangers of over-easy welfare and means-tested benefits in particular. Yet modern British governments learnt nothing from this wealth of history – this long tradition of understanding of the dynamics of welfare. In the 1920s and 1930s, then again in the 1960s and 1970s and once more in the current decade, they have just blindly competed to please voters by giving money to the poor without discrimination or intelligence. They have turned the social security aspect of the welfare state into a catastrophe.

It would have been better if modern social security – as initiated by Lloyd George and Churchill and soon corrupted – had never been started. Britain today would be a better place with better people. There would be fewer who were seriously poor in monetary terms and in their spirit.

THE DAMAGE DONE BY SOCIAL SECURITY

1. Mass, long-term unemployment.

2. Through unemployment, people have been made poorer.

3. Through unemployment, people have become depressed and alienated.

4. Alienation has led to incivility and crime.

5. Millions have been tempted into defrauding the system.

6. Fraud has damaged the honesty and self-respect of those who commit it.

7. Through means-tested benefits, saving has been discouraged.

8. Through means-tested benefits, work and extra work have been discouraged.

9. Through the discouragement of work and saving, self-reliance and self-respect have been diminished.

10. The cost of social security has greatly increased taxation.

11. Because of high taxation and unemployment, Britain has had lower growth than it has been capable of.

Nine out of the eleven kinds of damage have mainly affected the poor. Further damage described in the chapter on broken parenting also has damaged the poor disproportionately. Social security, intended to help the poor, has damaged them instead.

CHAPTER 3

The NHS: like a train crash every day

The man with the biggest single role in forming the NHS was Aneurin Bevan. What drove him?

He was born at 32 Charles Street, Tredegar, Monmouthshire on 15 November 1897 'of good dissenting stock'.[1] His mother was a Methodist and his father a Baptist. The two had first met as members of the choral society attached to the chapels. His father was a miner and used to leave the house by 5.30 in the morning to catch the colliers' train. They lived in a poor Welsh mining community. That description will evoke, for some, an image of unrelieved oppression. But Michael Foot, in his superbly written account of Bevan's life, depicts a proud, self-respecting family, astonishingly rich in culture, energy and intellectual life. Bevan's mother was strong-willed, ran her own business for a while and bore ten children, of whom seven survived beyond the age of eight. Aneurin was the middle one of those who lived.

From an early age Aneurin was a rebel. In the 1960s he would have been called an 'angry young man' except that he started being angry before he was even a teenager. One day at school, the headmaster demanded to know why another little boy had not been to school the day before. The boy replied that it had been his brother's turn to wear the shoes. The headmaster mocked the poor boy and other children tittered at the child's humiliation. But not Aneurin Bevan. He was outraged. He picked up an inkwell – which would have been made of china or glass – and hurled it at the headmaster. Later he was summoned to the headmaster's study to be punished for this gross misbehaviour. But he made such a show of aggression and willingness to fight back, that the headmaster decided better of it. This is an archetypal Bevan story. There are plenty more. It is hard not to warm to this bolshie boy, ready to take on anyone in defence of the weak and poor.

No one, not even his ambitious mother, detected any sign that he was bright enough to get into the secondary school. So in November 1911, he set out for his first day working in the mines, like his father and brother before him. He was just turning fourteen.

It was quite a moment for someone with a rebellious nature to start working in the pits. That year there had been a ten-month strike in the Rhondda valley which had ended in bitter defeat for the miners. In the first full year of his work there was a six-week national strike ending in victory for the workers that was soured by claims that the government had tricked them and the union leaders had let them down. South Wales mining towns and villages were the scene of tremendous revolutionary debates. Karl Marx was one whose ideas were discussed. But at that time he was not picked out so much as he is now from many other theorists and leaders. Bevan and many other young miners said that Noah Ablett was the most powerful intellectual influence of their youth. Ablett argued that the industrial power of the workers was mightier than that of any political debate. The miners had power through their work and should use it to change British society. Of democracy he said, 'Why cross the river to fill the pail?'

Bevan thrived in this atmosphere. He was a wonderful debater and became chairman of his lodge of the union at the age of only nineteen – the youngest since the union had been founded. He moved from pit to pit because of the heated arguments which his feisty attitude got him into. He came to be known as 'that bloody nuisance Bevan'. The young revolutionary was deliberately sent to one pit where it was thought he would find few supporters for his union activism. He was greeted by the manager saying, 'So this is the great Aneurin Bevan. The son of David Bevan, I believe. I used to know him well.' 'In that case', Bevan tartly replied, 'you knew a better man than yourself!'

He hated the idea that anyone should be considered better because they were of a different class. He viewed things in terms we would now call neo-Marxist, developing a contempt for the customs of 'capitalist society'. As far as he was concerned, he was in a class struggle for the dignity of the working man. Once he had a violent argument with the manager of the Tredegar Iron and Coal Company. It ended with the manager saying, 'Look here, Bevan, there isn't room in this company for you and me.' 'I agree,' replied Bevan, 'and I think you ought to go.'

Infuriating and magnificent at the same time, he was angry about many things, even including the waste he thought the mining companies were letting pass to their own advantage. Though he was a socialist, he was never completely devoted to any dogma. One of his contemporaries during his twenties said, 'He believed the test of any idea or theory was how it worked in practice.'[2]

As his political career progressed he fell out with the union and had bitter arguments with most of the major figures within the Labour Party. One of the things he argued with them about was the likely outcome of the 1945 election. He believed the Left would triumph after the war, when weaker souls in the party had little hope of that and were content to cooperate with the Tories. Bevan was a firebrand – a clever, high-quality, eloquent, principled firebrand.

He was right about the election. Labour won in 1945 with a big majority. On the first day in the House of Commons, Labour MPs sang 'The Red Flag' – the anthem of communism. As Foot, who later became an MP for the same constituency as Aneurin Bevan, ecstatically remarked, 'No Socialist who saw it will forget the blissful dawn of July 1945 ... Eyes were fixed on the promise of a new society. Suddenly the vision of the Socialist pioneers had been given substance.'

Despite being no great friend of anyone in the elite of the Labour Party, Bevan was impressive enough for the new Prime Minister, Clement Attlee, to put him in charge of health and housing. When Bevan arrived at the ministry, the idea of a

Michael Foot wrote of Aneurin Bevan (pictured left), 'Marxism taught him that society must be changed swiftly, intrepidly, fundamentally, if the transormation was not to be overturned by counter-revolution.'

National Health Service was already there. He did not invent it. But the previous minister had been negotiating with the medical profession. 'Negotiating' is the word.

Bevan was willing to discuss and debate. But he was not like some others might have been – ready fundamentally to compromise and dilute an idea. His thinking was 'rooted in Marxism' however much he might have made his own modifications. In Foot's words, 'Marxism taught him that society must be changed swiftly, intrepidly, fundamentally, if the transformation was not to be overturned by counter-revolution.'

Bevan was there to bring to reality part of the socialist dream he had been fighting for during the past thirty-four years. He had guile, charm, a terrific memory and great debating skills. Many members of his own party wanted him to fall flat on his face but he did not. He outwitted the general practitioners. He bribed the consultants. He carried it through – the most radical state take-over of healthcare anywhere outside an avowedly communist country. He had the convictions and talent to put into action the socialist spirit of 1945. He wiped away the old system. He did it so effectively that today most people have no idea what existed before the NHS. It is as if 1948, when Bevan's plan was put into action, was zero hour.

Many people may think that there simply was not much healthcare at all before 1948 – a few hospitals and then only for the rich, perhaps? The less well off went untreated? Is that why so many children – and indeed adults – died? Is that why three of Bevan's own brothers and sisters died before reaching their ninth birthday? Is that the heritage which Bevan was getting rid of 'swiftly, intrepidly, fundamentally'?

*

Rahere was something of a social climber and hanger-on at the court of Henry I in the early twelfth century. He was a friar, but very different from the idea of a friar that most of us have today. He was wealthy, for a start, wealthy enough to go on a pilgrimage to Rome. Unfortunately, while he was in Rome, he fell seriously ill. He was in grave danger of dying and as he lay there in great pain and full of fear, he made a solemn vow: if God would spare him, he would return to London and found a priory.[3]

Rahere survived the crisis and resolved to do as he had promised. He returned to London and applied to Henry for land. He was granted a site just outside the walls of London – an area that had been used as a market and a recreation ground in Smithfield. Here he built his priory and dedicated it to St Bartholomew, possibly because he had made his recovery on Tiber Island in Rome, where the relics of St Bartholomew were kept.

The priory he created was not a normal one. Rahere was an Augustinian friar and the Augustinians were a relatively new order, which – unlike some others – was encouraged to interact with the secular world, offering care and hospitality to the sick, the poor and the aged. These activities were 'corporal acts of mercy' which would help to save the souls of those who performed them. The new priory founded by Rahere had a master, eight brethren and four nuns. From the very start, they looked after the sick.

As the centuries passed, the brethren and sisters who looked after the ill acted increasingly independently of the rest of the priory. There were even some disputes between the two sides. But in due course, the hospital side was allowed to keep the money that was given directly to it by benefactors. The hospital grew from strength to strength so that by the late Middle Ages it was a large, sprawling institution.

Some of the benefactors gave land, which produced a growing income for the hospital from rent. More money came from rich pilgrims and travellers, who used the hospital as a sort of hotel. Sick people who were treated and who were also wealthy gave donations. Money was left to the hospital in wills. The brethren also collected money and food from local homes and shops. As well as caring for the sick, the hospital provided shelter for the homeless and alms for the poor.

Then came Henry VIII's expropriation of the monasteries and other religious foundations, which had such a devastating impact on welfare provision in Britain. St Bartholomew's priory was dissolved in 1537. Much of its property was sold off. But somehow the hospital survived – probably because its work was considered so important. Sir Richard Gresham petitioned the king to refound the hospital in 1544 – in other words, to put it on a sound new legal footing. This was agreed and it took on some aspects of a municipal institution. In 1547, the city authorities put in charge of the hospital four aldermen and eight commoners, all presided over by the Lord Mayor. It was an arrangement that was to last more than four hundred years.

The emphasis moved from wide-ranging help for the unfortunate to a greater emphasis on medicine. In 1549, three surgeons were appointed and in 1551 the number of nursing sisters was increased to twelve. During the 1550s, the hospital had about a hundred beds. In 1568, the hospital's first physician, Sir Roderigo Lopez, a Jewish refugee from Portugal, was appointed. A surgery room for the poor was built in 1597.

The hospital's long history and prestige attracted eminent doctors. William Harvey, who discovered the circulation of blood, was the chief physician from 1609 to 1633. The hospital naturally developed a role as a place of instruction. Medical students were first recorded in 1662 but were probably being taught earlier. Funding for the hospital continued to come from old endowments and new gifts and legacies. It was, in effect, a charitable hospital for the benefit of the poor. There were no 'pay beds' at all.

Famous and powerful people gave their money and time to the hospital in each century. In the eighteenth century, William Hogarth heard that a foreign artist was going to charge the hospital a considerable amount for some painting; he provided two large new paintings himself instead. They remain among the hospital's most important treasures.

An outpatients' department and a residential college for students were created in 1842. In 1850 one of the pioneers of medical careers for women, Elizabeth Blackwell, studied at the hospital. An anaesthetist – a new profession – joined the staff in 1875. This made surgery a far better bet than it had been and the number of surgical procedures carried out rose to 2,446 in 1899. It became a constituent college of the University of London – cementing its teaching role – the following year. By the middle of the twentieth century, St Bartholomew's – affectionately known to most people as 'Bart's' – had become one of the best-regarded and most famous medical schools in the world.

St Bartholomew's Hospital circa 1930. Many celebrities, such as Hogarth, gave their money and time over the centuries.

The story of Bart's suggests that there was a long history of medical care in Britain and a long history of treatment of the poor, too, for centuries before the NHS. But was Bart's a freak – a beacon of hope in an otherwise dark world?

Up until the eighteenth century, there were only two hospitals in London, Bart's and St Thomas', along with one or two special institutions.[4] But the population of London at the time was much smaller and medicine was often of little benefit or even positively harmful. George III, the king who showed signs of madness, had the best doctors money could buy but his life was nevertheless shortened by their well-meant ministrations. Then, in the eighteenth century, in less than three decades, starting in 1720, five new general hospitals were created in London: Westminster, St George's, the London Hospital, the Middlesex Infirmary and Guy's.

Who created them? The second president of St George's was the Prince of Wales. Among the 'five-guinea subscribers' were Lord Chesterfield, Sir Robert Walpole and David Garrick, the actor. The

London Hospital was supported at first and for years to come by members of the Buxton, Barclay, Cherrington and Hanbury families.

A leading spirit of the Westminster Hospital was Henry Hoare of the banking family. Guy's was founded by a single man – Thomas Guy – who made a fortune first by importing copies of the English bible from Holland and then by making a killing in the South Sea Bubble. In the same period the Foundling Hospital, 'the most imposing single monument created by eighteenth century benevolence', was founded by Thomas Coram with the support of six dukes, eleven earls, city magnates and professional men. George Frederick Handel was a benefactor, as was Joshua Reynolds, the artist.

So the hospitals were founded by the great, the good, the rich and media stars. The modern equivalent would be for a hospital to be founded by the Duke of Westminster, some business magnate like Richard Branson, a clutch of pop stars, some of the remaining dotcom millionaires, David Beckham and other top soccer players along with a score of the top companies. The equivalent of a foreign-born musician like Handel could be Madonna.

Was all this happening in London while the provinces missed out? London was the centre, certainly, but also founded at that time was Addenbrooke's in Cambridge, the Bristol Infirmary and hospitals in Edinburgh, Winchester, York, Exeter, Northampton, Shropshire, Liverpool, Worcester, Aberdeen, Cork, and three in Dublin. All were founded before 1750.

This great expansion in charitable hospitals, though, was as nothing compared to what happened in the following century. Out of the 550 or so hospitals for infectious diseases in the provinces in 1906, more than four hundred had been founded since 1850.[5] In London today, at least thirty-six out of its sixty-four hospitals were founded in the nineteenth century. They were founded by public subscription, by groups of people and by individuals.

The nineteenth-century hospitals varied enormously in their aims. The Brompton Hospital in Fulham was founded by a solicitor after a colleague with consumption (as tuberculosis was then called) was unable to find hospital care. The hospital was specifically to treat people with consumption. Moorfields Eye Hospital was founded in 1805, when soldiers came home from the Napoleonic Wars infected with trachoma and infected their neighbours too, with the result that thousands lost their sight. Moorfields became a world leader in the treatment of blindness. The New Cross Hospital was founded in 1877 'for pauper patients afflicted with smallpox'. For many years it was attached to Guy's. It was closed when owned by the NHS, in 1987. The Royal Free Hospital, in Hampstead, was founded in 1854 by a young doctor with help from members of the Cordwainer's Company and much royal support.

No one should pretend that this was a paradise of charitable healthcare. There were problems. The donations hospitals received varied from year to year. A hospital could be founded, but then find itself unable to finance all its beds. Hospitals were often in a state of persistent financial crisis.

Sometimes people showed great enterprise. Dr George Field became the Dean of St Mary's Hospital in London in 1883. To raise money he sent out six thousand invitations to

John Burton, 99, recovering from a successful eye operation at Moorfields Eye Hospital, 1934.

a *conversazione* in the hospital. The place was transformed for the occasion. William Morris, the leader of the Arts and Crafts movement, in cooperation with Messrs Gillow, the furniture-manufacturers, decorated the reception for free with pictures and other works of art lent by various owners. The Grenadier Guards, hand-bell-ringers, the Gala Choir and Mr Plater's Glee Singers provided musical entertainment in various parts of the building. Marshall and Snelgrove – one of the leading stores in London at the time – decorated the medical school. The latest medical inventions were exhibited, as was the most recent Victorian technological triumph: electric light. The refreshments were high quality and included a great novelty – bird's nest soup. The venture was a great success. The rapid expansion of the hospital continued. It was in this hospital, in a laboratory paid for by such means, as well as through fees and subscriptions, that Alexander Fleming was soon to discover penicillin.

There were Sunday collections in churches on behalf of hospitals. To these were added Saturday collections from workplaces. The royal family played a major role throughout, Edward VII first among them. He was the leader of the King's Fund, which, with his prestige and through the trust he inspired, was able to accumulate investments of over £1.8 million by the time of his death in 1910 – a fabulous sum which could provide a continuing income.[6]

Alongside the charitable hospitals were the local-authority hospitals. Most of these began life as Poor Law workhouses where the infirm could go if all else failed. Local authorities which ran them took civic pride in developing them. In 1861, they provided four out of five hospital beds – although the inmates tended to be those with long-term, chronic diseases and these hospitals performed a lower proportion of operations. Patients were asked to pay if they could. They would be interviewed by an almoner who would require the better off to pay up.

As charitable hospitals boomed, they began to catch up in the number of beds and overtook the local authority hospitals in active treatment. By 1936, the charitable hospitals took in 60 per cent of all patients requiring acute care.[7] By 1948 the proportion was probably higher still.

Charitable hospitals were also finding new and more reliable sources of finance. An increasing number of patients were paying, one way or another. In 1936 St Thomas' had forty pay beds, Guy's seventy-one and Manchester Royal Infirmary one hundred. Some people paid cash, others insured themselves against the cost of possible hospital treatment. But the

THE LIFE OF A CONSULTANT BEFORE THE NHS
Frederick Nattrass qualified as a doctor in 1914 and had to go off to the war straightaway. He was made a prisoner and only returned to Britain in 1919. At first he had difficulty finding a position, so he coached students to earn money. At last, he got a job as assistant physician at the Royal Victoria Infirmary in Newcastle, where he stayed for many years, eventually becoming a consultant neurologist. His daughter, Anne Whittingham, recalls his routine:

'He went to work at the hospital in the morning. All for free. It was a charity. Then, to get an income he took private patients at our home between two and five in the afternoon. This wasn't unusual at all. All his friends did it. All consultants did.'

Frederick Nattrass went on to become a professor and, among many other things, founded the Muscular Dystrophy Group.[11]

THE WHIFF OF DETTOL

'I remember the whiff of it. The smell of Dettol was all over the place. Antibiotics only became readily available after I graduated so the only thing we could rely on to stop infection was antiseptics. Hygiene was rigid. It was the first thing everyone learnt. Everyone was terrified of the sister. Obedience was expected. Respect was expected. You can't imagine the difference between then and now. You are not going to have cleanliness without strictness or encouragement.

'I remember going into the hospital when I was a child on Christmas Day. We used to do nursery rhymes and so on for the patients. They were lying in bed to attention! Their sheets were across them, all white, sparkling and firm. Everything was absolutely spick and span. If anything wasn't, sister or nurse would spot it.'[12]

Dr Anne Whittingham on the Royal Victoria Infirmary, Newcastle, between the wars.

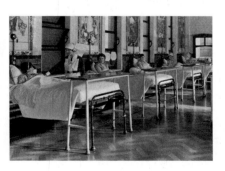

biggest development was a rapid increase in the number of people who paid through regular contributions to a hospital, which entitled them, if the need arose, to hospital treatment. It was a kind of health insurance which was arranged directly with a hospital. By 1943 there were 191 such schemes, most of which had been created in only the previous fourteen years. They had attracted, in this short time, nearly ten million regular subscribers.[8] Their families were covered too, so approaching twenty million people enjoyed this protection.

The proportion of charitable hospital income coming from paying patients was therefore rising dramatically. It jumped from 9 per cent in 1891 to 52 per cent in 1938[9] and very probably more in 1948. Not that the charitable side faded away. It was just joined and supported by payments. The result was that in 1935, the voluntary hospitals had an annual surplus of over £1 million despite the economic depression.[10]

Hospitals up to that time benefited from one remarkable advantage which most people know nothing about today except those old enough to have experienced it. The highest rank in the medical profession, the consultants, typically gave much of their time and effort for free. Being a doctor then was a vocation as well as a profession. It was normal for them to see patients without charge in hospital

CARY GRANT DISCOVERS CHARITABLE HEALTHCARE

There is no folk memory of healthcare before the NHS. Perhaps that is partly because few films concerned themselves with medicine. But one did.

In *The Amazing Adventure* (1936), Cary Grant plays a rich young man who is feeling out of sorts. He goes to see a Harley Street doctor about it. The eminent Sir James Aldroyd becomes angry with Grant's character – called Ernest Bliss. He says the only thing wrong with him is that he has too much money. He should give up his pampered life for a year and live on what he can earn as a working man. He only wishes some of Bliss's great wealth would go to his charitable clinic in the East End. The doctor refuses to shake Bliss's hand.

Bliss bets the doctor he will do exactly as he prescribes, saying he will stake £50,000 for Sir James's charitable clinic against 'an honest handshake'.

In his year as a working man, Bliss works for a while as a taxi-driver. By coincidence he is called to drive Sir James one evening to see a patient twenty miles away from his East End clinic. Sir James does not recognise him. They drive to the house of the patient, and Bliss waits. When Sir James emerges from the house, he tells the husband that his wife's crisis has passed. She will

Cary Grant and Mary Brian in
The Amazing Adventure.

be all right. The husband is worried about paying Sir James's fee. 'There is no fee,' says the doctor.

Ernest Bliss decides at that moment that regardless of whether he wins his bet or not, he will give £50,000 to the doctor's clinic. Before the NHS, it was normal for consultants to work for a large proportion of each day without charge.

and then to see private patients at another time of day. The private patients provided the incomes of the consultants. Why did they work for free? They learned in the hospitals as students. When they became specialists, they gained prestige for being a consultant to a hospital, they gained wide experience and as part of the deal, they were expected to hand on their expertise to the next generation of students. It is also only fair to suggest that they did the work partly out of a sense of philanthropy and duty. Some of the nurses, too, gave their services for modest amounts or for free. The nurses in some hospitals, such as the Hospital of St John and St Elizabeth in London, were nuns.

General practitioners would often treat patients without making a charge, too. They would adjust their fees according to the means of the patient. It is has been estimated that 20 per cent of the population received free services from a GP in the early twentieth century. Free treatment was also provided by the outpatient departments of charitable hospitals, the Poor Law hospitals and by charitable dispensaries (charities with benefactors, like the hospitals, but for outpatients only).

A small number of – mostly richer – people paid cash when they needed a doctor but the great majority made regular payments in various ways. Many – well over half the population – would pay for their GP through membership of a friendly society.[13] Being a member of a friendly society, you and your family could go to the doctor appointed by your local lodge for free or for a reduced amount. Alternatively, your friendly society might issue an approved list of doctors. You could choose which one you went to. A third system was for a society to create its own 'medical institute' – a place where doctors would work full time as employees of the society, while another way of financing GP care was for workers to arrange with their employer for an agreed sum to be deducted from their pay each week to create a fund. Miners and steel workers in the Welsh valleys did this, creating 'medical aid societies'.

> **'I never put off going to see a patient on account of the weather, except on two or three occasions when the roads were completely blocked with snow. Nor did I make any difference between the rich and poor in the attention I gave them.'[14]**
>
> **William Robinson on his time as a country doctor in the 1880s and 1890s**

Doctors themselves also organised contributory schemes. You could pay your local GP a regular sum and he would not make a charge when you needed him.

There were also 'provident dispensaries', which were hybrids – half-way between charities and self-provision. Benefactors would contribute to the cost but the patients would also make regular contributions. The idea of the creators of such dispensaries was that it was better even for the poor to make a partial contribution to their own well-being than to get it entirely free.

How GP services were paid for in the 1890s

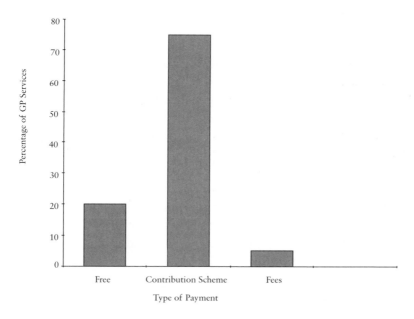

The free services were from hospitals. The contributory schemes were run by friendly societies, charities, unions, employers and provident dispensaries.
Source: David Green, 'Medical care without the State'[15]

Overall, the vast majority of people paid to see a GP one way or another. But the poor could normally see one at a discount or for free. In 1911, out of the twelve million who were covered by the new national health insurance, nine million were already covered by one type of contributory scheme or another. Of course, once they were obliged to have the national insurance imposed by David Lloyd George, they gave up the schemes they had voluntarily joined.

By 1939, nineteen million people had compulsory national health insurance – two-fifths of the population. But the other 27.5 million still obtained the services of GPs through direct payment, friendly societies, dispensaries, and so on. The proportion needing to rely on free services had probably fallen below 15 per cent.

The great variety of people and institutions who bought medical services before 1948 meant that there was competition among doctors to serve them. Doctors could not be sure of a job unless they pleased their patients. They could only charge what the market would bear – which meant they had to charge less than they would have liked. In Reading, the prices charged by doctors under the auspices of the British Medical Association (BMA) were the lowest in the country because in the same town, friendly societies had created a rival medical institute. That is why, when the BMA was discussing the future of medicine under the NHS, it was keen that medical institutes should not be allowed.

Alexander Fleming discovered penicillin in 1928.

So, before the NHS was created, British medicine included plentiful hospitals, rising self-provision and competition among practitioners. It was also a world leader. Students came from all over the globe to learn and patients to be treated here. We also had an unrivalled record in making major medical breakthroughs.

To gauge Britain's role in the most important medical advances, I asked three doctors with different backgrounds what they considered to have been the five biggest medical breakthroughs in world medicine between 1750 and 1948. The consensus was, in date order:

1. The proof that the source of cholera epidemics was the water supply;
2. The development of vaccines;
3. The use of anaesthetics;
4. The use of antiseptics;
5. Penicillin – the first antibiotic.

There is something remarkable about this short list. It is the place where most of the major breakthroughs originated.

The proof that the source of cholera epidemics was the water supply was made when Dr John Snow drew a map of where people lived who were affected by an epidemic of cholera in an area near Carnaby Street in London. He showed that those people who were infected were concentrated around a single water pump. Those who were nearer to other pumps, with clean water, did not get the disease. At the time, cholera was a major killer disease. Now, in advanced countries, it is not.

The pioneer of vaccines was Edward Jenner, a private doctor in rural Britain who developed a vaccine for smallpox in the eighteenth century. Other notables in the development of vaccines were Louis Pasteur in France, who developed a vaccine for rabies, and Sir Almroth Wright in Britain, who developed one for typhoid. Sir Humphrey Davy in Britain first suggested the use of nitrous oxide or 'laughing gas' as an anaesthetic in 1800. Anaesthetics were very important in making prolonged surgery possible.

The importance of antiseptics was proved by Ignaz Semmelweis in Vienna before 1850. Pasteur advanced research on putrefaction and bacteria. Joseph Lister pioneered the use of antiseptics in operations in 1865 using creosote (impure carbolic acid). Many people used to die of infections which entered an open wound during surgery before antiseptics were introduced.

The five major medical breakthroughs 1750–1948

1. Cholera	1854	UK	Dr John Snow	Understanding of cholera epidemics
2. Vaccines	1798–1896	UK/ France	Dr Edward Jenner (small-pox, 1798), Louis Pasteur (rabies, 1885), Sir Almroth Wright (typhoid, 1896)	Prevention of many diseases. They have saved millions of lives
3 Anaesthesia	1800/53	UK	Sir Humphrey Davy, Horace Wells (dentist)	Made prolonged surgery possible and no longer extremely painful
4. Antiseptics	1865	UK	Ignaz Semmelweis, Louis Pasteur, Joseph Lister	Made surgery far less dangerous
5. Antibiotics	1928–41	UK	Sir Alexander Fleming, Howard Florey, Ernst Chain	Killed bacterial infections

Penicillin was discovered by Alexander Fleming in St Mary's Hospital, one of the charitable hospitals, in London in 1928. Its potential was brought to fruition by Howard Florey and Ernst Chain, working in a laboratory in Oxford in 1941 largely funded by the Rockefeller Foundation.

Looking through these five most important medical breakthroughs over 198 years, it is clear that Britain played a major role in all of them. Other countries certainly made important contributions. Also some doctors might consider that the development of X-rays should be in the top five, in which case Wilhelm Röntgen, working in Germany, and Marie Curie, in France, would get most of the credit. Meanwhile Frederick Banting and Charles Best in Canada are the people most closely associated with the development of insulin for the treatment of diabetes. Pasteur crops up again and again in the advances of nineteenth-century medicine. All the same, there is no getting away from the fact that Britain was a leading player, probably *the* leading player.

So the inheritance which Aneurin Bevan was intent on replacing, far from being small and insignificant, was impressive.

Hospitals and beds were plentiful. Britain was a leader in a wide variety of specialities. A great richness of hospital existed in 1948. They were world leaders and world teachers.

Most people were charged. They often made regular contributions of one sort or another so that if they needed hospital treatment, it would not be a catastrophic financial blow. But the hospitals also offered free treatment for the poor. Consultants gave their time free of charge and typically spent much of the time treating the poor as well as the rich. General practitioners were plentiful. They had many different paymasters including friendly societies and medical institutes as well as individual patients, so they had to compete with each other on price and quality of service, to the benefit of patients. Doctors would informally adjust their fees according to the means of patients who, in any case, could also go to the outpatient departments of hospitals or get free treatment from the local authority. Most people, before national insurance in 1911, relied on friendly societies, unions and other similar bodies for their primary healthcare. Many still relied on them in 1948. Britain had established the best record in the world for achieving major medical advances and had just developed the landmark drug of the twentieth century: penicillin – the first antibiotic.

It was not a perfect system. There were surely some poor people who received inferior treatment or none. But the vast majority of the poor were treated – in many cases by the top specialists of the time.

Some people may think that this account is one-sided and that there must have been grave flaws in medicine in 1948, otherwise why would the Labour Party have been so keen to change it? Certainly there were flaws. Undoubtedly the Labour Party and some others, too, thought it could be better. But looking at what was written at the time – and even since then – the remarkable thing is how little people found to criticise. In Michael Foot's biography of Bevan, I have been able to find only a single page in which a case is made against healthcare before the NHS out of a total of 1,164 pages. This is in a book all about the man who thought it necessary to revolutionise the old system.[16]

On this single page no source is quoted. No mention is made of waiting lists. There is no description of poor hygiene. Foot makes no suggestion that British treatment was inferior to that of other countries. He makes no complaint that the poor went untreated. There is no complaint about treatment of patients at all. His main complaint is that there was no 'system'. All sorts of people were doing various things without central control. There were too many small hospitals, he suggests. But he makes no suggestions that they were too expensive or did not cure people. He makes no mention, either, that the many small hospitals meant more people had the advantage of a hospital nearby. He then takes the opposite tack and complains that there were not sufficient teaching hospitals – only thirty. At the time Foot was writing, of course, he did not know that a future government would try to close down Bart's, the oldest and most famous of them all. He complains: 'Many doctors gave their services on an entirely voluntary basis in the time they could spare from their private practice.' Again, he criticises the nature of the system. He does not criticise the outcome – the quality of the treatment.

For a fuller critique of medical care before the NHS, one can look to a pamphlet issued by the Labour Party in April 1943 which sets out Labour's case for a revolution in healthcare. I have obtained an original copy. It is printed in black on white with no pictures. It cost twopence. Here, surely, the case against pre-NHS healthcare would be made as graphically as possible.

Front cover of the 1943 Labour Party pamphlet calling for a 'national service for health'.

It is most cleverly written. The writer was perhaps Michael Young, who went on to write the Labour Party manifesto (see Chapter 5). Whoever the author may have been, he or she invites the reader to consider what medical services we need and portrays the image of a health service which many people – then and now – would find attractive. The first item 'needed' reveals the mindset of the reformers: that medical services should be 'planned as a whole'.

The pamphlet goes on to examine 'our existing medical service'. It is criticised for being a curative and not, additionally, a preventive service. It is said not to be 'open to all' but the author has to admit that 'to some extent the gap [between rich and poor] is narrowed by the public provision of free medical services.' He or she goes on to list a wide variety of these free services. But then the author comes back to what seems to be the main objection to the pre-1948 service – that it is 'unplanned' and 'a medley of public and voluntary institutions'. Criticisms of the actual standard of healthcare are very thin on the ground.

In a footnote, one can find reference to 'a great shortage of beds for the treatment of rheumatic diseases'. But this is the only reference to waiting for treatment of any kind in the entire pamphlet. No numbers of patients waiting or the length of their waiting times are given. We can only assume that in all other areas of medicine, such as surgery and getting an appointment with a consultant, waiting was not a problem. There is not a word of criticism about hygiene. There is not a word against the quality of the treatment. There is no suggestion that people are dying or incapacitated because treatment has been delayed or refused. The charitable – or 'voluntary' – hospitals, far from being criticised, are said to 'have rendered great service'. They 'have been maintained by devoted effort,

> **THE MEDICAL SERVICE THAT WE NEED**
> 1. Planned as a whole
> 2. Preventive as well as curative
> 3. Complete
> 4. Open to all
> 5. Efficient and up to date
> 6. Accessible to the public
> 7. Confidence between doctor and patient preserved
> 8. Equitable for the medical profession
> 9. The medical service should be so organised as to enable the medical profession to pull its weight effectively in all those tasks of democratic government which affect the nation's health
>
> **Paraphrased from *National Service for Health*, issued by the Labour Party, April 1943**

much of it unpaid'. Hardly a grievous criticism.

Foot explains what drove Bevan as the minister responsible for health. Bevan's job enabled him to illustrate the 'three strongest strands' in his political creed:

1. 'his detestation of a class-ridden society';
2. 'his belief in a collectivist cure';
3. 'his dream ... that democratic processes and democratic vigour, intrepidly unleashed, could accomplish revolutionary ends'.

The driving ambition does not come from failings in the existing healthcare system. It comes from a political ideology.

No doubt Bevan and the rest of the Labour Party believed that a centrally planned medical service would be more efficient and would treat people more equally. In this, he and others were influenced not only by Marxism but the apparent success of government organisation of the war effort. He also thought that the democratic accountability of the Secretary of State for Health would ensure it worked well. His much-quoted comment was: 'Every time a maid kicks over a bucket of slops in a ward, an agonised wail will go through Whitehall.'[17]

The medical profession was far from convinced. Many GPs were violently opposed to it, even though an NHS would mean they would have one rich paymaster in place of many individuals, some of whom were poor and some of whom were slow paying their bills. They believed it would damage the independence of doctors and thus the standard of medical care.

At a meeting of one thousand doctors in Wimbledon Town Hall in 1946, one called it the 'biggest expropriation of property since the dissolution of the monasteries'.[18] He had a point. In retrospect, there were two major expropriations of property in British history. One was done by a greedy, selfish tyrant – Henry VIII – who thereby damaged provision for the poor for years, perhaps centuries, to come. The second was the take-over of charitable and local authority hospitals by a zealous, socialist government.

What would be the effect of this second expropriation? Who would be right – the passionate reformer Aneurin Bevan or the doctors, who were against it from the start, and who were only persuaded, bullied and bribed to accept it against their better judgement?[19]

Let us judge the NHS by the standards the Labour Party prescribed in its 1943 pamphlet. This was what it said a medical service 'should be':

1) *Planned as a whole, so that there are no gaps in it*

The National Health Service must be regarded as a success as far as the first phrase is concerned. (We will come later to the question of whether there are no gaps.) There can be no doubt that the NHS is very much 'planned'.[20]

Maurice Slevin, a consultant oncologist (cancer specialist) at Barts and The London NHS Trust, decided to try to measure the extent of planning and managing. He set out to discover how many managers there are and how their numbers compare with the numbers of nurses. He looked at 'full-time equivalent' figures, which give a more accurate picture than the bare 'headcount' figure. He discovered that were 269,080 managers, administrators and support staff compared to 266,170 nurses. It seemed astonishing that there should be more administrators than nurses. So Dr Slevin went to some length to make sure the comparison was fair.

> 'The trust board has demanded we have six clinical governance half-day meetings a year – bringing the whole hospital to a standstill apart from emergencies ... Perhaps the most wasted half-day in my management dealing was a business planning meeting where many of the senior clinicians gave up their commitments to discuss the hospital's business plan ... only to be told at the conclusion of the meeting that the business plan had already been written.'
>
> Consultant at a large London hospital, 2003

He then took away from the management staff those he regarded as not really management after all: doctors' secretaries, whom he regards as part of the medical teams, those who do maintenance and those who operate ambulances. But even after making these adjustments, there were still eight managers and support staff for every ten nurses. This, he explained, was probably an under-estimate of the ratio because many nurses do the work of managers rather than nursing itself.

> 'The Office for National Statistics [ONS] ... reported that public-sector employment has risen by 142,000 in the last year to its highest level for over twenty-five years. The ONS estimates that 6.5 million people work for the public sector, amounting to one in four of the workforce.'[21]
>
> News item, February 2003.

'Ah yes,' some people may think. 'But to be efficient, an organisation does need managers.' So Dr Slevin also looked at a private hospital to see how many managers and so on it required. He found that it had 240 nurses and forty-three managers, administrators and support staff. The ratio was 1.8 managers to every ten nurses. His calculation showed that the NHS employs more than four times as many managers and support staff per nurse than a private hospital.

> 'An estimated thirty-five managers meet fortnightly at Chelsea and Westminster Hospital to monitor the "four-hour trolley waits". Meanwhile there is usually one casualty doctor at night.'
>
> Doctor at the Chelsea and Westminster Hospital who wishes to remain anonymous

The emphasis on management was still increasing, too, when he made his study. Between 1995 and 2001, the number of nurses increased by 7.8 per cent but the number of managers jumped by 24 per cent. The number of senior managers soared – by 48 per cent. But this is not just a recent thing. It has been going on for decades.[22]

University College London Hospital NHS Trust provides an example of modern NHS planning. It has a department manned by thirty people processing instructions from the Department of Health and demon-strating that the trust is fulfilling targets, thus falling in fully with central plans so that it is entitled to receive various grants and extra payments. These thirty people with their desks, computers and pension schemes do no treatment of patients. They are just part of the planning.

> 'NHS administrators are like the Chinese Red Army. Shoot one and three more spring up in their place'
>
> Richard Littlejohn, *Sun*, 4 February 2003

So yes, the NHS is certainly planned. It is, perhaps, the most heavily planned and managed structure in Britain.

2) Preventive as well as curative

The NHS is certainly working towards being 'preventive' as well as 'curative'. It tries to ensure that as many people as possible are vacci-nated against serious diseases such as tuberculosis. It has screening programmes for breast and cervical cancer. The NHS in the widest sense – including the rest of the government – has heavily taxed ciga-rettes and banned most forms of advertising for tobacco. All these measure are designed – wholly or partly – to prevent illness.

On the other hand, every other advanced country in the world has similar programmes without requiring an equivalent to the NHS. The NHS also has no programme of screening for prostate cancer – a test which is routine for men over fifty in many advanced countries. In America, many men are screened for prostate cancer every year. This probably helps explain why 92 per cent of people diagnosed with prostate cancer survive for another five years or more in the USA whereas in Britain, only 49 per cent survive as long.

An annual check-up can be preventive. It can result in a doctor saying, 'You need to exercise much more often and change your diet if you don't want to die of a heart attack.' But the vast majority people with an NHS GP get no annual check-up and receive no diagnostic tests except when a particular crisis arises – which is often too late.

The elderly, in particular, can benefit from check-ups. Without them, they are less likely to realise that they are, for example, eating insufficiently, taking too little exercise so that their muscles waste and they lose mobility, or developing osteoporosis, in which the bones become brittle and can easily break.[23]

3) Complete – covering all kinds of treatment required
Is the NHS 'complete – covering all kinds of treatment required' as the Labour pamphlet said it should be? Does it have 'an all round service of specialists' and 'good hospitals with enough beds'? Presumably all this was intended to mean that people would be treated in a timely and effective manner.

Mavis Skeet had cancer of the oesophagus.[24] Radiotherapy was tried but failed to halt the cancer's spread. On 5 December 1999, nearly a year after the initial diagnosis, she was scheduled for an operation which could save her life. She was told there was a 60 per cent chance of success. The surgery would take place at Leeds General Infirmary. She was there and ready on the appointed day. The operation could have gone ahead but the anaesthetist had flu. So it was postponed.

This was an urgent case – not something that could be allowed to drag on. But the operation was not rescheduled until more than two weeks later. She again prepared herself for the operation which might save her life. But many people were suffering from flu at that time with the result that there were no intensive-care beds available for her recovery after the operation.

So the operation was postponed again. A third date was made. A third time, Mavis Skeet prepared herself for this operation which, by now, had a reduced chance of success. A third time it was cancelled. So, for a fourth time, a new date was made for an operation that was becoming increasingly less likely to succeed. For a fourth time, Mavis prepared herself. A fourth time, the operation was cancelled.

In January 2000, a scan was done to see how far her condition had deteriorated in the meantime. It showed that the cancer had spread to her windpipe. An operation could not succeed at all. There was no point in rescheduling the operation. She was certain to die within months.

For many years, every assertion that something was going wrong with the NHS was countered by someone else replying that they – or a relative – had been treated very well. It was one anecdote against another. But then, starting in the 1990s, international comparisons began to be made. The Imperial Cancer Research Fund looked at one of the best measures of a medical service – how long patients survive after being diagnosed with various kinds of cancer. One of the cancers they looked at was cancer of the oesophagus – the one from which Mavis Skeet suffered. In Britain, they found, 7 per cent of patients survived for five years after being diagnosed with it. In Germany 8 per cent survived and in America 12 per cent.[25] In other words, somebody getting cancer of the oesophagus in Britain had only 60 per cent of the chance of survival of someone in America. Mavis Skeet was not exceptionally unlucky. She was one of many.

Cancer of the oesophagus is one of the less common forms of cancer. How does the NHS perform with other cancers? Breast cancer, for example.

The European Union funded the Eurocare study of survival of people diagnosed with breast cancer between 1990 and 1994 across nineteen European countries. The survey included some of the poor countries of Europe which had previously been part of, or satellite states of, the Soviet Union, such as Poland, Estonia and Slovakia. Sweden, Finland and France came out best with over 80 per cent of those diagnosed still being alive a year after first being diagnosed with breast cancer. The former communist states did worst, which is not surprising given their circumstances. Among the western European countries, the one with the third worst performance was England. The second worst performance was that of Scotland and the worst of all was that of Wales, where fewer than 70 per cent survived. To put it another way, a woman diagnosed with breast cancer in Britain was 40 per cent more likely to die within five years than one living in France.[26]

A similar story can be told for nearly all the cancers. In the Eurocare survey, out of eight major Western countries, including France, Germany and Italy, Britain came sixth for leukaemiain men and seventh in women, seventh for non-Hodgkins lymphoma in men and eighth in women, third for cancer of the head and neck, and last for prostate cancer and lung cancer as well as breast cancer. Overall, Britain was certainly the worst of the eight. In lung cancer, for example, the survival rate of only 7.7 per cent was less than half that of France In another survey of colon cancer, the British survival rate was shown to be 36 per cent compared with an American survival rate of 60 per cent.[27] Professor Colin Pritchard of Southampton said that even black people in the USA – a group of people less likely than whites to have medical insurance – had a better survival rate than people depending on the NHS.

How many are still alive a year after being diagnosed with lung cancer?

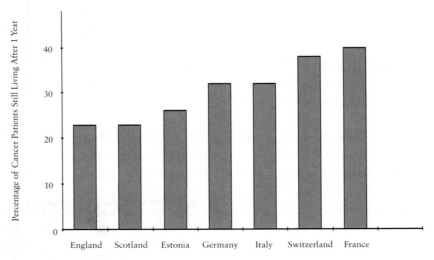

Source: Eurocare III study for 1990–94 followed to 1999

Professor Karol Sikora, Visiting Professor of Cancer Medicine at Imperial College, University of London and former head of the World Health Organisation's cancer forum, looked at various cancers and the effectiveness of Britain in treating them. He calculated how many patients' lives would be saved if Britain performed as well as other countries. His conclusion was that 10,000 people a year would be saved from death if Britain matched the average performance of medical services in Europe. Putting this the other way around, some 10,000 people a year die of cancer in Britain because of the inferior nature of NHS treatment.

Is the inadequate treatment of cancer patients one dark patch in an otherwise bright picture? Does the NHS treat people with other diseases well even if its cancer care is below standard?

Bob Golightly put his trust in the NHS.[29] He was a deputy headmaster and reckoned himself pretty fit. He worked out and played golf. But towards the end of 1998, he felt chest pains while exercising on a running machine. Prudently he went to see his GP, who told him that he might be suffering from angina. He was referred to South Cleveland Hospital in Middlesbrough. The tests took place quite a while later in September 1999. They confirmed that he had blocked arteries. The next logical thing was to see a specialist. There was another six-month delay before Mr Golightly was able to see him. The specialist told him he needed a triple bypass but assured him it was not urgent. He was asked if he would, perhaps, like to delay the operation to September, the start of the academic year. No, he said, he would like it as soon as possible. He was told he would probably have to wait five months anyway – until August. Mr Golightly was concerned. He phoned the hospital every two weeks to get a date. He and Ann, his wife, discussed going privately. She said later, 'If they had told us, "You're sitting on a time bomb," . . . we'd have gone privately immediately.' Her father would have paid.

But no, they put their trust in the NHS.

In June 2000, eighteen months after he first went to his doctor with chest pain, Bob went with his daughter Kirsty and his grandchildren, aged eight and ten, to watch Darlington FC play Peterborough at Wembley. On the way, he had a heart attack. He died in the arms of twenty-year-old Kirsty and in front of his grandchildren.

Was this just a one-off? A freak misdiagnosis that could happen in any system? What is the overall picture?

World Health Organisation statistics show how many men per 100,000 die before the age of seventy-five of coronary heart disease in different countries. The figures are 'age adjusted' so

Bob Golightly with his wife Ann and daughter Kirsty. Bob and Ann put their trust in the NHS.

they take account of the fact that older people are more likely to die than younger ones.

How likely are men to die prematurely from coronary heart disease?

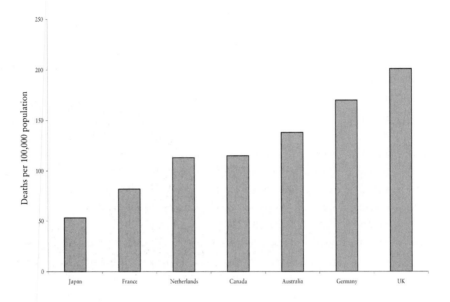

Source: World Health Organisation figures published 2004 relating to 2003 and earlier

Former communist countries such as Latvia have easily the worst figures. Leaving them aside and sticking only to advanced countries, Japan and France have easily the best results: only fifty-three per 100,000 died in Japan in 2002 and eighty-two in France in 2000. But deaths from heart disease reflect more than just the quality of the medical service. Diet and smoking make a big difference. To be fair to the NHS, we should look, perhaps, only to those countries where diets are not so very dissimilar to our own. In Australia, for example, 138 died per 100,000 men. In Germany the figure was 170 and in the Netherlands 113. What was the figure in Britain? The death rate was 201 per 100,000.[29] To put it another way, a man living in, say, Australia, is 31 per cent less likely to die prematurely of coronary heart disease than someone in Britain.

This evidence is not conclusive in itself, however. It would be possible that – even between Britain and countries like Germany and Australia – differences in lifestyle could entirely account for a greater risk of dying of heart disease.

But if Britons do have a particularly high propensity to suffer heart disease because of their lifestyles, one would expect Britain also to have a particularly high rate of heart bypass operations. It does not.

Around 2000, British surgeons performed open heart surgery, for example, 645 times for every million people compared with 907 times in Switzerland, 904 in the Netherlands, 1,061 in Sweden and 1,191 in Germany.[30] If Britain does indeed have a higher propensity to heart disease, this lack of treatment is all the more dramatic and disturbing.

You are also much less likely to be treated with angioplasty, in which a balloon is used to reopen blocked coronary arteries. Professor Keith Fox of Edinburgh University studied the medical histories of more than three thousand patients in twenty-nine countries. He found that in Britain, angioplasty

> 'Things are in such a mess, much worse than I would have imagined possible. I'm hearing over and over again that there aren't enough beds. In some places, elective surgery has just about stopped.'[31]
>
> **Sir Peter Morris, President of the Royal College of Surgeons, December 2001**

was used for a mere 1 per cent of those who had suffered a heart attack compared with 19 per cent of French and German heart attack victims. Among those with unstable angina – increasing episodes of chest pains – only 19 per cent of British patients received angiography, a diagnostic test which reveals the state of the arteries. In contrast, two-thirds of French patients received it. He also found that British patients are given shorter times in which to recover in hospital – eight days, while German heart patients get an average of eleven days. As time goes by, Britain has increased the number of bypasses and other interventions for heart diseases. But it has been 'behind the curve' – always trailing what other countries are doing.

Diagnostic techniques are important in this, as in other areas of medicine. Bob Golightly, mentioned above, died because the gravity of his condition was not recognised. This could just have been a mistake by the consultant. Then again, it could be a kind of mistake which regularly happens. There is a wide variety of diagnostic techniques in heart disease. One is an ultrasound technique known as echocardiography. An image is made of the heart which shows how well the muscle is contracting. It can often help establish the cause of heart failure and helps a doctor decide on the best use of drugs. In 1995 a study was done in Scotland of how much echocardiography was used.[32] The researchers found that heart failure patients in general practice were given echocardiography in only 30 per cent of cases.

There are many other measures of how well the NHS treats those with heart disease. Nearly all of them show that it treats patients poorly and considerably worse than in other advanced countries. No one, as far as I know, has estimated how many avoidable deaths have resulted from the relatively poor treatment by the NHS of those with heart disease. No doubt such an estimate is fraught with possible errors. Nevertheless it may be useful to make some calculations which may give an indication.

Let us suppose – as seems likely – that the higher rate of premature deaths from heart disease in Britain is indeed due to inferior treatment. If the death rate here was the same as in other advanced countries with similar diet and lifestyles, how many lives would be saved?

The average premature death rate for Australia, Germany and Canada is 185 men per 100,000, compared to 265 in Britain. That suggests that 30 per cent of the 30,000[33] men who die each year would not do so if they enjoyed a better health service. It follows that 9,000 men a year could be dying because we have the NHS instead of an averagely good medical service.

Coronary heart disease is a less common cause of death for women – 12,135 a year die prematurely. In Australia, Germany and Canada, 33 per cent fewer women die on average compared with Britain. That suggests that a further 4,000 people may die because Britain has the NHS instead of average medical care.

I don't pretend these figures are authoritative. But it appears that British treatment of heart disease and strokes is inferior and that a considerable number of people die as a result each year.[34]

The figures suggest the NHS is far from being 'complete' as the 1943 Labour Party pamphlet said it should be. But what do patients – the customers of the service – think? To begin with, in 1948, they thought it was perfectly satisfactory. This is crystal clear because in 1955, the first year for which figures are readily available, only 1.2 per cent of the population went to the expense of buying private medical insurance. Five years later, however, the idea of 'why pay twice?' was beginning to lose ground. People were starting to discover that the NHS did not offer them as good a service as they had been accustomed to. The proportion jumped to 1.9 per cent. There was another sharp jump five years later and, again, five years after that. In fact over every five-year period from 1955 to 1990 – whether the government was Labour or Conservative –

the proportion of people 'paying twice' and buying private medical insurance significantly increased.

The proportion reached 11.6 per cent in 1990 and did not rise at all over the next decade. That may lead some people to think that a plateau had been reached. But there were other ways in which people were resorting to private-sector medical care. Company health insurance plans kept on increasing the numbers covered during the 1990s. Also important were 'health cash plans', in which someone who becomes ill gets cash which covers some but not necessarily all the cost of an operation. These plans are more affordable.

> **The increasing number of people who resort to 'going private' (or abroad) for treatment without delay almost certainly reduces the number of people who die from cancer and heart disease in Britain. No estimate has been made of how many more people would die prematurely if there was not this large minority getting prompt treatment. It is very likely that Britain's record would be even worse.**

Some people have more than one plan so we must be careful of double counting. But the Family Resources Survey of 1998/9 showed that the proportion of the population with insurance or a cash plan or both had reached 19 per cent. If the trend has continued to the present, one in five of the population now finds the service offered by the NHS so 'incomplete' that they feel they must take out some form of private insurance.

On top of that, as insurance has become more expensive, partly due to less favourable tax treatment, people have turned instead to direct payment – or 'self-pay'– for medical services. Between 1992 and 2002, the proportion of self-pay treatments in independent hospitals jumped from 13 per cent to between 22.5 and 25 per cent.[35]

If that is a good indication, it means that as much as 5 per cent of the population self-pay and a full quarter of the population now use private medical care for some or all of their hospital treatment.[36]

Considering how expensive it is to 'pay twice', this is a damning indictment – by the customers themselves – of the NHS.

The NHS has not lived up to the standard which the Labour Party set in the pamphlet. It is not 'complete'. It does not offer 'for every citizen . . . whatever medical treatment he requires'.

4) Open to all, irrespective of means or social position

This is the very heart of the ambition of the NHS. In the ringing words of the pamphlet, 'Poverty must be no bar to health, no bar to a man's right to life.' And again, 'There should be no lower limit of income . . . for access to the benefits of the entire services.' Even if the NHS looks after patients less well than other countries, does it at least look after the poor – albeit in this second-class way?

Chris Davies[37] began to get angina – a heart problem causing a pain in the chest. After some years he was referred to a large regional cardiac centre, where he saw a consultant and had angiography in 1996. He was told, 'I don't think you need surgery yet.' Only the right coronary artery was blocked, which was less important than the left. To the consultant, it did not seem too bad.

It was bad enough, however, to force Mr Davies to stop work a year later. He was getting chest pains after walking only fifty yards. He asked to be put on the waiting list for bypass surgery. Come back for another angiogram, he was told. He was then given to understand that a bypass would only be offered by the NHS when more than one artery was blocked. He knew the other artery had narrowed, but there was nothing he could do.

On his next visit, the surgeon agreed that the left artery could be operated on but said it could be risky and might not be needed for some years yet. Mr Davies insisted – in a way that many, less confident and articulate people would not – that he be put on the waiting list for surgery.

He waited. And waited. Finally, after eight months, he took action. He demanded a copy of his angiogram and flew to Belgium. 'My journey to the modern teaching hospital at the University of Louvaine took just over two hours.' The cardiologists there told him, 'You need three grafts. The right coronary is fully blocked, as it has been for some years. There is now a 60 to 70 per cent stenosis [narrowing] on your main left artery and a 90 per cent stenosis on the first diagonal branch.'

At last, he says, he 'had a cogent explanation of what was wrong and why a bypass might help'. The operation was described as 'routine' and the wait in Belgium would be three months at most. Mr Davies did the paperwork which enabled him to get the operation done at the same net cost as for a Belgian citizen – 25 per cent of the total cost. In March 1999, the operation took place. 'My ordeal was over,' said Mr Davies, who was now completely free of discomfort and 'for the first time in twenty years, I need no medication for angina.'

It is a story with a happy ending. Why? Because Mr Davies had the intelligence, confidence and enterprise to deal with the problem. He came out smiling because he was a member of the entrepreneurial middle class.

Here is a second story about waiting for heart surgery.

Rodney Spriggs was on the waiting list at Bristol Royal Infirmary. He waited and waited and then he died. He was only forty-seven. I don't know how rich or poor he was, but his wife Brenda said afterwards, 'My husband died while on a waiting list and since his death other people have died too. Unfortunately my husband's problem was that he didn't complain enough.' His wife thought that if he had been more demanding, more proactive, he would have lived.

> 'The waiting list to begin radio-therapy in many parts of the country is three months – and that's ridiculous.'
>
> **Professor Karol Sikora, 1999**

The Bristol Royal Infirmary's own chief of cardiothoracic surgery, Franco Ciulli, became so angry and disillusioned about deaths like that of Rodney Spriggs that in May 2001 he did something very unusual for any doctor.[38] He publicly announced that fifteen people on his waiting list for surgery had died. He and his team revealed there was a sixteen-month waiting list compared to two months in France and Germany. Mr Ciulli declared, 'The longer the waiting lists are, the more deaths you get. This is fifteen too many. This is fifteen people who were never able to get access to services in Bristol.'

How many patients have to wait over four months for surgery?[39]

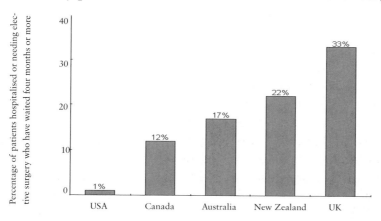

Who are most likely to be denied 'access to services'? Those who are not well educated and articulate enough to find out about their condition, those without the confidence to demand that it be dealt with and – if it is not going to be dealt with – to find some other way, those without access to the internet and those without medical friends who can advise them. The people who are likely to be left behind are the poor and the less well educated. Consequently, they are ones most likely to suffer and die.

The NHS is therefore not truly 'open to all, irrespective of means and position', as it was claimed it would be. It is egalitarian in theory only – not in practice.

One way in which it is not genuinely 'open' is through the waiting for treatment. How can a service be fully 'open' if it keeps on delaying entry? One observer of the medical scene observed that the NHS waiting list grew by a quarter of a million every decade. So after five decades, with 1.25 million on the list, it was going according to schedule.[40] The length of the waiting lists has been a major political issue for many years now. In 1997, the list stood at over 1.3 million. In 1998 it rose to 1.5 million. Since then, after many millions of pounds spent on treatment by private hospitals as well as NHS ones, it has been reduced to 800,000. Even at this level, it means that out of every hundred people in England, 1.6 are waiting for in-patient hospital treatment.

> **'60 per cent of doctors, polled several weeks ago by the British Medical Association News Review, said that they had first-hand experience of politically-motivated goals distorting clinical priorities'**
>
> *Guardian*, **21 January 2003**
>
> **The phrase 'distorting clinical priorities' usually means that someone with a relatively minor problem has been treated ahead of someone else with a life-threatening condition. A political goal is achieved because the operation is quicker and makes the waiting list shorter**

But there is every reason to doubt that waiting list figures can be trusted any more. Hospital managers are under pressure from the Department of Health to keep them down. They are given targets and if they can't meet them, they have an incentive to cheat. One method of cheating is to move patients from the waiting list onto the 'suspended list' – those who cannot have an operation for one reason or another. The Department of Health considers that as many as 5 per cent of patients could reasonably be on the suspended list. But in August 2000 half of all NHS trusts were above that level.[41] In the worst case, Wrightington Hospital in

> **'No one has any faith in the validity of waiting list figures now. The Department [of Health] has been silently complicit on waiting list manipulation.'[42]**
>
> **Dr Evan Harris, spokesman on health for the Liberal Democrat Party, 2003**

Wigan, the suspended list amounted to a quarter of the waiting list. Many people on the Plymouth Hospital NHS Trust suspended list were not aware they were on it. It was suggested at the time that as many as seventy-five thousand patients might be being hidden in this way.

In December 2001 the National Audit Office described a raft of ways in which hospitals manipulate the figures. Salford Royal Hospital, for example, was not reporting those who had been waiting for over eighteen months.

The Audit Commission similarly looked at the waiting lists of forty-one NHS trusts. Errors were found in nearly half of them.[43] Three were discovered deliberately misreporting the figures. In half the cases, hospitals were manipulating the lists with 'sharp practice', for example offering appointments at very short notice (sometimes as little as twenty-four hours) and then 'restarting' waiting times if patients could not attend.

The commission chairman, James Strachan, commented, 'Some trusts have lost sight of the real priorities, which are about improving the NHS for the patient, not just meeting government targets.' The government itself seemed to have lost sight of the real priorities, too, since the outgoing chairman of the commission revealed that it had put pressure on the commission to water down its findings. In addition to all this, there is the waiting list to get on the waiting list. The ill person has to get to see a consultant who orders the operation. But it can take a long time even to see consultants.

The much-publicised waiting lists have therefore become untrustworthy. They have become like an article in *Pravda* in the 1960s or 1970s announcing that wheat production has gone up again according to targets in the ten-year

> 'Some hospitals are playing fast and loose with patients' lives. Can you imagine the trauma of waiting six months for a scan, only to be told that, if you can't make it tomorrow, you are going right back to the end of the queue again?'
>
> 'In one case, 5,000 patients at one hospital alone were treated like this.'
>
> **Source quoted in Audit Commission report on waiting lists, March 2003**

> 'Tony Blair is throwing his weight behind an audacious strategy that would in effect abolish NHS waiting lists, guaranteeing that no patient would wait more than three months for any treatment.'
>
> **Headline and opening sentence of article by Polly Toynbee and David Brindle, *Guardian*, 31 May 2000**

Cartoon by Dave Gaskill, *Sun*, 21 August 2002.

plan. The figures are false. Everyone knows they are false. The behaviour of communist propagandists is now being repeated in the British medical service.

The Prime Minister, Tony Blair, and his ministers have started many 'initiatives' to deal with the problem. But Britain still has waiting lists for treatment of a length completely unknown in any other advanced country. The waiting lists are a means by which the poor get inferior treatment to the rich and the middle classes. As a result they are more likely to suffer and die.

Is there another group of people, apart from the poor, who have reason to feel that the NHS is not 'open to all'?

In 2001 the Association of Community Health Councils did a survey of how long patients had to wait for treatment in accident and emergency departments. It found that patients under forty had an average wait of something under three hours. But those over sixty were kept waiting an average of nearly five hours. In 2002 the King's Fund[44] contacted senior managers from health- and social-care services across England and found that three-quarters of senior managers thought that age discrimination occurred in their area.

Discrimination against the old has been measured and demonstrated in many ways. Breast cancer screening is offered every three years to women aged between fifty and seventy. Then the offer stops. Curious, since the risk of getting breast cancer does not disappear with age; it increases. One possible justification could be that older women do not benefit from treatment. A study was done in the Netherlands and described in the *International Journal of Cancer* in 1996. It showed that regular screening of women over sixty-five and up to seventy-five at least could reduce breast cancer deaths by about 45 per cent.[45]

The charity Age Concern did a survey of GPs in 2000 which showed that an upper age limit exists for heart bypass operations and kidney dialysis, too. The NHS is short of capacity so it decides, to put it simply, to concentrate on the young. This means, in many situations, that the old are allowed to die.

The 1943 pamphlet argued that a medical service should be 'open to all'. But the NHS discriminates against the poor and the old especially. It cannot be described as 'open to all'.

5) *Efficient and up to date*
The creators of the NHS were keen that the suggested new service would be up to date. Is it?

CT scanners per million population

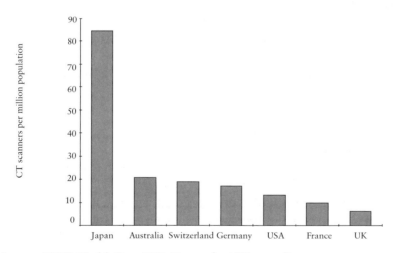

Source: OECD Health Data 2001. Figures for 1999 or earlier

Some of the most important tools for diagnosis are scanners. X-ray machines were the most important of the early ones. Since then, a great variety of machines has become available. One of the most important has been the CT (computed tomography) scanner, which shows doctors exactly what and where many troubles are. It can help a doctor see whether a patient has cancer or not, and if so, the precise location. The OECD keeps account of how many CT scanners each country has. Japan, despite its relatively low spending on medical services, has by far the most – ninety-three per million of population.[46] France, Germany, Italy and the United States have 8.4, 14.7, 24 and 13.1 respectively. So how many does Britain have? Only 5.8, fewer than any other advanced country – fewer, too, than Turkey and the Czech Republic.

Even more recent and advanced than the CT scanner is the MRI (magnetic resonance imaging) scanner, which avoids giving the patient a dose of radiation and can distinguish between different tissues more precisely than CT scanners. Again the Japanese are prodigious buyers and have 35.3 per million of the population. Iceland comes next with 17.3, followed by Switzerland with 14.2. Britain has 5.2 – more than France, with only 2.8, but far below the average for thirteen advanced countries of 9.6. Even if Japan is excluded

> **'Entering a British hospital, I had the impression I was in a museum.'[47]**
>
> **Ukrainian nurse, 2003**

as a distorting anomaly, Britain remains well below the average of 7.5 for the rest.[48]

The lack of the latest scanning equipment means that Britain relies more heavily on the older technology – X-ray machines. In what sort of condition are they? Dr Colin Connolly, a former chief scientist for the Department of Health, carried out an audit on behalf of the World Health Organisation.[49] He found that over half of them are past their recommended safe time limit. He audited other equipment used in British hospitals, too, and he found that about a fifth of the equipment used in cancer treatment is obsolete. More than half the anaesthesia machines need replacing. The majority of operating tables are over twenty years old – double their safe life span. And over half the machines used for intensive care are past their use-by dates.

One may think that in many cases, old equipment works perfectly well. But according to Dr Connolly, 'Out-of-date equipment can be life-threaten-

> **'An NHS consultant was asked to use a dessertspoon instead of a proper surgical instrument during hip replacement operations, a tribunal has heard. Godfrey Charnley, a consultant orthopaedic surgeon ... later used £150 of his own money to buy the correct implement.'**
>
> **BBC News, 19 February 2003**

ing. The state of NHS equipment is a key issue for patient safety and effective treatment.' He added, 'In cancer care there is undoubtedly a lack of investment that has had a harmful effect on patients.'

Britain, therefore, has less of the latest equipment and the old equipment is often being kept beyond the time when it is safe. The NHS is not, as it was suggested it would be, 'up to date'.

This section of the 1943 pamphlet also stressed the importance of research for good medical care. 'The service must be amply equipped and endowed for research,' it states. We have already seen that prior to 1948, Britain was a world leader in research. Just before the creation of the NHS, the crowning achievement of British medicine had been achieved: the first deployment of penicillin. But the creators of the NHS thought it would do even better. So how does British medical research rate now?

I asked the same three doctors whom I had asked about major advances between 1750 and 1948 to make their best guess about what could be the major medical breakthroughs of the next ten or twenty years. The consensus was:

1. Transplants of animal organs into humans, saving people with heart or liver disease;

2. Gene therapy may be developed to enable doctors to 'turn off' genes which give people afflictions such as cystic fibrosis and Parkinson's disease;

3. A cure for heart disease;

4. A vaccine to prevent AIDS.

It is an exciting prospect.

Where, then, is the work going on which may bring about these extraordinary advances?

The companies working on the use of stem cells include Geron, Stem Cells and Advanced Cell Technology. These are all American. In gene therapy, the leading companies include Genvec, Genentech and Genzyme. These, too, are American. The companies working towards a cure for heart disease include Scios (which has already produced an important new drug in the fight against heart attacks), Vaxgen, Genentech, Amgen and Biogen. Once again, these are American. And so it goes on.

The lead taken by America is unmistakable. Britain's former pre-eminence has completely gone. Britain is no longer expected to contribute in a major way to any of the medical advances which will save and improve lives in years to come. True, there are some biotech companies in Oxford, Cambridge and London. Elsewhere in Europe, there are also some in Sweden and Germany. But these are small beer compared to the enterprises in America, particularly in California and Massachusetts. Some of the large, old-established European pharmaceutical companies, such as Novartis of Switzerland, have also moved much of their research to America.

Money spent on research by commercial companies here is tiny compared to that in the USA. The market capitalisation – i.e. the value ascribed by stock market investors – of a single American biotech company, Amgen, was US$74 billion in 2004[50] – more than all European biotech companies put together.

The ambition of the creators of the NHS that British medical research would be particularly good has not been realised. Britain has changed from being a leading country – or the leading country – making medical breakthroughs to being an also-ran.

6) Accessible to the public

The creators of the NHS thought that a good medical service should offer local hospitals with an emphasis on 'local'. A GP should be able to direct patients to 'a centre not too far from home', the 1943 pamphlet asserted, and there they could 'be examined by specialists'. If a patient was not able to travel, 'the doctor should be able to call in a specialist to the patient's home.' What has actually happened?

A new hospital was built in Kidderminster in the 1870s. As usual at that time, it was paid for by members of the public who subscribed money.[51] It was their hospital and one which, like other charitable hospitals, would look after the poor as well as the rich. Even after the hospital became part of the NHS in 1948, there was strong local support for this hospital – not just emotional support but hard cash, too. Despite the fact that the NHS is, in theory, meant to provide a complete and modern service, local people, through the Hospital League of Friends and other organisations, contributed about £3 million during the 1990s to try to keep it up to

'Roland Moyle, Minister of State ... told Parliament: "I think the homely atmosphere of a small hospital is no less important – it may indeed be more important – in urban community hospitals than in a rural community hospital." Yet his department has systematically closed over 100 hospitals in the period 1975–7.'[52]

David Widgery, Health in Danger

scratch.

But in 2000, the Kidderminster hospital was closed. At a stroke, 110,000 people who were within five miles of the hospital lost the 'accessibility' which was meant to be part of the NHS. When a child now breaks his arm falling off a bicycle in Kidderminster, he must be taken fifteen or twenty miles to get to an accident and emergency department in Worcester, Redditch or Birmingham. When an old lady needs to have an operation, she must go to a town she does not know well, where she feels less at ease and where it is more difficult for friends and relatives to visit. Some twenty-five thousand people in the countryside outside Kidderminster are now up to thirty-five miles away from emergency care.

'To see equipment and furniture, much of it purchased by local people, loaded onto removal vans was devastating,' said Dr Richard Taylor, a retired rheumatology consultant. Petitions were got up with as many as sixty-six thousand signatures, showing overwhelming support for the hospital from the people of Kidderminster. But it made no difference. People were powerless.

> 'Sir,
> The Government, while in opposition, promised to save and restore St Bartholomew's Hospital. Though Bart's has been kept open, the vitally important accident and emergency department remains closed ... The department proved its worth ... at the time of the Old Bailey terrorist bomb and the Cannon Street rail disaster. Many lives were saved as a result of the proximity of Bart's ... Reinstatement has the support of ... the Royal Hospital of St Bartholomew Charitable Foundation, and is backed by a petition of more than 22,000 signatures.'
>
> Peter Carter-Ruck, letter to the *Daily Telegraph*, 14 May 2002
>
> The A&E department remains closed.

Outrage was so great that Dr Taylor stood for Parliament in the 2001 election on the issue. Normally, single-issue candidates get nowhere and he was up against David Lock, a junior minister with a 7,000 majority.[53] But that majority melted like snow in a kettle, such was the heat of the disappointment of local people. Dr Taylor was elected with a majority of 17,630.

The NHS has not established a record of opening local hospitals; on the contrary, it has closed them. Closures are often disguised as 'mergers'. The Chelsea and Westminster Hospital was created out of five hospitals. To put it another way, four hospitals were closed. Often governments claim that mergers mean no loss of capacity in the NHS. Do the figures bear this out?

Available NHS beds in England

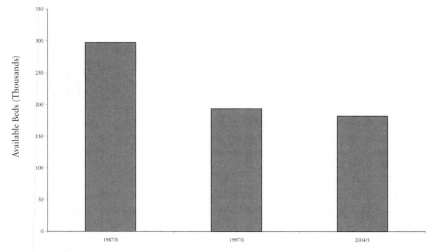

Source: Department of Health

One of the periods of fastest closures was the later 1970s. 'There are over 100 gone since the cuts began, and probably a further total of 500 under threat,' wrote David Widgery in *Health in Danger*, subtitled *The Crisis in the National Health Service*.

Is there a bed available?

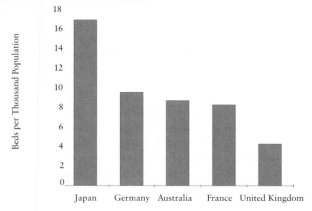

Source: *Prospect*, quoting OECD and WHO.

In 1990/1, there were 255,000 hospital beds in England. Ten years later, the figure was down to 186,000 – a drop of 27 per cent on top of similar big declines in previous decades. After these closures, Britain now has one of the lowest numbers of beds per person of any advanced country. Japan has the most with 16.5 per 1,000 people. Germany has 9.3, Australia 8.5 and France 8.1. Britain has a mere 4.2.[54]

St George's Hospital was founded in 1733 and lasted nearly 250 years until the NHS sold the building, which has now become the Lanesborough Hotel (pictured). St George's was merged with at least ten other hospitals.

The most important beds are those devoted to intensive care. They cost more but they are needed for the most serious conditions. The second cancellation of Mavis Skeet's operation was due to the lack of an intensive-care bed. How well off is Britain for intensive care beds? France has thirty-eight per 100,000 people and Spain 14.8. Britain has five.

Since the NHS was created in 1948 very few new hospitals have been created. I have not been able to identify a single hospital in London, for example, which was not founded before the creation of the NHS. Instead, the NHS has closed hundreds of hospitals around the country. The NHS is less accessible than the service which existed in 1948.

> **'60 hospitals face axe in NHS reform'**
>
> **Headline, *Observer*, October 2002**

As for the idea that 'if necessary, the doctor should be able to call in a specialist to the patient's home,' it is rarely achieved. It is difficult enough to see a specialist in a hospital, let alone in one's home. The fact that the pamphlet mentions the idea suggests that consultants did visit patients in their homes prior to 1943. The practice has fallen into such disuse since the NHS that it now seems barely comprehensible.

7) *Preserve confidence between doctor and patient*

The 1943 Labour pamphlet declared: 'Good doctoring is a very individual business.' It was important that people should have confidence in their doctors. It was important, too, that they should be able to change them if dissatisfied. How has that idea worked out in practice?

Doris Wood, 71, suffered a burst blood vessel in her stomach in February 2000 and she went to hospital in Hillingdon, in west London. There was a delay of three days before she was given an ultrasound scan

> **'We are expected to see unreasonably large numbers of patients in an increasingly small time and use obsolete equipment in grubby wards and outpatient clinics. Patients complain that staff are aloof and unfeeling but have no idea how worn down, burnt out and, indeed, clinically depressed many staff now are.'**
>
> **Sarah Burnett,
> consultant radiologist,
> *British Medical Journal*, March 2002**

and she died. Her son, Mike, said afterwards, 'We were not kept informed and there was very little communication. We had to push and wring every bit of information out of them. The patients seemed to be an inconvenience to the doctors there.'[55]

It should be said that this sort of treatment is far from universal. Many people have experience of doctors working within the NHS being patient, helpful and informative. But this is just pitting one anecdote against another. For an objective assessment, we can go to a survey done by Harris Interactive. The polling company and its associates around the world polled 1,400 people in five countries about how they were treated by GPs. Were they treated with dignity and respect? Were they listened to carefully, provided with all the information they wanted and given enough time? Did the doctor know their family situation and was the doctor accessible by phone or in person? On these six measures, Britain came out last in four and second from last in two. It had the worst overall score.

It is not surprising when one considers that the average time doctors get to spend with patients is typically only six or seven minutes. That is as much as they can spare when they work for the NHS. They would all like to spend more time with their patients. They are very much aware

How British GPs are rated in a league table of five countries

	Position
Treating patients with dignity and respect	4th
Listening carefully to health concerns	4th
Providing all the information wanted	5th
Spending enough time with patient	5th
Knowing patient and family situation	5th
Being accessible by phone or in person	5th

Survey of people in Australia, Canada, New Zealand, United Kingdom and USA by Harris Interactive[56]

that some patients do not reveal what is really worrying them until they feel comfortable – perhaps near the end of a consultation. General practitioners dislike the situation as much as anybody. It means that patients do not have the confident, trusting relationship with doctors they might otherwise have.

Do people have more confidence in hospital doctors? The Picker Institute asked people in five countries about their stays in hospital.[57] Were they told about the purpose of the medicines they were given? Were they told of the danger signals to watch for at home and given advice about resuming work or other activities?

Each country was given a score – the higher the number, the worse the advice. The best scores were achieved by American and Swiss doctors, with ratings of 28.4 and 30.0 respectively. Somewhat worse were the ratings for Germany and Sweden at 40.6 and 40.2. But the worst rating of all was given to British hospital doctors at 45.1.

Advice in hospital to patients about medicines and danger signs when back at home

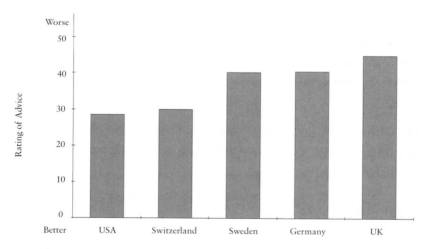

Source: Picker Institute adult inpatient surveys 1998–2000

It appears that the relationship between doctors and patients is worse than in other countries. It seems likely that confidence of patients in their doctors has declined since the creation of the NHS.

8) Equitable for the medical profession
The Labour Party in 1943 was keen that the doctors should not feel

---

'APART FROM MOTIVES OF DUTY . . .'

'The doctor on his part, if it was in the night, had to saddle and bridle his horse . . . then would come a journey of possibly an hour's dura- tion, attention to his patient and the drive or ride home, and after that the necessary attention to his horse . . . Tiring, responsible and wearing work, yet it had to be done, for more than one reason. Apart from motives of duty, family practice could not be established or main- tained without it.'

'Medicine is a vocation to the service of Humanity.'[58]

Life in a country general practice in the 1870s, recalled by H. W. Pooler MB

---

threatened by its proposals. It reassured them that Labour wanted to give a 'fair deal' to the medical profession. The nation 'must tolerate no sweating or overwork of doctors, nurses or other health workers', the pamphlet declared. This would be achieved through 'ade- quate specialist services' and 'sufficient doctors'. The pamphlet powerfully declared that the 'burden' of achieving the equal service being created must not 'fall on the shoulders of the most self- sacrificing members of a generous profession'.

It is worth noting, in passing, the way that in 1943, the Labour Party described doctors as members of 'a generous pro- fession'. That shows how great was the respect with which doctors were regarded. It is also testimonial to the way members of the medical profession then worked with a sense of philan- thropy and public service just as strong – and perhaps stronger – than exists in the state-controlled service today.

But the whole idea of doctors getting

Practising physicians per thousand population	
Italy	4.1
Belgium	3.9
Switzerland	3.6
Austria	3.4
France	3.4
Germany	3.4
Sweden	3.3
Spain	3.2
Netherlands	3.1
Norway	3.1
Denmark	2.9
Luxembourg	2.7
Finland	2.6
Republic of Ireland	2.6
Australia	2.5
USA	2.3
New Zealand	2.2
United Kingdom	2.2
Canada	2.1
Japan	2.0

Source: OECD Health Data 2005[59]

a fair deal in the NHS and not being overworked depended, as the creators of the health service said, on there being 'sufficient doctors'.

Even after recent increases, Britain has significantly fewer doctors per thousand population than most of the world's advanced countries. It has 2.2 doctors per thousand whereas the Netherlands has 3.1 and France and Germany each have 3.4.

There are shortages of staff all across the front line of the NHS. There is a chronic lack of cancer specialists. In Britain there is only one for every 119,000 patients compared with a European average of one for every sixty thousand patients.[60] That explains why many people with cancer do not see a specialist at all.

There have been serious shortages of nurses and other kinds of staff too. Successive governments – having failed to train and retain sufficient staff within Britain – have resorted to hiring staff abroad – from Spain, Trinidad, the Philippines, anywhere they can get staff. But still the shortages continue. In 2002, the BMA said that 'thousands' of GPs had closed their lists to new patients. The reason? Doctor 'shortages' and growing workloads. Dr John Chisholm, the chairman of the BMA general practitioners' committee, said, 'We are approaching meltdown in general practice, with a dire shortage of doctors.'[61]

Some GPs say that they would like to have 1,500 patients on their list because with that number, they can give each patient the sort of time that they would like. But GPs can have as many as 3,500 on their list.

The lack of medical staff means that those who hold the fort are under considerable strain. In a survey, two-thirds of GPs said they suffered from low morale and 82 per cent said they suffered stress.[62] Nearly 96 per cent believed that too much was expected of GPs.

The pamphlet of 1943 suggested that a good medical service would be 'equitable for the medical profession' and that there would be sufficient doctors. But after fifty-five years of the NHS, doctors' morale is low and there is 'a dire shortage'.

9) *The Medical Service should be so organised as to enable the medical profession to pull its weight effectively in all those tasks of democratic government which affect the nation's health*

It is not really clear what this last part of 'The Medical Service We Need' means. But it is unlikely that the modern medical profession feels it has much power in the organisation of healthcare. This section may seem to some to be little more than an attempt to flatter the medical profession into acceptance of the plan. If that is what was intended, it did not work. Doctors voted again and again against the plan that Aneurin Bevan put forward. The medical profession was forced to accept it because the government was democratically elected and the minister was determined.

The Labour Party pamphlet of 1943 described what was in the minds of those who created the NHS. The NHS has clearly failed to come up to the standards which Labour set itself. The shocking thing, as one looks at scores of assessments of medical performance, is how frequently Britain comes right at the bottom among advanced countries. It appears to have the least successful medical service in the advanced world.

There are two criteria, however, which the Labour pamphlet did not mention in 1943. It did not state 'hospitals should avoid infecting their patients.' Nor did it say 'hospital patients should be treated with care and consideration.' It probably did not make those demands because these things were taken as read. The medical service at the time had good standards of hygiene and looked after patients attentively. These are things which – surely the Labour Party would have agreed – should be part of 'the medical service we need'.

Does the NHS provide them?

Hospitals should avoid infecting their patients

Leyla Sanai was a consultant anaesthetist at the Western Infirmary in Glasgow – someone at the top of her profession. But she herself became ill and instead of looking after others, found herself on the receiving end of hospital care. She was astonished by what she found. 'The truly gobsmacking revelation I had as a patient was the total neglect of ward cleaning,' she says.[63] 'In the olden days, matron would cause hearts to quake when she scrutinised the area under beds and ran her finger along ledges, looking for dust.'

> '**Last week it emerged that consultants at Queen Alexandra Hospital in Portsmouth were refusing to operate because of filthy surgical instruments. Infection rates from MRSA at the trust are doubling each year.'**
>
> **Daily Mail, 23 November 2000**

Dr Sanai had to be moved from hospital to hospital, giving her a great deal of experience. 'In all the hospitals I was in, with the notable exception of the Royal Free in London, there was an appalling lack of any form of ward cleaning.' She recalled what happened on one ward: 'Each day a weary cleaner would appear . . . [She had] minutes to attend to each room. She never changed the fetid water in her bucket or added detergent to it. The areas where hygiene was truly important ... received scant attention.'

Dr Sanai caught MRSA – methicillin-resistant *Staphylococcus aureus* – a dangerous kind of infection because it resists being destroyed by antibiotics. She was put in a room by herself to reduce the chance of her passing on the infection. But even then 'not once did a cleaner bring the mop into the bathroom, nor did it happen on any of the subsequent forty or so admissions.' She tried an experiment in one room: 'I kicked a pubic hair from the previous occupant into a corner of the bathroom. It remained there.' She was in that room for 'a few weeks'.

Lord and Lady Fitt – 'I love you more than my life, no one could have a better man,' she wrote.

There are many anecdotes of poor hygiene that could be told. I quote this one because the source is a former consultant who knows how hygiene should be and who had wide experience of different hospitals.[64] And this is why it matters:

Gerry Fitt became well known, well liked and much respected as an MP from Northern Ireland. After he left the House of Commons, he was made a member of the House of Lords. In 1996, his wife Anne was admitted to Chelsea and Westminster Hospital in London with asthma.[65] Lord Fitt visited her there every day. On the second day, Anne pointed to an old lady at the end of the ward who had been screened off from the other patients. Anne said she had heard doctors discussing the fact that she had a bug 'called MRSA'. Gerry Fitt did not know about MRSA at the time, but he still exclaimed, 'Oh my God, Anne, if there's a bug in here, you're going to get it too.'

Two days later, she did. Soon after that she died. Anne Fitt died because she got MRSA in hospital, not because of her asthma. Lord Fitt still carries around in his wallet a fading note from his late wife which has the last words she wrote before she died: 'I love you more than my life, no one could have a better man.'

How widespread is poor hygiene in hospitals? The National Audit Office (NAO) report in 2000 remarked, 'There is ample evidence that compliance with hand-washing protocols is poor.'

How actively is hygiene pursued? 'There may be a growing mismatch between what is expected of infection control teams in controlling hospital infection and the staffing and other resources allocated to them,' according to the NAO. Some people are inclined to blame private cleaning contractors. But the ultimate responsibility lies with the management – indeed the government. The role of management is revealed in the following shocking fact discovered by the NAO: 'A quarter [of hospital infection control teams] were never consulted on the letting of cleaning, or catering or laundry contracts.'

One way to combat MRSA is to isolate those who have it, as Leyla Sanai was isolated, so that the bug does not spread to others. How well is this done? 'The number of isolation facilities within individual NHS trusts have been greatly reduced over the last five years and over 40 per cent of infection control teams were dissatisfied with the facilities available in their Trust,' reported the NAO. Private hospitals, of course, nearly always have separate rooms for each patient, considerably reducing the risk of cross-infection. Private hospital groups also take other measures which substantially reduce the risk and typically they claim that there are no MRSA deaths in them whatsoever.[66] In 2004, BMI Healthcare, one of the major groups, with forty-seven hospitals, asserted that it had 'never' had a patient who had acquired blood-borne MRSA. In contrast, according to Dr Barry Cookson of the Public Health Laboratory Service, understaffing, overcrowding and poor hygiene have created a 'cauldron' of infection in NHS hospitals.[67] MRSA in Britain is something for which the NHS bears responsibility.

> 'It is shocking that one of the richest countries in the world has this problem, which can largely be solved by hand-washing'
>
> **Dr Natasha Crowcroft, consultant in public health medicine, Public Health Laboratory Service**

How many people die because of hospital-acquired infections – particularly MRSA – every year? One figure often quoted is 5,000. It appeared in a report by the NAO published in 2000. It should not be treated as reliable, however. As the report clearly stated, it was based on a study done in the USA and a 'crude comparison' or hypothesis that 'if US rates were applicable in the United Kingdom, 5,000 deaths ... might be primarily attributable to hospital acquired infection and in a further 15,000 cases ... hospital acquired infection might be a substantial contributor.'[68]

There is every reason, however, to think that the incidence of deaths in Britain from infections caught in hospitals may be substantially higher. A study by the European Antimicrobial Resistance Surveillance System looked at samples of the bacterium *Staphylococcus aureus* taken from hospitals in different countries around Europe.[69] The idea was to see what proportion was methicillin resistant – the most dangerous kind. The results showed a clear north–south divide. Countries surrounding the Mediterranean had a much higher incidence of it. However, there was one

> '**I thought I was coming to First World nursing ... I could not believe it, because even the mission hospitals in Zimbabwe were cleaner and better run.**'[70]
>
> **Zimbabwean nurse, 2003**

break in the pattern. In Britain, the proportion of MRSA was 46.1 per cent – above the levels even of the Mediterranean countries and far higher than that of other northern countries. The report described the British figure as 'alarmingly high'.

Percentage of *Staphylococcus aureus* samples resistant to antibiotics taken in hospitals

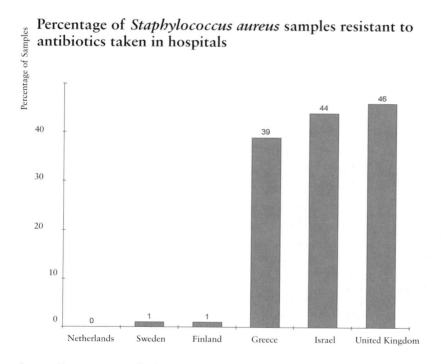

Source: European Microbial Resistance Surveillance System bulletin, 2002

Another reason for thinking that deaths from hospital-acquired infections may be far higher is that the incidence of MRSA in British hospitals has been rising fast. In 1995, 189 hospitals were known to have had outbreaks of MRSA.[71] In 1998, there were 1,597 incidents – eight times as many. The disease was advancing at a gallop.

A third reason for thinking that deaths from hospital infection are higher comes from a study by the London School of Hygiene and Tropical Medicine and the Public Health Laboratory Service. They looked at people who died in hospital and found that, in normal circumstances, 8 per cent of elderly patients who go to hospital die. But of those elderly patients who pick up an infection in hospital, 38 per cent die. After adjusting the figures for types of illnesses, sex, age and so on, they found that catching an infection in hospital increased a person's chances of dying by seven times.

In most instances, hospital infection does not appear as the cause of death. But if the infection had not been caught, six out of those seven people would not have died.

> **FAMOUS HOSPITALS INFECTED**
> Christopher Malyszewicz, consultant chemist and microbiologist, took swabs from toilet flushes, door handles and seats in casualty departments and public areas at five of Britain's largest hospitals: Leeds General Infirmary; Leicester Royal Infirmary; Addenbrooke's, Cambridge; St Mary's, Paddington; and Bristol Royal Infirmary. In every one of them he found MRSA.[72]

It remains difficult to say how many people are dying because of MRSA. Only relatively few death certificates name it as the cause. Hospitals are short of staff and have no inclination to spend time deciding whether a patient was killed by his or her original problem or by MRSA. Indeed they have a reason to avoid finding out. If relatives discover MRSA had a role, they may sue, causing the hospital huge costs and damaging the careers of those involved.

It seems likely that the widely quoted estimate of 5,000 deaths a year being directly due to hospital-acquired infection is a gross under-estimate. The suggestions that in another 15,000 cases it is a 'contributory factor' is also likely to be a major under-estimate. Moreover, the so-called 'contribution' of hospital infection will – in the vast majority of cases – be the difference between someone living and dying.

What about the other desirable aspect of a medical service that was considered unnecessary to mention in 1943? Are patients treated with consideration when they go to hospital?

Hospital patients should be treated with care and consideration
A nurse who moved from the West Country to work in London said:

> I thought I would see the very best in nursing. I expected to feel
> like a real country bumpkin, coming up against the highest stan-
> dards. But I got the biggest shock of my life. I went to three
> hospitals: Ealing, Hammersmith and Charing Cross. The care
> was pretty appalling.
>
> Patients were not treated in a respectful way. They were manhan-
> dled, really. Elderly people who had had strokes and needed total
> care were toileted in the ward with gaps left between the cur-
> tains. People could see them. Sometimes care could be good. But
> it was random whether patients received good care or bad.
>
> I don't know if NHS nursing suffers from low morale or whether
> they have just lost focus on what nursing is all about. Does the
> training put people off who would have been good nurses? It is
> so academic now – a three-year degree course for everyone. Pre-
> viously there were enrolled nurses, who had a simpler, two-year
> course with practical work, as well as the state-registered nurses
> who studied for three years. But nursing is still practical work.
> The attitude has changed. Often it is: 'I've got a degree. I am not
> going to get involved in giving personal care.'
>
> On one occasion when I was a patient, I asked for pain relief – I
> suggested an anti-spasmodic drug. An hour and a half later, I
> still had not been given any. I rang the bell. A nurse came and
> said 'Yes!' in an angry, impatient voice. I asked again. She said,
> 'I'll see.' It was more than five and half hours later, at 12.45 at
> night, that a nurse finally came with a tablet.
>
> On the ward, there were nurses who were simply lazy. On one
> occasion I saw two nurses playing solitaire on the computer for
> over three-quarters of an hour. Of course there are times on a
> ward when there is nothing urgent to do. But they could have
> been reading up the notes of their patients or talking to them.

Many of the nurses were imported. Battling with the language problem, they got irritated about repeating themselves. There were three or four Philippine nurses who did work hard. They were very caring and meticulous. But they still could not talk to patients because of the language barrier. I was worried about the language problem when it came to them reading drug charts [showing which drugs each patient should receive].

There was one night sister who was fantastic. She spent time with every patient. She delegated staff effectively. You had no doubt that you were getting the right medication or that drains [which remove blood or other fluids after an operation] *would be checked. She spoke to patients about their surgery. She read their notes and talked to them about their anxieties. It was nursing as it should be. But this was exceptional.*[73]

It should be emphasised that there are nurses, doctors and other front-line staff in the NHS who do a wonderful job and who show great humanity and kindness as well as professional dedication. Nothing in this chapter – or indeed the book – should be taken as a criticism of such people. Indeed, their behaviour is all the more remarkable in view of the circumstances in which they work. But the purpose here is to look at the experience of patients generally. Largely because of the working conditions they find themselves in, the front-line staff do not always provide the service which they – as well as the patients – would like.

The overall experience of people in hospital has been monitored by the Picker Institute.[74] The study looked at five countries: Germany, Sweden, Switzerland, the USA and Britain. People in the USA probably have particularly high expectations. Nevertheless, the experience of the British in hospital was rated lowest on six measures out of the seven. Britain was the second worst in the seventh case. The measure on which Britain was particularly bad was 'respect for patients' preferences'. The British score was 50 per cent worse than that of any of the other countries.

In 1943, the authors of the Labour pamphlet took it for granted that hospitals would be kept clean and patients would be treated with consideration. But after fifty-five years of the NHS, high standards which once were considered normal have seriously declined.

Avoidable deaths

It may seem a gruesome question to ask, but how many people die unnecessarily each year because of the NHS? It seems possible to put some figures on avoidable deaths whereas it is not possible to put a number on unnecessary suffering. One can measure the tip of iceberg more readily than the much larger, submerged part. A precise figure, of course, is not possible – even of deaths. But one can get some idea of the scale.

Professor Karol Sikora estimated that 10,000 people a year die who would not do so if only Britain had an average European medical service. Unfortunately, no estimate with such authority exists for coronary heart disease. My own calculations above suggested that it could be as many as 13,000, but I exclude these from a minimum total because it lacks expert authority. Deaths from hospital-acquired infection according to the NAO could be 5,000 in which it is a direct cause. Of course other countries have some deaths from this cause but as 5,000 is likely to be a gross under-estimate for reasons given before, the figure is included in the minimum.

It has been estimated that there are 41,650 avoidable deaths each year because of blunders or, as they are known in health policy jargon, 'adverse events'. All medical services, however, make such mistakes and I know of no study which measures whether there are more in Britain than elsewhere. Therefore they are not included in a minimum figure.

England had the highest proportion of avoidable infant deaths in a comparison of ten countries between 1993 and 1998 – 53.5 per cent, compared with an average rate of 44.9 per cent for the others. The difference between the two – 8.6 per cent – is the proportion who probably die in Britain because our standard of care for babies is below the average. More than 1,600 babies die each year in Britain, so it seems likely that about 140 of them die because of our substandard care.

Minimum number of deaths resulting from the NHS being 'below average' among advanced countries

Cancer	10,000
Hospital infection	5,000
Infant deaths	140
TOTAL	15,140

Sources: Professor Sikora, estimate based on WHO figures for infant deaths and estimate quoted by NAO

Adding together only the avoidable deaths in Britain of which we can be most confident, the 10,000 estimated by Professor Sikora, 5,000 from hospital-acquired infection and the 140 baby deaths, makes a total of

15,140 deaths. That is a conservative, minimum estimate. It is readily conceivable, sad to say, that 13,000 also die of coronary heart disease, more from strokes and from other major diseases and, say, 20,000 from hospital infection (especially allowing for the cases where it is a so-called 'contributory factor'). That would make a total of about 48,000 deaths a year.[75] Unfortunately, even that figure should not be regarded as a maximum.

Sticking only to the minimum of 15,140 deaths a year, the figure is shocking enough. People became angry and indignant, quite understandably, when thirty-one died in the Paddington rail crash on 5 October 1999. The subject dominated news broadcasts for long afterwards. There were interviews with people who had lost their loved ones. Television cameras followed the funerals of those who had died. The Prime Minister, the Deputy Prime Minister and many other politicians extensively expressed their sorrow, dismay and anger. Yet the deaths which take place in Britain because we have the NHS, instead of an averagely good medical service, are more than equivalent to a Paddington train crash every day. Should there not be a correspondingly massive sense of outrage?[76]

Why does the NHS perform worse than other systems?

Why doesn't the NHS work well? Why do so many patients suffer avoidable deaths and many more suffer in its care? A huge amount of money is spent on it. Why does the money not achieve good results? Why have the aspirations of Aneurin Bevan and his colleagues been unfulfilled?

We might learn something of the reasons through the experience of another country.

In Stockholm, in the late 1980s, the medical services were also in a bad way. Health services in Sweden are run by the local governments and in 1991 one of the local governments – that with responsibility for Stockholm – did something different. It started what has become known as the 'Stockholm transition'.[77]

It changed the way hospitals were paid. Hospitals, in future, would be remunerated according to how many operations and procedures they carried out. This improved productivity. Three years later, one hospital in Stockholm, St Goran's, was made into a separate, limited company. It would thrive or flounder according to its own efforts. This caused another boost in productivity for this particular hospital.

Services such as X-rays and pathology were thrown open to competition over the next few years. People who were formerly employees of the local authority started their own independent enterprises. Then in 1999 Stockholm sold St Goran's to a commercial company, Capio. The hospital would still be paid in the same way. It would sink or swim according to whether it could deliver services more cheaply than other hospitals still controlled by the local authority.

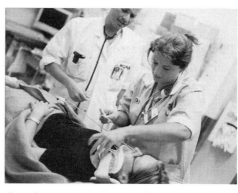

A patient receiving care at St Goran's Hospital in Sweden.

As a result of the changes, Stockholm developed distinctly more productive medical care than elsewhere in Sweden. The effect was dramatic. In 1991, the first full year of the new scheme of payment to hospitals for each procedure and operation, there was a 19 per cent improvement in productivity. This was followed by further improvements in productivity at St Goran's, both when it became independent and again when it was handed over to a commercial company. The opening of services such as X-rays and pathology to commercial competition also helped.

Because more medical throughput was being achieved, waiting times fell.

Treatment of patients was guaranteed within three months. Outside Stockholm, the ambition was the same but it was not reliably achieved. There patients had to wait up to two years for knee replacement surgery. In Stockholm, the wait came down to between two and ten weeks. Outside Stockholm, the wait for hernia surgery could be ten months. In Stockholm, it became one month or less. The Stockholm transition brought about a big improvement in medical care in the Swedish capital. Why? And how does it help explain why the NHS has disappointed?

One thing the transition did was to completely change the incentives for hospitals. Under the old system – as in the NHS – the more they did, the higher their costs and the more they would run at a loss. Under the new system, the more they did, the higher their income. The incentives were aligned with the desired result.

How did Capio manage to compete with local-government hospitals and still make a profit and expand? What changes did it make to the hospital it acquired?

When St Goran's was owned by the local authority, 'parts of the hospital such as radiology and diagnostic services were open six to seven hours a day,' according to Per Båtelson, the chief executive. Capio extended the hours they were used to between seven and ten. Capio also started using the facilities for non-emergency operations a great deal more – in some instances as much as twenty-four hours a day.[78]

Capio set about using the staff more productively. 'A typical problem was that nine people were waiting for the tenth person to arrive,' says Batelson. It became imperative to manage the personnel so that such waste occurred as little as possible. Much of the management effort went into making sure that the front-line people – doctors, radiologists, nurses and so on – were able to do what they are expert in, instead of doing things such as ordering equipment, filling in forms, managing personnel . . . and waiting.

Capio tried to incentivise staff by giving them more autonomy, creating independent units where possible – in diagnostics, radiology and pathology. These semi-independent units have gone on to obtain a large part of their work from outside St Goran's.

When Capio took over, it found high staff turnover. Normal commercial incentives made Capio want to end this waste. Capio therefore worked hard to keep staff. Pay is now higher and every year the hospital arranges skiing trips, parties at the hospital and summer get-togethers in pubs. Turnover of staff has been considerably reduced.

The great improvements in Stockholm point to the weakest features of the NHS.

Incentives, productivity and waste

Hospitals in the NHS have little incentive to maximise productivity, whereas in Stockholm they are paid per operation. Hospitals have little independence so they have little incentive to excel – they cannot keep any surpluses. Hospitals and services like radiology have little incentive to keep costs down and quality up, since they have no competition. The practitioners and management have no personal financial stake in the units, so they have less incentive to make sure resources are not wasted. Again and again, one comes back to the word 'incentive'.

The NHS is a non-profit-making, highly planned monopoly. This is not just a description. It is the problem.

Money is wasted in a great variety of ways. Bevan thought a state-owned, centrally planned system would be more efficient. There would be no 'gaps'. But the centrally planned system appears to stifle incentive and allow waste.

We can see this in action. In 2002, the Audit Commission found that NHS trusts had spent 'significant sums of money on apparently sophisticated computerised systems' but that in many cases 'the emphasis seems to have been on developing IT systems rather than on identifying and capturing the information needed to plan and run an efficient operating theatre.' In other words, money had been spent but results had not been obtained. People had gone through the motions of modernisation but no one had had the authority and incentive to ensure that money was well spent.

One of the reasons for poor use of operating time available was cancellations. The commission reported that one in ten operations was cancelled. It argued that 'with good management' there should be half as many. Many NHS operating theatres – unlike those of Capio – are only used in business hours. It is like having an airport and only using it from nine to five. The waste is appalling.

> **TRAINING AND WORKING**
>
> 'I acted for six months, whilst still a student, as Dr Heath's assistant at the old Eye Infirmary.'[79]
>
> **William Robinson, medical student in the 1870s**
>
> 'I continued to dispense until I qualified in the Spring of 1889. It was hard work, even then, to combine medical training and earning one's own living.'[80]
>
> **Dr H.W. Pooler, 1948**

A study was reported in the *Journal of the Royal Society of Medicine* looking into how efficiently a consultant's time is used in the NHS.[81] The researchers attended consultations at an urology outpatients clinic. They found that the mean time for each consultation was 8.2 minutes but only 4.8 minutes was actually spent with the patient – 41 per cent of the time was spent on other things. On average nearly a minute was used up trying to find missing results. The diagnostic results of one patient in every four were missing. The most common thing missing – in 71 per cent of cases – was an X-ray or some other scan.[82]

The shortage of doctors itself appears to result from central planning. Before the NHS, doctors generally paid for their own training. They did related medical jobs to pay their way through universities and medical schools. They worked long hours and hard.

Then came the NHS and state-financed university teaching. The obvious expectation was that more students would become doctors. But the opposite has happened. Governments – in cooperation with the royal colleges of various branches of medicine – have decided how many student places should be made available. Governments have, of course, been under pressure to keep taxes down in the very short term. Meanwhile the result of having too few doctors does not become apparent until the long term, when the politicians concerned have moved on.

In the absence of incentives and the profit motive, waste in the NHS is extensive. Until recent times nurses were trained like apprentices. Now, in the words of an a retired nurse, 'they contribute virtually nothing to healthcare during their three years of training'[83] and at the end of the training, they are less well equipped to be good nurses. Some of the nursing students go through eighteen months of academic courses which can include subjects like 'assertivism' and 'communication skills'. Such things doubtless have their value, but any system that cared primarily about results and costs would count the loss of the work of those trainees against the intended gain in 'communication skills' and the like.

A magazine was created for NHS staff. The cost was £900,000 over the year to November 2001.[84] How many people bought it? Twenty-two.

Many quangos have been created to help decide policy, check up on patient safety and so on. According to the Royal College of Surgeons, four of these cost £63 million a year.[85] That is not counting the cost of the time of doctors who must interact with these agencies.[86]

Nigel Crisp, the NHS chief executive, ordered trusts and hospitals to improve the reputation of the NHS through public relations. The cost was reportedly up to £18 million. The press office – or Communications Directorate as it is now called – of the Department of Health has 106 officials listed in the booklet issued to journalists – many more even than six years ago without any noticeable improvement in the service offered to the press. It also does not include further press officers (and support staff) for the Health Development Agency, the Health Service Commissioners, the National Institute for Clinical Excellence and so on and on.

Money gets spent on non-core activities which surely would not be spent so freely by any commercial organisation trying to maximise sales and minimise costs. The fact the NHS does not have 'sales' and does not need to bring its costs below the price of supplying those 'sales' is a root cause of its waste.

Money is wasted because elderly people continue to occupy hospital beds which they no longer need. Hospital beds cost a great deal to service. Elderly people able to live elsewhere, in a nursing or residential home, do not go there, partly because hospital and social services are not proactive in arranging it and partly because there is limited access to such care homes – another part of the welfare state. The NAO reported that there were six thousand beds occupied in this way in 2000.

Waste through paperwork in the NHS has become legendary. A GP registering a mother and baby as new patients once required two forms to be filled in. Now it apparently requires nineteen. The Audit Commission, in looking at why public servants gave up and left their work, found that paperwork and bureaucracy were the biggest of all factors. They have created waste twice over – once though the demand of time and second through early retirements.

A consultant surgeon wrote to a newspaper in 2002:

Sir,

The crisis in general practice relating to recruitment and retention is reported to be due, in part, to excessive bureaucracy, form-filling and red tape (report Aug 21). I can readily sympathise with the GPs. However, their bureaucratic problems probably pale into insignificance compared with the burdensome scrutiny endured by hospital doctors. I list below the various bodies that are assessing/appraising/ validating my performance and activity as a professor of surgery and consultant surgeon. Each requires a significant amount of form filling.

National:
  General Medical Council revalidation procedures
  UK Council for Regulation of Healthcare Professionals
  National Clinical Assessment Authority
  National Care Standards Commission
  Commission for Health Improvement
  National Patient Safety Agency
  Cancer Accreditation Teams

Hospital:
  Clinical Governance Committee
  Continuing Professional Development Committee
  Professional Advisory Panel
  Clinical Auditing Committee
  Annual Consultant Appraisal
  Junior Doctors Hours Action Teams
  Pre-registration House Officer and Senior House Reviews for Post-graduate Dean

*Specialist Registrar Review for Postgraduate Dean and Royal
College of Surgeons*

University:
Internal Quality Assurance Committee
Staff Review and Development Committee
Annual University Appraisal
Quality Assurance Agency
Research Assessment Exercise
Peer Review of Teaching
Research Governance Committee.

Professor Irving Taylor,
Professor of Surgery,
University College London.[87]

Paper-chasing takes up time that could otherwise be used by nurses and doctors to do what they were trained to do. And without the paper-work, fewer staff would be needed. Moreover, as well as causing early retirement,[88] paperwork – and perhaps other frustrations in centrally planned organisations – leads to a high level of absenteeism in the NHS, as in other public services. The Work Foundation found that public-sector workers take off 17.5 days a year compared to only 7.2 days in the private sector.

The scale of waste in the NHS is a reason to doubt that spending more money on it will get a good return. Expenditure on the NHS increased by 21.5 per cent between 1999 and 2002, yet the number of patients treated only rose by 1.6 per cent.

The total money wasted in the NHS is difficult to estimate. In 2001, however, one civil servant – Stuart Emslie – had a stab at it. No official report ever emerged and his figures only appeared in news reports.[89] Nevertheless, it may be interesting to see what a civil servant thought 'unofficially'.[90]

He estimated the waste as follows:
Avoidable management and legal costs: £100m
Hospital-acquired infections and clinical negligence: £1,400m
'Bed-blocking' – beds occupied by elderly people who should have been moved into care: £2,000m
Staff absence and sickness: £2,000m
Fraud: £3,000m
Wasteful prescriptions: £300m–£600m
Total: £8,800m–£9,100m

The total amounted to a fifth of all the money then spent on the NHS and that was without including many of the other kinds of waste described in this chapter such as the low usage of operating theatres and other equipment, the cost of early retirement and the over-employment of staff.

Bevan thought that the clear responsibility of the health minister would mean that, through the democratic vote, the top person would have a strong incentive to make the NHS successful. But a strong incentive for one person at the top appears not to be good enough. In fact a powerful incentive for that one person in some ways damages the effectiveness of the NHS.

The BBC did a survey of senior managers in the NHS in cooperation with the Institute of Healthcare Management. They asked whether there were circumstances when the managers, personally, had felt it was necessary or justified to file a report about their organisation which they knew to be 'inaccurate'. One in twelve said 'yes'.

As one explained, 'I have filed inaccurate reports under pressure from the regional office, i.e. regular phone calls after the first submission of waiting list numbers saying, "Do you realise if you submit these you'll be an outsider?"' Another said, 'All chief executives in the region contrived to make the same 100 per cent return to the Department of Health on absence of waits in the A&E. This was done with the encouragement of the regional director because we all agreed the requirement was meaningless.'

The centre – trying to motivate people through orders and threats – says, 'Here are the targets – you had better meet them or else!' The result is that those in the field say, 'Yes, we have met the targets,' whether they have met them or not. The government then proudly announces that targets have been met. This is not true management of a medical service. This is political propaganda. Politicians, finding it too difficult to make the NHS work well in reality, have turned their attention to something easier: improving perceptions of how it works.

But the biggest response to the BBC survey was to a question that goes to the heart of the way the NHS now works. The managers were asked if they 'felt able to raise their concerns without fear of reprisals'. More than half replied 'no'.

The BBC researchers were surprised at how vociferous the accompanying comments were. One manager said:

I have worked for the NHS as a manager for more than thirty years. I am well respected by colleagues, but since the arrival of a new chief executive, I have been threatened with disciplinary action and suspension because one patient referral went over the target number of weeks. I have no confidence in my situation now.

Another called the NHS 'an organisation ruled by fear, even for senior managers'. A third said, 'I raised valid concerns in the past. I lost my job due to a "breakdown in relationships". The trust used its financial resources and solicitors to force me out.' Yet another said, 'There is a bullying culture from the top. If I managed my trust in the same way that I am treated I would have a major rebellion on my hands.' One personalised his bitterness: 'It is a brutal environment. The current secretary of state is a bully and his staff reflect that behaviour.'[91] One said simply, 'Most CEOs [chief executive officers] I know have an exit strategy.'

> **'You are welcome to use any of the information but I would prefer to remain anonymous. I'm too young to be chucked out!'**
>
> **Consultant in an e-mail to the author, 2003**

A picture is drawn of a culture of fear like that in a totalitarian state. One could argue that fear helps to motivate people to put in extra effort and perform well. But the other comments indicate that sometimes the fear is created in order to fake figures rather than make the service better. Fear and lies demoralise. In doing so, they put up the cost of finding people prepared to go through this. If the process weeds out those with integrity, it is hardly a desirable process.

Even those who are disposed to support the NHS find the management style worrying.

One of the establishment aristocrats of health policy is Julian Le Grand, who has advised the Department of Health and the European Commission among many others.[92] He remarks that senior NHS managers 'have been subject to a continuous stream of target-setting and other directives from the centre, coupled with threats to their job-security if they fail to deliver'.[93]

The NHS tries to motivate through fear. In doing so, it encourages lies. In the process, focus on actually serving the public well is blurred. The Stockholm system and the system in Britain which pre-dated the NHS both motivated people through a sense of their own achievement and their attempts to make successes of their own enterprises.

Can the NHS be made to work better?

Whatever may be wrong with the NHS at any time, there is always a political party which reckons to have the answer. Sometimes the answer is simply 'more money'. Sometimes it is a reorganisation on different lines. It is very tempting for the electorate and the media to think, 'Yes, that sounds like a good idea' and 'Let's give them a chance. It could work.'

Such a response exists only because, in the nature of things, most voters and journalists have not followed the story of the NHS closely over the past fifty-five years. The truth is that a long procession of previous governments have expressed confidence that they had the answer and have been proved wrong. In 1974, for example, Keith Joseph was the secretary of state and thought he had got it. He shared with many people at the time a remarkable faith in management consultants. He brought in the American firm McKinsey and experts from Brunel University.[94]

> 'Nothing gets time to settle down without some new, radical change ... They [politicians] can't resist interfering or trying to interfere.'
>
> **Sir Peter Morris, President of the Royal College of Surgeons, December 2001**

The search was on for 'managerial efficiency'. Joseph replaced seven hundred hospital boards, boards of governors, management committees and so on with a different structure of fourteen regional health authorities, ninety area health authorities and two hundred district management teams, each with a community health council to watch over it. There was also a network of advisers for each tier of management. As Nicholas Timmins in his biography of the post-war welfare state remarked, 'It looked beautiful on paper while proving something of a disaster on the ground ... The one issue which was almost totally neglected was the management of the hospitals in which patients were actually treated. They did not even appear on the McKinsey and Brunel's beautiful organograms.' The reorganisation was 'an absolute shambles' according one of the civil servants on the implementation team.

So, after fifty-five years of reforms and repairs, the engine still does not

> 'New figures showed that NHS funding increased by 21.5 per cent between 1999 and 2002 – but the number of patients treated rose only by 1.6 per cent.'
>
> *Daily Mail*, **9 January 2003**

work. The detail of how and why it does not work suggests that state control has a great deal to do with it. It is surely no coincidence that Britain has the worst performing medical service in the advanced world and also the most state-controlled. The state pays for the NHS, decides where and how patients will be treated and provides the treatment. No other country outside former communist states has a system that completely controls all three of these stages.[95]

Bevan thought that a centrally planned NHS would be efficient. In fact, the NHS has turned out to be remarkably inefficient and riddled with waste. One of the leading medical services in the world has been turned into the worst among advanced countries after fifty-five years. The NHS is causing a minimum of 15,140 avoidable deaths a year compared with what an average medical service would achieve. Patients have deserted it in growing numbers. So have doctors and nurses. It would be better if it had never been created. The structure that pre-dated the NHS was better.

CHAPTER 4
Education: eleven years at school and still illiterate

W. E. Forster was an unlikely revolutionary. Married to the daughter of Dr Thomas Arnold, the archetypal Victorian head of a private school, he was MP for Bradford and vice-president of the Education Department in William Gladstone's gov-ernment. But W. E. Forster – no one seems to use his first name – nonetheless stood up in the House of Commons in 1870 and announced the beginning of a revolution in British education.

Was Forster – like Aneurin Bevan in healthcare – a passionate rebel who wanted to tear down privilege and destroy the bourgeois establishment? Not exactly. He introduced state education with great caution – even concern. He verged on being reluctant about it. He said, 'we must take care not to destroy ... the existing system'. There should be 'the utmost endeavour not to injure existing and efficient schools'.

W. E. FORSTER

W. E. Forster began the state take-over of education.

He said he did not want that the state's involvement to cause parents 'to neglect their children'. He insisted that the money should not come from central government. 'Consider ... the enormous power it would give the central administration,' he warned. He wanted parents to keep on contributing to the cost, asking, 'Why should we relieve the parent from all payments for the education of his child? ... The enormous majority of them are able ... to pay these fees.' Nevertheless, he acknowledged that under 'special circumstances' in places of 'exceeding poverty', local authorities should have power to create free schools. In general, though, he wanted to keep 'the present proportions – namely of one-third raised from the parents, one-third out of the public taxes, and one-third out of local funds [either charity or local rates]'.

The law he brought forward allowed the creation of state schools. Its purpose was not to wipe out the existing private and charitable schools but 'to complete the present voluntary system, to fill up gaps'.

So the politician who began the process which resulted in the gradual destruction of the vast majority of independent schools had no intention of doing any such thing. He did not want to displace independent and charitable schools, only to complement them. He would have been appalled by how his own law and the apparently logical subsequent changes introduced by people such as David Lloyd George and Winston Churchill, created schools that were dominated by central government and were free to all.

The gaps

What were 'the gaps' that Forster said he wanted to fill? How many children were not going to school before the state decided to create its own schools? It is rather like asking 'Where is the bullet?' at a moment between the firing of a gun and when the bullet hits something. The bullet is moving so fast, it is hard to be sure.

Observers in the nineteenth century remarked with awe at the speed at which education for the poor was expanding. A parliamentary select committee reported in 1817:

There is the most unquestionable evidence that the anxiety of the poor for education continues not only unabated but daily increasing; that it extends to every part of the country, and is to be found equally prevalent in those smaller towns and country districts, where no means of gratifying it are provided by the charitable efforts of the richer classes.[1]

In the first comprehensive survey, it was found that about 7 per cent of the entire population, including all adults, were being schooled in 1818. Only ten years later, Henry Brougham did a follow-up survey and was astonished to find that the number of pupils had doubled.

Numbers at school

1818	478,000
1834	1,294,000
1851	2,144,378
1858	2,535,462

Sources: 1820 select committee, 1835 parliamentary survey, 1851 Registrar General, 1861 Newcastle Commission[2]

Of course, the population of Britain was rising too. Allowing for that, the proportion of the entire population which was at school rose from 7 per cent in 1818 to 13 per cent in 1858 – a near doubling in forty years. Education was taking off like a rocket – and this was all happening when there were no state schools.

Proportion of entire population at school

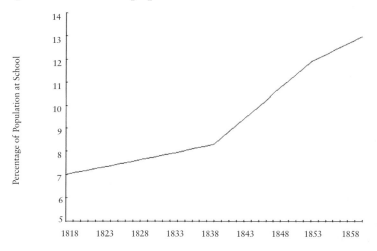

Sources: 1820 select committee, 1838 select committee, 1851 Registrar General, 1861 Newcastle Commission[3]

It is no exaggeration to say that the first half of the century saw an explosion of schooling and that it took place with very little involvement of the state. As Professor E. G. West remarked, 'When the government made its debut in education in 1833 mainly in the role of a subsidiser it was as if it jumped into the saddle of a horse that was already galloping.'[4]

Where, then, had this galloping reached by 1870? The Newcastle Commission in 1861[5] sought to discover how many children were at school and then estimate what percentage of all children must be receiving schooling. The figure the commissioners came to was 95.5 per cent. Even this may have been an underestimate. Elsewhere in the research was evidence that children spent slightly less time at school than the commission had assumed.[6] If the average time spent at school was less but numbers at school were the same, an even higher proportion of children must have been to school than the commission had estimated: virtually 100 per cent.[7]

Numbers at school, though, tell only half the story. Were the children learning? Perhaps the schools were all Dickensian horror stories, imposing sadistic discipline and misery in dreadful conditions.

Here is a report:

> *We noted the grim approaches ... rubbish dumps on waste land nearby; the absence of green playing spaces on or near the school sites; tiny play grounds; gaunt looking buildings; often poor decorative conditions inside; narrow passages; dark rooms ... unroofed outside lavatories ... books kept unseen in cupboards for lack of space to lay them out ... and sometimes all around, the ingrained grime of generations.*

For some people, this will confirm their worst suspicions about education in the nineteenth century. However, I have copied a little trick (formerly played by Professor West). The above is paragraph 133 of the Plowden Report of 1967 about state schools. It is a reminder – including to myself – of two things. First, that we often cling to prejudices like a young child to its mother. Second, that one should never rely too much on a single anecdote. Bearing that in mind, here, nonetheless, is an anecdote about a school that really was placed squarely in the mid-nineteenth century.

The Reverend Richard Dawes was a fellow of Downing College in Cambridge who might have hoped to become the Master. Unfortunately, he was passed over, so instead he became the vicar of King's Somborne, a village of 1,125 people in Hampshire.[8]

There was no school there, so he set about creating one. He persuaded the lady of the manor to donate a site. To create a building, Dawes contributed £500 of his own money – a considerable sum in those days – and obtained a matching grant from the government. But he wanted the school to become self-supporting. He insisted that the parents, many of whom were far poorer than almost any parents today, all had to pay – and promptly at that. He believed that people do not value what they do not pay for. The amount they paid varied according to their circumstances. Labourers were charged a few pence a week while those who earned higher wages were charged six to ten shillings a quarter – which must have been about four times as much. The school opened with thirty-eight children but quickly grew. By the end of the fourth year, it had 158 pupils.

What did the school teach? Dawes followed his own ideas and others he had picked up from reading Jean-Jacques Rousseau and William Cobbett. If parents liked what he produced, he had a school. If not, it would collapse.

They clearly liked his regime, which was like this: the children were taught reading as a beginning. He tried to make this pleasurable and relevant to their lives. They had to write down the names of their brothers and sisters and all the things in their house and the names of

King's Somborne School, a charitable school founded in the nineteenth century. Fees varied according to the incomes of the parents.

the birds, trees and plants they knew. To help them practise writing, they were asked to write about the food used in their homes, about animals, agricultural equipment, the river Test nearby, the neighbouring town, Stockbridge, the sun, the moon and the stars. As soon as they had mastered reading, they were introduced to the finest poetry and prose in the English language.

To teach history he took his pupils to the Roman road from Old Sarum to Winchester. He gave special attention to the way people lived at different periods – what sort of houses they had, what they ate and how they were clothed.

He taught nature through the direct observation of local plants and trees, and through the study of birds and of their migration. Under the supervision of the assistant master, the pupils kept records of barometric pressure and temperature. They kept a journal in which they recorded events such as the arrival of the first swallow, the coming of the cuckoo, the earliest pear and apple blossom and the first ears of wheat or barley.

Dawes wrote about his method:

A teacher may talk to them about a thermometer, and find in the end, they just know as much about it as they did when he began; but if he shows them one, and then grasps it in his hand, telling them to look at the fluid as it rises, or plunges it into hot or cold water, and lets them see the effect, they then begin to open their eyes in a wonderful manner.

In mathematics the older boys learnt algebra and the subject matter of the first three books of Euclid. Again they used actual objects known to them – surveying the land around them and measuring in a carpenter's shop. Dawes proudly wrote: 'Writing in my study, I heard a noise of joyous voices, which I found proceeded from half-a-dozen boys, who after school hours, had come to measure my garden-roller.' They wanted to practise calculating the weight of a cylinder using measurements of the size and knowledge of the specific gravity of the material from which it was made.

King's Somborne, in the 1840s, gave instruction and encouraged inquiry. It was a kind of school which one might wish one's own children could attend. Of course, King's Somborne was one of the best. No one would pretend its standards were run of the mill. But it is an excellent antidote to the impression that many have of nineteenth-century schools from Dickens's melodramatic depictions of the worst ones imaginable in *Nicholas Nickleby* and *Hard Times*.

There were all sorts of schools that sprang up in that explosion of education between 1818 and 1848. There were, of course, very many Anglican schools, funded by the established church and its supporters. There were Quaker schools such as Ackworth, where the Friends Provident society had its origins. There were purely commercial schools – 3,754 of them in 1850 according to the 1851 census.[9]

The Brook Street, New Road, Ragged, Industrial, Sabbath and Free-day Schools founded in Birmingham, 1843.

Something like a quarter of all working-class children at elementary school attended private schools – schools outside the control of any church.[10] Phil Gardner, who has rescued such schools from historical invisibility, passionately describes how working-class parents often chose them because they were flexible and responsive to their wishes. The children spent their time on subjects which the parents wanted rather than being taught what their upper-middle-class 'superiors' thought was good for them. The parents, being poor, sometimes needed their children at different times of day or year. The school would accommodate their needs instead of scolding them. The parents did not feel patronised or resentful. Education was something they showed their commitment to by paying. But education was under their own control. There was a 'close cultural link between home and school which the public [government] system sought to break down'.[11]

Some of these establishments were 'dame schools', which date from at least as far back as 1742. Women would take children into their homes and, for a few pence each, teach them. Standards varied, of course. Some modern historians are dismissive of dame schools, basing their scorn largely on the comments of professional educationalists of the nineteenth century. But nineteenth-century officials condemned such schools for not teaching middle-class morality, failing to teach much beyond the three Rs and for having modest premises. They were sometimes impressed, however, by the effectiveness of the actual teaching. One official remarked in the Newcastle Commission Report of 1861, 'I very much doubt if any public [government-supported] school could teach [reading] so quickly as was done in some small schools of the class which I visited.'[12]

There were also the so-called ragged schools. They began with John Pounds, a Portsmouth cobbler who was concerned about the very poorest boys in his neighbourhood.[13] He tempted them into his workshop, so the story goes, with hot potatoes, and taught them reading while continuing at his work. Many similar efforts took place around the country and they came to be known, collectively, as the ragged schools. Lord Shaftesbury took the spontaneous movement under his wing in 1843 and by 1849 there were eighty-two ragged schools with eight thousand pupils. They were taught by over a thousand teachers, of whom nearly nine out of ten did the work without payment. Twenty years later, the number of such schools had multiplied. There were 204 day schools, 207 evening ones and 226 Sunday schools. They had twenty-six thousand pupils of all ages.

Sunday schools were widespread and the various sects of Christianity had their own. Aneurin Bevan went to one.

There were schools based on a system of teaching used by Andrew Bell and Joseph Lancaster. Bell was a missionary in India, where there was a shortage of teachers. To overcome the problem, he used senior pupils to teach junior ones. When he returned to England he wrote pamphlets describing his work. Meanwhile Lancaster started a private school in Southwark, London. He used a similar method, deploying pupils as teachers, whom he called monitors, to teach and do much of the administration. In this way, teaching could spread from a single adult to many pupils at a low cost.

Another kind of education started at Glasgow University in 1760.[15] Professor John Anderson began to hold evening classes which he encouraged working men to attend. The idea was more fully developed by a successor of his, George Birkbeck. He was lecturing on medicine and needed local artisans to help with the apparatus. He found the men so intelligent and eager to learn that he started lectures in mechanics 'solely for persons engaged in the practical exercise of the mechanical arts'. The experiment proved successful. 'For three successive seasons I had the gratification of lecturing to 500 mechanics. An audience more orderly, attentive, and apparently comprehending I never witnessed,' he reported.[16] The idea spread across the country so that by 1851 there were 610 mechanics' institutes with a membership of 600,000. The London Mechanics' Institute later developed into Birkbeck College and became part of London University.

This is not the end of the extraordinary diversity and growth of edu-

> **THE BIRTH PANGS OF A RAGGED SCHOOL, BY CHARLES DICKENS**
> 'The pupils ... sang, fought, danced, robbed each other – seemed possessed by legions of devils. The place was stormed and carried, over and over again; the lights were blown out, the books strewn in the gutters, and the female scholars carried off triumphantly to their old wickedness. With no strength in it but its own purpose, the school stood it all out, and made its way. Some two years since I found it quiet and orderly, full, lighted with gas, well whitewashed, numerously attended, and thoroughly established.'[14]
>
> Dickens documenting an actual school, not a fictional one.

cation in the nineteenth century. Education at home, or self-education, is another subject in itself. It was important for several people described in this book – Bevan and Thomas Chalmers among those mentioned so far.

There were, of course, some bad schools. Some inspectors wrote scornful accounts of such places. But the litmus test of education is the outcome. Could the great mass of people read and write before the state took over?

Could they read?

The Council on Education wanted an answer to the very same question in 1840. An assessment was made on its behalf of the literacy of miners in the coalfields of Northumberland and County Durham. It was found that a large majority of them, 79 per cent, could read while just over half, 53 per cent, could also write.[17]

A survey was made twenty-five years later of men in the marines and the navy which showed that 80 per cent of the marines and 89 per cent of the seamen could read.[18] These men would have been educated, on average, a decade or more earlier. But of the boys newly recruited out of school 99 per cent could read. Literacy was bounding ahead.

Ability to read was always in advance of ability to write because, at the time, reading was useful and pleasurable whereas writing was not necessary for most occupations, which were still manual. But the ability to write was catching up fast, all the same. In 1840, half the women who got married in England and Wales signed the register with a mark rather than a signature.[19] By 1870 the figure was down to 27 per cent and by 1891 it had fallen to only 7.3 per cent. For men, the figures fell similarly so that by 1891 only 6.4 per cent were signing with a mark. Men on average married at the age of twenty-eight and left school at eleven, so the vast majority of those signing in 1891 would not have been affected by W. E. Forster's Elementary Education Act. This was a nation racing towards literacy.

If the 'galloping horse' of independent education in the nineteenth century had been allowed to continue its charge, we might by now have schooling in Britain of an extremely high standard. The willingness of ordinary working people to purchase education was demonstrated by the extraordinary growth in schooling and literacy in the nineteenth century. Britain is a vastly richer country than it was in 1870 so it is all but certain that the massive increase in wealth would have produced a

> ### COULD PEOPLE READ IN THE NINETEENTH CENTURY?
>
> **Thomas Paine's *The Rights of Man*, published in 1803, sold one and a half million copies. William Cobbett's *Address to the Journeymen and Labourers* sold two hundred thousand copies in only two months. His writings 'were read on nearly every cottage hearth in the manufacturing districts of South Lancashire'.[20] Serialised fiction such as the works of Dickens sold in huge numbers and regular reading of the Bible at home was traditional and widespread.**

major development of the extent and quality of schooling. Yes, there were 'gaps' when Forster proposed the law which was to transform British education. But they were relatively small and closing fast.

Forster's Act was not meant to interfere with the rapid growth of independent education. It was meant to preserve charitable and private education while allowing local-government schooling for any children who might be left out. The almost complete take-over by the state which happened subsequently was not what Forster and Parliament intended. In fact it would have horrified them. True, there were some people who wanted full-scale state education. But others, too, were against even the early stages of the state's involvement.

Edward Baines wrote a book called *Education Best Promoted by Perfect Freedom, Not by State Endowments*, which was published in 1854.[21] He thought the state would take away the 'happy social influence' of the churches and benevolent individuals. Parents would lose influence over their own children. He warned that state enterprises were inefficient and developed large bureaucracies which would waste time and money. He suggested that the state would settle on particular ways of teaching, which would mean a lack of valuable innovation and flexibility. He suggested that teachers' salaries would eventually be reduced. The government would be generous to begin with, he asserted, but such largesse would not last.[22]

Baines was not the only one to be against the state take-over. Thomas Daniels had charge of St Paul's Church of England schools in Manchester. The publicly funded Manchester School Board wanted to take over his schools since they were 'not flourishing'. Daniels angrily replied that their difficulties were due to the actions of the board itself, which had acquired a Jewish school in the same road and lowered its fees to below those of St Paul's.[23] His schools were not alone in suffering from this predatory pricing by publicly funded schools. The Wesley School in the same area was also 'not flourishing' due to the same 'unfair competition'. Members of Christian churches had made 'great sacrifices of time and money to erect schools', he said. They were now also taxed as rate-payers in addition to supporting their religious schools with money. He refused to hand over his schools to the board because it would be 'a breach of trust'. The schools were 'subscribed for as Church of England Schools and the trust deed sets forth the same object'. It was a brave, principled stand. But hundreds of independent schools were wiped out or taken over in this way.

The state increasingly and over several generations took over assets built up over years by charitable and private schools. The local boards of education, funded by rates, gradually destroyed independent schooling by offering a free alternative. Only independent schooling for the rich survived this competition. Even one of the school inspectors regretted 'the disappearance of different and interesting types of school, adapted to the varied social requirements and religious convictions of different classes'.[24]

From 1880, education was made compulsory. This meant all the more pressure to make state schooling cheap and, ultimately, free. The history of British education is truly of one thing leading to another. All state primary schools became free in 1918 during David Lloyd George's premiership, causing the demise or takeover of yet more independent schools. Over time, this was another case of the state expropriating or destroying what had been built up by charity or commercial enterprise.

The full story of the development of state education has been told elsewhere (see box overleaf for a brief summary). Rather than repeat it, let's ask a basic question about it.

What was state education meant to be for?

What were the intentions of those who established the state education we have today? They have changed a deal over the years.

H. A. L. Fisher, whom Lloyd George hauled out of Sheffield University to bring forward the Bill to make all state primary schools free, offered the following reasons for the Bill to the House of Commons in 1917.[25] He wanted to raise 'the general standard of physical health among the children of the poor'. He said that the war had created an 'increased feeling of social solidarity'. It was only fair, he implied, that the poor, who had been asked to 'pour out their blood', should be con-

A BRIEF HISTORY OF STATE EDUCATION –
OR HOW ONE THING LEADS TO ANOTHER.

1833: The first government grants are made to charitable, church schools. The idea is to give a bit of help. Once the principle is established, it is extended. More grants are given.

1839: Inspectors are appointed to examine schools. If government money is going to be spent on them, the schools have to be suitable.

1870: Forster's Elementary Education Act empowers local boards to create elementary schools to 'fill up gaps' in independent provision. But the existing schools, which charge fees, are not able to compete with the growing number of free state schools, so from now until 1918, increasing numbers go out of business, quite contrary to what Forster intended.

1876: Lord Sandon's Elementary Education Act prohibits employers from taking on children who had not been to 'certified' schools. The government wants children to go to good schools and therefore wants to rule out other schools, even if parents prefer them. Another swathe of independent schools is forced to close.

1880: Elementary schooling is made compulsory for all aged five to ten.

1902: Arthur Balfour's Education Act empowers local authorities to create secondary schools. If education is good for small children, it is good for older ones too.

1917: The first government grants are made to Oxford and Cambridge Universities. The government is helping out universities who have been nearly bankrupted by the war, just as it has helped out schools from 1833. The universities are similarly assured that there is no question of reducing their independence.

1918: H. A. L. Fisher's Education Act (while Lloyd George is Prime Minister) abolishes all fees for children in state elementary schools and raises the compulsory leaving age to fourteen.

1944: Under 'Rab' Butler's Education Act the government pays more money to church schools and, in return, achieves control of most of them. Their independence is gradually reduced over the next six decades. School is made compulsory for fifteen-year-olds (and later sixteen-year-olds).

1961: The first university is created by the state (Sussex). The old universities become increasingly dependent on government money.

1963: The Robbins Report recommends that higher education should be available to all who qualify for it.

Today: The state has taken over the vast majority of schooling (although it originally only wanted to 'fill up gaps'). Control that was once intended to be local has effectively become central. The state has taken indirect control of all universities except one (Buckingham) although originally it wanted them to remain independent. It has taken control of most church schools, although it originally wished them to remain independent, too. Property which had been paid for by churches and generous individuals has effectively been expropriated by the state.

sidered full citizens and get 'any form of education from which they are capable of profiteering [*sic*]'. Industrial workers, he said, wanted education as 'an aid to good citizenship'. They also wanted it as a 'source of pure enjoyment' and 'a refuge from the necessary hardships of a life spent in the midst of clanging machinery'. Fisher remarked that 'fierce rivalry' and 'hostile feeling' in Germany against Britain might not die down after the war. So 'the youth of our country' had better be given 'the best preparation which ingenuity can suggest'. Implicitly, education would help equip them to fight Germany again if need be. Another of his reasons was that the vote was being given to more people. 'How can we expect an intelligent response' unless money is paid 'to form and fashion the minds of the young'?

So the growth of state education in 1918 was to make people healthy, to make things fairer, to give pleasure, to help fight the Germans again if necessary, and develop people fit to use the vote. It was assumed that schools would maintain the same standards as before.

H. A. L. Fisher, the academic whom David Lloyd George hauled out of Sheffield University to make all state primary schools free of charge.

David Lloyd George, who appointed H. A. L. Fisher to be in charge of education, was ultimately responsible for making state primary schooling universally free. As a matter of interest, what was his own education like? What sort of standard was it? He himself had not been to a state school of course. He came from a lower-middle-class family in a remote part of Wales and went to an Anglican school, leaving at fourteen. Was he therefore poorly educated?

Not at all. He had written précis of some of Macaulay's essays and *The Theory of Moral Sentiments* by Adam Smith. He had access to all the books which had belonged to his father, a teacher who died when he was very young, such as Gilbert Burnet's *History of the Reformation of the Church of England* and François Guizot's *History of the English Revolution*. He read Thomas Macaulay's *History of England*, Charles Rollin's *Ancient History*, Edward Gibbon's *Decline and Fall of the Roman Empire* and classic fiction including novels by Charles Dickens and Victor Hugo.

He had won a school scripture prize and throughout his career was able to cite relevant passages of the Bible at will. He had learned algebra and Latin. Later in life, when asked when he realised he was a genius, he said half-humorously that it was while he was in the upper branches of an oak tree reading Euclid.[26]

His family believed in self-help in education as in all other things. To pass his law exams, Lloyd George had to master two foreign languages. His school had taught him Latin, but did not offer French. So Lloyd George's uncle – who knew no French himself – set about learning it and then teaching it to David. Overall, Lloyd George left school better educated than many a university graduate today.

Returning to the intentions of those who created state education, 'Rab' Butler was appointed by Winston Churchill, the Prime Minister, as his education minister in the Second World War.[27] Butler, in his White Paper introducing another important education Bill, had similar ambitions to those of Fisher – although preparing children to fight the Germans again had been dropped. Additionally he argued that his extension of state education would make for 'a happier childhood' and 'means for developing the various talents' of young people.[28] He said it would 'enrich the inheritance of the country'.

In more recent times still, the reasons given for extending state education have changed much more substantially. Politicians now emphasise education as a means for creating economic prosperity above all else. Tony Blair said, 'We know education is the key to ... Britain securing its future. In the modern knowledge economy ... the brains of our people are our number one asset.' The second main theme has been that education for the less well off creates greater equality of opportunity.

Since people have such different ideas about education, let us judge state education by the intentions of all those who created it. Has it achieved the various things which they claimed it would?

State education for high standards

The one ambition that they all shared – explicitly or otherwise – was that state education would be of a high standard. Forster even said that 'the schools which do not receive government assistance are, generally speaking, the worst schools'. He expected state-assisted education to improve standards. So how high is the standard of education now provided by the state?

Most people probably think state education is like the curate's egg: good in parts. They will have heard of sink comprehensives but also of the London Oratory School, where Tony Blair's sons have gone. They could be comforted by the publicity given to some international assessments of British education such as the massive PISA study by the OECD, in which Britain came seventh out of thirty-one countries.[29] These included much poorer countries such as Mexico, but even among the advanced countries, Britain was above average. Not brilliant, but above average. Many people believe the emphasis on literacy and numeracy in recent years has put right the thing that was most wrong.

Is this correct?

Tom Burkard and his wife Felicity had a son called Arthur. The boy had every advantage. His parents were loving and well educated. Every day they read to their beloved child. They spent a lot of time with him, so he gained a wide vocabulary – using three- and four-syllable words even before he started school.

The Burkards thought Arthur would 'come up trumps in any school'.

The Burkards sent Arthur to a school in the suburbs of Norwich – a well-regarded school, like many state-aided Roman Catholic schools. During Arthur's first year in reception class, Tom says he and Felicity did not pay much attention to Arthur's progress. 'We didn't want to come across as pushy parents.' He thought that education might not be as rigorous as it had been a few decades before, but he was confident that Arthur, as a bright boy with supportive parents, would 'come up trumps in any school'.

When Arthur was in year 1, the Burkards became concerned when he started coming home from school 'in a bit of a sulk'. It emerged that he had been falling behind other children whose reading had developed through practice with their parents – rather than learning at the school. The teachers had discovered that Arthur had not experienced the same assistance and he was now under strict instructions from the school to read a story – *Butch and his Bone* – to his parents. Tom sat down with Arthur to hear him read and was astonished. 'Right away, I noticed that the words Arthur was saying were not the words on the page, even though they captured the gist of the action.'

He decided to cover up the pictures on the next page and have Arthur simply read the words. There was silence. Tom pointed to simple words like 'the' and 'of'. Still Arthur was silent.

Tom then pointed at a letter and asked what it was. More silence. Arthur did not know any letters apart from the ones in his own name (which his parents had taught him themselves). Tom was appalled. He wrote to the headmistress of the school asking 'if it was usual to expect children to read before they knew the alphabet'.

The headmistress replied that Tom would have to come in 'to see how they did things these days'. They had a discussion that became strained, to put it mildly. Arthur's form teacher was there. She angrily asserted she did not believe in teaching children the alphabet first. She associated such a thing with a strict, unfeeling attitude to children. 'I will NOT have my children sitting in neat little rows!' she exclaimed, shaking with anger. 'I will NOT have them chanting mindless drills!'

Tom had been naïve. He did not know that a generation of teachers had been through a training which made them see things in a very different way.

> **SENDING CHRISTMAS CARDS**
> 'About three million people have such poor literacy they will not even attempt to write a message to their friends and family ... Any cards they send are unlikely to reach their destinations anyway because the addresses are so badly misspelt on the envelopes. More than 50 million cards are thought to be lost in the post as a result.'[30]

There are, of course, things to be said for and against all sorts of methods of teaching. If Arthur could not read any words at the age of five or six, perhaps that did not really matter. The important thing could be that Arthur and other children read at, say, nine. By eleven, anyway. Certainly by the time they leave school, whenever that might be.

So can they?

According to the Department for Education and Skills, one out of every five adults in Britain is 'functionally illiterate' – that is to say, he or she cannot find the section for plumbers in the Yellow Pages or cannot see where a pop group is giving a concert even though it is stated on a simple poster.[31]

This is quite an astonishing admission for the welfare state to make about itself. It can only be regarded as failure on a spectacular scale. Whether it is due to fashionable teaching methods or anything else, the fact remains that children have been compelled to go to school for eleven years of their lives. They have been put in the hands of qualified teachers employed by the state. Yet after eleven long years, the state has failed to teach one in five of them how to read properly. It is nothing but a scandal, pure and simple.

> 'After the report by Sir Claus Moser, it is now established even more firmly than before, that Britain has a high rate of adult illiteracy. Only Poland and Ireland are worse than Britain according to a comparison of 12 countries printed in the report.'
>
> *Daily Telegraph*, 28 March 2002

In recent years, people have put their hopes on the 'literacy hour' upon which David Blunkett, when he was Secretary of State for education, insisted. But, if one stands back, his intervention seems extraordinary. Here was a minister suggesting that the British teaching profession was failing to concentrate on the three Rs sufficiently and had been doing so for years.

If we assume for a moment that Blunkett was right, then many millions of people had passed through schools which were failing to teach the basics. Literate people reading these words may have found school a bore. But imagine what it was like for children who could not read and who were forced to stay on, year after year until sixteen. Books would have been put in front of them – Shakespeare, Dickens, books on history, geography or science. But they could not read them. It must have been a ghastly, infuriating experience – a monstrous farce.

> 'We published a paper in 1990 showing that Zulu children could spell better than UK children, and English is their second language.'
>
> **Nick Seaton, chairman of the Campaign for Real Education.**[32]

It would be terrible if that was the only damage and if everything had now been put right. But has it?

There is an exam which children now take aged eleven, at the end of what, in current educational jargon, is called

Key Stage 2. The exam includes a test of literacy. A mark or 'level' of four is meant to represent a reasonable level of literacy for this age. The proportion gaining level four soared from 48 per cent in 1996 to 75 per cent in 2002. This was taken by many to be a great success even though Blunkett's target was not quite reached. Was it a success? Even according to this official test, a quarter of children in Britain's schools still were not achieving a reasonable level of literacy. But were the official figures reliable?

Durham University conducted an experiment. For five years it conducted the same test of reading and vocabulary for eleven-year-olds in 122 primary schools. It found that between 1997 and 2002, there was no improvement whatever.

The contrast between the government's figures and Durham University's is vast. What could be the explanation? Professor Peter Tymms, in charge of the experiment, suggests that the government's exam was a 'high-stakes test' on which much depended for the schools and their heads. Many primary schools virtually stopped teaching in the normal way for ten

HOW MANY 11-YEAR-OLDS CANNOT SPELL...

Environment: 82%
Necessary: 82%
Extremely: 80%
Pollution: 62%
Pierce: 59%
Structures: 50%
Passenger: 44%
Expensive: 41%
Century: 40%
Preserve: 40%
Gleaming: 38%
Generations: 37%
Foundations: 33%
Difficult: 32%
Importantly: 29%
Complete: 28%
Castles: 25%
Weight: 25%
Climbing: 21%
First: 8%

Source: Qualifications and Curriculum Authority.[33]

weeks before the tests. Instead, day after day, they worked through previous tests and practice papers. The schools were 'teaching to the test'. They managed to create the illusion of literacy rather than the thing itself.

It might be thought that perhaps teaching children to read and write is particularly difficult. Should we expect about a quarter of children not to make the grade?

There is a school in Whitechapel, east London, which serves one of the poorest areas in Britain. Two-thirds of the children qualify for free school meals. The vast majority of its pupils come from immigrant Bangladeshi families where little or no English is spoken at home. If

Kobi Nazrul school teaches children to read fluently at seven.

ever there was a school which would have plausible excuses for poor English literacy, this would be it. Yet something strange happens at the Kobi Nazrul Primary school. The children can read fluently at the age of seven. And not only a good percentage of them. All of them.[34]

How is this remarkable result achieved? The school, turning aside the conventional wisdom of British teaching over the previous two decades, has been teaching literacy with 'phonics' – a fancy name for teaching children their letters and what sounds they make, alone and in combinations. The remarkable thing is that, after at least twenty years of ineffective teaching of reading and writing, most state schools are only reluctantly thinking of moving to this proven technique.

Not that it takes a new technique to teach children the basics. Those surveys of coal-miners, seamen and marines between 1840 and 1865 suggested that between 80 and 90 per cent of adults could read and that the proportion was rising rapidly. It seems possible that the rapid advance of nineteenth-century literacy was not merely slowed but actually put into reverse by state education.

> 'A government survey ... found 47 per cent of the adults in England – or 15 million people – had a lower level of mathematical knowledge that was needed to gain a grade G at GCSE.'[35]
>
> BBC News online, 31 October 2003.

EDUCATIONAL ACHIEVEMENT AMONG BRITISH ADULTS OF WORKING AGE IN 2005

26.6% Degree and qualifications such as teaching or nursing certificates (National Vocational Qualifications (NVQ) level 4 or 5)

19.4% Two or more A-levels, City and Guilds Advanced Craft, trade apprenticeships or other qualifications at NVQ level 3

21.4% Five or more GCSEs at grades A–C, City and Guilds Craft, RSA diplomas and other qualifications at NVQ level 2

19.6% One or more GCSEs but fewer than five at grades A–C, YT certificates, foundational General National Vocational Qualification or other pass at NVQ level 1

13.6% No exam passes at all

Source: Department for Education and Skills[36]

Reading is only one subject, though. How high a level of attainment do children reach generally? What do the exam results suggest?

According to the Department for Education and Skills, 34 per cent of the population has not achieved five GCSEs at grades A to C.[37] Given that anything less than a C may not reflect true understanding or competence in a subject, it is a disturbing statistic. And some 13.6 per cent of the adult population in England have obtained no exam passes at all.

How many people is 13.6 per cent? No fewer than 4.2 million – individuals who have been totally failed by state education. It would have staggered those who created state education, from W. E. Forster to David Lloyd George to 'Rab' Butler.[38]

More recently, nearly one in four children in their final year of compulsory education failed to achieve even one GCSE C grade in 2003/4.[39]

What about the standard of the exams which these children do not pass? Is it, perhaps, very high and demanding?

The issue of whether exams have been dumbed down has been debated for many years. What is the truth of it?

Here is a question from a geography A-level paper:

Give a reasoned account of the distribution of plantation agriculture in India, Ceylon and Bangladesh.

And here is a question from a different geography A-level paper:

Label this sketch [an illustration of a house, apparently in Britain] *to show the characteristics and quality of the housing and environment.*

The question is accompanied by photographs.

Let me ask you, the reader, which question you would find easier to answer right now, without any preparation? My own answer would be this: by chance, I happen to have a smattering of knowledge of plantations in India, Ceylon and Bangladesh. But I don't have enough knowledge to answer the former question with any confidence. But the house in the sketch looks British and I come from Britain. The sketch contains a great deal of information and the photographs (though I have not seen them) presumably contain even more. This looks like a test of observation and intelligence as much as a test of knowledge. I would be happier with the second question.

> '**A quarter of eleven-year-olds fail their basic tests and almost half of sixteen-year-olds don't get five decent GCSEs.**'
>
> **Tony Blair, Labour Party Conference speech, October 2001**

The first question, requiring actual knowledge of plantations, was set in 1975. The second, with the visual aids, was set in 2002.[40]

In an English A-level exam of 1955, students were asked to put four out of eight passages from Shakespeare in their contexts and comment on their significance and on any phrases or allusions that might need explaining. This is one of the passages.

Forgive me this my virtue;
For in the fatness of these pursy times
Virtue itself of vice must pardon beg,
Yea, curb and woo for leave to do him good.
                    (Hamlet)

The speakers in the various short passages were not revealed. Students had to know the plays well enough to identify the speakers and contexts themselves. The Shakespeare paper produced by the same Cambridge board in 1995 was very different. Long extracts were given and the speakers were identified. Students were asked to comment on the extracts without having to mention the contexts. It was possible to answer the questions with only a cursory knowledge of the play.[41]

The proportion of good GCSEs has doubled

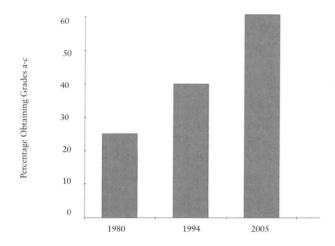

Thirty and forty years ago, students doing exams sat for three hours without aids. Now they can often take in mathematical formulae, calculators and other assistance. They are given information within the questions. If they cannot answer the earlier part of a mathematical question, they are given enough information to carry on with the latter part. They are given points for working in the right direction, even if they are actually wrong.

Above all, the difference lies in coursework, which now accounts for 60 per cent of GCSE scores. The *Times Education Supplement* has reported how schools are able to manipulate the system to achieve better scores.[42] One supply teacher told the *TES* how students at a private school in Lancashire were allowed up to six 'drafts' of English course-work before submitting a final version for marking.

> **'If 725 tons 11 cwts 3qrs 17lbs of potatoes cost £3386 2s. 2d., how much will 25 tons 11 cwts 3qrs 17lbs cost?'**
>
> **Question in Post Office entrance exam for women and girl clerks, 1897**

Several contributors to the *TES* magazine's website have reported the increasing use of what are called 'writing frames'. These are suggested outlines for an essay. They allow some schools to provide virtual model answers. A former head of English at a secondary school in the north of England said it was 'common to provide a structured plan, paragraph by paragraph, for course-work assignments'. There is also copying of course-work from the internet. The *TES* entered the phrase 'GCSE course-work' into an internet search engine. Up came more than ten British sites offering access to course-work essays. The *TES* said that examiners could tell if essays had been obtained from the internet. But I have found no mention on anyone testing this claim. There are no figures available for the number of GCSE entries rejected because the content was detected to have come from the internet. Moreover one must wonder why more than ten websites would continue doing this business if no one used their services.

> **FEWER FAIL THEIR A-LEVELS**
> **1980: 20%**
> **2002: 5.7%**
> Proportion of papers failed

Perhaps the most rigorous independent test of British exams was done by Dr Robert Coe of Durham University.[43] He used the International Test of Developed Abilities (ITDA). This involves no course-work and is simply a test of knowledge and ability.

In 1988, the average score of students taking the ITDA biology test was 63.7. A decade later, the average score had fallen to only 53.4. Was

'90 per cent of me wants to go out and celebrate, but the other 50 per cent asks: were they dumbing down?' Mac cartoon, *Daily Mail*, 15 August 2002.

this reflected in a similar decline in A-level exam grades? No. On the contrary, although the ability of the students was going down according to the ITDA test, the grades they got at A-level improved. At the beginning of the study – using a scale of A grade = 10, B = 8 and so on – the average A-level grade was 4.33. A decade later, it had risen to 5.24. Expertise was declining but the A-level marks were going up.

Was this just happening in biology? No, it was happening in all the subjects for which measurements go back to 1988: English literature, geography, history and, most spectacularly, mathematics and French.[44] In French, the ITDA score fell from 58.2 to 55.2 but the A-level grade average soared from 3.77 to 5.90.

The rise and fall of geography exam results

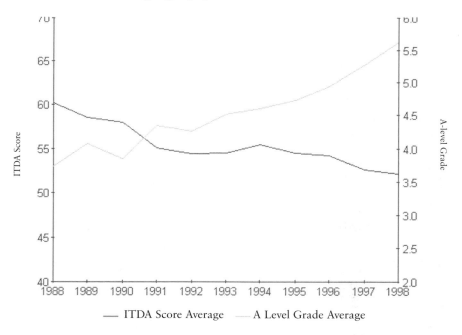

— ITDA Score Average   — A Level Grade Average

Source: Curriculum, Evaluation and Management Centre, Durham University

Dr Coe estimated what a student with a score of 60 on the ITDA test would typically have achieved in their A-levels at the beginning and the end of the period. His conclusion: 'A-level candidates across a range of subjects achieved over a grade higher in 1998 than candidates of the same ability had done in 1988.[45]

But what about those international comparisons, some of which suggest that British education is not really so bad? The PISA 2000 study – a huge exercise organised by the OECD – put British students in seventh place out of thirty-one in literacy, fourth in 'scientific literacy' and eighth in 'mathematics literacy'.

Unfortunately people with highly contrasting views have queued up to pour scorn on the methods of the PISA study, particularly when it comes to inter-country comparisons. One reason is that not all the schools invited to join the study agreed and the proportion varied considerably from country to country, so the study may not be an accurate reflection of average national ability. The PISA study is not without all merit, but the inter-country comparisons may be the least reliable part of it.

Another study, however, has attracted less criticism. It contains fundamental mathematical sums like 6000 - 2369. How did Britain do in this, the Third International Mathematics and Science Study (TIMSS)? England came twenty-fourth out of forty and Scotland twenty-eighth. We came a very long way behind the best-performing countries, Singapore, Korea and Japan.[47]

But of course most advanced countries have a high proportion of state education. So doing well or badly in such league tables does not – in general – tell us whether state education delivers high standards.

> 'At A-level, I did not read all the set texts. I only read six to eight of Blake's poems. I did not read most of the Sylvia Plaths and I made a point of not reading Sean O'Casey's *The Plough and the Stars*. I did not read Mary Shelley's *Frankenstein* either. I just read synopses and descriptions of the themes in the *Oxford Guide to English Literature* and then skipped through the texts picking out a few quotes. The exam papers included a great deal of the texts so I got by pretty well. I got a grade A.'[46]
>
> **Student now at London University**

What about quality in our universities? Can we still be proud of Oxford and Cambridge, two of the oldest and most famous universities in the world? London University now also has claims to be ranked with the other two. There are others, which have, in their time, been home to Nobel Prize-winners. Can we be comforted that in university education, at least, Britain still leads the world?

Early in 2003 Margaret Hodge, the higher education minister, referred to 'Mickey Mouse degrees'. A reader wrote in to the *Daily Telegraph* education editor, John Clare, to ask what she meant.[48] He offered for con-

British maths teaching – not as good as Singaporean

1.	Singapore	643
2.	South Korea	607
3.	Japan	605
4.	Hong Kong	588
5.	Belgium	565
6.	Czech Republic	564
7.	Slovakia	547
8.	Switzerland	545
9=	Netherlands	541
9=	Slovenia	541
11.	Bulgaria	540
12.	Austria	539
13.	France	538
14.	Hungary	537
15.	Russia	535
16.	Australia	530
17=	Canada	527
17=	Republic of Ireland	527
19=	Israel	522
19=	Thailand	522
21.	Sweden	519
22.	Germany	509
23.	New Zealand	508
24.	**England**	506
25.	Norway	503
26.	Denmark	502
27.	USA	500
28.	**Scotland**	498
29.	Latvia	493
30=	Iceland	487
30=	Spain	487
32.	Greece	484
33.	Romania	482
34.	Lithuania	477
35.	Cyprus	474
36.	Portugal	454
37.	Iran	428
38.	Kuwait	392
39.	Colombia	385
40.	South Africa	354

Scores in TIMSS, 1995[49]

sideration an honours degree offered by Barnsley College and validated by Sheffield University. This was a 'modular, multidisciplinary degree' including study of English, geography, history, and politics. The government's own Quality Assurance Agency had inspected the course and commented that any links between the subjects studied were 'fortuitous'. The claim by the college that it was teaching the 'heartlands' of the subjects was untrue. Students were able to predict their exam questions 'with a high degree of confidence' and then regurgitate their course-work. The inspectors had no confidence in standards being achieved. Perhaps this was a 'Mickey Mouse degree', he suggested.

How much educational attainment do you need to get into a British university? This is the view of Professor Alan Smithers of Liverpool University:

The School Curriculum and Assessment Authority conducted a survey in 270 schools.[50] They asked nine-year-olds the following question:

Pam has £1.37. She wants to buy a box of crayons which costs £2.75. How much more money does she need?

This is a calculation which adults should be able to do in their heads. A child of nine should readily be able to do it with pencil and paper. But the survey showed that fewer than one in five could manage it. Another question was even simpler:

What is 56 x 100?

Again, fewer than one in five answered correctly.

> *It is quite possible to get into some universities having totally failed your A-levels. At some of our newer universities, there are students who didn't get good A-levels who nonetheless finish up with a first. The result is that you can no longer tell what a first means. The devaluation of degrees is so serious that foreign governments like that of Singapore now only recognise qualifications from a limited number of our universities.*[51]

It is a humiliating observation. The country which produced Isaac Newton and Dr Johnson while Singapore was a bare, sparsely inhabited little island is now regarded as second rate by the same place.

Can it be true that 'it is quite possible to get into some universities having totally failed your A-levels'? In August 2002 the *Sunday Tele-*

graph tested the proposition. A reporter posed as a student who had not obtained a single A-level. He told universities that he had got seven GCSEs and two AS-levels. He was offered places at Greenwich University, Portsmouth University, the University of Glamorgan and the University of East London. The last of these told him, 'That is lovely. I can make you an offer on the spot,' inviting him to take a degree in sociology.

> 'More will mean worse.'[52]
>
> **Kingsley Amis, on the expansion of higher education.**

But even if many students should not really be at university at all and others do 'Mickey Mouse' subjects, is the teaching good?

One might rather ask, 'How much teaching takes place?' since there has to be a fair amount of teaching in order for its quality to matter. Here is a letter from one parent:

> *My daughter is a first-year student on a BA course in theatre, film and television at York St John College. She's had no feedback on her work since she enrolled last September.*[53]

The letter appeared in February. In other words, her daughter had been on a course for a full term – her first – and had not received any response to what she had done. Responses from lecturers and professors is a key part of what a university is meant to offer, but she was not being taught badly so much as not at all.

Professor Anthony O'Hear used to hold the Chair of Philosophy at Bradford University. He says that in the 1980s, on the course he was teaching, the university was penalised if it took more than thirty students in a year.[55] But

> 'In a poorer university ... you are more likely to experience what is called "student-centred learning" or "open and flexible learning", meaning that you will be left to get on with it with relatively little personal contact from your lecturers ... Lecturers are under increasing pressure to publish research. They have to teach more and more students in larger and larger classes. They have been distracted by research assessment exercises and teaching assessments. And too much of their time and mental energies is spent in committee meetings fighting over university, faculty and departmental policy to deal with financial cuts.'[54]
>
> **G. W. Bernard, *Studying at University***

by 2002 the same department had fewer members on the teaching staff. He had to 'aim for 50 or 60 [students], and for a time we took 80 or 90'. The individual attention to students could not possibly be up to former standards.

Dr George Bernard, a reader in history at Southampton University, says, 'The main reason why first- and second-year students are set little work to do is that there are increasingly large numbers of them and no more of us. We simply could not cope with the marking load if we set our students more essays.'[56]

> 'Every university teacher knows ... the average quality of education that undergraduates receive in all but a handful of universities has declined significantly, and this has been disguised by a ... reduction in degree standards.'[57]
>
> **Gordon Graham, Regius Professor of Moral Philosophy, Aberdeen University**

What about Oxford, Cambridge and London? Do they, at least, still maintain their pre-eminence and their high standards?

Robert Stevens was educated at Oxford and Yale. For most of his long academic career as a law professor, he worked in American universities before returning to Oxford to become Master of Pembroke College. He is in a better position than most to judge Oxford on a world scale. What is his view? 'While Oxford does have a number of distinguished departments, it is already hanging on by its fingertips in claiming to be an international university.'[58] He points out that Oxford has no Nobel Prize-winners, compared with eighteen from among current and emeritus staff at the University of California. Oxford has only ever had one winner of a Nobel Prize in economics, whereas Chicago University has won nine over the last thirty years.

The tutorial system has distinguished Oxford and Cambridge. Students have traditionally gained the advantage of direct contact with a top academic every week. The student is set work and then comes with one or two other students to see the tutor. One of them reads out his or her essay which is then criticised and dis-

Oxford: easier by degrees?

	Firsts	Thirds
1960	8.5%	33%
2005	25%	9.0%

Degrees awarded by Oxford University.[59] There are three possible explanations: students became cleverer; they worked harder; or good degrees became easier to get. In view of the other evidence, the last of these appears the most likely.

THE INTENTION ...

'The administration of the government grants to the universities ... was entrusted ... to a University Grants Committee composed of eminent academic people ... The fear that government finance might involve government dictation has thereby been exorcised.'[60]

H. A. L. Fisher, education minister 1916–22, in his autobiography

... AND THE REALITY

Governments now tell universities how many students they may take in certain subjects, how they should choose which students to admit, whether tuition fees should or should not be charged and how much lecturers may be paid.

cussed. Such close contact with a first-class academic can, at its best, be bracing and stimulating. According to Stevens, that system is now under threat, with subjects such as geography and law being increasingly taught in seminars instead. The college system is supposed to provide a community of people in which the expertise of the dons rubs off on the students during informal contact as well as in tutorials. But the college system is also being undermined. Fewer dons actually live in the colleges. Much of the funding is now in the hands of the universities. 'The long-term fate of the colleges is likely to be that of glorified dormitories,' says Stevens. He warns that, on current form, British universities 'will follow the German and French universities into a state of serious – and perhaps terminal – decline'.

Even the *Financial Times* – a newspaper generally sympathetic to the welfare state – admits that Oxford and Cambridge are falling from the top level. 'It is debatable', Martin Wolf wrote, 'whether the UK has any world-class universities. Judging from my own discipline, economics, I would argue strongly that it does not.'[61] He suggests that if the trend continues, 'the UK will become an intellectual backwater, perhaps forever'.

The British also-rans – Nobel Prize-winners 1980–2005 from selected universities

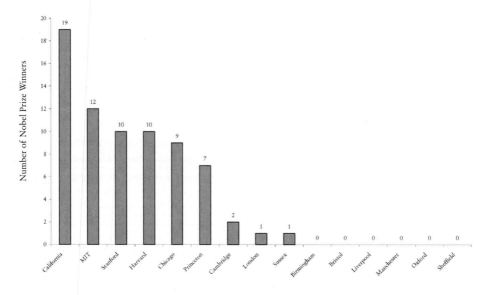

The prize-winners from all the British universities put together are a fraction of those from just one American university, the University of California. Birmingham, Manchester and Sheffield all won Nobel prizes in previous decades – mostly before the Second World War.
Source: Nobel website

Looking at both our schools and our universities, it seems clear that state education has been bad for standards. But what about another very important aim of those who created state education?

State education for fairness and equality

H. A. L. Fisher implied in 1918 that it was only fair that the poor, who had been asked to 'pour out their blood', should get 'any form of education from which they are capable of profiteering [*sic*]'. After the Second World War, this sort of ambition was raised even higher. Some wanted 'equality of opportunity' through education. Professor A. H. Halsey went further: 'Some people, and I am one, want to use education as an instrument in pursuit of an egalitarian society.'[62]

Serious consideration was given, after the Second World War, to abolishing fee-paying schools altogether. In the end this was not done. But some politicians tried other means to create as much equality as possible. As Tony Crosland, the education secretary from 1965 to 1967, said, 'If it's the last thing I do, I'm going to destroy every fucking grammar school in England and Wales and Northern Ireland.'[63]

Has the aim of fairness and equality been achieved?

Peter Lampl went to a grammar school and from there to Oxford University. He spent twenty years in America and made a fortune. Then, in 1996, he returned to Britain and was surprised by what he found. 'My state-educated friends were sending their kids to private schools. What was going on?' He soon discovered that state schools were no longer getting as good results as they had when he was a child. 'In terms of opportunities for bright kids from non-privileged backgrounds, Britain had actually gone backwards since I left.' The statistics on this were, to use Lampl's word, 'outrageous'.

The children of people in professional or 'intermediate' careers are five times more likely to get their A-levels than children whose parents are partly skilled or unskilled. More than three-quarters of the children of professionals go on to higher education but only 14 per cent of the offspring of the unskilled do.

The poor also go to lower-quality universities. Since they have inferior A-levels, they are the ones who have to resort to the 'Mickey Mouse' courses with little actual teaching and low standards. More than half the undergraduates at Oxford and Cambridge attended independent schools even though only 7 per cent of children go to such schools. This is not because of bias in favour of them. On the contrary, dons are keen to bring in children from state schools and are under increasing political pressure to do so. Their problem is that the state schools are just not effective at enabling children to get even the debased A-levels.

'But there are some very good

Who gets two A-levels or equivalent?

Socio-economic groups

Professional and intermediate	51%
Skilled	41%
Partly skilled and unskilled	8%

Source: Hilary Metcalf, *Class and Higher Education: The Participation of Young People from Lower Socio-economic Groups*[64]

Who gets higher education?

Professional class	76%
Intermediate	48%
Skilled non-manual workers	33%
Skilled manual workers	19%
Partly skilled	19%
Unskilled	14%

Percentage of each class obtaining higher education

Source: Age Participation Index[65]

state schools,' people say. Perhaps. But who goes to them?

One of the best primary schools in London is Our Lady Of Victories in South Kensington. A governor on the admissions committee says that again and again the applicants are wealthy bankers or lawyers. The London Oratory is another of the better state schools. Nine out of ten children who sit their GCSEs there get five or more A–C grades.[67] Who has gone there? The children of the Prime Minister. They crossed London in order to reach one of the better state schools.

> 'In Hackney schools, only 9 per cent of black boys get five decent GCSEs ... I really wasn't prepared to put my son through that system.'[66]
>
> **Labour MP Diane Abbott explaining why she was sending her son to a private school**

Not far from The London Oratory is another state school, called Phoenix High. Only 21 per cent of its students get five or more A–C grades. Who goes there? Children of poorer people. Four times as many of them have 'special educational needs'. The school gets a large number of asylum-seekers – 18 per cent of their total pupils. How many asylum-seekers go to the school attended by the Prime Minister's sons? None.

A house within the catchment area of a good primary school can cost as much as a third more than a similar home in the next street. This gives a significant advantage to those who are richer.[68] Professor Paul Cheshire of the London School of Economics, who studied this phenomenon, remarked, 'Our results confirm that getting your children into a better school is conditioned on income.'

> 'I know that all secondary schools are not identical. As a teacher, I go into some schools and think, "I would like to work here," but there are some I wouldn't touch with a bargepole.'[69]
>
> **Estelle Morris, education secretary, June 2002**

The bourgeois get the best of state education – the better schools and then the better universities. The poor get the leavings – what Alastair Campbell, the Prime Minister's former spokesman, called 'bog-standard comprehensives'.

The poor do well to get A-levels at all and are extremely fortunate to get to any university, let alone a good one. Among the lowest socio-economic group only 12 per cent get some sort of further education. A mere 1.7 per cent go on to receive a university degree – less than one-twentieth of the proportion among the top socio-economic group.

The idea of equality in education has not even begun to be met. The balance of the evidence suggests that the very opposite may have taken place and that state education has increased inequality.

A bright girl born into a low-income family in 1958 had a four in ten chance of getting a degree. But the chances of a similar girl born twelve years later were less than three in ten. Conversely, a low-ability girl from a wealthy background increased her chances from 5 per cent to 15 per cent, according to the Institute of Education and the Centre for Economic Performance.[71]

David Lloyd George was brought up by his uncle, a cobbler. He went to school in Llanystumdwy in a remote part of north-west Wales before education was made free. Yet he rose to be Prime Minister. Would a cobbler's son rise to be Prime Minister now? Aneurin Bevan was a poor miner's son yet he had a better education

---

University degrees for the rich

Socio-economic group

Professional class	19.9%
Intermediate	13.5%
Skilled non-manual	7.8%
Skilled manual	3.2%
Partly skilled	1.3%
Unskilled	1.7%

Percentage of each socio-economic group going on a degree course. Excludes higher education diplomas and other lower-level qualifications

Source: *Family and Working Lives* survey[70]

---

before the state fully took over than poor people do today. A child sent to a state 'bog-standard comprehensive' receives an unspoken sentence of low achievement.

Instead of reducing the impact of a privileged background, state education appears to have increased it.[72]

Education versus immorality, drunkenness and crime

Many in the elite in the nineteenth century thought that education would counter the immorality, drunkenness and crime which they thought – without much objective data – was commonplace among the working classes. Sir Charles Dilke argued for free compulsory education because 'the state suffers by crime and outrage, the results of ignorance.'[73] They believed education would inculcate morality, being strongly religious in character at that time.[74]

In fact, crime has increased very dramatically since the state took over our education. Sex outside marriage, which Victorians regarded as immoral, has become routine. Binge drinking and even drug-taking are

> The chief preventive of crime is 'the general and enlightened education of the people.'[75]
>
> **Frederick Hill, prison inspector, early nineteenth century**

now *de rigueur* among older children, while they are still undergoing the state education which the Victorians thought would reform them. The streets of London near the university are splashed with vomit after Saturday nights.

Is it possible that, instead of reducing crime, state education has actually contributed to making it worse? This may seem far fetched. But let us consider how it might be possible.

We have seen that a large minority of children do not manage to achieve a single GCSE pass. According to Ofsted 'a large number of pupils become disaffected with school during Key Stage 4 [ages fourteen to sixteen].'[77] Such children effectively disengage from their education, yet they are still obliged to attend school. They are likely to be in schools with a considerable number of other, similarly alienated children. They may often become bored and irritated. Could continued, compulsory attendance at school for such youths create a group of people prone to turning towards delinquency?

> 'Every child denied a place in a good school is more at risk of falling into crime.'[76]
>
> **Tony Blair, sharing with the Victorians the belief that schooling counters crime**

In 1959, the Crowther Committee, though arguing that the last year of compulsory schooling should be raised to sixteen before too long, noticed a curious fact. In 1946, when the last year of compulsory schooling was fourteen, children aged thirteen – in their last full year of compulsory education – had the worst record for criminal behaviour. Then the school-leaving age was raised to fifteen in 1947. There was 'an immediate change over'. The thirteen-year-olds were straightaway outdone by the fourteen-year-olds.

In other words, the oldest year group which was kept compulsorily at school was consistently the most delinquent. The final age of compulsory schooling has long since been increased further to sixteen and most children continue schooling or training until they are

> 'The data suggests that violent students are more likely to be those who have given up on school, do not care about grades, find the courses irrelevant, and feel nothing they do makes any difference.'[78]
>
> **US National Institute of Education**

> **PROPORTION OF CRIMES COMMITTED BY TEN- TO SIXTEEN-YEAR-OLDS DURING SCHOOL HOURS**
>
> Street robberies 40%
> Car thefts 33%
> Burglaries 25%
> Criminal damage 20%
>
> Estelle Morris, education secretary, speech, April 2002[80]

seventeen or eighteen. The age at which crime is most common among teenagers has risen through this period and is now eighteen.

Two out of five street crimes are now carried out by ten- to sixteen-year-olds in school hours. So are a quarter of burglaries, a fifth of criminal damage and third of car thefts.[79]

The police and education welfare officers once did a sweep for truants in east London, taking the children back to their schools. This resulted in a 39 per cent drop in burglaries. It also seems that those who get into the crime habit at this age often keep it going. Thirty per cent of prisoners admit that they were regular truants from school.[81]

Compulsory schooling, contrary to what nineteenth-century reformers expected, has not reduced crime. The indications are, if anything, the other way around: that compulsory schooling has contributed to the rise in crime.

> '68% of the robberies and 50% of the assaults on ... youths aged 12 to 15 ... occur at school.'[82]
>
> US National Crime Survey

Education for health and fighting wars

Has state schooling made children healthier? Are they made into better fighters? We may not now care too much about the latter, but health, at least, is still considered desirable.

School meals for poorer children may have helped some avoid malnutrition but the money allocated to school meals is now so very small that the nutritional value may be modest. Meanwhile, nearly one in five secondary school children does not take part in any sport at all, which may have contributed to obesity among children becoming an epidemic.

An anti-competitive spirit has spread around state schools. A study of more than three thousand children showed that 38 per cent of secondary school children do not take part regularly in football, rugby, hockey, netball or other 'invasion' games.[83] The armed forces complain that recruits have a lower level of fitness.

Education for enjoyment

'Rab' Butler hoped that more schooling would bring children 'pure enjoyment' and a 'happier childhood'. For those who remain functionally illiterate at school and unable to pass a single exam, it seems unlikely that school can be a satisfying experience. By making school compulsory up to the age of sixteen, the state has ensured that those who do not enjoy it are made to stay anyway.

Does state education 'fill up gaps'?

Has state education at least achieved the first aim for which it was originally started? W. E. Forster was concerned – although he was wrong about the figures – that some children were missing out on education or, in other cases, on an education worth having. Has state education at least succeeded in 'filling the gaps'? In a sense it has. Virtually every child now goes to one school or another. We have 'education for all' in form. But what about the substance?

At state primary schools, 5.9 per cent of children are missing each day. At the secondary schools, 8.7 per cent of children are not in class. Some have reasons such as illness. But the number of absences is more than twice the level experienced in independent schools. Even these figures understate the problem. They are averages for all ages. But of course younger children are not in a good position to truant at all. The truanting takes place mostly among the older children and there the level is much higher. Secondly, also among these older children, more unofficial truancy takes place than official truancy. The children register their presence in the morning but then absent themselves from

---

Hengrove Comprehensive in Bristol had a student absentee rate of 23 per cent in 2002 – nearly one child in four. A new head introduced new systems for monitoring absences, and he made more contact with the parents, with follow-up visits to them, letters stressing the need for attendance and, in some cases, prosecution of parents. Through this mixture of persuasion and the threat of court action, he got the absentee rate down to sixteen per cent by early 2003.[84]

classes or leave the school premises altogether. But even the official, average figure of about one in eleven children not actually attending school suggests that many parents, as well as their children, have simply given up on schooling.

This giving up on school represents a kind of gap. Various governments have been disturbed by the high level of disaffection. They have blamed irresponsible parents. There must, indeed, be some irresponsible parents. But there is another possible cause that governments are less keen to mention.

Tracy Hornsby said that her daughter, Toni, had truanted from school because she had been kicked, punched and beaten.

Tracy Hornsby was taken to court by the government for her daughter's truancy and could have opted to remain anonymous. But she waived her right and spoke out. She wanted people to know the reason she was not making her fifteen-year-old daughter, Toni, attend St Chad's School in Tilbury, to the east of London. Toni had missed more than two-thirds of her lessons. Tracy described the school as 'a war zone'. Her daughter had been kicked, punched and beaten at the school since she was eleven. 'There has been bullying, continual disruption in the classroom, violence towards my daughter and the selling of drugs in that school,' she said.

In some cases the decision of a parent not to force a child to go to school is perfectly rational – indeed, wise and in the best interests of the child. A significant proportion of truancy is actually caused by state education. Disorder, low achievement and sometimes bullying turn people away, creating a large gap. It is also a kind of gap that 14 per cent of

---

How many truant?

Between once a week and every day	9.9%
One to three times a month	12.3%
Less often	13.6%

Year 11 students, all types of truancy including post-registration. Even these figures are known to be underestimates, being based on a survey of children in schools. The most persistent truants, of course, were not present to answer the survey.

Source: D. J. O'Keeffe (ed.), *Truancy in English Secondary Schools*, prepared for the Department for Education.[85]

British adults have not passed a single GCSE or its equivalent at all.

The gaps in education are perhaps more serious now than they were when Forster was worried about them. In numbers, the children seriously missing out on education might be about the same. But in Forster's time, most of them were learning a trade. Now, enforced theoretical attendance appears to encourage an apprenticeship in crime instead.

Education for economic growth

The most important reason given currently for state education is to promote economic growth.

'Can I remember a time when Karl was not bullied? Only since we buried him.'

Headline above interview with the parents of Karl Peart, 16, who committed suicide after years of being bullied at state school in Gateshead, Tyne and Wear

In 2002, Tony Blair said: 'We know education is the key to individuals making the most of themselves. It is also the key to Britain securing its future. In the modern knowledge economy, we will never compete on the basis of labour costs alone. The brains of our people are our number one asset.'[86] Margaret Hodge, when Blair's minister for higher education, went so far as to say that the target of 50 per cent of young people going on to higher education was 'totally set in the needs of the economy'.[87] It may seem strange that a Labour government wants more education in order, so it thinks, to accelerate capitalist growth – but that is the way it is. The previous Conservative administration had a similar view. It may seem obvious that a more educated workforce will be more economically productive. But is it true?

Chris Mole got a grade E in his A-level physics, a D in technology, and completely failed the chemistry exam.[88] His parents and teachers were keen for him to resit the exams. 'At school the advice was to go to university at all costs and that basically we wouldn't get anywhere if we didn't.'

But Chris decided not to take the advice everyone was giving him. When stuck on a question in the physics exam, 'I started to wonder whether I would ever get to university. I realised all my classmates would be going and for some reason, I started wondering where they would get their computers from.' He came up with the idea of a business selling computers to students. He sought out a company which would make the computers at a competitive rate and struck a deal with the National Union of Students to sell computers to their members. After five months trading, his company, studentdesktops.com, had sold £300,000 worth of equipment and sales were projected to reach £4 million after a year. Viewed purely from a financial or economic point of view, not going to university did Chris Mole no harm. It might even had done him good because he focused on active business rather than studying.

It is only an anecdote. But there are quite a few of the same ilk – some of them on a much bigger scale.

Alan Sugar never dreamed of going to university. But although computers are surely a 'knowledge business', he, too, made his fortune in this sector. He sold millions of computers and other electronic gadgets. The company he started was called Amstrad.

Another entrepreneur who achieved great riches despite not going to university was Richard Branson. In fact a list of the most successful entrepreneurs is cluttered with people who did not go to university. It is easier to think of the ones who did not go to university than of the ones who did. One might almost think that going to university damaged one's chances of entrepreneurial success.

Another young man went to university but dropped out without finishing the course. He started a business and went on to become the richest man in the world. His name was Bill Gates. The business he started was Microsoft.

Warwick University conducted a study of how much university-leavers earn compared to those who did not

SOME SUCCESSFUL PEOPLE WHO DID NOT GO TO UNIVERSITY

Bill Gates

Alan Sugar

Richard Branson

Paul McCartney

David Lloyd George

Leonardo da Vinci

Aneurin Bevan

Jim Callaghan

John Major

The Duke of Wellington

Sir Winston Churchill

Isambard Kingdom Brunel

Henry Royce

Ferdinand Porsche

Jane Austen

Charles Dickens

William Shakespeare

Florence Nightingale

George Orwell

William Caxton

go to university. The researchers found that, over their lifetimes, university graduates make £220,000 more. That sounds like pretty convincing evidence the other way. It is the sort of evidence which has also persuaded governments that university education benefits the economy as a whole. If graduates earn more, they must be of greater value to the economy.

> **'What do you say to an English Literature graduate?'**
> **'Big Mac and fries, please.'**
>
> **Joke doing the rounds at University College, London, Spring 2004**

But the devil is in the detail. The extra money earned by graduates depends a great deal on the subjects studied. Those who read law or medicine earn 25 per cent more than non-graduates. But law and medicine are vocational subjects. They are professions where entry to the highest levels is all but barred to those who do not take degrees. The extra money is not exclusively created by the educational value of the course, but also by the way entry to these professions is limited. This could be a major cause of the higher pay.

What of the graduates who did arts subjects such as history, politics, philosophy and English literature – subjects where education was pursued for itself without a vocational element or the advantage of leading to a profession with limited entry? In those cases, the graduates earned less than those who had not been to university – between 2 and 10 per cent less. So the

> **'Twenty years of schoolin' and they put you on the day shift.'**
>
> **Bob Dylan, 'Subterranean Homesick Blues'**

economic benefit of higher education in arts subjects appears to be nil. In fact, it is a luxury in the sense that it costs money rather than yielding it. It is a luxury paid for out of general taxation, including taxation of the poor.

Nevertheless, it appears that grouped together, those who have more education gain higher incomes. So does this reflect a benefit to the economy?

There are three problems with this proposition. First, the government has to spend more money on education than the individual. So although education may be highly profitable for an individual, the investment return to the nation as a whole is far lower. Second, those with the greatest ability and those from the most ambitious families tend to get highly educated. Some of the high pay they get when they work is due to the fact that they were bright or strongly encouraged and helped.

These two factors bring the national rate of return on education crashing down. 'The long run social rate of return [to higher education] ... has run at about 7 to 9 per cent,' reported the Dearing Committee of Inquiry into Higher Education in 1997. 'This is above the six per cent rate regarded by the Treasury as a minimum acceptable return on public investment.' Yes, the return was above the rate required by the Treasury but only by a whisker. It was hardly the 'economic imperative' suggested by Hodge. It is more like a 'just about worth it provided all the statistics and the analysis are right'.

But nearly all analysis of the economic return of education misses out a third problem – one that has been mentioned previously. Some professions are well paid for reasons which do not reflect real economic benefit. The high salaries may reflect the existence of a cartel in a profession.

In America, some of the best-paid people are lawyers. They are well paid because it is a long and difficult process to become one, and American society is extremely litigious. The earnings of lawyers significantly boost the apparent 'social return' on higher education. But it is an illusion. Their earnings do not reflect high productivity. Japan gets by with a sixth as many lawyers per head as America and is almost as rich.[89]

If one adjusts for the fact that the extra earnings of many graduates do not truly reflect higher productivity, the 'social rate of return' surely falls below the 6 per cent which the Treasury has considered a minimum. In other words, higher education is a bad investment of public money, looked at from an economic point of view. Governments have simply been wrong.

That is specifically considering university education. What about publicly funded education overall? If publicly paid-for education contributes significantly to economic success, we would expect to be able see the impact.

Here are ten countries which spend contrasting amounts of their gross domestic product on government schooling. Alongside is an indication of the level of the economic prosperity of those countries in 2001, which allows some time for the impact of government schooling, if any, to emerge.

Percentage of GDP spent on government schooling

	1960	1980	1993	GNI (US $) per capita
Japan	4.1	5.8	4.7	35,610
Spain	1.3	2.6	4.7	14,300
Germany	2.9	4.7	4.8	23,560
Italy	3.6	4.4	5.2	19,390
United Kingdom	4.6	5.6	5.4	25,120
USA	4.0	N/A	5.5	34,280
Switzerland	3.1	5.0	5.6	38,330
France	2.4	5.0	5.8	22,730
Australia	1.4	5.5	6.0	19,900
Sweden	5.1	9.0	8.4	25,400

Education spending from *Does Education Matter* (op. cit.) and per capita incomes for 2001 from World Bank, using the Atlas method.

There appears to be no correlation between the public money spent on education and economic performance. Japan and Spain were both low spenders in 1993. One was the fifth richest country in the world eight years later. The other was less than half as prosperous. Switzerland, the most successful major economy in the world according to this measure, has been middle of the road in its spending. Sweden has been the biggest spender of the ten but has produced an economy which ranked only twelfth in the wealth league table. Australia was one of the biggest spenders in 1980, yet it ranked a lowly twenty-ninth in the table. As for higher education, Switzerland has a lower than average proportion of university students.

What does history suggest? Prior to 1918, a mere 1.8 per cent of British GDP was spent on public education, yet the growth rate was phenomenal by modern standards. It seems possible that economies do better with little or no public spending on education.

> **'Among the most successful economies, there is in fact no clear link between growth and spending on education, let alone between growth and central government involvement in education planning.'**
>
> **Professor Alison Wolf, Institute of Education, University of London**

The idea may seem extreme but it gains support from World Bank analyses of developing countries. Egypt had a big push to increase public education between 1970 and the 1990s. The proportion of children going to secondary school soared to 75 per cent. The proportion going to university nearly doubled.[90] With what effect? In 1980, it was the forty-seventh poorest country in the world. Fifteen years later it was the forty-eighth poorest. In Africa and South America, a great deal of public money has also gone into public education with similar lack of success. Hong Kong, in contrast, has rather lagged behind in its public spending on education but it is now richer per capita than Britain – in thirteenth position. Many people long to believe that state education is the key to economic growth. But the unglamorous truth is that the evidence is the other way round.

The last throw of those who long to believe in it is to claim that the future will be different. We are in a new technological age where creativity and education will be at a premium. But in truth, only a minority of the population is involved in anything which could possibly be regarded as requiring higher education. The single fastest-growing occupation in the 1980s was postman. In the 1990s it was probably care assistant. The greatest shrinkage of jobs has been among skilled and semi-skilled manual jobs. Services – such as serving in restaurants and working in call centres – have been major areas of growth.

> **'People who look at this issue in detail have almost unanimously concluded that ... we definitely over-educate.'**
>
> **Professor Alison Wolf, Institute of Education, University of London**

It is true that the number classified as managerial/professional/technical has risen to 36.6 per cent of the workforce. But this category includes very large numbers of owner-managers of small shops, hotels and other small businesses. It is hard to argue that a higher education degree is really necessary for being good at this sort of work.

If one thinks about it with simple common sense, the idea that public education – especially higher education – is a poor investment is not strange at all. Why should anyone expect that sending a person to a second-rate university to think about the media or philosophy would increase economic growth? It is surely more likely to put into someone's head thoughts of a non-economic sort which could actually divert him or her from making an economic contribution of any substance. Even if some of them are eventually well paid, how useful are they? As the *Daily Mail* columnist Lynda Lee-Potter put it, 'I have often been in urgent need of a plumber. I have never desperately thumbed through the Yellow Pages trying to find a sociologist.'[91]

So the argument that ever more higher education is vital to our economic future is not proven at all. The public spending could even be damaging our economic growth.

Looking back at this and the other targets of those who created state education, it seems that every one of them has been missed. State education has not made children happier or healthier. It has not been of a high standard. It has not made adults more equal. It has not even given equal opportunity. It has failed in everything it set out to do.

Most people understand much of this, even if they resist admitting it openly. Opinion polls have shown that most people who send their children to state schools would send them to private schools if they could afford it. Even among those who support the Labour Party, 51 per cent would send their children to private schools.

But *why* has state education done so badly? Why has it left us with 20 per cent functional illiteracy? What is the root cause of the failure?

Why has state education disappointed?

One way to get ideas about what is wrong with British state education specifically is to look at those countries which do better. All economically advanced countries have state education, which limits the field. Yet still there may be signposts.

The country which came top by a long way in the most authoritative survey, the TIMSS, was Singapore. How does education operate there?

There are quite a few contrasts with Britain:

• A much higher proportion of schools have a significant amount of autonomy. Among secondary schools, 36 per cent of children are at schools which are 'aided', 'autonomous' or 'independent'.[92]

• All schools charge the parents. The charges are small – the most prestigious secondary school, the Raffles Institution, demands only S$200 a month (about £100). But a charge is made, which might have some effect. In the top schools, scholarships are available. So no bright child need go without an education which will stretch him or her.

• Singapore has not followed Britain in adopting GCSEs. Instead it has stayed with O-levels, set by the Cambridge Overseas Examination Board.

• Testing is frequent. Getting into the best secondary schools depends on test results.

• Competition and elitism are fostered. The system is meritocratic. Not everyone gets a prize. Those who obtain good marks and get into the best schools are likely to gain entry to university and then get the top jobs.

• Homework starts at the age of six and lasts half an hour to begin with, rising to an hour at age nine. Private tutoring and cramming are normal.

• Teachers are well paid and widely respected.

The next two countries were Japan and Korea. Again, there is a much higher proportion of private schooling than in Britain. More than half the children in Japanese junior high schools (mostly state schools) go on, in the evenings, to private schools called *juku*.[93] Such extra tuition is commonplace and private-sector companies compete to get the business. One of the techniques used is the Kumon method of teaching maths, which has become successful not only in Japan but around the world. Many an ambitious mother in Britain has her child practising Kumon exercises.[94] The sums – done for a short time every day – are within the ability of the child but gradually they build up in difficulty. There are rewards for progress.

The senior high schools, for fifteen- to eighteen-year-olds, are considered the crucial stage in a child's progress. More than a quarter of them are private. As in Singapore, Japan's system is meritocratic and competitive.

A larger proportion of education is private in these two countries than elsewhere in the world. The same goes for South Korea, too, despite active opposition by the government for nearly two decades after 1980.[95] Despite this opposition, Korean parents spent US$25 billion on private education in 1996 – 50 per cent more than the government's education budget. A survey showed that 70 per cent of elementary schoolchildren took private lessons and half of middle- and high-school students. A Korean family typically spends 15 to 30 per cent of its budget on private education.

These facts about the best performers in the world may provide clues about what actually works. Let's look at some of the reasons which have been put forward to explain the poor performance of British state education.

Is it the money?

Those keen to defend state education point first to one thing: money. They say it would be better if it were not 'underfunded'.

Is it underfunded?

The average cost of secondary schooling was £4,855 per student in 2001/2.[96] Independent day schools cost an average £6,364 in 2001/2 according to one estimate[97] and £6,006 in 2002 according to the Independent Schools Council. So yes, state education costs less per pupil than private schooling. But the difference is not a chasm. The state spends 24 per cent less or 19 per cent less, depending on which estimate one takes of average private school fees. There are some private schools, such as Hillgrove School in Bangor and Tower College in Prescot, Merseyside, which provide education at a similar and even a lower cost than the state.[98]

One should also bear in mind that the price of private schooling may be higher partly because a higher proportion of children go private in central London, where costs are higher. Moreover some of the money goes on activities outside education per se, such as prize-givings and sports days.

State schools certainly feel themselves to be seriously short of money. Could there be a problem in the way the money is used? Some of the money is taken out of the pot by central government, which has its five thousand departmental civil servants to pay for plus over 150 quangos and myriad 'initiatives'. Nick Seaton closely examined the initiatives listed for 2001/2 and found the cost came to £4.1 billion – about 8 per cent of the total money spent on state education. It therefore appears – and I must emphasise 'appears', given the labyrinthine nature of government funding of education – that, at the very most, 92 per cent of the money allocated to education in the Budget is passed on to the local authorities.

Of this money, only two-thirds actually goes on to the schools, according to one study, rising to 75 per cent if one adds in money given to schools as 'grants' by central government which are not permanent sources of funding. As only 92 per cent of the state money goes to the

> '**Ofsted might like to vacate its expensive West End offices, and the Qualifications and Curriculum Authority might decide that a Piccadilly address really is not the best way to spend our money.**'[99]
>
> **Phil Taylor, suggesting a 'revolution' in education**

local authorities and only three-quarters of that proceeds to the schools, an absolute maximum of 69 per cent of tax-payers' money actually reaches schools and the real figure could be closer to only 60 per cent. That is a big handicap for state schools to live with.

Some people may wonder, 'Can there really be so much spending outside the schools?' Here is a story from the *Times Educational Supplement* which may help to explain:

> *The nightmare began when the dreaded OFSTED team arrived at Downs infants school in Brighton, last Monday.*
> *Shortly afterwards, head Regine Kruger got a phone call from Her Majesty's Inspectorate wanting to send someone to inspect the inspectors. She reluctantly accepted.*
>
> *But the next day, Regine received a call from Full Circle, the contracting firm providing the OFSTED team, asking if it could send a team to inspect the inspectors who were (keep up) of course already being inspected. They also told her that Her Majesty's Inspectorate wanted to send another inspector – to inspect their inspector inspecting the inspectors who were trying to inspect the teachers.*[100]

All these people are, of course, trying to do their best and they often do make useful contributions. The only question is whether the money could be spent more effectively.

Fundamental to an understanding of what is wrong is the recognition that bureaucracies have a natural tendency to grow. Let us take just one quango: the Qualifications and Curriculum Authority, which has responsibility for maintaining the national curriculum and monitoring qualifications. When it first came into existence, in 1988, its budget amounted to £10 million. By the turn of the century, the budget had increased to £60 million. Admittedly it had been given responsibility for national testing, but this was a remarkable six-fold rise.

Ofsted, which was originally set up to inspect state schools, has also increased its remit. It had a budget of £86 million in 1999/2000. This was set to be £197 million in 2003/4 – a rate of increase of 31 per cent a year.

Why has the bureaucracy of state education, like that of other government departments, grown so much? The explanation written many years ago in *Parkinson's Law* cannot be bettered:

We must picture a civil servant called A, who finds himself over-worked ... For this real or imagined overwork there are, broadly speaking, three possible remedies. He may resign; he may ask to halve the work with a colleague called B; he may demand the assistance of two subordinates, to be called C and D.

A will undoubtedly choose the third option. Why?

By resignation he [A] would lose his pension rights. By having B appointed, on his own level in the hierarchy, he would merely bring in a rival for promotion to W's vacancy when W (at long last) retires. So A would rather have C and D, junior men, below him. This will add to his consequence and, by dividing the work into two categories, as between C and D, he will have the merit of being the only man who comprehends them both.

In due course, C and D will also find they are overworked and they in turn will need two assistants. 'With the recruitment of E, F, G and H the promotion of A is now practically certain.' Meanwhile, seven people are now doing the work formerly done by one. But this does not mean they are idle. Far from it. They are extremely busy.

Imagine a document comes in:

Official E decides that it falls within the province of F, who places a draft reply before C, who amends it drastically before consulting D, who asks G to deal with it. But G goes on leave at this point, handing the file over to H, who drafts a minute that is signed by D and returned to C, who revises his draft accordingly and lays the new version before A.

What does A do?

A, one must appreciate, is very busy and would have every reason not even to read the draft before signing it. By this time he knows he is going to replace W and he must decide which of C and D should succeed him in his current job. He has many staff issues to attend to.

Nevertheless, A is a conscientious servant of the people and reads the draft with care.

[He] *deletes the fussy paragraphs added by C and H, and restores the thing to the form preferred in the first instance by the able (if quarrelsome) F. He corrects the English – none of these young men can write grammatically – and finally produces the same reply he would have written if officials C to H had never been born.*

All these people have done their honest best. A does not get out of the office until late. 'Among the last to leave, A reflects with bowed shoulders and a wry smile that late hours, like grey hairs, are among the penalties of success.'

Parkinson's Law makes sense of the way bureaucracies always seem to grow. Northcote Parkinson also discovered some striking examples of the phenomenon. Between 1914 and 1928, for instance, the number of major or 'capital' ships in the navy collapsed from sixty-two to only twenty but the number of officials in the Admiralty soared – by 78 per cent.

The full extent of the bureaucracy in state education is not definitively known. That may seem a bizarre statement but it appears to be true. The main difficulty is in knowing how many people work for local authorities administering and advising on education. I have asked the Department for Education and Skills and obtained no reply. Others have tried to answer this question on my behalf, without success.

I can offer some figures from one local authority as an indication. The Education and Libraries Directorate of Newcastle City Council has, when up to full strength, 963 employees.[102] There are 107 schools in Newcastle, so there are nine local civil servants for every school. To put it another way, there is one civil servant for every forty children. If one takes this figure as typical and then adds into the stew all the central-government civil servants, inspectors and those examining exams and working on other

> 'Enthusiasm for educating the young is often accompanied by an utter carelessness of the money of the taxpayer ... At present there is a vast amount of waste in unnecessary luxuries, in the building of ornamental palaces, in the multiplication of clerks, inspectors, and so forth.'[101]
>
> **G. R. Porter,** *The Progress of the Nation,* **1912**

quangos and 'initiatives', it seems probable that, overall, there is one civil servant for every class in a state school. Or more. Teachers have longer holidays than civil servants. So the working hours of civil servants are equivalent to at least one and a half teachers. In working time, there may be well over one civil servant per class. This would lend support to the claim made by the Conservative Party in 2003 that there were 731,000 non-teaching employees employed by local governments and working in education compared to a much smaller number – 504,000 – of teachers.[103]

It is true that the bureaucracies in charities and commercial companies also have a tendency to grow. But the evidence of history is that state organisations are the least successful in resisting the tendency. So much of the money does not get through to the schools, putting them at a disadvantage to private schools. The amount of money that could be better spent in state education is vast.

Is it the class sizes?
What else could explain the disappointing performance of state education? Some people think it would be all right if only class sizes were smaller.

Do class sizes matter or not? When the OECD tried to make sense of the issue, the researchers found that for different countries the results were wildly different. They were also confusing even within countries. But attainment in all OECD countries taken together was significantly better for those children with student/teacher ratios of less than 20:1 compared to those with more than 30:1.[104]

In a study of ten thousand children in three hundred state schools, it was found that a drop in class size from twenty-five to fifteen produced a gain in literacy of a full year among children in the bottom 25 per cent of a class. The effect was far less marked for the better-performing children. Professor Peter Blatchford, who led this study, was very specific in saying small classes were effective 'particularly for literacy for the smallest children'.

Project STAR in Tennessee was, perhaps, the most determined attempt to decide the issue one way or another. It tracked seven thousand children from eighty schools. The children were divided into those who would attend larger classes of twenty-two to twenty-five and those who would attend classes of thirteen to seventeen.

In 1990, an assessment was made of how the children had done. Those who had spent their first four years of schooling in smaller classes clearly outperformed those who had been in bigger classes. A follow-up study ten years later showed that the benefit lasted though secondary education.[105]

Nothing is proven beyond all doubt, but the balance of the evidence is that children do progress better in classes of below twenty and that this is particularly important for younger children and low achievers. The size of the impact is significant but not massive. Class sizes may explain part of the underperformance of state education, but perhaps only a modest part.

Order and disorder
Helena Zeffertt was a teacher in primary and secondary schools but after twenty-four years wanted a change.[106] She wanted to go on teaching but do it without the form-filling, the 'pointless meetings' and the feeling that she was a cog in a machine. So she decided to become a supply teacher. She was sent to schools which temporarily needed someone to fill in for a teacher who was away for some reason. In the next two years as a supply teacher, she visited forty different schools.

The thing that struck her most was the number of pupils with 'behavioural and social problems' for whom school was just something to be endured. She found she was not actually expect to teach the children anything. 'My task is simply to prevent them from wrecking the classroom and injuring each other.'

'Many' of the schools were 'not for the faint-hearted'.

The pupils are bad mannered, disaffected and often violent. They shout, swear, throw books around the classroom, kick over chairs and tables, laugh in your face, call you names, and threaten to 'have you done' if you remonstrate with them.

Almost daily, I suffer abusive behaviour, foul language, personal insults and comments of a sexual nature too disgusting to repeat. When I first walk into a classroom, it is not unusual to be greeted with the comment: 'Just another f***ing supply teacher'.

She noticed that mobile phones were more common than pens or pencils and that pupils clicked through dozens of ring tones and called each other up throughout the day. The boys looked at an 'incredible amount' of pornography on the internet and always referred to girls as 'slags'. Between classes, 'the children surge up and down the staircases

shouting expletives, kicking, shoving and grabbing each other's bags.'
Her experience might not be typical. It could be that supply teachers go
to a disproportionate number of the most difficult schools and get the
worst classes.

So what is the overall picture?

The Association of Teachers and Lecturers did a survey of children,
asking them about their own experiences. A third of pupils had been
bullied in the last year
and a quarter claimed
they had been threatened
with violence. A large
minority felt that teach-
ers were not aware of the
bullying going on. In
middle and secondary
schools, 13 per cent of
children reported having
been physically attacked
in the past year.

A third of children had been bullied in the last year.

Fear of violence was
remarkably widespread. A large minority of girls – 44 per cent – and
not many fewer boys – 39 per cent – were worried about it. More than
one in ten were so frightened that they had missed school specifically
because of it. A quarter of children said
they were worried about travelling to
and from school because they were
afraid of bullying or attacks. The eleven-
year-olds were the worst affected,
perhaps because many are in their first
years of secondary school. More than
half reported incidents of bullying. It is
an extraordinary statistic. If it does not
shock, perhaps it shows how inured we
have become to the idea of aggression in
schools.

It is possible that children exaggerate
the problems for dramatic effect. But it
is also possible that boys, in particular,
downplay the degree to which they are
frightened.

> 'Two out of three teachers
> said they had lessons dis-
> rupted every week by
> badly behaved children.
> Eighty per cent said pupils'
> behaviour had deteriorated
> during their teaching
> careers. Not only were
> pupils becoming more dis-
> ruptive, but they were
> doing so at an earlier
> age.'[107]
>
> **Warwick University
> research report**

Perhaps the best overall picture comes to us thanks to Terry Haydn, a lecturer at the University of East Anglia.[108] He created an index of what classes are like, ranging from 10, in which the teacher feels completely relaxed and class control is not a problem, down to 1, which is awful.

Using this index, the journal *Education Today* surveyed student teachers, asking them what their experience of classes had been like. The result was that the teachers reported an average level on the Haydn Index of 7 in semi-rural schools. That is the level defined as: 'the pupils are not actually going out of their way to challenge your authority but there are rowdy interludes.' The average level in inner-city schools was 6.5 – half-way towards level 6, in which 'you don't really look forward to teaching the class; there is a good deal of noise; it is difficult to get some pupils to work; and by the end of the lesson you are feeling rather drained.'

These were the averages. But even in the country, some student teachers reported classes at level 3, where pupils throw things when you write on the board and pay little or no attention. In the inner city, they reported classes at the lowest possible level where 'your entry into the classroom is greeted by jeers and abuse; you wish you had not gone into teaching.'

> **'I was thrown against the door and pushed into a wall and door frame. Because it was said that I could not immediately identify the children concerned, no disciplinary action was taken. I was pregnant at the time and subsequently miscarried.'[109]**
>
> **Amy Blackburn, teacher, giving evidence in court about her work at Islington Green School (the school Tony Blair's children would have gone to if he had not got them into the London Oratory School, some miles away)**

How much does this disruption matter?

Among other things, the PISA study by the OECD set out to measure how a big a difference good discipline makes. They related academic achievement to the level of discipline reported by students and the degree to which they said they got on well with their teachers. They found that these factors were among the most important of all in determining whether children do well or badly. Among factors relating exclusively to schools – that is leaving out the impact of parents – they were the second and third biggest factors. If you combine them, they were the most important.

Lack of discipline and respect for teachers is therefore likely to be an extremely important reason why state schools do badly. But that leads to the follow-up question, 'Why is discipline so bad in many state schools?'

A lot of teachers would say that was an easy question and point accusing fingers at the parents. Is that fair?

Parents themselves – not to mention their children – have increasingly become violent and threatening. One mother, aided by her fourteen-year-old daughter and a teenage girl from a related family, attacked a school governor at Southfield Primary School in west London. Five people tried to defend the governor. One of them, a woman, was knocked to the ground and had a finger broken. Another, a female governor of the school, had clumps of hair pulled from her scalp. According to Colin Lowther, the headmaster, it was the culmination of a five-month 'reign of terror' by the family involving bullying, violence and intimidation against both pupils and other parents.

The case is extreme. But no one should be under the illusion that all parents are upright citizens. Parents make a major difference to how well children do at school academically. That is overwhelmingly clear from the PISA study. It would be surprising if their influence did not also affect how well behaved their children are. There appears to be an epidemic of children whose home life has left them disturbed in various ways, making it more difficult for schools to succeed with them. Parenting appears to be at the root of this and I have examined how the welfare state may have contributed to this problem in a following chapter.

> **'50 per cent of boys have largely lost interest in school by the time they are 15.'[110]**
>
> **Permanent secretary for the Department for Education and Skills**

But do schools themselves contribute to the discipline problem? Since eleven-year-olds just starting at secondary school are the most likely to suffer bullying, it seems likely that much of what they suffer is perpetrated by the fifteen- and sixteen-year-olds, at the end of their school careers, perhaps those who have given up on education.

Jason James: 'Everyone wants to be part of a group'.

Jason James got only three GCSEs and admits he did not reach his potential.[111] 'Everyone wants to be part of a group,' he explains. 'I had to pick one to be part of for friendship and security.' In each group in a school there is a hierarchy. 'The people at the top don't go to lessons,' he says. 'They are always in the centre of the trouble.' To stay in with such a group, all the members have to adopt a similar attitude. 'If you want to be part of the cool group, you have to do that [cause trouble] a little bit yourself.'

Jason James describes the sort of thing anthropologists study – a society within a society: groups of children, boys in particular, who have given up on school society and created a subgroup in which they find meaning. The subgroup is male and assertive, and finds the way to status is through demonstrating power – against school authority and other children.

> **'When the schools are in session it's like *Animal Farm*. The children attack each other in wolf-packs. It becomes totally horrific. As an old-age pensioner, you walk down there and you just get insulted. You're expected to move out of the children's way.'[112]**
>
> **Pensioner living in Highbury, London, 2002**

If these fifteen- and sixteen-year-olds were not legally obliged to be at school, they probably would not be there causing misery and under-achievement among others. They would not be caught up in that subgroup. If they were, for example, apprenticed or in jobs, they would be surrounded predominantly by adults. These adults would then be their role models instead of other children who had become something like tribal or pack leaders. In other words compulsory schooling up to the age of sixteen probably contributes to the indiscipline in British schools and is therefore one of the reasons why British state education does so badly. Other children suffer because of the ones who are compelled against their will to stay. The ones compelled to stay also suffer, because they are more likely to become delinquent and then criminals.

> **'Llantwit Major comprehensive has been forced by an appeals panel to take back an eleven-year-old boy whom the head had excluded. The boy had shot a teacher in the neck with a plastic pellet.'**
>
> ***Times Educational Supplement,*** **14 February 2003**

Is there anything else that could cause the indiscipline? Let us go back to the story of the attacks on a school governor in the playground.

Colin Lowther, the headmaster, decided to suspend the two families at the heart of the violence at his school. He accepted at face value the government's pledge of 'zero tolerance' of violent parents. But when he told the local authority education department, he was told in no uncertain terms that he was exceeding his powers and could not exclude the pupils. He was told that his own role was to be reviewed – which he took as an indirect threat of the sack. Meanwhile he heard that another part of the council was advising the families about possibly taking legal action against him. The lack of support was total. He was strongly discouraged from exercising real discipline.

> 'I have seen for myself how a school's ethos and discipline can make a world of difference to standards. Yet there is no doubt that behaviour has deteriorated over the past 20 years. Parents and teachers are right to be concerned.'[114]
>
> **Tony Blair**

Helen Zeffertt, the supply teacher, similarly noted, 'Not only am I not allowed to use any physical force but I am prohibited from responding to their abuse . . . in any way that might be considered insulting to them.' A 'softly, softly' approach is insisted upon by the bureaucracy and by government. Why?

One of the motives is a desire to treat aggressors as victims of circumstance – as they quite often are – who need to be persuaded towards more civilised behaviour. Next there is the problem: 'If we exclude children from schools, what will we do with them?' The first thing that will happen is that they will cost more money. They will have to be given tutors or – if kept in school – put in much smaller classes. Daniel Cowan, aged only six, was excluded from three schools because of his unruly conduct. North Tyneside Council had to find him a place at a special boarding school at a cost of £94,000 a year.[113]

> 'According to a poll last year, a majority of parents want to see a return to corporal punishment in school. Experts were appalled.'
>
> *Daily Telegraph,*
> **17 November 2001**

The intense desire to be 'inclusive' led the incoming government in 1997 to reduce exclusions as a matter of policy. So keen was the government to avoid exclusions that up until 2002, a pupil found carrying a knife or knuckle-duster could not be permanently excluded. Eventually the policy was reversed because the bullying and violence, according to the government's own research, was getting so much worse. But as the case of Colin Lowther shows, this reverse in policy has not gone far. The state education system is extremely reluctant to enforce discipline.

Is it the way they teach?

What about the actual teaching? Most parents – let alone other members of the public – have little idea of what goes on after they leave little Johnny or Lucy at the gates of the school.

We have already seen how Tom Burkard discovered that the teaching of reading has changed out of all recognition and become less effective. How did that happen?

During the 1980s, teaching experts asserted that the old-fashioned way of learning to read was didactic, boring and stultifying. Children should pick up reading and writing as they went along instead. They could be helped along by pictures which would give them clues to what the words were. The stories would relate to things they knew, so they would enjoy the process of learning. They would learn for themselves instead of being told. It was called 'whole-word' learning in which they would recognise whole words rather than letters. The children would read 'real books'.

The technique sounds appealing – gentler than the old method, more fun and natural. How well did it work?

Martin Turner, an educational psychologist working for Croydon education authority, noted in 1990 that reading test scores in the area had been going down for five consecutive years.[115] He remarked later, 'The psychology service was being asked all the time to help these children. Were they dyslexic?'

He came to the view that many of them were not dyslexic at all. They were simply not being taught reading in an effective way. Through his efforts, the performance of eight local authorities was measured. All showed the same downward trend in reading attainment since the new technique was introduced.

Turner was treated badly because his research offended the new orthodoxy. But over the next thirteen years, official bodies began – extremely slowly and reluctantly – to acknowledge that he was right. The vast majority of children taught in the 1990s experienced the whole-word method – a method now admitted even by the government to be defective. The government is now trying to introduce more learning of letters through phonics. But the introduction is slow and patchy.

What about other subjects?

The teaching of all subjects is, of course, handicapped by the failure of many schools successfully to teach children to read. The great amount of time now spent labouring to teach reading also reduces the time left for other subjects. Teaching of most subjects has also been influenced by the following ideas:

• that schools should not stunt creativity;
• that it is better for children to discover things for themselves than just be told them;
• that children should enjoy the learning experience.

Again, it is easy to see the appeal. We would all like our children to enjoy their lessons and be creative. We all recognise – like Richard Dawes at King's Somborne School in the nineteenth century – that something discovered may be more profoundly learned than something taught. But these attractive concepts have moved from being part of what schools try to do to being heavily dominant. They have caused major changes in teaching techniques:

• a drastic reduction in direct instruction;
• children sitting in groups facing each other instead of the teacher;
• learning, or attempting to learn, a great deal through discovery;
• little if any 'rote' learning of things such as multiplication tables;
• mistakes going uncorrected in case children find corrections discouraging;
• studying around a subject instead of the subject itself;
• less teaching of grammar in English and foreign languages.

Do these changes matter?

The National Institute of Economic and Social Research did a comparative study of teaching methods in England and Switzerland.[116] In an English biology lesson, the children spent their time measuring each other's hand sizes, thumb lengths, colour of eyes and so on. They were asked to think about how to record, analyse and present this information. But they did not in fact gather what all the data was intended to mean. This is typical of the new orthodoxy. But the researchers found that the children had 'gained only a superficial idea of the principles underlying their individual experiments and some had developed a wrong understanding'. The teachers were reluctant to tell them outright. You might even say the teachers were reluctant to teach.

In Switzerland, meanwhile, older methods were used. Two-thirds of the time was devoted to continuous interaction between the teacher and the whole class. The teacher started with a problem. He or she worked towards solutions and key concepts through questions and instruction. The pupils were guided towards the answers in logical stages. The teacher could see by their responses which students understood and which needed further help. Researchers in this study were struck by the contrast between England, where there is a 'long tail' of under-achieving pupils, and Switzerland, where most students kept up so well it was 'a revelation'.

In England they found: 'For most of the time pupils are left to their own resources. The teacher's role is mainly to help individual pupils when there are difficulties and to check their work.' But often many pupils want help at the same time. They cannot all get it at once so they form a queue. In some cases, the teachers have a rule limiting the queue to 'not more than four waiting at my desk at a time'. The pressure of the time of the teachers thus becomes intense and each child often only receives a 'cursory' check of his or her work. The children do not receive adequate support. 'Average pupils, and more so those who are below average, consequently suffer.'

> **'I once asked a schools inspector what was the one single thing he would do to improve education standards. His reply was unhesitating: "Burn down all the teacher training colleges."'**[117]
>
> **Keith Waterhouse**

The new theory and practice of teaching means that in science, scientific principles are learned ineffectively. In maths, multiplication tables are not learned because learning by rote is disapproved of. In writing and many other subjects, children are not told about their mistakes. Grammar is not widely and rigorously taught because children are expected to discover it for themselves. In English literature, schools and local authorities frequently do not insist that the greatest works of English literature are read. They consider it would be too dogmatic.[118] In history, children are supposed to develop skills of historical research, which sounds fine until you realise that it means they will not actually learn many of the events of the past. They may emerge from a study of Roman civilisation without knowing anything substantial – or perhaps anything at all – about Julius Caesar, Augustus, Tiberius, Nero or the rise and fall of the empire. Geography is used as an opportunity for children to learn and discover for themselves and to glean, as absolute truths, theories about 'sustainable development' which are, in fact, highly contentious. Children do not have much time left afterwards to be instructed in where places are in the world or how to read maps.

Just as English grammar is not extensively taught, similarly there is a reluctance to teach the grammar of foreign languages. John Gordon, the admissions tutor in modern languages at the University of East Anglia, took the students who had just arrived at the university to study German in the autumn of 1994 and gave them a test. They were asked to translate very simple sentences into German such as:
- I like to drink Chinese tea
- I prefer to drink strong coffee
- The train you came on was twenty minutes late
- The teacher gave the pupil the book.

How many of them could translate the sentences correctly? Out of forty-three students, seven could manage the first, four the second, ten the next and eight the last. Gordon commented that the final sentence 'was once widely used to introduce learners to the use of the indirect object. Until recently the use of this sentence in a test after the first year of German would have been regarded as some kind of jest . . . It would have been regarded as an insult to the students.' But these were under-graduates who had achieved As and Bs at A-level.

How much damage have recent educational theories done to British state education? It is impossible to quantify, but the impact must have been immense. Reading opens the way to a vast continent of knowledge but this door is now closed to many. The new teaching theories treasure creativity above all things and we can all agree that creativity is 'a good thing'. But it is being valued at the expense of knowledge and under-standing. Nor is it clear that creativity is actually damaged by learning in the old way. Shakespeare – not one whose creativity was obviously stunted – went to a school where he learnt by rote.

Why did damaging education theories gain such a strong hold in Britain? Why did parents not object?

Parent power

Some of them did. They questioned teachers and were told, like Tom Burkard, that they did not understand modern teaching methods. They also discovered that they had no power. The only real power that parents have in a school is to take their child away and place him or her in another school.

What power do parents have in the state system? Typically there may be only three schools or so available within a reasonable distance of a home because state schools tend to be big. The effective choice is likely to be limited. The number of appeals against rejection by schools has been rising year by

> '**The reason teachers can indulge in folly is that parents have virtually no say in the way their children are educated.**'[119]
>
> **Professor Kenneth Minogue,**
> ***Civil Society and David Blunkett***

year. Among secondary schools, the appeals nearly doubled between 1995/6 and 2001/2. There was about one appeal for every ten admissions.

Appeals lodged by parents against rejection by secondary schools[120]

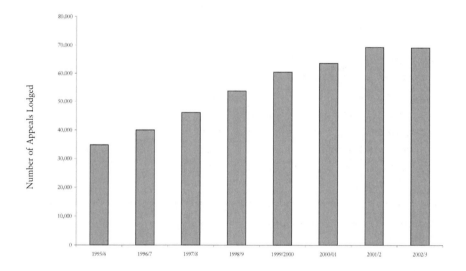

Considering the likelihood of failure of such appeals and the time, effort and confidence that is required, one in ten is a substantial number. Naturally, the better off and more articulate are the parents most likely to appeal. They are also the ones who will go to great lengths to get their children into the better state schools in the first place. They will use an affiliation to the Roman Catholic church or move house to get into the right catchment area.

But the most worrying aspect of the lack of parent power is that bad schools and bad teaching methods can go on forever.

So who does have power?

> '**My daughter and her husband have had to move to Mansfield in Nottinghamshire. Unfortunately, they bought a house that is just outside the catchment of the Brunts, the only comprehensive in the area that seems worth considering. The council says my grandson should go to Queen Elizabeth's, where only 16 per cent of the pupils pass five GCSEs ... By chance my other daughter, who is single, does live within the Brunts catchment, so my married daughter is wondering whether she could say she's left her husband and gone to live with her sister. Do you think anyone would check?'**
>
> **Letter to the education editor of the *Daily Telegraph*, 11 March 2003**

Government power

Power is shared between the national government, local government, heads of schools, teachers (including their unions) and members of the bureaucracy such as inspectors and education advisers. Does this combination work well?

Does the central government, in particular, use its power well? In 1997, the new government promised to link schools up to the 'information super-highway'. To many electors this will have sounded extremely up to the minute. Since then, over £1.8 billion has been spent on the government's commitment to computers and internet connections. The commitment has become deeply embedded. Computer science or 'IT' (information technology) has reduced the time left for other subjects or even pushed some – such as French, to a large degree – off the timetable altogether. The IT idea has become a major part of how other subjects are now taught too.

John Clare, the education editor of the *Daily Telegraph*, visited Hall Green, a comprehensive in Birmingham. He sat through five lessons in which, so the headmaster had told him, he would see computers being used effectively. The first was an English class for low-ability twelve-year-olds. The topic was Shakespeare. But they did not read one of his plays. Instead, the head of English had spent an hour selecting internet websites. He told the children to look through them and transfer bits they found interesting into their computer folders.

*Most of them spent the 35 minute lesson scrolling aimlessly
though the sites, pausing occasionally at the pictures. Whenever
Mr Kennedy [the teacher] was not looking, one played a video
game. At the end, I asked him what the pupils had learnt about
Shakespeare. 'Good question,' he said, as if the idea had not
occurred to him.*

Clare sat through four more lessons with computers. In each case, the
subject that was supposedly being studied wasn't. 'In all five lessons,
the subject had become subservient to the technology. Far from moti-
vating the children, it distracted them.'

I visited a special computer centre for the Royal Borough of Kensington and Chelsea in Notting Hill Gate. It was a large building,
decorated in a modernist way with many offices for local-authority
officials working on education. I was taken to three rooms with hi-tech
equipment. Only in one of them was some equipment being used.
There were two Apple computers with extra-large flat screens, which,
at the time, must have been extremely expensive. Two girls sat at one of
these superb computers. They were selecting pop songs from a play list.

Academics in abundance provide evidence
that computers – as they have been used
thus far, at least – provide no measurable
educational benefit. Two professors took
advantage of a natural experiment that
took place in Israel. In 1996, some schools
were given computers and the rest were
not. There was no evidence that increased
educational use of computers actually
raised test scores. In fact the best estimates show that the mathematics scores
of pupils in schools that received the new
computers actually went down.[121]

The PISA report tried to establish if
there was any correlation between computer use and academic attainment. The
research found no statistically significant
effect.

> **DO CHILDREN
> SUFFER BECAUSE
> OF TEACHER
> SHORTAGES?**
>
> 'The quarter of schools
> where principals are least
> concerned about teacher
> shortage score, at 556
> points, significantly above
> the quarter of schools
> where principals are most
> concerned (507
> points).'[122]
>
> OECD report on Britain.

The government itself commissioned a
report by the British Educational Communications and Technology
Agency which followed the progress of seven hundred pupils. This

research also found 'no consistent relationship' between computer use and pupil achievement in any subject at any age.[123]

Computers and the internet, as currently used, are of no educational benefit. They consume a vast amount of money and time. Yet the government, its inspectors and advisers continue to insist that the money must be spent on them. The government uses its power badly. Unfortunately, this is not an isolated incident. The waste and mis-spending caused by government is extreme.

• Individual Learning Accounts were created to help people to continue their education into adulthood. The scheme came to be so riddled with fraud, costing millions of pounds, that the government finally gave it up.

> **DEALING WITH THE TEACHER SHORTAGE**
>
> **David Daniels, the head teacher at White Hart Lane School in north London, was twenty teachers short. In desperation he asked agencies to recruit abroad. He got them in the end so that he had a total of thirty-nine overseas teachers out of a total of eighty-seven.**
>
> *Daily Mail* **20 June 2002**

• Teachers are trained for three years at considerable expense and taught education theories which are ineffective. Worse still, 40 per cent of those in the their final year of teacher training never go into teaching.[124] The training budget in 2000 was some £245 million, so this is an annual loss of £100 million. Another 18 per cent leave teaching within five years. There is a vast army – far bigger than Britain's real army – of teachers who don't teach: an estimated 296,200 people.[125] The waste is staggering.

• The government contributes to the shortage of teachers actually working. Professor Alan Smithers and Dr Pamela Robinson interviewed former teachers to discover their reasons for leaving the profession. These were the top three:

Primary schoolteachers		Secondary schoolteachers	
Workload	58%	Workload	74%
Government initiatives	42%	Pupil behaviour	45%
Stress	26%	Government initiatives	37%

'Government initiatives' were specifically named by former teachers as either the second or the third most significant reason why they left.[126] So government control has helped to create the teacher shortage.

Schools then try desperately to fill the shortage by hiring teachers from abroad. They are sometimes very good. But they are likely to work for shorter periods and some are not able to speak English very well.

The *Times Educational Supplement* generally takes it for granted that state education is a good thing. But even in this journal, an adverse – or merely useless – role for central control is often suggested, as in this column by David Winkley:

> *'To read or not to read...', one irritated head teacher said to me last week, tossing me a recent booklet. This heavyweight publication was from the Qualifications and Curriculum Authority, itemising arrangements for the administration of the 2003 key stage 2 tests.*

> *It turned out to be a revelatory example of hyper-bureaucracy: a hundred pages of utterly pedantic instructions.*[127]

> **'Are teachers over-inspected? Is the Pope a Catholic?'**[128]
>
> *Times Educational Supplement*

One page of instructions was devoted entirely to the subject of unwrapping the tests. Winkley remarked that the 'Byzantine' document added to the 'mountain' of instructions that clutters up 'every head teacher's office'. Winkley reflected at the end of his column, 'just think how much this document cost to produce and how many hours heads have wasted reading it.'

But is this just moaning by the teachers' trade paper? Should they really be grateful for the guidance they get from government? Do the children indirectly benefit, at any rate?

> **'The basic problem is this: there are far too many people being funded to monitor, advise and even direct the far too few actually doing the work.'**[129]
>
> **Jim Hudson, head teacher of Two Mile Ash Middle School, Milton Keynes**

The PISA report set out to discover the effect of outside control on schools. After studying the figures from over twenty countries, the researchers came to the conclusion that autonomy for schools was a mildly positive factor. 'Students tend to do better on average in countries with more [school] autonomy, particularly in choice of courses and budget allocation.'[130] Or, to put it the other way round, control by government was mildly negative. The government does more harm than good and uses up money which could have been used more effectively.

Teacher and union power

What about teachers – and their unions? Do they use their power to good effect?

There has been very little examination of their role – surprising considering their undoubted muscle. But there are, at least, three things they have done which are likely to have affected the quality of state education.

The National Union of Teachers, the biggest of the unions, has resisted the idea that teachers should be paid on the basis of their performance. This means that good teachers are no more encouraged to stay in the profession than bad ones. This must tend to damage the interests of children. The teachers' unions also have resisted the idea that any of their members should ever be fired unless their behaviour reaches an undoubted extreme of negligence or incompetence. This again is likely to be against the interests of children.

> 'British education has grown worse precisely in proportion to the increasing control of the ministry of education.'
>
> **Professor Kenneth Minogue,** *Civil Society and David Blunkett*

Teacher power also means less work. According to government figures 56 per cent of teachers average ten days off sick a year – that is two weeks out of the relatively short school year. The proportion of state school teachers off sick is 50 per cent above the rate in non-state schools.[131]

Can the state ever succeed at education?

We have looked at a considerable number of possible reasons why state education should have disappointed. Could state education be improved if these problems were dealt with?

Yes, it could. But is the state capable of dealing with these problems? Would the state, for example, make hundreds of thousands of administrators redundant? Would it be willing to let schools become autonomous and – for example – punish and exclude children much more enthusiastically than now? Would the state give parents choice to the extent that some state schools were closed down? All this seems unlikely.

The problems of state education derive from the fact that it is provided by the state. To ask the state not to waste money or be bureau-cratic is like asking a zebra to give up its stripes.

'But there are some very good state schools!'

One likely counter to all the above is: 'But there are some very good state schools. We don't need private ones. Allowing for their superior intake, they are not much better.' There are undoubtedly some good state schools. But how many? And how good are they, really?

How many were in the top ten for their results at A-level in 2002? We should bear in mind that 93 per cent of children start off at state sec-ondary schools,[132] so their intake must necessarily include many of the brightest and best. They include many grammar schools, which still remain despite the best efforts of various politicians over the years to get rid of them. How many were in the top ten? I have asked several people with different attitudes and experiences to guess. They have usually suggested that perhaps two or three state schools were in the top ten.

The answer is that there were none. What about in the top twenty? Still there were none. The list, which could be seen on the BBC News website, showed one private school after another. At number nineteen was the Jaamiatul Imaam Muhammad Zakaria School, a non-selective private school. Did any state school at all get into the top thirty schools in the country ranked by A-level performance? No. The first state school in the league table came in at number thirty-five: Queen Eliza-beth's School in Barnet, north London. It is selective. In the first fifty schools in the country, a mere four were state schools. Out of the top hundred, only twelve were state schools. The dominance of private schools among the top performers was stunning.

It is true of course, that private schools have certain advantages. One of them is that the chil-dren tend to have parents who are more ambitious and well educated. But such parents are not confined to private schools. Let us look at a school known for the ambition of two of its parents at least: Tony and Cherie Blair. They surely chose the best school they could get into in London within the state system. Many other highly motivated, upper-middle-class families

> **'43 per cent of those getting three As at A level have been to inde-pendent schools, even though only 7 per cent of the population is edu-cated in them.'**
>
> **G. W. Bernard,**
> *Studying at University*

have also gone to some lengths to get their children into the London Oratory School.

So how did the London Oratory do at A-levels? It came 760th. Within the same London borough – Hammersmith and Fulham – it only came fifth out of seven schools that had substantial numbers of students. The top three schools in the area were all private.

Let's look at the Henrietta Barnett School in north London. Parents fight like cats to get their children into this selective girls' school. There are nine applications for every place. To gain entrance is to be very bright, to have seriously pushy parents or both. At the time of the last Ofsted inspection, there were 683 children, of whom only four were eligible for school meals – the usual blunt way of identifying less prosperous families. The inspectors remarked, 'The surrounding area is affluent, with a markedly higher proportion of families in favourable socio-economic circumstances than nationally.'

I talked to a former pupil. She told me the school was very keen to get good exam results. 'If you didn't get the grades, you weren't welcome,' was her slightly bitter description. She herself was told not to take history at A-level because she had only got a C in the GCSE. She did the subject anyway but 'I knew a lot of girls who did subjects they didn't want to do.' The idea was to get the grades, whatever the interests of the girls.

Parents, though, did not rely on the school's efforts. Like Tony Blair, who hired tutors for his children from Westminster School, they too hired private tutors. Tutors were even used to get children into Henrietta Barnett in the first place. Six children applied from the primary school of the former pupil I spoke to. Five had been helped by tutors. That gives an idea of the motivation and family background of Henrietta Barnett girls.

In the former pupil's history class at Henrietta Barnett, two out of six children had private tuition. She was told by a friend doing economics that virtually everybody in that subject had a tutor – the same one. 'There was a lot of pressure from oneself, the parents and the staff,' she said. When she did her GCSE in physics, she taught herself to a large degree using revision textbooks. With pupils selected from so many keen candidates, Henrietta Barnett should be able to compete with any school in the world. It is certainly higher achieving than the vast majority of other state schools. But how did it do compared to private schools? It came forty-sixth in the overall table – beaten by some non-selective private schools and others selective only in name.

Private schools with better results included some which are second, third or even fourth choices for parents. St Paul's gets the best results among private girls' schools in west London. The Godolphin and Latymer School is well liked but is regarded as less of an academic hot-house. Then there are Francis Holland School (Westminster) and Notting Hill and Ealing High School. These two would be regarded by some parents as third or fourth choices. Yet all these schools beat Henrietta Barnett. The girls at them are probably not as inherently clever, on average, as those at Henrietta Barnett. But they did better in their exams all the same.

> **British private schools had the best attainment of any kind of school in any of the twenty-six countries examined by the OECD – an average score of 614 compared to a score of 515 for state schools and a lowest score of 484 for a major advanced country (Germany).**[133]
>
> **PISA report, 2000**

What does the dry, objective research say about state schools compared to independent ones? The PISA report noted a massive difference between the performance of British private and state schools. On the literacy test, the difference was one hundred 'scale points'. The OECD researchers then made adjustments for 'all other factors'. Most importantly, they adjusted for the higher average socio-economic status of private-school parents. But even after every possible adjustment, the private schools still outperformed by forty-eight scale points, which, in case of doubt, they said was 'statistically different'.

Evidence that independent schools do better than state ones is not confined to Britain. The World Bank studied government and private schools in Tanzania, Colombia, the Dominican Republic, the Philippines and Thailand – dramatically different countries in different continents.[134] The researchers went to great lengths to 'control' for factors which could influence the results – particularly the wealth and background of parents. The conclusion of the report on Thailand was that 'students in private schools perform significantly better that their public [state] school counterparts'. British people may wonder, 'Yes, but how much more did the private schools

> ### SCHOOLS FOR TEACHING?
>
> **'Private schools emphasised teaching and learning more than public [state] schools did and ... provided rewards that were contingent on good performance.'**
>
> *Public and Private Secondary Schools in Developing Countries (World Bank, 1994)*

cost?' The answer is that they did not cost more at all. Their unit costs were 'much lower' than in the state schools, partly due to the fact that so many lower-income parents send their children to private schools in Thailand. The schools have to be low cost.

> **'Our results are robust. The estimated private advantage is large and empirically important.'**
>
> **World Bank report on Colombia and Tanzania, 1989**

Reviewing the five countries studied, the World Bank remarked, 'Private school students generally outperform public school students on standardised math and language tests.' This was achieved despite the fact that the unit costs in private schools were generally lower. Private schools gave a bigger educational bang for each pound spent.

The World Bank's explanation for the superior performance of the private schools can be summarised in one word: incentives. Private schools had strong incentives to produce what the parents wanted – namely educational advancement. The study found that 'private schools emphasised teaching and learning more than public schools.' In private schools one-third of the time in teacher meetings was devoted to discussing teaching practices. In state schools it was half that. The heads of private schools spent more time actually teaching. Of course they needed to spend less time on communicating with state authorities and doing administration.

Who makes the decisions?

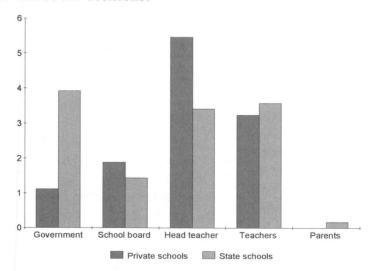

Decisions in schools in Colombia, Dominican Republic, Philippines, Tanzania and Thailand analysed by the World Bank[135]

Private education is widespread across the world, providing a wealth of evidence that it is better than state education and often cheaper, too.

Eleven years at school and still illiterate

The story of education told in this chapter is an extraordinary one. Until 1870, all schooling was provided by independent schools and universities. Virtually every child had five to seven years' schooling. The amount and quality of instruction was improving by leaps and bounds. Then Parliament passed a law intended only to 'fill up gaps' in independent provision. But this new law – quite against the wishes of the man who proposed it – led, over the following seventy-four years, to the almost complete destruction of independent schooling.

As the state increasingly took over, various politicians who took part in the process expressed what they expected from state education. Their intentions varied over time, although the basic, common ambition was to provide a good education for all – whatever that meant during their lifetimes. State education, though, has failed to reach every single target they described. The standard has fallen. Illiteracy is now widespread. It must be considered astonishing that state education has proved so incompetent that, after eleven years of compulsory schooling, it still cannot teach a significant minority even to read. Poor families have ended up with their children at the worst schools. Compulsory attendance at inferior schools has bred alienation and incivility to the point of encouraging crime. The ambition that state schools would create equality – or at least equality of opportunity – has failed too. It may even have had the reverse effect of reducing the chances for the children of poorer families to use education as a way up. No one has done worse out of state education than the poor.

State education has been a disaster. It has wasted what was developing so excitingly before. The assets of the independent schools – built up over centuries in some cases, like those of the hospitals – were taken over for free or at knock-down prices. Vast amounts of money have been wasted on layers of bureaucracy. The state has imposed what it considers the right methods of teaching – which have actually been poor methods – and has quashed innovation and competition between alternative methods. This is one of many failings which some people, such as Edward Baines, had the remarkable prescience to warn about from the outset in the nineteenth century.

It is a tragedy that independent education was not allowed to continue to grow. It is a shame that the state take-over of education ever happened.

CHAPTER 5

Housing: from 'homes fit for heroes' to Rachman and Damilola Taylor

Michael Young was a mild-mannered, rather badly dressed young man. Yet despite his modest appearance, he was also brilliant and energetic. In later life he would go on to create *Which?* magazine among many other unique achievements. During the Second World War, his talents saw him rise rapidly to become a secretary of the Labour Party research department. He wrote the Labour Party manifesto for the 1945 election. He was a bright, rising star of the left and might easily have gone on to become a leading Labour politician.

But at that moment he veered away from the predictable. He went to Chicago to learn about the relatively new subject of sociology. This was not because he was disenchanted with Labour. On the contrary, he was pleased with the work he had done for the party and believed in the welfare state. But he had the honesty to feel that a gap was opening up between the Labour government and its supporters.

After his studies in America, he and his former colleague at the Labour Party research department, Peter Willmott, decided to conduct research which would get them close to the people. They would discover how Labour reform was really affecting the working classes by investigating one of the most famous working-class districts in Britain: Bethnal Green.

Bethnal Green has long been a symbol of working-class England. In *Oliver Twist*, Bill Sikes, the burglar and thug who eventually murders his girlfriend Nancy, lives in the area. It is described as 'a maze of mean and dirty streets'. Elsewhere in the book Charles Dickens describes a nearby part of east London: 'The air was impregnated with filthy odours … Covered ways and yards which here and there diverged from the main street, disclosed little knots of houses, where drunken men and women were positively wallowing in filth.' Bethnal Green and environs were the sorts of place which nineteenth-century reformers wanted to clear as slums.

Young and Willmott arrived in the area as dedicated socialists with a certain idea of what they would find. They knew of previous studies of the conditions of the working class. They knew that Charles Booth, in a previous age, had reported on barefoot children in the street, under-nourished babies in the tenements, young mothers dying for want of food and medical care and so on. They looked back to Helen Bosan-quet, who had written about the neighbouring borough of Shoreditch and how, in 1896, a typical man there was mean with his money, forced his wife into sex (making her pregnant against her will), often became drunk and then turned violent. Not a pretty picture.

This would surely be a place that was desperately in need of help from the Labour government. The residents were bound to benefit from rehousing and better planning. Young and Willmott set about their work thoroughly. Both worked in the area throughout the three years during which the research was done. One of them lived in the borough with his wife and children, who went to the local schools. This was in-depth research.

In the course of the project, one thousand people were interviewed out of the fifty-four thousand living in Bethnal Green. They were chosen by picking every thirty-sixth name from the electoral register. This they called their 'general sample'. But then they interviewed a second or third time a smaller sample of couples with young children.

What they discovered was not at all what they had expected. It was so very different, in fact, that they decided they had to change the whole focus of what they had originally intended to do. 'As happens so often with research, more interesting than what we were seeking was what we stumbled on,' they wrote. They found a Bethnal Green that bore little relation to that described by Dickens, Booth or Bosanquet. The report they wrote was not about mud, filth, barefoot children and oppressive, drunken husbands.[1] It was about families.

What struck them was the extent of the family networks which had built up in Bethnal Green over the years. In one street of fifty-nine households, they found thirty-eight people had relatives in other house-holds in the same street. These people would bump into their relatives in the street without even trying. They also set out to meet up regularly, which was easy to arrange. Young and Willmott discovered a vast network of emotional and practical support. Of course, living cheek by jowl could cause problems, too. A young couple might have to stay with one of the sets of parents until they could get a place of their own. This could cause tensions, particularly between the women. But, in general, the family networks offered more benefits than drawbacks. Help of any sort was only a short walk away. Guidance and care for the children was readily to hand. It is the sort of thing we may associate with southern Europe – in countries like Italy or Greece. But Young and Willmott found it in east London.

A small boy came home from school one day, saying that the teacher had told the children to draw pictures of their families. The boy had drawn his mother, his father and his brother. 'But isn't it funny,' he said, 'the others were putting in their nannas and aunties and uncles and all sorts of people like that'.

Among the many families which Young and Willmott sought to interview was that headed by Mr and Mrs Banton in Minton Street. When they arrived at the address, they found a typical two-up, two-down cottage with a scullery at the back and outside lavatory at the far end of the small backyard. They knocked at the door. Mr Banton opened it – a small, downright man in shirt-sleeves and braces. He was suspicious at first and kept them on the doorstep. But after a few minutes' conversation – intently listened to by the neighbours – he let them in and called his wife.

Young and Willmott talked to them about their families. Mrs Banton said she went to see her mother nearby several times a day and got her shopping for her. Her mother, although getting on in years, returned the

East End children racing each other as part of the coronation celebrations in June 1953. The people of Bethnal Green had 'pride in themselves, their community and their country and ... an overwhelming vitality'.

favour by looking after Mrs Banton's children when need arose. The story was typical. Young and Willmott found that 68 per cent of married men and 75 per cent of married women lived near their parents.

Mrs Banton also told them about her grandfather, who used to live in the next street. This was a sadder story. He used to be looked after by an aunt who lived nearby. But then the council pulled down the aunt's house, declaring it a slum. She was then moved 'to one of those estates outside London'. Sadly, without her support, the grandfather had been obliged to go into an old people's home.

Relatives in Bethnal Green provided childcare, care for the elderly, financial assistance in times of trouble and peer pressure on each other to behave decently. Young and Willmott had discovered what they called an 'older organisation' which preceded the welfare state – 'a method of government not only in Bethnal Green but in most of the world'. It was not something that the state had created or planned. It was not subsidised. It was the extended family.

What effect did this way of living have on the people of Bethnal Green? Young and Willmott recalled that manual workers over the years had been portrayed as 'shiftless, lazy, improvident, rascally, uncultured, acting for themselves alone'. But that is not at all what they found. On the contrary, they found them in some respects to be 'a model for those who were (and are) doing the denigrating'. They were poor, yes. But if so, this was accompanied by 'a sense of family, community and class solidarity, by a generosity towards others like themselves, by a wide range of attachments, by pride in themselves, their community and their country and by an overwhelming vitality'. They were poor, but in some ways they had a quality in their lives that many, far richer, would envy.

The original point of Young and Willmott's investigation was to study the effect of policies on people. The policy in question was that of moving people away from the 'slums' of Bethnal Green to vastly better homes. So Young and Willmott followed those who were moved – as part of this policy – to a suburb they called 'Greenleigh', although that was not its real name. Greenleigh was designed to be a new utopia for the working class. On one side of the Underground railway were cows grazing in the fields. On the other, a brand new housing estate. In place of the jumble of blocks created by Edwardian philanthropists and old privately built cottages in Bethnal Green, there was a large expanse of semi-detached homes – each with its own garden and net curtains in the front window. What could be better, thought the planners.

Young and Willmott went there and, again, conducted many interviews. They found there were indeed some advantages to Greenleigh. Families had gardens to sit in and more space. They had indoor lavatories and baths with running hot water.

They talked to Mrs Harper, a 'stout, red-faced woman her late thirties' who moved with her husband from Bethnal Green in 1948. She had come from a large family – six girls and two boys – who had all lived in Bethnal Green. She recalled how 'we were always in and out of each other's houses.' When she went to the shops she called on her mother 'to see if she wanted any errands'. Every day she dropped in on one sister or another and would see a niece or an aunt at the corner shop. Her many long-standing family relationships were being constantly renewed. Her relations came to her during her confinements – 'my sisters used to come in and make a cup of tea and that.' And every Saturday and Sunday night there was a family party at her mother's place. 'We all used to meet there weekends. We always took the kiddies along.'

That busy, sociable life had now gone. Shopping in the morning, surrounded by the chrome and tile of the Parade at Greenleigh, was a lonely business compared with the familiar faces and sights of the old street market in Bethnal Green. The evenings were quieter too. 'It's the television most nights and the

A new council estate, *circa* 1952. In such estates, contact with extended families fell by as much as 75 per cent.

garden in the summer.' She had tried to make friends with neighbours but not very successfully. She disliked the loneliness and the 'quietness'. She thought the quietness would, in time, 'send people off their heads'. Her husband was less gloomy. But then he still went to work in Bethnal Green and could still see relatives there easily. That was typical. The women, who formerly had the most contact with family members, had the least after they moved to Greenleigh.

Young and Willmott found that the Harpers' story was typical. Before leaving Bethnal Green, husbands saw members of their extended family fifteen times a week on average. Once they moved to Greenleigh, they saw them only 3.8 times a week – a drop of 75 per cent. The wives had seen members of their extended family 17.2 times a week in Bethnal Green. Once in Greenleigh, they saw them only three times a week – a decline of 83 per cent. After a couple more years, the frequency of family contacts declined still further.

At Greenleigh, it was further to get to a pub to have a drink with friends or relatives. Friendships with neighbours did not work out well in many cases. Young and Willmott found that the idea of keeping 'themselves to themselves' was widespread. People tended to judge each other by their possessions and where they had come from (since they had not all come from Bethnal Green). People became house centred instead of kinship centred. Young mothers, children and the old had particular reason to regret the reduced support from extended families.

The story of Young and Willmott's investigation is one of the most poignant descriptions of how the welfare state's well-intentioned actions can misfire. It is all the more telling because it comes from people strongly sympathetic to the ideal of the welfare state. Their description – while highly suggestive of how the welfare state has changed the character of Britain – only describes relatively mild problems. But the state's well-intentioned attempts to do good in housing had far more dramatic and damaging effects than Young and Willmott examined, as we shall see.

*

The state's intervention in housing started in the nineteenth century with slum clearance. If there was bad accommodation housing dirty, poor, dishevelled people, the idea was simply to get rid of it. Later it was considered harsh to take people's homes away without replacing them with something else. So slum clearance led to the provision of council housing.

But was it a good idea to 'clear' those slums in the first place?

One MP got up in the House of Commons and suggested that certain small, mean, unkempt terraced houses should be cleared. They were disgusting. Some of the residents

> 'In a Corporation [council] estate there is an uncomfortable, almost prison-like atmosphere, and the people who live there are perfectly well aware of it.'[2]
>
> **George Orwell, *The Road to Wigan Pier*.**

> **'In perhaps half the cases, I found that the people in Corporation [council] houses don't really like them. They are glad to get out of the stink of the slum ... but they don't really feel at home. ... The typical slum-dwellers miss the frowzy warmth of the slum.'[3]**
>
> **George Orwell, _The Road to Wigan Pier_.**

kept pigs in the basements. The rooms were small and there were plenty of people in each of them.

The usual thing said about slums – often by people who had never actually visited them – was that they were dens of drunkenness and moral laxity. Ironically one of the pictures regularly used in histories of housing to demonstrate the misery, poverty and all-round awfulness of the slums reveals, if one looks closely, a group of men and women dressed perfectly decorously. The women don't seem so drunk that they cannot stand still for the slow process (as it then was) of taking a photograph. Their bodies are fully covered, as strict Victorian morality required. The men are mostly wearing hats and sober expressions.

As it turned out, the mean, disgusting terraced houses the MP referred to, were not cleared and it is now obvious that there would have been no purpose in clearing them. The houses were not particularly well made, it is true. But they were sufficiently well built to be still standing today. The only thing wrong with them was that the people inside were poor. There was no purpose in punishing them for being poor by destroying their homes. The 'slums' were in Notting Hill Gate and formed part of what estate agents now call 'Hillgate Village'. The houses are now considered charming. John Cleese used to live in one. Lord Lamont, the former Chancellor of the Exchequer, currently lives in another. The 'slums' – their essential structure unchanged – now change hands for £700,000 to £1 million.

At this distance of time, there is not enough evidence to assert that all the slum clearance was mis-

The 'slums' of Hillgate Place now exchange hands for between £700,000 and £1 million.

guided. But it is certainly true that some of the clearances were not so very philanthropic and had an element of the middle classes trying to protect themselves from sights and smells that they found offensive. There is also evidence from the modern Third World that even shanty towns are not such a bad thing as people normally assume. John F. C. Turner in his book *Housing by People*[4] told how people have felt good about designing their own homes, building them and then progressively improving them as they could. This has been seen to bring psychological benefits which renting a council flat does not.

But there was another thing the state did apart from slum clearance and subsequent council housing that was far reaching and undoubtedly catastrophic in its effect.

To get an idea of what happened and why, we need to go back to the Second World War and the arrival in Britain of a refugee from Poland. Of course there were many Poles who came to Britain at around that time. The overwhelming majority were a credit to their origins and to their adopted home. But this one turned out differently. He started work very modestly, working for an estate agency in Shepherd's Bush, west London, not far from where the BBC's television studios are now. But Perec – or Peter as he was called in Britain – saw an opportunity to make serious money. He bought the leases of flats with tenants. They did not cost much, for reasons that will become clear. The flats he bought were in Notting Hill, now a fashionable place, but at the time, full of rented properties in a terrible state. After buying the leases, he set about persuading the tenants to leave.

First, he would offer a modest sum of money. If that did not work, he would, for example, let one of the rooms in the building to eight West Indian musicians, telling them that he liked parties. Their noise, if nothing else, would give the other tenants a powerful reason to go. If that still did not work, he got rough. The heavies – ex-wrestlers and boxers – were sent in. Tenants were intimidated and sometimes assaulted. They might have their furniture destroyed. Peter's henchmen would cut off the electricity or the water. They might break the lock or destroy the lavatories. It was terrifying for the tenants. The Peter in question who was inflicting all this misery was, of course, Peter Rachman.

Most references to the story of Rachman do not bother to ask why he behaved as he did. Was he mad? Did he do it for the pleasure of causing pain? What logic was there to his behaviour? Normally, landlords want to keep tenants. So why did Rachman – and others at that time – want to get rid of them instead?

For the answer to that question, we need to go back still further – to Glasgow in 1915. It was the second year of the First World War. The government was organising the manufacture of munitions in Glasgow. This intensified work brought new people into the city and increased rents. Meanwhile, the Labour Party had a particularly strong following in the city. Seen from a Marxist point of view, the rent increases were a simple matter of the bourgeoisie exploiting the working class. And to make it worse, the bourgeoisie were also using workers to fight and die in one of their wars. Glasgow became the centre of a strike in which it was demanded that landlords should not take advantage of the housing shortage to raise rents.

The strike endangered the war effort and politicians feared it would spread, even leading to a neo-communist revolution. The government also included some people sympathetic to the Marxist interpretation (even if they did not wholly subscribe to it). So it rushed through emergency legislation forcing rents back to whatever level they had been at the beginning of the war. This was meant to be a temporary, wartime measure to protect poorer people. Higher rents were excluded. But then, when the war ended, any government which had announced that rents were to be suddenly jacked up would have made itself very unpopular. The talk was of providing 'homes fit for heroes', not of rent hikes. So the law remained for years afterwards and then for decades.

Why was Peter Rachman determined to get rid of his tenants?

The effect was described in *A Social History of Housing*[5], which was sympathetic to the idea of council housing. The Rent and Mortgage Restriction Act of 1915 was described as an 'immediate ... cause of the post-war housing crisis'. The author, Professor John Burnett, explained that 'the fact that rents were now artificially pegged to levels of a vanished age meant that few, if any, speculative builders would come forward to build low-cost houses at uneconomic rents.' Although there was a national housing shortage, he wrote, it was 'concentrated among the lower-paid workers'. The need was mainly for houses rated at not more than £13 a year or £20 in London. But 'these were precisely the kinds of houses which private enterprise could not now be expected to supply.'

In other words, legislation intended to benefit the working class had caused a shortage of housing for that very class. A short-term benefit changed quickly into a long-term crisis for poor people.

In the previous sixty years leading up to 1911, the numbers living in cities had tripled – from 9.7 million to 28.5 million. But the housing had more than kept up. The number of people per dwelling actually fell from 5.46 to 5.05.[6] Burnett remarks in his history that it was 'remarkable' how, in the long term, house-building proceeded as closely in step with demand as it did. The building industry was 'small-scale, traditional ... and in no way equipped to make nice calculations about demographic trends'. Yet it provided housing for nineteen million town dwellers in sixty years, with improved standards.

The damage done to market provision of housing started even before the emergency legislation of 1915. Five years earlier land values duties were introduced. The result was that, whereas about eighty-five thousand new houses had been built each year up to 1910, immediately afterwards the number fell rapidly. In fact, in London, more rooms were destroyed than built between 1911 and 1915.[7]

The rent controls of 1915 were eased a little in 1923 so that the rent would be decontrolled on a change of tenant. But then in 1939, rent controls were made more widespread than before, applying to all properties except those with the highest value. It even applied to newly built properties. The result was a prolonged decline of rented housing in Britain. At the beginning of the century, most people rented their homes. As late as 1961, rented property still accounted for 32 per cent of households. The decline continued far below the proportion in most advanced countries. It was fast and relentless. At the bottom, rented property accounted for a mere 9.5 per cent of homes. The rental sector had been all but destroyed.

This brings us back to the question posed earlier: why did Peter Rachman, the notorious landlord, do every vile thing in his power to get his tenants to leave? It was because the tenants in the flats were on rents fixed by either the 1915 or the 1939 rent Acts. The rents were now far below the open market level. The tenants were getting an absolute bargain and the landlords had effectively lost their money. A building with flats let at tiny, controlled rents was worth virtually nothing since the tenants could not legally be made to leave. Landlords were left with no reason to improve or even maintain the properties. So buildings that had once been good, or even grand, became slums. The rents were so low that tenants hung on in them all the same. Never mind that they might have reason to move to another part of town or to move into a house to start a family. It was financial madness to give up a rent-controlled flat. So they stayed and civilised landlords just gave up – depressed and effectively robbed. They sometimes sold. That was when someone like Peter Rachman had his chance. If he could get the sitting tenants out, the value of the property would be transformed. He could relet to new tenants at the market price or sell the property using the magic words 'with vacant possession'.

The rent Acts thus created new slums where there had been none before. The Acts gave rise to Rachman and his like. Rachman is sometimes wrongly cited as a vicious example of capitalism. He is actually a vicious example of what happens when the state blunders into the market place. The unhappiness caused by the state through the rent Acts is hard to comprehend, so extensive and persistent was it.

The decline of rented accommodation was also not, as sometimes suggested, just a matter of people deciding they preferred direct ownership – though they often did. It was government destruction of a kind of housing tenure which suited many millions. At last, in 1987, the law was changed allowing landlords to evict tenants again and charge market rents. As a result, rented accommodation has begun to grow again. The state-induced nightmare has begun to disappear.

Where we have lived

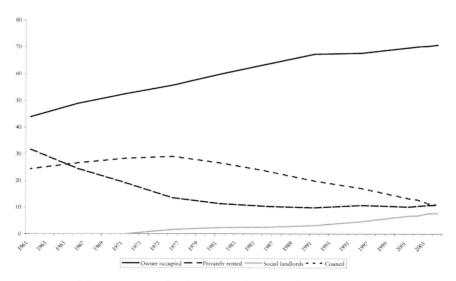

Dwelling stock by tenure in England. The 1961 figure was for 1 April, the figures for 1966 to 1986 were for 31 December and the remaining figures were for 31 March. The figures for England have been used instead of those for Great Britain because there is a longer statistical series.
Source: Office of the Deputy Prime Minister.

One effect of the shortage of rented accommodation which the state caused was that people were all the more dependent on housing provided by the state: council housing – the main focus of this chapter.

After the Second World War, the Labour government strongly pushed ahead with new council housing. Unfortunately, the quantity of new housing it was able to build was far below what it had expected. Meanwhile the government also made it hard for the private sector to fill the gap. Not only was there rent control – inhibiting the creation of building for buy-to-let investors – but the private sector was rationed in obtaining building supplies. Builders also needed to get licences. As a result of all this, despite all the propaganda about building homes, fewer dwellings were constructed than after the First World War. The Conservatives, when they came to power, freed up the private sector a good deal but still pursued council house-building as fast as possible. How did this great post-war emphasis on council building work out?

One day in 1959, the leaders of the council in Birkenhead woke up and looked forward to a great event, a landmark moment in the history of their area: the opening of a major new housing project. They would have the satisfaction of doing good – delivering brand new homes to families who would probably otherwise be living in slums. They would be giving them something special: the latest, most modern thing – flats in three ten-storey blocks. The height was impressive by the standards of the time. The government in Whitehall was encouraging these high blocks. There were good reasons – most obviously that by building upwards, a given amount of land could yield more accommodation and, at the same time, wide open spaces at the bottom – far more spacious than the tiny backyards of old Victorian terrace houses. The councillors undoubtedly felt a sense of civic pride. The design was considered so good it was circulated to other local authorities as a model. This was a triumphant day to be a civic leader in Birkenhead.

But after the local newspaper reporters had filed their stories, the life of those three ten-storey blocks did not continue as everyone hoped and expected. The common parts became dirty and unpleasant. The lifts were fouled and jammed.[8] Windows were smashed. Sabotage of the electrical system caused black-outs. Sabotage of the fire-fighting equipment caused floods. Fires were started. Tenants began not to feel safe, let alone happy. The spiral of decline reached the point where nobody wanted to live there at all.

Fifteen years after that auspicious, hopeful day in 1959, the three blocks were completely empty. Five years after that, in 1979, the burghers of Birkenhead invited observers from other local authorities to witness another, very different civic event. This time, they invited their colleagues from other councils to see the same three ten-storey blocks being blown up.

The blowing up of the Birkenhead flats in 1979 appears to be the first occasion on which council blocks in Britain were destroyed. It was not the last by a long way. Among the many estates to be totally destroyed in following years was Hunslet Grange in Liverpool. The residents of the Netherley estate, also in Liverpool, campaigned for five years to have their estate flattened. In 2000, Birmingham announced that it intended to demolish three hundred of its tower blocks.

Some of the many council tower blocks that have been demolished. These ones were in Hackney.

Total destruction, by its nature, is an acknowledgement of failure. It says, 'This estate has not merely done badly; it has done disastrously. We confess that the public money spent on it was wasted. We don't even pretend that with a little reform here or there it could be put right.' But for every council estate where failure was admitted this way, there were – and still are – many other failing estates. The Department of the Environment even developed a term for it: estates were designated 'difficult to let'. One that became 'difficult to let' was Everton Heights, in Liverpool – better known as 'The Piggeries' – built in 1966. The three blocks rose even higher – to fifteen storeys. At the time, the greater the height, the more prestigious and modern the building was considered to be. Within twelve years the Piggeries were completely wrecked. No one wanted to live there. They were offered for sale to any taker on a 99-year lease. It took three years before they were sold. They were eventually demolished.

Sometimes estates moved from being 'great works of the welfare state' to 'complete disasters and wastes of public money' astonishingly quickly. The Divis flats on the Falls Road in Belfast were completed in 1972 and were dubbed 'the youngest slum in Europe' the very next year. The Noble Street estate in Newcastle, built between 1956 and 1958, was 'from its inception, the most notorious street in Newcastle'.[9] The Broadwater Farm estate in north London, built between 1967 and 1970, was classed as 'difficult to let' three years later. Eventually it degenerated into a no-go area even for the police. Then, in 1985, a particularly serious riot took place. One of the policemen sent in to quell it, PC Keith Blakelock, was knifed to death.

The North Peckham estate in south London became afflicted by gangs of youths or, rather, children. One local mother said,

Just a few months ago, around 3.25 p.m., I was in my flat when I heard the most terrible racket outside. I looked out to see what on earth was going on. And saw a gang of teenage girls from Warwick Park and Waverley School outside on the green.

It started as a fight between two girls. By the end there were forty or fifty of them there and I have never seen weapons like the ones they had in my life. They had baseball bats, knives and clubs, and they were girls.

This was the estate where Damilola Taylor, a charming, hard-working boy who had only recently come to England, was attacked and bled to death in 2000.

Of course not all estates have ended up this way. But this kind of result has been widespread and well documented – as we shall see. The gap between what reformers expected from council housing and what has actually taken place is vast. Workers who moved into council houses and flats often did not live the bright, cheerful, clean lives that well-meaning politicians expected. Something went wrong. But what? What was the problem?

What went wrong?

We have already been offered one idea of what went wrong. Michael Young and Peter Willmott showed how extended families were broken up. The network of family relationships had been a kind of social cement which was dissolved when extended families were separated by new council housing. Several other studies have testified to the great importance of this.[10] What else contributed to the way so much council housing went to the bad?

Ten years after the destruction of the Birkenhead tower blocks, Alice Coleman, an academic at London University, set out to suggest a second reason why council housing kept on failing. She studied the part that design might have taken. The project was massive. It took five years and was the work of up to six people. They studied 4,099 blocks of flats containing 106,520 homes and of course many more people.[11] For good measure, they threw in 4,172 houses, too. The flats and houses they studied were mostly in the London boroughs of Southwark and Tower Hamlets – therefore including council housing in Bethnal Green, where Young and Willmott had trod the streets a generation before. They also included the North Peckham estate, where Damilola Taylor would be murdered two decades later.

Coleman put forward fifteen different aspects of design which she thought might contribute to the decline of an estate. These included the use of walkways above ground level, the raising of blocks of flats on stilts, the number of storeys in the blocks and so on. She and her team went to all 4,099 blocks, noting down their features. They also tried to measure the degree to which each estate had degenerated. They noted the amount of vandalism, litter and graffiti. They looked at the amount of excrement on each estate and, after their initial work, decided they should subdivide it into the separate categories of urine and faeces – not very pleasant work. They discovered the number of children taken into care on each estate.

At the end of this enormous exercise, they collected together the thousands of figures they had amassed. The results were overwhelming. The association between certain design features and the degeneration of an estate was astonishingly close. You could pretty well predict how bad an estate would be simply by getting a list of its design features. The more pronounced the feature, the worse condition a block would be in. Coleman developed a league table of bad design. At the top was

THE RISE AND FALL OF COUNCIL HOUSING

1845–1914: 'Five per cent philanthropy' – philanthropic building of housing for the working classes. They reach four per cent of dwellings in 1885. Massive building of private housing which more than keeps up with the rapid growth of population

1851: First act allowing local councils to provide housing

1868: Torrens Act gives councils the right to demolish individual 'unfit' houses. In one case, local rents double after demolition

1875: Councils permitted to clear whole areas of 'unfit' housing

1890–1914: Ten per cent of new homes built by councils

1915: Glasgow strike against rent rises leads to the introduction of controlled private rents as a 'temporary' measure

1919: Councils given duty to provide housing and central subsidy to pay for it. Another 'temporary' measure

1919–39: Councils build over 1.3 million dwellings. Council dwellings rise to more than ten per cent of total housing stock

1939: Council tenants' rent strike in Birmingham against increasing rents for better-off tenants so as to offer rebates to poorer ones. Rent controls on all except the highest-value private property

1945–51: Boost to council house-building created by Aneurin Bevan. Eighty per cent of all new dwellings built by councils. But the new building falls well short of the numbers planned and is as much as two-thirds over budget. Private sector restricted by rationing on building materials and licensing of builders. Fewer dwellings built than after the First World War

1957: Publication of Young and Willmott report on how people formerly living in 'slums' in Bethnal Green lost the support of their families through being moved to council housing in the suburbs. Other similar reports

1965–72: Construction of North Peckham estate in London

1966: Construction of 'the Piggeries' in Liverpool

1977: Councils provide twenty-nine per cent of all dwellings in England, the all-time peak

1979: First demolition of a council tower block takes place, in Birkenhead

1980: Council tenants given right to buy. During the next ten years, 1.5 million council dwellings are sold. Controls on private rent eased, leading to the beginning of the recovery of the rented sector

1985: Backlog of repairs needed to council housing estimated at £19 billion. Murder of a policeman on the Broadwater Farm estate, London

1987: New laws on private renting give greater freedom to charge rents and enforce eviction of tenants, leading to further recovery of the rental market. 'Buy to let' begins to develop as a common way of investing

2000: Councils apply to transfer three hundred thousand dwellings to 'social landlords' to avoid further liability for repairs. Damilola Taylor murdered on North Peckham estate; a £260 million demolition and redevelopment programme gets under way

1997–2002: New Labour government continues to let state-subsidised housing decline as a percentage of all housing. Council housing falls to 14.5 per cent of all dwellings in 2001 and social-landlord housing reaches 6.5 per cent

the feature most likely to lead to vandalism, graffiti and the rest. It was a single entrance leading to many dwellings.

This is not surprising if one imagines living in such a place. If you have an entrance shared by a thousand people, they will not know each other even to nod to. They will not know who has real business in the entrance way and who is an intruder. Even if they suspect someone is up to no good, they will not feel it is their own space which they can ever hope to defend. This lies at the root of a breakdown in how safe a place feels and how safe it actually is, too. Coleman and her researchers found that if a block was finely subdivided, creating entrances for fewer dwellings, it was only half as likely to be abused as even the smallest blocks where there was no such subdivision.

Next in the league table of design features was the number of dwellings in any particular block – pretty much a measurement of the same sort of thing. Next came the number of storeys per block. Again, the more storeys, the more people coming and going who will not know each other. The use of overhead walkways was another major factor. These walkways could be used as escape routes for vandals and criminals. They created areas which were neither properly public nor clearly private. That too is what is meant by the number five in the league table of design features. Bad 'spatial organisation' is the design of spaces which, again, are neither public nor private. It could be an area of land between three or four blocks of flats. It does not belong to one family or even one block. No one is responsible for it and no one feels able to defend it from the encroachment of litter, graffiti and damage.

> 'I have been here two years and I hate it ... People throw bottles, fish, condoms and other rubbish out of windows and it lands on the porch roof outside my window.'[12]
>
> **Donna Barron, resident of Grayson Heights, in Leeds**

You might have thought that after Coleman had done her extraordinary research effort and showed the government the figures that, horrified, they would have mended their ways. Not a bit of it. On the contrary, the reaction she met was wholesale denial. The ministry would not accept that design was any part of the problem. It blamed the tenants. This, too, is not so surprising if you imagine yourself as one of the civil servants involved. For the past generation you and your colleagues have been superintending the design of council housing. How keen are you

Why have so many council estates become miserable, graffiti-ridden places that are 'difficult to let'?

to admit that you have made serious mistakes? The question only needs to be asked for the answer to be obvious. It would also have been a dramatic volte-face for the government to accept the central and most radical recommendation which Coleman made: a complete stop to the building of council flats at all. The record of houses was so very much better.

Alice Coleman made a strong case that bad design was an important factor in the failure of council housing. But why was it designed badly?

Almost incidentally to the study she was making, Coleman took a sideways look at housing produced by the private sector. She recorded the design features of privately owned flats in Southwark in the same way as she had done for the council homes. After doing her studies of how bad design affected behaviour, she had created a design 'disadvantagement score'. Her finding was that the design disadvantagement score for privately owned blocks was 4.0 – less than half the disadvantagement score of 9.1 for council housing in the same area.

Where would you *least* like to live?

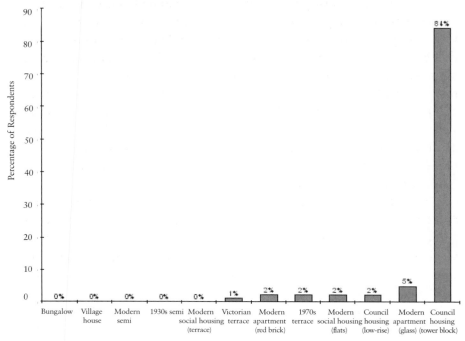

In 2002, more than one thousand people were interviewed in random locations and asked what kind of housing they would least like to live in. Source: MORI

Coleman remarked, 'Market forces appear to be a positive power for good in housing design.' She went on to offer an explanation which is a classic of how and why the private sector often provides a better service than well-meaning public servants. 'Private builders', she wrote, 'cannot survive unless they can profitably meet both the tastes and the price range of purchasers. Designs which sell quickly tend to be repeated, while those that hang fire are discontinued.' This, she explained, was what had led the private sector to produce mostly small, low-rise blocks subdivided into sections with few dwellings per entrance – exactly the sort of blocks least likely to suffer graffiti, violence and so on. Individuals making thousands of personal decisions were better at selecting good, safe design than all the 'experts' in council offices, Whitehall and the top architectural practices in the country. It is an extraordinary testimonial to the wisdom of the ordinary person – or rather, a powerful testimonial of how people make better decisions when they themselves are going to live with the consequences. Ownership concentrates the mind wonderfully.

Ownership appeared to have other advantages, too. Coleman could not account for the vastly lower rate of graffiti and violence in privately owned blocks entirely by the better design. Something else was at work. Ownership seemed to bring a second benefit. She does not attempt to define it but the benefit is implicit in the psychology of housing which she describes. Many of the bad design features are ones which make it more difficult for humans to exercise their natural instinct to defend and protect their territory. What she does not say, but is surely common sense, is that the instinct to protect and defend territory must be all the greater when a person actually owns it. As long as the territory is rented, it only half-belongs to a person. Once he or she has bought it, commitment to it is all the greater.

When Margaret Thatcher brought in the right to buy council houses and flats, you could see the effect of ownership. Doors were painted a colour chosen by the proud owner, instead of the council. Faulty equipment and damage was not left in place until the council might do something about it. It was repaired as quickly as possible. Action and self-reliance replaced a culture of complaint.

We now have three reasons why council housing got into such trouble. First, the breaking up of families, then the bad design and, third, the absence of the beneficial effect of ownership.

But, for most of the postwar years, the government did not think the real problem lay with any of these things. The real problem, it reckoned, was the people. There were too many children going round in disruptive groups. Government research indicated that the estates with bad problems had a higher ratio of children to adults. The other people blamed by central government were their colleagues in local government. Bureaucrats in Whitehall considered that other bureaucrats, in town halls, were messing things up. They did not look after the estates well enough, they did not do repairs promptly and so on. The views of the civil servants were not wholly without merit. But they were missing the point. The reason so many children were in some blocks was that the government had put them there. As Coleman had showed, if couples with young families made the decision for themselves, they would go for houses rather than flats.

Council estates became places for people already in difficulty: lone mothers whose boyfriends or husbands had left them, those unable to get a good job or people made homeless in one way or another. Such people would probably tend to be less confident and assertive than average about maintaining a clean, law-abiding environment. Many would be on social security benefits which – as we saw in Chapter 2 – can have a demoralising effect on those who receive them. They are less likely to organise neighbours into making sure a community takes control of its own destiny. The people and, in particular, their benefit dependency are surely part of the problem on many council estates.

Council housing was not originally intended for them. It was meant for the working class, with the emphasis on 'working'. Here we come to the most basic of all reasons why council housing was always likely to fail. If it was reserved for the working classes, it was unnecessary. They could look after themselves. If, on the other hand, it was reserved for those really who could not manage, council housing was bound to concentrate despair in one place. Either way, council housing did not make sense.

The failure of many local authorities to look after estates well also goes back to the effect of ownership. People working in local councils were never going to look after homes as well as owners. Ownership transforms people's attitudes and behaviour. This is a systemic fault – not just a matter of some feckless local government officers.

We have now built up six factors which are possible contributions to the problems of council housing: the breaking up of families, revealed by Young and Willmott; bad designs of block of flats, copiously documented by Coleman; the way council housing takes away the positive power of ownership; two ideas promoted by Whitehall in the 1980s – that there are too many children in some blocks and that some local councils look after their estates badly; and the way that council housing tends to bring together people who already in difficulty and who may be demoralised by welfare dependency.

Which of these factors is the most important? Which one stands out? I don't know of an objective way to rank them. Instead, I would point to the one thing which each of these factors has in common. They all originate with the state.

- The state broke up family networks of support.
- The designs were chosen by the state – and would never have been chosen by individuals.
- The state removed personal ownership.
- The state put children in tower blocks.
- The state appointed local authority civil servants to look after the housing.
- The state brought together people with problems and made many of them welfare dependent.

The state, through housing, has done extraordinary damage to people's lives. The state destroyed rental housing with the rent Acts of 1915 and 1939, creating – quite unnecessarily – new slums and slum landlords like Peter Rachman. Because of the state, millions of people in Britain over decades could not get rented accommodation. That meant they had to rely all the more on council housing.

The rise and fall of council house-building

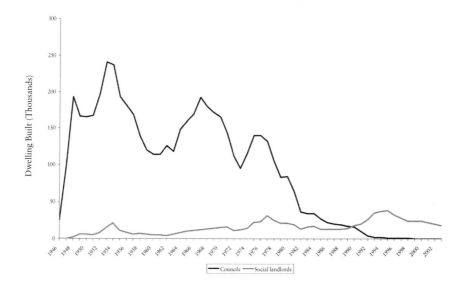

At the peak in 1953, 241,000 council dwellings were built. A generation later, the idea had been almost entirely given up. Only 250 council dwellings were built in 2003.
Source: Office of the Deputy Prime Minister.

Council housing has meant waiting on a council housing list. Those who have finally reached the top of the list have had a serious chance of facing disrepair, graffiti, vandalism and crime. At its worst, council housing has ended up with people living in an estate like that in Birkenhead, which eventually had to be blown up, or it has meant being in the North Peckham estate with its tens of thousands of syringes for drugs, its gangs and the murder of Damilola Taylor.

Council housing has not failed in every case, but it has condemned millions to a sense of hopelessness, to living – literally – alongside urine and faeces, to living with graffiti, to fearing violence and indeed to becoming violent children who end up in prison. Hundreds of thousands of lives have been ruined by state housing. Council housing and rent controls have caused suffering, fear, depression, squalor and violence on a massive scale. This aspect of the welfare state was truly disastrous. It is a blessing that it is being allowed quietly to fade away.

CHAPTER 6

Parenting: Diana and the habits of the apes

At 95, May Chapman was photographed with five succeeding generations of her family. Her daughter-in-law, granddaughter, great-granddaughter, great-great-granddaughter and her little great-great-great-granddaughter – only one year old.[1] Each of the five adult women had given birth to children. But the circumstances of the births were very different.

May Chapman and five generations of her family. The circumstances of the successive births were very different. From the left: Kaye, Shakiri, Christine, May, Sue and Pat.

May herself got married to Albert in 1927 and gave birth to two boys. The older one, Ronald, grew up and, at the age of twenty, married Pat. They had five children during their lives together, the second of which was Sue. Sue changed the pattern. In 1968, she gave birth to Christine without being married. Her mother, Pat, 'hit the roof'. She even wanted the baby to be adopted and said it would 'bring shame on the family'. Despite Pat's anger, Sue kept Christine. But the idea that one should get married was clearly still strong in the family. So soon after she did get married, albeit to a different man. With her new husband she went on to have two more children. Sadly the marriage did not last and they were later divorced.

Christine, the daughter whom Pat refused to give up, repeated the new pattern. She gave birth to Kaye when she was nineteen. The father was a 'boyfriend'. She went on to have three other children by a 'partner'. She has never married. Her daughter Kaye, aged seventeen, gave birth to Shakiri in 2001. The father is another 'boyfriend'. Mention of 'shame' is long gone.

These six generations headed by May Chapman illustrate an astonishing change. Right up to the 1960s, the overwhelming majority of children were born to married parents who nearly all remained married for life. Children were therefore predominantly brought up by two people with three shared characteristics: they were the natural or biological parents, they were married and they stayed together.

First marriages[2]	
1950	340,000
2003	185,000

The situation is very different now. Forty per cent of children are born to parents who are not married. Many of them are cohabiting and some ultimately do get married. But more than two out of five marriages end in divorce and an even higher proportion of cohabitations break up. So how many children are brought up now without one or more of the three characteristics that used to be normal?

At any one time, 21 per cent of children are being brought up by one natural parent alone and 8 per cent of households with dependent children are stepfamilies. So at least 29 per cent of children don't have both their natural parents. Some of the parents of the remainder are not married.

But a snapshot of a single moment in time can be misleading. Many of these children are caught only part-way through their upbringing – some will just have been born. So the proportion who will get through to their sixteenth birthday with both their biological parents still together must be lower – perhaps 60 per cent or less.[4] The proportion who get the full set – natural parents who are married and who stay together throughout – is sure to be down to about half. According to one estimate, it could be as low as 42 per cent. And since out-of-wedlock birth figures and the divorce rate have only recently become so high, inevitably even fewer children are going to get natural, married parenting up to the age of sixteen in the future. It will certainly be a minority. That is a great change, whether one approves or not.

How many relationships split up within five years of having a child?[3]

Already married at birth	8%
Married after birth	25%
Cohabiting	52%

Proportion of relationships that split up within five years of the birth of a child

What was the cause? What happened in the last century – mainly in the past fifty years – to change behaviour so much? Some people might say it has been a 'cultural change'. But that begs the question 'why there has been a cultural change?'

Some think it is just part of the modern world. The idea of marriage has generally been in retreat around the world. But that still does not explain the cause. In any case, the variations between countries are very large. There are sixty-nine divorces for every hundred marriages in Belgium but a mere eleven in the Irish Republic. And the world trend is not as universal and one way as one might assume. The proportion of births outside marriage actually fell – and by quite a large amount – between the late nineteenth century and the late 1960s in Italy, Norway, Portugal, Austria and Spain.[6]

Children living with lone parent	
1972	7%
1981	12%
1991/2	19%
2004	24%

Source: *Social Trends 2002* and *Social Trends 2003*;[5] Office of National Statistics website

Some will argue that women now have greater opportunities for careers outside the home. This, they say, offers women greater independence and therefore they are more willing to break away from a man. The idea has its merits but also one major problem. The new independent earners are not the same women as the ones who are becoming lone, unmarried parents. The women in the vanguard of the lone-parenting revolution are the least well off, most of whom will not take outside work at all while their children are young.

> **Births outside marriage were generally about four of five per cent of all births between 1900 and the early 1960s.[7] They have now reached 40 per cent.**

Could the pill have caused the change? Women can now have sex without fear of conception. This has, perhaps, made them more willing to have sex outside marriage, which, in turn, means that men can get sex more easily than before without marrying a woman. Therefore men have lost one of the reasons why they used to want to get married. This idea, too, has its appeal. But again, it has a flaw. Many women who start bringing up children without the natural father or marriage appear not to be taking the pill.[8]

Does the past provide any clues to the cause of this great change in behaviour? Perhaps. A long time ago, in 1600, when Elizabeth I was on the throne and Shakespeare was alive, it seems that about 3 per cent of births were outside wedlock.[9] Soon after, Cromwell, supported by many fervent Puritans, achieved power and the number of births outside marriage plummeted to a mere one per cent. This suggests that the views and laws passed by a ruling elite can have a powerful effect on the incidence of births outside marriage. With the restoration of Charles II in 1660 – a man who fathered many a child outside his marriage – the illegitimacy rate steadily began to rise again. But it took a century before it passed the previous peak. It continued rising until some time between 1800 and 1850. The exact moment is uncertain because methods of recording such things changed. But by 1850 at the latest, the rate was falling again. It fell from 6.5 per cent down to 4 per cent at the beginning of the twentieth century.

So from the low point during Cromwellian austerity, the rate soared by at least 500 per cent. Then from the high point of illegitimacy in the early nineteenth century, it fell by a third. These were major movements. They all took place before the pill was invented, before the word 'feminism' was coined and before the 'modern world' could have any influence. As for the independent earning power of women, that increased substantially in the second half of the nineteenth century, yet the illegitimacy rate fell.

So what else could possibly explain the rise and fall of illegitimacy between Cromwell and the late nineteenth century?

All sorts of ideas could be put forward. But we can look at what certain people who studied the matter believed in 1833. Royal commissioners investigated the operation and effect of the Poor Laws as they stood at that time (see also Chapter 2). They received reports from all around the country from overseers and others who administered the laws. Why did *they* think women at the time were having so many births outside marriage?

In Holbeach, Lincolnshire, the master of the workhouse told the story of an unmarried girl who was leaving the workhouse after giving birth to her fourth child. As she was leaving, she said to him, 'Well, if I have the good luck to have another child, I shall draw a good sum from the parish; and with what I can earn myself, shall be better off than any married woman in the parish.'

Some while later, the master saw her again and she had got her wish. She was five months pregnant with a fifth child. The master explained the economics of lone parenthood in that parish in the early 1830s. For each of her children born outside marriage she received two shillings a week from the parish. In addition, she would be able to get work paying five shillings a week. So her income could readily amount to fifteen shillings a week. Her income was tripled through her illegitimate children. Her costs were increased, too, but not by as much.

An overseer from a different parish, Battersea, reported that 'as soon as the children can run about' they could be taken into infant schools which charged twopence a week. In other words, five children could be consigned to a school all day for less than a shilling a week.[10]

Several parishes reported their disgust at the fact that they were compelled to pay more to women who had given birth outside wedlock than to married women who had been widowed. A woman in Swaffham, Norfolk, who had seven children outside marriage received two shillings for each of them, making fourteen shillings a week. But if she had been a widow with the same number of children she would have received four or five shillings less.

In theory the fathers of illegitimate children were meant to supply the money for the mother, precisely the same idea Margaret Thatcher had when she created the Child Support Agency. The man was meant to be pursued to support the child he had helped to create. But it did not work out well in practice, said people on the ground. Many men left the area if they were named. Sometimes a poor person – who had no cash he could pay – was named as the father so that the real father could get off scot free. Either way, the parish would have to stump up the money.

Another effect, reported from Bray in Berkshire, was that an unmarried woman who had sex with a man and produced a baby would get either the support of the parish or, if he married her, a husband. It was, in this sense, a 'no lose' situation. Accordingly, there was a high proportion of marriages in which the woman was pregnant – nineteen out of twenty, according to a clergyman at Bulkington in Warwickshire and another at Beckenhill in the same county.

The financial incentives created by the Poor Laws as they stood in the early 1830s were thought to have changed ideas of morality – in other words, to have changed the culture. From Cumberland it was reported that even the daughters of farmers, who would be relatively wealthy and think themselves respectable, would claim an allowance from the parish for children born out of wedlock. Sometimes it would even be claimed by the women's fathers and deducted from their contributions to the poor rates (local taxation). 'Parish aid has a tendency to remove all shame,' commented the correspondent from Cumberland.

Among all the creators of the Poor Laws – and there were many between Henry VIII and 1834 – surely none intended that relief for the poor should 'remove all shame'. They intended alleviation of suffering, yes. But as Christians, they certainly did not intend to encourage what they regarded as sinful. Yet, in Cumberland in the early 1830s, it was believed that their good and kind intentions had resulted in precisely that.

> **'Parish aid has a tendency to remove all shame.'**
>
> **Report from His Majesty's Commissioners for inquiring into the Administration and Practical Operation of The Poor Laws, 1834**

The report of the Royal Commission, published in 1834, shocked the governing class and brought about a fundamental change in policy. The new law – though not always enforced countrywide – was that parish aid could be given only inside the workhouse. The poor, unemployed, incapable, pregnant – whatever it might be – were entitled to benefits only if they went to live and work in the workhouse. It was a draconian change that a modern parliamentary democracy would probably never make. But it provided a real-world experiment. This change would reveal whether the welfare benefits regime could have a major impact on the incidence of births outside wedlock. Did it?

Behavioural change was not instant, but quite quickly, in the second half of the century, out-of-wedlock births fell by a third. It makes sense that the change should not have been instant. Men and women about to indulge in sexual intercourse generally do not make fine calculations about the financial consequences. The culture – what their parents said to them as they grew up, what their teachers and friends said at school – strongly influences whether or not they get to the situation where unprotected, full intercourse might take place. Only over a period of decades do the new financial consequences change the advice which parents, teachers and friends give. In the end though, the 'culture' changed in response to the new, more austere welfare system.

The story of the nineteenth century suggests that a change in welfare benefits can powerfully affect the incidence of lone parenting. Is there any more recent experience which also suggests such an influence?

The welfare plan outlined by William Beveridge in his 1942 report had no special provision for lone parents at all. Everything was based on his idea of compulsory national insurance. The level of payments under his plan was deliberately intended to be a 'minimum' for 'subsistence'. But even this minimum could only be obtained by making contributions over a period of time to qualify. If you had made the necessary contributions, you could claim benefits only on becoming unemployed or incapable of work, or on reaching pensionable age. A lone parent would probably fit into none of these categories. So a lone parent would probably get no national insurance but have to rely, instead, on national assistance. National assistance benefits were intended to be even less generous. Beveridge said national assistance must be felt to be less desirable than the insurance scheme 'otherwise the insured persons would get nothing for their contributions'.

National assistance would only be given 'subject to proof of needs and examination of means'. Beveridge was keen, too, that people should genuinely and effectively be seeking work, so national assistance was to be 'subject also to any conditions as to behaviour which may seem likely to hasten restoration of earning capacity' (s369).

For lone parents – particularly teenage mothers – this was nothing like the benefits of today. 'Examination of means' would include the family and home in which she was being raised. She would be expected to stay in that home. That indeed, is what many young *married* people did, let alone unmarried girls. For an unmarried teenager in 1950 there was no council flat, no rent rebate, no rate rebate, no housing benefit or anything of that sort at all. There would probably be little or no national assistance. The burden of supporting her and her child fell, above all, on her family.

One can imagine that the father and mother of an unmarried teenager who got pregnant would not be at all pleased. Instead of their daughter marrying a man who would support her, the mother and father would have to support her themselves for years to come – and the new baby, too. Their home would probably become crowded if it was not already. They might also, very probably, be furious with the young man who made her pregnant. It is easy to believe that the financial realities created a culture in which having children outside marriage was thoroughly disapproved of.

What about married parents bringing up children? How was that kind of family supported – or penalised?

They received no benefits and neither were they penalised. The state was not involved except in those cases where a family obtained subsidised council housing. Even then, the subsidy was relatively modest at that time. As for penalties, a family on average income or less with a couple of children paid no income tax at all. The personal allowance – the amount of income on which no tax is paid – was relatively large and there was a married-couples allowance and tax allowances for each of the children.

Generous tax allowances used to lift most families with children completely out of income tax

Average earnings for male manual worker	£363
Family allowance (two children)	£13
Total taxable income	£376
less	
2/5 of earnings relief	£145
Married couple's allowance	£180
Tax allowance for two children (2 x £60)	£120
Total reliefs/allowances	£445
Income liable to tax	zero

Based on the average weekly earnings of a male manual worker in April 1949 and on the taxes and benefits of 1948–50[11]

The typical working man and his wife in 1950 lived an income tax-free existence. They could keep every penny they earned. This simple fact made the two-parent family eminently viable. It had every chance of success because it was not hindered. It was not given special advantages of any great size. It was just left alone.

Now, more than fifty years later, the situation has dramatically changed. A lone parent is likely to receive, sooner or later, free accommodation. She – it is predominantly a she – will get a council house or a flat, a place in a hostel or 'bed and breakfast' accommodation on a temporary basis. In due course, there is a good chance she will eventually get a flat or a house. The rent will be paid for her. So will the council tax. She will not be required to seek work until the children are aged sixteen. Her children will get free milk and school lunches. She will get free prescriptions, free glasses or contact lenses, free dental work, a Sure Start maternity grant of £500 and, if she takes part-time work, a childcare subsidy of £67.50 per week for one child or £100 for two or more. She will receive cash in the form of income support, the level of which will depend on a wide variety of adjustments. She will also get child benefit.

Meanwhile the situation of a working couple bringing up children has also changed dramatically. They face income tax whereas in the 1940s they did not. They may be given some of their tax back, but only some.[13] And only a minority of such parents will get the free housing and 'passport' benefits received by a lone parent.

So since 1950, the relative positions of a lone parent bringing up children and a couple doing the same have been transformed. Lone parents used to get nothing and now get a great deal. Working couples used to face no income tax but now they are caught in the tax net even if they earn well below average incomes. The state has even brought about a situation where, in some cases, two parents are considerably better off living apart than together.

How income tax spread to the poor

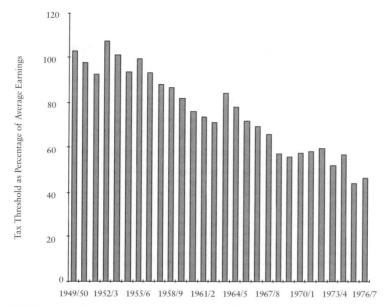

In 1949/50, a married couple with two young children paid no income tax at all if they were on an average income. Gradually governments levied income tax on couples with lower and lower incomes. By 1975/6, under a Labour government, such couples earning only half average incomes were liable to tax. It has been politically easy to let inflation silently reduce tax-free allowances. Newspapers, television and politicians concentrate on rates of income tax and rarely notice personal allowances.
Source: Hansard, 19 May 1976.[12]

Tracy Goodheart[14] became pregnant by her boyfriend when she was nineteen. The boyfriend, Bob Meanwell, made himself scarce as soon as he heard. He did not want the 'commitment'. But they continued to live in the same district and gradually, after the baby was born, they

The change from non-interference to heavy interference

	1950	2003
Lone parents	State offers little or no cash	State pays income support
	State may offer subsidised housing	State usually offers free housing
		State provides 'passport' benefits
Two-parent families	State may offer subsidised housing	State levies tax on income

began to re-establish contact. By June 2001, Tracy had got a council flat while Bob was still living with his parents, rent free. He sometimes went round to visit Tracy and played with their baby, Eve. He thought he might like to get together with Tracy after all and even marry her.

But then they did some calculations. If Bob married and moved in with Tracy, she would lose housing benefit of £45.60 a week. Tracy would also lose her income support of £86.30 a week. It would actually cost them money to get married – a net £65.82 a week. That sum may not seem very large to some. But it is very serious money to them – 28 per cent of their cash income. Tracy and Bob would be penalised by the state for getting married. This is a fictional story but the figures are all too real.

The state's impact is not always so negative but in most situations the state has inadvertently arranged for there to be some disadvantage to marrying or even cohabiting.

This is why, in recent times, we have had a second experiment. Since 1950, benefits for lone parents have been very substantially increased and working couples who used not to be taxed now are taxed.[15] Has this had any impact? It certainly looks that way. In 1950 most children were brought up by their natural married parents. Now the proportion is falling below 50 per cent. It would seem likely that, once again, a change in welfare benefits has changed the culture of bringing up children outside wedlock just as it had (in the opposite direction) in the nineteenth century.

If Bob married Tracy

	Living apart	Married
Earnings (Bob)	£143.50	£143.50
Income tax (Bob)	(£8.05)	(£8.05)
National insurance (Bob)	(£5.65)	(£5.65)
Rent and council tax	(£56.00)	(£59.30)
Children's tax credit	0	£8.05
Working families' tax credit	0	£71.73
Child benefit	£15.50	£15.50
Housing benefit (Tracy)	£45.60	0
Council tax benefit (Tracy)	£10.40	0
Income support (Tracy)	£86.30	0
TOTAL	£231.60	£165.78

Cost to the couple of getting married = £65.82 a week (28% of their previous income).

But there will still be some who think that cultural change – whatever its cause might have been – came first and that change in welfare benefits and tax merely followed and reinforced that change.

Richard Burton and Elizabeth Taylor divorced twice. Has the elite led the lone-parenting boom?

There is one way of testing. If culture were the prime mover, rich and poor would be likely to participate in a similar way. In fact the rich would probably lead the change and be the ones who became lone parents most frequently. This, in fact, is what is argued by some commentators who have said that writers and upper-middle-class people such as members of the Bloomsbury Group, D. H. Lawrence and, after the war, people such as Antonia Fraser, who left her husband for Harold Pinter, and Elizabeth Taylor, who became a child star in 1944 and got her first (of eight) divorces in 1951, led the way, creating moral precedents for the less well off.

Has the elite led the lone-parenting boom? Certainly not among teenagers. According to an analysis of the government's Family and Working Lives Survey in 1994/5, only 2 per cent of women whose fathers are top professionals became teenage mothers at that time.[16] The incidence of teenage mothering among the elite turns out to be tiny. But among the girls whose fathers are unskilled workers, 23 per cent became teenage mothers. The lowest socio-economic classes are eleven times more likely to have babies in their teenage years – normally outside marriage. These young mothers then go on to constitute 31 per cent of all lone parents.

What about divorce? Has the elite led a 'culture' of divorce? It does not seem so. According to a study of

Class and teenage motherhood	
Social class	Rate of teenage motherhood (%)
A	2
B	5
C1	7
C2	12
D	13
E	23

Social class of the teenage girl's father when she was 14

Source: Karen Rowlingson, 'The Social, Economic and Demographic Profile of Lone Parents'[17]

divorce made by the government in 1984, the divorce rate among the least well off is more than four times higher than among the socio-economic elite.[18]

The poor divorce much more

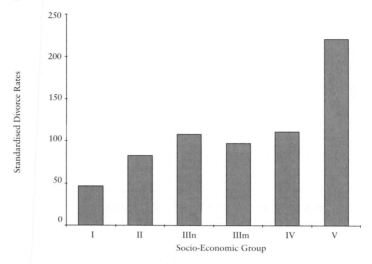

Source: J. Haskey, 'Social Class and Socio-economic Differentials in Divorce in England and Wales'[19]

Some may think that there is something about those who are poor which makes them inherently more likely to divorce. But historically, divorce has actually been more common among the rich. Up until recent times, divorce was something that only the rich would undertake. Only they could afford the proceedings and the expense of maintaining separate homes. Henry VIII could indulge himself with six wives because he was the richest and most powerful man in the country. But poor men and women had to stick together with more determination. The welfare state has turned all that on its head so that now the financial effect of divorce is least bad for the poorest and, correspondingly, most common among them.

The elite has not led the cultural change so it seems clear that the state, by taxing married couples and giving money and other benefits to lone parents, actually created the cultural change which primarily affects the less well off. The welfare state created the lone-parenting boom.

Some will object: 'Surely you are not saying that people deliberately become lone parents just to get a council flat and benefits?'

The divorce boom

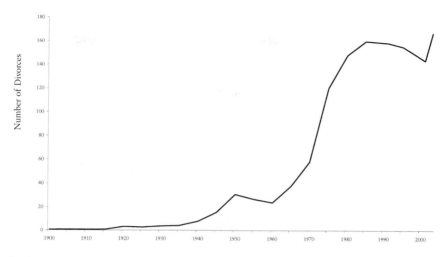

The divorce boom got going from 1960, in parallel with the rising tax on married couples with children and rising benefits for lone parents. The recent decline from the peak is only because there are now fewer marriages left to break up.[20]
Source: Office of National Statistics.[21] England and Wales only

No. While there is some anecdotal evidence that this takes place, there is not enough other evidence to be conclusive. However, it is reasonable to surmise that many less well-off young women end up becoming pregnant because they – and their parents – know at the back of their minds that the state will, in all probability, pick up the tab.

'My father told me that welfare is probably the worst thing that ever ... happened to black people. There was a time, after slavery, when a black man was as likely to have a child within the confines of marriage as was a white man. Look at the census data ... What happened? We launched Lyndon Johnson's War on Poverty, essentially going door to door and encouraging people to get on welfare. ... Fast forward to the year 2000: nearly 70 per cent of today's black children are born out of wedlock.'[22]

Larry Elder, author of _The Ten Things You Can't Say in America_.

That knowledge is likely to change how they think and what their mothers say to them as they grow up. Instead of saying 'Don't, for heaven's sake, get pregnant. It would be a disaster', any warnings offered are likely to be made in more moderate terms.

Similarly boys are probably not warned against getting girls pregnant in the way they once were. Parents don't tell them it would be immoral to ruin a girl's life by getting her pregnant without marrying her because they know that the girl will not, in fact, be ruined. Unmarried parenting will not be – or rather will not be perceived to be – a disaster for her.

An international study of the influence of welfare benefits on the number of single parents concluded that a ten per cent increase in benefits could increase the prevalence of single mothers by 17 per cent.[23]

Those who accept that the welfare state has played the leading role in creating the lone-parenting and divorce epidemics of the past fifty years still have one crucial question to consider: does it matter?

Who cares if the welfare state created a lone-parenting boom? You could call it a by-product of trying to look after the poor – an innocuous cultural change in a worthy cause. Many people argue there is

---

THE LONE-PARENT CULTURE

'I became fully aware of the attractions of early pregnancy to many girls when teaching in Wythenshawe in the early 1980s ... For girls in the middle and lower streams of a large comprehensive, getting pregnant was the first simple step in the process which would solve all their perceived problems:

1. it gave you a perfect excuse for doing no school work.

2. it would give you a flat of your own – infinitely preferable to the 'prison' of the run-down council house which your extended family occupied in Benchill.

3. it would automatically guarantee the respect of your peers: there was great pressure to choose this life-style and older sisters and friends were models.

I made something of a 'study group' of the girls in my form who left in the summer of 1985 ... Within two years of leaving school, of the 14 girls in my group, all but one had had a baby and two were about to give birth again. None were married. About 90 per cent of them had been provided with council flats. None of them had a resident male.'

Mr E. C. Mackrill, former teacher, Birchwood, Cheshire[24]

nothing wrong with lone parenting. There are positive advantages. The mother and father can see who they like instead of being stuck with a spouse who may infuriate them. The children might be better off too, it can be argued, without their parents fighting each other. In any case, all types of family are 'valid'.

It is true that some separated parents are happier than they would have been together. Sometimes the children are happier, too. But we need to ask: are such cases the general rule or the exceptions?

In the early 1980s, 404 mothers in Islington were interviewed by social scientists at London University to discover their state of mind and – in particular – whether or not they suffered from clinical depression.[25] Their conclusion was that the risk of an onset of depression was 7.9 per cent among women who were married but 16 per cent among the single mothers. Single mothers were twice as likely to suffer serious depression.

The researchers were so struck by the extent of the extra unhappiness among single mothers that they suggested the rising number of single mothers in Britain may have 'raised the prevalence of depression in the population at large'. The average level of misery

> 'Many out-of-work lone parents experience a malign spiral of hardship, poor health and low morale ... The experience of the 1991 cohort was particularly interesting. They started out in 1991 somewhat healthier than other British women of a similar age. Then their health deteriorated until a third were suffering long-term problems by 1998. Part of this deterioration appeared to have its origins in injury sustained during separation from violent partners, and part was connected to poor health behaviour, including high rates of smoking.'[26]
>
> Alan March, 'Helping British Lone Parents Get and Keep Paid Work'.

throughout Britain could well increase solely because so many more people were becoming single mothers and because single mothers are so prone to depression.

Why should lone parents be so prone to depression?

One reason is money. As we have already seen, lone parents tend to be from the poorer end of society in the first place. Many expect that life on benefits with their child will not be too bad and that it has some advantages. They may see friends in the same position. But the initial acceptability of lone parenthood turns out to be a trap – a bait which lures them into a relatively poor social and financial situation over the long term.

Lone parenting on benefits provides little opportunity to rise above a very low standard of living. For a teenager, the money from welfare may seem better than pocket money. But it does not go up. It remains low while the lone parent sees friends and relations who have married and/or who are working achieve a gradually rising standard of living.

The Department of Social Security, in 1995, surveyed lone parents about how they felt about money. One of the questions asked was: 'Have you been worried about money in the past few weeks?' The answers were desperately sad. Approaching half of them said they were worried 'almost all of the time'.

Household incomes of lone mothers are very low far more often than those of married couples. Single mothers are five times more likely than married couples to have a household income of £150 a week or less. Of course the figures are affected by the fact that the poor are more likely to become single mothers than wealthier people in the first place. It is also true that a married couple naturally needs more money and potentially there are two adults who can bring in money instead of only one. But the figures are so dramatic that it seems inescapable that lone motherhood is a route to being poor over a long period.

Worried about money in the past few weeks?

Almost all the time	45%
Quite often	22%
Only sometimes	23%
Never	10%

Survey of Lone Parents. Source: Department of Social Security Research Report No. 40, 1995.

Who is poor?

Married couples	10%
Cohabiting couples	15%
Separated mothers	26%
Divorced mothers	28%
Single mothers	51%

Proportion with a usual weekly household income of £150 or less

Source: *Living in Britain*[27]

Even cohabiting does not bring the financial security of marriage. The chances of a couple being seriously poor are 50 per cent higher if they are not married. It seems that marriage, over the long term, is the route to financial security while lone parenting or cohabiting means – in hundreds of thousands of cases – being persistently less well off. That is likely to contribute to making lone parents depressed.

But lone parents have other reasons to be depressed, too.

Many psychologists believe that contentment depends on satisfying two needs: status and emotional attach-ments. Most lone parents in Britain do not have a job. They depend on benefits. That is bad for anyone's sense of self-esteem. Someone who is poor, but paying their own way, feels better about themselves. Work is also likely to involve personal interactions in which the worker has a recognised role. A lone mother claiming benefits, however, plays only one role repeatedly – that of a supplicant.

Most lone parents have cohabited or been married before becoming a lone parent. So being a lone parent usually means having experienced a major break-up of an emotional attachment. After some months or a few years, many will have a new boyfriend or girlfriend. They may cohabit again. But, if so, they have a higher than average risk of a second break-up. Instead of deriving a sense of stability and contentment from one persistent attachment, they may well have a series of partings.

Oliver James, the psychologist, said:

We have inherited a tendency to develop warm feeling and intimate relationship and ... if we do not, we are penalised by loneliness and ill health. Unfortunately. we divorce and separate from our partners vastly more than in 1950. The collapse of marriage and of the close social networks that characterized our ancestors is a major cause of ... depression, aggression, compulsions. It is partic-ularly visible among young women today.[28]

Then there is the violence.

Samantha Bottarelli, a lone parent, met Terence Le Page and thought he was 'lovely'. After only four months, he moved in with her and her little girl. They did not get married. After a while, he began to give Samantha a shove now and again. Then he started hitting her. After that, 'he was constantly threatening me with knives, saying if I push him I was going to get it.' Samantha went to the police – several times. There was plenty of scope for her to pursue charges against him. But she did not go through with it. Terence's family persuaded her not to.

> 'We have been losing each other so fre-quently that, in terms of the emo-tional effects, it is as if we have been living through a psy-chological Third World War.'[29]
>
> **Oliver James,**
> ***Britain on the Couch***

The violence continued until she couldn't face any more. She gathered all her resolution and finally walked out in

April 2000. Then she agreed to meet him again. She took the precaution of meeting him at the home of his parents. But 'Terry lunged at me with the knife.' A picture of her afterwards shows one cut all the way from near the middle of her back to the side of her right breast. There were other cuts and scratches, too, a bandage on her neck and another very large one over another part of her back. She was taken to hospital. She lost one of the arteries going to her heart, leaving her with three instead of four. She lost five pints of blood.

This grim story was one of four cases of women being injured by men that appeared in the *Sun* on 30 May 2003. The newspaper did not draw attention to whether or not the women were married. But on reading the stories carefully, it becomes clear that three out of the four women were unmarried. Is that just chance? Or does it reflect something about reality?

The British Crime Survey of 2001 looked at how likely adults were to be subject to domestic violence.[30] For married people there was a tiny 0.2 per cent risk. Those who cohabited were more than five times as likely to be victims, with a 1.1 per cent risk. Single people and the divorced were in still greater danger – seven and nine and a half times more at risk respectively than married people. Those described as separated were the most at risk, being more than twenty times more likely to suffer domestic violence. No condition was anything like as safe as being married.

That series of figures does not precisely pick out the risks attaching to lone parents. Nor does it exclude other factors which might influence a person's risks. More detailed analysis was done by the US Department of Health and Human Services in 1994.[31] Researchers tried to identify the strongest 'predictor' of someone being abused. They looked at race, age, education and housing conditions. Each has an impact on the likelihood of someone being hurt. What was the strongest predictor? Whether or not they were married. One finding was particu-

> **MARRIED MEN LIVE HAPPIER, HEALTHIER LIVES THAN THOSE WHO STAY SINGLE**
>
> Ninety per cent of married men who are alive at forty-eight will still be alive at sixty-five, compared to only sixty per cent of single men. Married men are half as likely to commit suicide as single men.
> Single men drink twice as much as married men of the same age.[32]
>
> **Source: Linda Waite and Maggie Gallagher, *The Case for Marriage***

larly chilling. Unmarried women were three to four times more likely than married women to be physically abused by their boyfriends while pregnant.

The evidence that lone parents – and indeed those who cohabit – are more likely to be victims of violence is worldwide, consistent and overwhelming.

What about the children? Are they, at least, just as well off being brought up by a lone parent or cohabiting parents?

They are certainly poorer on average. Lone parents are poorer so, inevitably, their children are poorer, too. It is not surprising, therefore, that the proportion of children who are relatively poor has risen in parallel with the increase in lone parenting. If this had been brought about by an open government edict, it would have been a scandal. The headlines would have been 'Government puts children in poverty' or 'Children to be brought up in homes on benefits.' This has, in effect, been the result of government actions. Governments encouraged lone parenting and the children of lone parents are relatively poor. So governments arranged things so more children would be brought up in relative poverty. There has been no scandal about it, but there should have been. As a result of the welfare state, children are now brought up in homes which are poorer, compared to the average, than ever before in British history.

Unmarried parenting leading to children being relatively poor

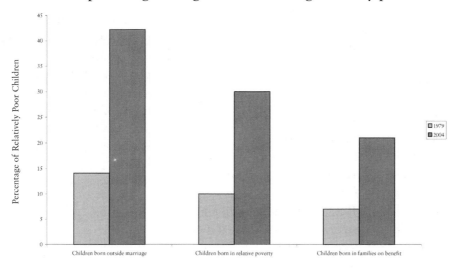

Sources: *Social Trends 34*, Office for National Statistics, Department for Work and Pensions

There is no crime in being poor, of course. Children can be brought up in poor families better than in rich ones. They can be happier, do better at school, achieve more in their lives and have every kind of desirable quality.

Unfortunately, relative poverty is not the only problem that children of lone parents tend to face. We already know that lone parents are more likely to be clinically depressed than married parents. It follows that the children of lone parents have an increased chance of being brought up by someone who is clinically depressed as well as poor.

What else is likely to happen?

There is a good chance that the child will find, within a few years, that his or her lone parent has found a new mate. What is that experience like?

Many men and women who take on the role of a step-parent try their best to be as loving and kind as possible. I have several friends who have become step-parents with a sincere desire to do their best. But does it come easily to be loving to a child who is not your own? Is there something about human psychology which means it is easier to, say, forgive a difficult child or to spend an extra hour playing with one you know is your own?

Writers over centuries have certainly taken this view. Virtually every culture in the world has stories about children being maltreated by step-parents. In *Cinderella*, the stepmother makes Cinders into an insulted servant. In *Snow White*, the stepmother, the new queen, orders a huntsman to murder Snow White. The root of that well-loved story is attempted infanticide by a stepmother.

Charles Dickens in *David Copperfield* wrote one of the most disturbing evocations of the arrival of a step-parent. David Copperfield's natural father has died. He returns from a stay away to find

In *Cinderella*, the stepmother makes Cinders into an insulted servant.

that Mr Murdstone – whom he has never met before – has married his beloved mother and now dominates the household. Mr Murdstone stops his mother hugging David and expressing affection as she used to. His 'old dear bedroom' is no longer his. Instead, he has to sleep far away in a strange room. On his first night back, he cries himself to sleep. But he is woken by his mother and Peggotty. His mother is now openly loving towards him. But then Mr Murdstone comes in. He tells David's mother to leave and makes Peggotty go, too. He shuts the door and holds David – looking steadily into his eyes.

> 'David,' he said, making his lips thin, by pressing them together, 'if I have an obstinate horse or dog to deal with, what do you think I do?'
> 'I don't know.'
> 'I beat him.'
> I had answered in a breathless whisper, but I felt, in my silence, that my breath was shorter now.
> 'I make him wince and smart. I say to myself, "I'll conquer that fellow"; and if it were to cost him all the blood he had, I should do it.'

Over the following days, David is belittled, insulted and beaten. Eventually he is sent away. Thus begins his story.

Of course this is only fiction. But the way that stories around the world – fairy tales, in particular – featuring maltreatment of stepchildren have remained popular for centuries suggests there is something about them which we instinctively recognise and accept. Even the *Harry Potter* series, in our own time, features a couple caring greatly for their own natural child while treating Harry, whom they have reluctantly taken in, cruelly.

This phenomenon has been studied, and perhaps explained by evolutionary psychology, which is based on the idea that our behaviour is determined by millions of years of evolution. Psychologists consider our own human behaviour in the light of the theory – initiated by Charles Darwin – that each of us is trying to survive personally and pass on our genes to another generation. They have also studied the behaviour of monkeys, apes and so on, to see how our close relations behave.

In 1971, Sarah Hrdy, a tall, blonde oil heiress, was studying anthropology as a graduate student at Harvard University.[33] She heard about infanticide committed by hanuman langur monkeys in India. No one had succeeded in explaining the phenomenon. With financial help from her mother, she set off for the desert land of Rajasthan and the medieval towns of Jodhpur, Jaipur and Mount Abu.

There she studied these hanuman langur monkeys – elegant creatures with long limbs and tails, their black faces and hands contrasting with lighter, grey hair on the rest of their bodies. They sit confidently outside temples, hoping to be fed, looping their arms around the monkey in front, their nimble fingers lazily searching for ticks among the hairs of a friend. Langurs, like humans, can be friendly and sociable. We go to the pub, play golf and meet for coffee. They look for ticks.

But there is another side to their nature. Hrdy saw that about once a year, the dominant male in the group was supplanted. Every time this happened, the new male killed all the suckling infants belonging to the previous dominant male. The females would try to protect their offspring but without success. The new male would chase each nursing female, steal her suckling baby and bite its head in two. Why did the male do this?

According to the old idea of animal psychology – popular right up to the late 1960s – overcrowding was probably the reason for such killings. But Hrdy saw there was no overcrowding. She came up with an interpretation which, though controversial at the time, has since come to be widely accepted. She argued that the new male killed the infants that were still breast-feeding because this would make the female monkeys fertile again as soon as possible. The new male would then be able to inseminate them and breed his own children. His over-arching impulse was to create his own natural children and, moreover, to ensure that his children would not have to compete for maternal care with the children of other males.

Of course, we are not monkeys. But we share a common evolutionary root. We share 98.4 per cent of our DNA with chimpanzees and 97.7 per cent with gorillas.[34] Many other species too – up to and including lions – share the same driving concern for their own genes. It would, in fact, be strange if we did not share this instinct. It would be strange if we cared as passionately for children who do not have our genes as for those who do.

There is, though, research specifically about how humans feel about their stepchildren. In 1975, Lucile Duberman was upbeat and confident about the prospects for stepfamilies. She worked on an interview study of 88 of them – not average ones but stepfamilies with good chances of success. The adults were married and middle class. Duberman did not, however, find what she hoped for and expected. She was obliged to acknowledge, 'There were very few step-parents who reported wholehearted love for their stepchildren. Many expressed varying degrees of affection.'

'Varying degrees of affection' may be disappointing but it does not sound too bad. There is evidence, however, of much worse than that.

In one of the most extraordinary television programmes of recent times, a 71-year-old man admitted sexually abusing at least two of his daughters.[35] One, Karen, had grown up and become angry at what he had done to her and her sister. She felt the police had not pursued the case adequately. So, with the help of the BBC programme *Newsnight*, she visited and secretly filmed him. During the conversation, the man, known as 'Stan', admitted he had had sexual relations with her. The two daughters asserted that he had regularly raped them when they were children and even passed them on to his friends for their sexual pleasure too. To Karen, he admitted having sex with her when she was ten or eleven. Karen told the programme that the abuse had started at bathtime when she was only three. 'He used to say we weren't clean until we were clean down there. It graduated to full sex by the time I was four.'

Didn't her mother protect her, she was asked. 'Mum was a peculiar fish,' she replied. 'I told her what was happening, but she believed him and would beat me.'

The casual viewer of the programme might have concluded merely that some men do horrible things. But both the daughters whom Stan was said to have sexually abused were not his natural daughters. They were stepdaughters. Stan also had a natural daughter. She, apparently, had not been abused. It is pretty clear why. She was his own flesh and blood. 'Some men are horrible' would have been the wrong reaction of the story. The more accurate observation would have been that 'some men are horrible but they are far less likely to be so to their own children.'

In a British study of court cases, it emerged that the chances of a child of a lone mother being abused – whether violently or sexually – was fifteen times greater than for the child of natural married parents.[36] Children who lived with their natural mother and a cohabitee (not the natural father) were at even greater risk. Their chances of being abused were an astonishing thirty-three times greater than for a child with its natural, married parents.

The figure is so high that it takes time for the impact to sink in. So much newspaper and television coverage treats all families as more or less equal. It is widely acknowledged that lone parents tend to be poorer. But it is much worse than that. A child living with a lone mother accompanied by a live-in boyfriend is in a vastly riskier position than he or she would be if living with natural, married parents.

A child is safest with its natural, married parents

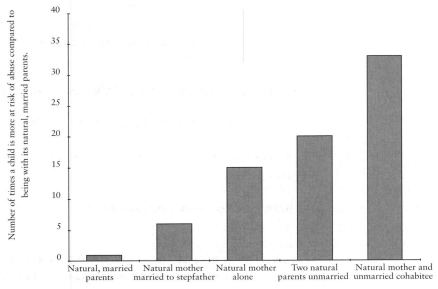

Source: Robert Whelan: *Broken Homes and Battered Children*[37]

Although the sample size was small, this study was particularly important because it isolated exact family types instead of mixing several types together.

Many other studies have fully supported the idea that the natural parents provide a far safer environment for children than families with a substitute parent.[38] An NSPCC study showed that families with a substitute parent yielded 32 per cent of 4,037 registered victims of intentionally inflicted physical injuries at a time when such families account accounted for only 3 per cent of the population.

Some people, I know, will suspect that the higher abuse suffered by children of lone parents and step-parents really reflects the fact that families with substitute parents tend to be poorer. They think the abuse is due to lower social status rather than the style of parenting. However, when the NSPCC controlled for differences in family incomes, children

> **HOW LIKELY TO BE SEXUALLY ABUSED?**
> Girls living with their genetic father: 0.2%
> Girls living with a stepfather: 3.7%[39]
>
> Questionnaire study of nine thousand fifteen-year-old girls in Finland.

WHAT CHILDREN SAY ABOUT THEIR STEP-PARENTS

'The third one [boyfriend of mother] used to go to the pub and come home and take it out on me. He put a knife to my throat.'

'My mum believes she asks for it. For the last nineteen years, lots of men have knocked her about.'

'My stepfather is violent, but my mum gives as good as she gets. She smashed his face with an ashtray.'

'The second one sexually assaulted me at nine. My mum didn't believe me.'

'He used to beat hell out of my mum, but when I was older I got sent to prison for two years. I tried to do him with a scaffold pole.'

'She [my natural mother] just disappeared when I was two. My stepmam used to cook for her own children but not for me, so me dad cooked for me.'

Comments from focus groups conducted by the Rowntree Foundation, a generally left-leaning research institution, which wanted to find out more about people suffering from 'social exclusion' on council estates. The researcher found, to his surprise, that they were most concerned about the kind of parenting they had experienced.[40]

from families with substitute parents remained nineteen times more likely to have suffered injury. It remains a simple story: a child with both natural married parents is dramatically safer than a child without.

Abuse – whether a child is hurt or sexually molested – is bad enough. But sometimes it goes further than that.

In June 2001, Sarah Hart, a teenager, had a baby with Ian Storer.[41] The baby girl, Jade, was 'bonny, happy and playful'. But not long before Jade's first birthday, Sarah and Ian split up. Sarah returned to her home town, Ramsgate, where she met up with a former boyfriend, Ross Hammond – a young man with tousled blond hair. They started going out together again.

Sarah found it convenient to leave little Jade with Ross from time to time. On 16 July, she discovered a large round bruise on the inside of Jade's thigh. Over the following days, more bruises appeared. Sarah's family

Jade Hart was 'bonny, happy and playful'.

urged her to take Jade to the doctor. At last, eleven days after she saw the first bruise, Sarah took Jade to the doctor, who decided the injuries could have been caused when she took her first, unsteady steps.

As time passed, Jade began to scream if Ross even looked at her. If he picked her up, the baby struggled. A bruise and a lump were found on Jade's head. Ross told Sarah that the little girl had fallen over during a stroll in a grave-yard. Sarah believed her boyfriend. Two days later, Ross again looked after Jade while Sarah was running errands. Sarah returned to find Jade 'floppy', continually falling asleep and vomiting. Sarah was worried but Ross tried to persuade her it 'isn't all that bad'. He warned that if they took Jade to hospital, the authori-ties would take the child away from her. Then Jade stopped breathing.

Sarah dialled 999. Jade was taken to hospital and pronounced dead shortly afterwards.

In court, it was revealed that Jade's injuries included a broken shin, nine fractured ribs, a brain haemorrhage, ruptured liver, a burnt foot and a severe black eye. Her fractured ribs

Ross Hammond. Jade began to scream if he even looked at her.

were caused by 'severe wounding or compression' – possibly a punch. The unnatural force required was 'equivalent to an adult standing on the chest of a baby'. The judge took the view that she had been sexu-ally abused too. Several jury members wept as medical experts described the suffering Jade had endured. Ross was convicted of mur-dering the child.

Are murders of children by step-parents more common than those by natural, married parents?

A study of children abused to the point of death in Britain between 1968 and 1987 suggested that a child with its natural mother and a cohabiting boyfriend was seventy-four times more at risk of being killed than one with its natural married parents.[42]

An extra risk factor of seventy-four times is extreme by any stan-dard. The result may seem so extreme as to be beyond belief. But it is supported by many other studies around the world.

A study of 279 child killings in the United States revealed that chil-dren with a step-parent were one hundred times more likely to suffer this fate than children with their two genetic parents.[43] Another study in Canada suggested that a child aged two was seventy times more likely to be killed by a step-parent than a genetic parent.[44] This study also looked at whether poverty was the underlying cause. It found that the enormous importance of step-parenthood in creating risk was hardly reduced at all when other factors such as wealth were removed from the equation.

Some may feel, 'Yes, but if a child is really looked after badly, it is taken into care by the social services,' the implication being, 'in which case, everything is all right'. But if a child is taken into care, its prospects become really bad. The child, if it is very lucky, may be taken early and quickly adopted. But it is more likely to spend time in a mixture of foster and children's homes. The least bad result is likely if the child spends plenty of time with one foster family. The worst results arise in institutional care. One study took nineteen children with foster parents and compared how they did with nineteen similar children in institutional care.[45] Fifty-six per cent of those in institutional care became markedly hyperactive compared to half as many in foster care. There are many examples of child abuse in council care homes.[46]

The inescapable conclusion of all the above is that unmarried parents and their children are seriously disadvantaged:
- A lone parent is likely to be poorer;
- A lone parent is more likely to be depressed;
- A lone or cohabiting parent is more likely to endure violence;
- A child is likely to be affected by all the above;
- The child is likely to receive a lower level of love from a non-genetic parent;
- The child is more likely to be hurt, sexually abused or killed;
- If the child is taken into care, the results are even worse.

Some people will nonetheless say, 'Yes, maybe, but children are tough little things. They bounce back. Who remembers anything about their first few years anyway? They probably have little lasting effect.'

Is that true? Sadly not. A great variety of studies show the same consistent result. Children brought up in the absence of their biological fathers are seriously affected throughout their childhood. They do worse at school, are more likely to have under-age sex, smoke more, take drugs more and are more likely to be excluded from school. In many cases – such as having under-age sex and being excluded from school – the absence of the biological father is associated with the problem being dramatically worse.

	Increased risk
Children of lone parents more likely to leave school at sixteen	60%
Sons of lone parents more likely to have sex before sixteen	80% (129%)
Daughters of lone parents more likely to have sex before sixteen	50% (65%)
Daughters of lone parents more likely to become mothers before eighteen	60% (60%)
Children of divorced parents more likely to become teenage mothers	100% (40%)
Fifteen-year-olds from lone parent families more likely to smoke	100% (50%)
Eighteen-year-old daughters of lone parents more likely to drink heavily	90% (similar)
Fifteen-year-old sons of lone parents more likely to have taken drugs	100%
Fifteen- year-old daughters of lone parents more likely to have taken drugs	25%
Teenage children of lone parents more likely to have taken drugs	(50%)
Sons of lone parents more likely to truant from school	(270%)
Children of lone parents are more likely to be excluded from school	325%
Eleven- to sixteen-year-old children of lone parents more likely to offend	25%
Young men from lone parent families more likely to offend persistently	25%

The figures in brackets are after adjustment for socio-economic status in all cases and for other factors such as sex and educational level in others. After such adjustment, the increased risk of children leaving school at sixteen is greatly reduced but a figure is not available. Figures from various sources cited in *The Fatherless Family* by Rebecca O'Neill (Civitas, 2002).

To put it the other way round, if natural fathers were a medicine, they would be regarded as a miracle drug. In virtually every case, even after adjustment is made for the fact that lone parents tend to be poorer, the disadvantage to the child of going without the natural father matters very much indeed.

What about when the children grow up into adults? Do they then, at last, recover from their disadvantaged childhood? This is the story of a sister and brother whose parents divorced.

The mother, Frances, went off with a 'tycoon', leaving behind four children: Jane, Sarah, Diana and Charles. Charles was three and Diana five at the time.[47] Charles said later, 'I can remember being told that my mother had gone away on holiday and I remember thinking it seemed a very long holiday.' His sister Diana told him later that she found him crying in his room, asking for 'my mummy'.

After a long gap, Charles, by then aged twelve, was on his way to carpentry class at school when he was called to the office of his headmaster to be told that his father had remarried. This came as a shock. He and his sisters had met the woman concerned and had told their father they were against him marrying her. Once she became their new stepmother, it seems likely that she did not love them as much as a natural mother. For their part, far from loving her, they positively disliked her.

Charles says that after the marriage, 'my father didn't seem so happy. And very soon after that he had a stroke which left him quite changed ... We suddenly had our family home being run by somebody who we didn't get on with and it made it very hard.'

Did this history damage the children into their adult lives? Diana certainly thought so. According to one confidante, 'I don't think [she] ever recovered from the thought of being abandoned ... She recognised it was the root of all her problems. But what can you do? We all want to be loved by our families. It wasn't an awful lot to ask.' She was insecure and desperate for love in adult life. She married but then had affairs and divorced. She suffered from anorexia and bulimia. Charles, her brother, similarly got married and then divorced. Eventually Diana died in a traffic accident in Paris. The Diana in question was, of course, Diana, Princess of Wales.

I have retold her story because, without most people realising it, it is probably the most high-profile illustration of the way the loss of a natural parent and the arrival of a substitute can be damaging. Diana suffered ruptured parenting and her life – while triumphant in many ways – became one of great pain.

Was Diana's experience exceptional? In one American study, between 20 and 25 per cent of children of divorced parents experienced long-term emotional or behavioural problems compared with only 10 per cent of children whose parents remained married. Children of divorced parents are more likely, like Diana and her brother Charles, to get divorced (or break up a cohabitation) themselves. Men with divorced parents are 90 per cent more likely to break up a partnership while women are 50 per cent more likely. Diana and Charles suffered the classic emotional effects of children whose parents divorce.

Diana: probably the most high-profile illustration of how the loss of a natural parent and the arrival of a substitute can be damaging.

Rod Stewart is famous for moving on from one young blonde to another. People tend to chuckle and think, perhaps, 'he's a bit of a one

– lucky devil.' At one point he married Alana Hamilton and together they had a son, Sean.[48] Stewart moved on, as usual, leaving Sean without the presence of his natural father. How did Sean do? In September 2002, he was sentenced to three months in jail for kicking a stranger unconscious outside a restaurant in Los Angeles. Stewart went to Los Angeles to support his son. That support might have been more effective if given when Sean was a child.

Barry Humphries – best known for playing Dame Edna Everage – is another much-married man. His third wife was an Australian artist, with whom he had a son called Oscar.[49] The couple divorced and he moved on to his fourth wife. How has Oscar done in the absence of his natural father? On Christmas Day in 2002 he was taken to hospital after trying to kill himself with a bottle of paracetamol tablets and a bottle of gin. He had a history of alcohol and cocaine addiction.

Jimi Hendrix had scores of affairs, like many rock stars. One resulted in a son called James, who was brought up by his mother.[50] How has James done in the absence of his natural father? In 2002 he was reported to be chronically shy and troubled. He was planning to have a sex change.

Amanda Barrie, the actress, was the daughter of a broken marriage.[51] Her mother took her away to live with her lover, an ex-army colonel. The man did not like Amanda and 'would make me stand outside the house at night if I misbehaved'. Barrie blames the fact that she has suffered anorexia, bulimia and a nervous breakdown on the childhood she endured in the absence of her natural father.

For rich and poor alike, broken parenting is damaging. The damage done to children by the absence of their natural fathers lasts well into their adult lives. They are far more likely to be jobless, unhappy and in prison.

	Increased risk
33-year-old men from 'disrupted' families more likely to be jobless	100% (40%)
33-year-old women from 'disrupted' families more likely to be on income support	35%
24-year-old women more likely to have had sexually transmitted disease	40% (53%)
*Children of divorced parents more likely to have long-term emotional or behavioural problems	100–150%
*By their early thirties, sons from one-parent homes more likely to have been in prison (or similar institution)	100%

Figures from various sources cited in *The Fatherless Family* by Rebecca O'Neill (Civitas, 2002). * US studies

The same US studies quoted in the table above also showed that children of divorced parents are likely to die younger by an average of four years.

To make matters worse, the children of broken parenting are more likely to go and do the same thing themselves. They are twice as likely to have their first child without cohabiting or being married.

Broken families are tragedies for those in them. But is everybody else all right? Are the rest happily unaffected by the ruptured parenting that has become so common?

Here is an example – admittedly an extreme one – of how other people can be affected. Two friends, Robert and Jon – both suffering from broken parenting – went to a shopping centre one day and started stealing things: batteries, enamel paint, pens and pencils, a troll doll, some fruit, sweets and trinkets.[52] They stole a wind-up toy and played with it on the escalator, tossing it down the moving steps. They teased an old woman, poking her in the back. Then they climbed over the chairs at a branch of McDonald's until they were chased out.

They played with a two-year-old toddler they came across and started walking off with him. The mother noticed and called her son back. Then the mother went into the butcher's. There was no queue so she left her toddler near the door. Jon went up to the little boy and said, 'Come on, baby.' The infant followed.

Jon and Robert took the little boy of two, James, out of the shopping centre. Once outside, they sometimes hit him. They sometimes dragged him along. After a long walk, Jon and Robert took James onto a railway line. They did a number of horrible things to James. One was to hit him on the head with bricks. Finally they left him to die on the railway track.

This was the death of James Bulger in 1993 – the murder which, perhaps, horrified Britain more than any other in modern times. One of the aspects of the murder which made it so terrible was the killing was done by mere children. What is not always remembered, though, is that these were children from broken families.

Robert Thompson's father beat his mother and then abandoned the family for good. Robert's brothers, without the father present, bullied each other and him. Jon Venables' parents had a tumultuous relationship too, at the end of which his father left.

If one looks closely at newspaper accounts of murders, it is astonishing how often the perpetrators came from broken families. Estate agent Tim Robinson was stabbed to death in 2002 by Dwaine Williams.

Williams had come from Jamaica, aged eleven, without a father. Kaiser Osman, fifteen, was killed in the same year by a boy also aged fifteen. The boy had been sent by his parents to live with relatives in Britain and then ran away from foster homes and children's homes. The parents of Richard Reid – known as the 'shoe bomber' after he tried to blow up an American Airlines plane in 2001 by igniting explosives in his shoes – divorced when he was four years old. Ian Huntley killed the young girls Holly Wells and Jessica Chapman in 2002. When he was thirteen, he found his philanderer father in bed with the babysitter.[53] His parents split up in acrimony when he was fifteen. Maxine Carr was the girlfriend who provided Huntley with a false alibi for his crime. She, too, came from a broken home. Her mother left her father when she was only two.[54]

In 1983, 32 per cent of all adult criminals were found to have lost one parent before the age of fifteen.[55] At the time, only eight per cent of the population at large had lost a parent in this way. The children of broken parenting were at much greater risk of becoming criminal. More recent research has shown that one third of people in prison spent time in a orphanage at some point in their childhood.[56] It is an extraordinary statistic – evidence of a very strong link indeed between psychological damage suffered by children and crime.

> 'On a recent visit to a prison I asked the deputy governor if he kept records of how many of the inmates were former system children [children taken into care who had not been adopted]. There would not be much point, he told me. Why not, I asked? Well, it's nearly all of them, he replied.'[58]
>
> **John Blundell, General Director, Institute of Economic Affairs**

Some people may object: 'What about Sweden? Sweden has seen a boom in divorce and lone parenting. It hasn't done them any harm, has it?' In fact, between 1960 and 1985, Sweden saw a 'widespread increase in lawbreaking'.[57] There was a five-fold increase in crime among eighteen- to twenty-year-olds in the three decades up to the mid-1980s.

There is not just one link between broken parenting and crime. There is a succession of links. The lack of the natural mother or father increases the risk of the child being hurt, abused or taken into care. That increases the chances of the child becoming a criminal when grown up. A broken family is more likely to be poor and live in a council estate with plenty of other children of poor, lone parents. That increases the risks still further. The children are more likely to receive poor and even neglectful attention from the lone parent and more likely to fall in with local gang culture. The risks of the child becoming a serious adult criminal thus increase yet again. One risk factor backs up and inflames another.

Broken parenting is responsible for a substantial amount of the dramatically increased level of crime in Britain (as described in Chapter 1). And crime is only the extreme form of incivility. Beneath the tip of that iceberg is the less easily seen mass of rudeness, callousness and lack of consideration.

The epidemic of ruptured and never-formed families has caused a great deal of unhappiness for the men and women concerned. Above all it has caused misery for the children. We must add to their suffering the aggression against society perpetrated by those worst affected, ranging from increased delinquency to major crime. The lives of such children have been ruined and they, in turn, have damaged the safety and quality of life of others.

The great increase in lone and broken parenting was brought about by successive governments increasingly taxing married, working parents with children while giving money and other benefits to lone parents. The epidemic was caused, pre-eminently, by the state – the welfare state. It constitutes one of the most important indictments against it.

The welfare state taxed married, working parents and gave money and other benefits to non-working lone parents

→ **Boom in divorce, separations and lone parenting, especially among the poor**

→ **Unhappiness and increased risk of violence for the lone parents**

→ **Increased risk of trauma, misery, underachievement, delinquency and crime for children**

→ **Rise in crime and incivility, affecting all society.**

CHAPTER 7
Pensions: Octavia warned us

In the grand surroundings of the Queen's Robing Room in the House of Lords, members of a royal commission arrive and take their seats. This is a royal commission like few others. To begin with, it actually includes a royal. The portly figure of the Prince of Wales, who will later be King Edward VII, arrives and takes his place.

He loves hunting and, like a future Prince of Wales, he has a mistress. In his case she is called Lillie Langtry. He has wide, philanthropic interests, supporting charitable hospitals though a special fund which raises enormous sums of money. And today, he is taking an interest in the burning issue of the time. The day, 6 June 1893, looks likely to be the high point of the commission's hearings on the subject. It is the day when Octavia Hill will give her evidence.

The Royal Commission actually includes a royal: Edward, the Prince of Wales.

The royal commission has been established – as so often – because the government does not know what to do. People are increasingly demanding that money should be given to those who are both old and poor – the 'aged poor', as they are known. A political head of steam has built up which seems hard to resist.

Charles Booth is prominent among those who have campaigned for government payments to the old. He is an enterprising, successful businessman who tried to get elected as a Liberal Party MP in the 1865 election. His life was changed as a result of canvassing from door to door in Toxteth. He was so shocked by the squalor and poverty that it contributed to him losing faith in a Christian God. In place of his religious devotion came a profound sense of duty to attempt to improve the conditions of the poor. His special contribution has been to document exactly how many seriously poor there are. He has recently published *Pauperism, a Picture; and Endowment of Old Age, an Argument*.[1] He argues that everyone over the age of sixty-five should be given five shillings a week out of taxation. Booth is a member of this royal commission.

But so is the leading speaker on the opposite side of the argument. Charles Loch's credentials as someone concerned for the poor are just as good as Booth's. He is the secretary of the Charity Organisation Society, which tries to help charities channel money to those in need without duplicating each other's work or doling out money in a way that could be damaging. He too is dedicated and energetic in fighting for his beliefs. He is convinced the state should go no further than it already does in providing for the old. He is driven by the spirit of Thomas Chalmers, the church minister who worked with the poor in Scotland and became well known for his view that indiscriminate aid did more harm than good (see Chapter 2). Loch backs up his passionately held views with research and analysis of his own.

As these two leading proponents of the opposite sides of the argument are both on the commission, it is doomed, some say, to end in disagreement. They even suggest it is *meant* to end in confusion. The government knows there is strong pressure for state old-age pensions and wants to appear open to reform. On the other hand it is worried about the cost. Anyway, it is not sure that pensions are the right thing to do in principle.

At last, Octavia Hill takes her seat to give evidence. Everyone knows her credentials. She comes from a well-to-do family where philanthropy was part of everyday conversation. Her grandfather was a pioneer of the movement for improving public health. She is an intimate friend of John Ruskin who, as well as being the leading writer on culture, has taught at the Working Men's College and advocated a form of Christian socialism. She has particularly tried to help the poor through housing. She has begun a project of renovating slums and then renting them to poor families. Ruskin has given her financial help for this. She has organised a corps of rent collectors who offer advice to tenants as well as collecting the money due. She has worked with the poor. She knows them. Her evidence is likely to be the moment when the conflict between the two sides will be most direct.

The Right Honourable C. T. Ritchie, who is chairing the proceedings, addresses her:

'Miss Hill, I think you have taken a good deal of interest in all matters connected with the social condition of the people, especially of the poorer classes?'

'Yes.'

The chairman establishes some of Miss Hill's opinions about the poor and how they provide for their old age. At last he comes to the central issue: whether or not there should be a state pension.

'Are you acquainted with any of the schemes that have been put before the public of late, in connection with annuities [pensions] from the state either without contribution from the people, or with contribution from the people?'

'I have read Mr Booth's scheme,' Miss Hill cautiously replies. She is referring to the proposal of Mr Booth, sitting right in front of her on the commission. She continues, 'but I cannot say that I have followed it in great detail, or studied it generally. I have only got a general impression from reading the account of it.'

Octavia Hill on the state pension: 'the most gigantic scheme of inadequate relief ever devised'.

'Could you give us what your impression is with regard to it?' asks the chairman.

Miss Hill takes a breath. The moment of confrontation has arrived.

'I should describe it shortly as the most gigantic scheme of inadequate relief ever devised by any human being. It seems to have almost every flaw in it. It would not be adequate. I cannot believe it would promote thrift. It seems to me it would do a great deal to destroy one thing that is most desirous to cultivate: the sense of responsibility of relatives.'

> **'It would not be adequate. I cannot believe it would promote thrift.'**
>
> **Octavia Hill on the proposed state pension**

It is out in the open now. Battle has commenced. The chairman asks if Miss Hill would condemn Mr Booth's scheme 'root and branch'.

'I should,' she replies. Then she adds, in a moment in which she recognises that Mr Booth, like Mr Loch and herself, has the interests of the poor at heart, 'I think I really should, except in its motive and desire to help the people, of course.'

Miss Hill is questioned in detail on her views about – and experience with – the poor. But her basic argument is in that opening, defiant attack on Mr Booth's proposal. She adds another element when she argues that the help of the state can be a cruel deception.

'A man asked the other day about sending some children to the convalescent home,' she says. 'He said he had done all he could for his children, and that the state must do the rest ... There is a dreadful expectation of what is going to be done for them. It is most pathetic, I think, because the expectation is so cruelly raised. I think it is so cruel to let them hope for what really will not be done.'

As her evidence continues, it is obvious that Miss Hill's opposition to state pensions is passionate. The Prince of Wales – impressed or astonished, one can't tell – asks her a question himself. He wonders how far she goes in opposing state provision. Does she object, he asks, to Post Office savings accounts or deferred annuities (pensions) purchased from the state on fair commercial terms?

'Not at all, sir,' Miss Hill replies respectfully.

> 'The poor ... are very much worse off wherever you get either uncertain action or such action as paralyses their own power, their own energies.'
>
> **Octavia Hill, evidence to the royal commission, 6 June 1893**

*

If the government intended that 1895 commission to be a delaying tactic, it certainly worked. The Prince of Wales withdrew before a conclusion was reached because he could see it was getting too political and controversial. The members could not even begin to agree on a unanimous report. They produced in the end four separate ones: two written by individuals on their own accounts; the majority report, signed by Loch and nine others; and the dissenting, minority report, signed by Booth and four others. The majority report rejected the idea of a state pension. The minority report complained that the members of the commission had such different views that it was not well designed for coming up with a concrete plan. Few could argue with that.

So, for the time being, the debate was won by the side of Loch and Hill. If it had been left at that, we would today have no state pension. But of course we know that the victory of Charles Loch and Octavia Hill was only temporary.

Why did Booth's side win in the end? Why were state pensions created?

To get the answer, one needs to put oneself in the shoes of Lloyd George, leading member of the Liberal Party. His famous old party is being squeezed to death, caught between the Tories, representing the status quo, and the fast-rising Labour Party, attracting the votes of discontented workers and radical reformers. What is an overwhelmingly ambitious politician like Lloyd George to do?

Along with Winston Churchill, he decided that the salvation of the Liberal Party lay in social reform. This would give the workers some of what their leaders were demanding but do it a way which would not frighten the bourgeois. Lloyd George and Churchill would offer sensible reform and thus save the nation from revolutionaries. In the process, they would keep their party and their personal ambitions alive. The social welfare programme they came up with was the 'Third Way' of the time. Voters loved it and the Liberals swept to a landslide victory in the 1906 election.

Herbert Asquith, the new Chancellor of the Exchequer, developed a plan for state pensions. He then became Prime Minister in 1908 and Lloyd George was made Chancellor of the Exchequer in his place. So Lloyd George saw the new legislation through Parliament while Churchill also contributed speeches in favour of the idea.

People called the new state pension created by the Liberals the 'Lord' George, because only a lord could be so generous. But the five shillings a week he dished out was only the small beginning of the British state pension. Over the next seventy years restrictions and qualifications that he introduced at the beginning were removed. The value was increased. Everything was made bigger and more generous. There was an almost continual upping of the promises made with regard to the state pension.

Now, nearly a century after the state pension first began, we have plenty of experience of how successful it has been. Governments have had every chance to deal with any problems. We can now judge how good were the arguments made back at that first royal commission in 1893–5. How well does Hill's evidence stand up now? In retrospect, was she just a blinkered reactionary, swimming against the tide of history? Or did her warnings and objections to state pensions have some merit?

Hill had four objections to the state pension, the first being that it would not be 'adequate'. Is it possible, after nearly a century in which the per capita income of British people has quadrupled,[2] that the state pension is not 'adequate'?

THE RISE AND FALL OF THE STATE PENSION

1895: Royal commission rejects Charles Booth's proposal of a universal five-shilling pension for the over-65s

1908: 'Lord' George's five shillings introduced for the 'deserving' poor over seventy

1919: The need to be 'deserving' is dropped

1925: Pensions linked to contributory health insurance

1942: William Beveridge's report confirms the idea of contribution-based insurance. He recommends that the state pension should be worth more than means-tested benefits

1948: Means-tested benefits barely worse, and in some ways better, than national insurance-based benefits[3]

1974: Labour Party October election manifesto promises to 'replace the unjust Tory pension scheme with ... adequate earnings-related pensions for everyone, fully protected against inflation' and to 'free future pensioners from the need for means-tested assistance'. State pension increased to highest-ever level – twenty-six per cent of average earnings

1975: Introduction of state earnings-related pension

1976: Labour government in financial crisis. Widespread spending cuts

1979: The incoming Conservative government decides that welfare benefits, including the state pension, will rise only in line with inflation. The pension therefore begins to fall compared with average earnings

1980s and early 1990s: The value of the state pension gradually declines. Labour promises to restore the link to earnings when next in government

1997: Labour re-elected. Does not restore the link to earnings

1998: Labour government pensions Green Paper states that, in the future, private and company pensions should provide sixty per cent of old-age incomes, instead of only forty per cent.[4] Implicitly the state is announcing that it is giving up on trying to be the overwhelmingly important source of income for the old

1999: Minimum income guarantee introduced – a means-tested benefit – at well above the level of the state pension

2003: Pension credit replaces the minimum income guarantee, attempting to reduce the penalty suffered by those with savings under a means-tested system

Is the state pension 'adequate'?

Let's take the financial year 2003/4, the latest period for which all the figures are in. The basic state pension is £77.45 a week, equivalent to £4,027.40 a year. Is that 'adequate'? Couples share £123.80, which is equivalent to £3,218.80 a year each. Is just over three thousand pounds a year 'adequate'? Of course, it depends what one means by 'adequate'. But to put the amount into perspective, it is less than the annual rent of a parking space in Notting Hill Gate – currently £3,700. It amounts to less than £8.82 a day and must cover food, heating, clothing, perhaps also insurance for the home or its contents, telephone, lighting, water and perhaps occasional travel. The amount of £3,200 to £4,000 a year per person would permit survival but most people would regard it as a meagre amount on which to live out one's old age. It is only 13 per cent of average earnings for full-time employees.[5]

Does the government itself regard the state pension as 'adequate'? Certainly not. The government has for some years now paid extra money to those who only have the basic state pension. It gives extra because it regards the state pension as unacceptably small. The extra – currently called pension credit – is means-tested. So the precise financial circumstances of each potential beneficiary have to be investigated. Forms must be filled in. Ironically this is not very different from what the Poor Law did in 1895 in large areas of Britain. In those days, some old people in need of financial support were obliged to enter the poorhouse to get it. But others were given money and allowed to stay where they were.

How many old people are now so poor that they are given means-tested benefits? According to calculations made by the House of Commons library, 57 per cent of pensioners were likely to receive them in 2003.[6] Even when on such extra benefits, people might still doubt that their incomes are 'adequate'. Under pension credit, a single person gets a minimum of £5,324 a year. A couple gets £8,124.[7] Some will also be getting subsidised housing.

What is the view of the government?

The government has a so-called 'poverty line'. Any household on less than 60 per cent of median income is said to be below it.[8] Median income in 2003 is approximately £17,350,[9] so the poverty line is £10,410. Those who get the means-tested minimum taking them above the basic state pension are still below the government's own poverty line.

But many old people do not even get the benefits they are entitled to. The old are more likely than others to be frail or weak. They are less likely to have heard about the means-tested benefits they could apply for. They are less likely to understand that it may be worth their while applying and more likely to be daunted by (or even incapable of) actually making such an application. Between a quarter and a third of all families entitled to the minimum income guarantee – the predecessor of pension credit – did not claim it in 2000/01. That is about half a million old people living below even the very low level of income provided by the minimum income guarantee.[10]

> 'There are problems if you move to too much means-testing, as you can see with pensioners who do not take up income support'.[11]
>
> **Tony Blair, 1998**

Most will agree that those on means-tested benefits are poor. It is also clear that some 57 per cent of old people are on means-tested benefits. It therefore follows that, after nearly a century of growing wealth and plenty of time for the perfection of state pensions, the welfare state has left a clear majority of old people poor. According to the government's own definition they are in 'poverty'. On this basis, state pensions can hardly be described as 'adequate'.

Deceived by politicians

Hill's second objection was that people would be 'deceived'. It may seem an extraordinary accusation. The state, in deciding to create state pensions, was trying to help the 'aged poor'. How could that be a deception? The intent was kind and generous – as well as being to win an election. How could provision be interpreted as deceit?

Let's look at what people have been led to believe about the state pension. Then let us see if they have been deceived.

The most important social-security document in the twentieth century was the Beveridge report in 1942. A pamphlet version was issued, and the contents were relayed to the armed forces by their officers as well as through the newspapers. Millions of people read some version of it. It was regarded, then as now, as the blueprint for the postwar welfare state. What did it say on the subject?

Any Plan of Social Security worthy of its name must ensure that every citizen, fulfilling during his working life the obligation of service according to his powers, can claim as of right when he is past work an income adequate to maintain him. This means providing, as an essential part of the plan, a pension on retirement from work which is enough for subsistence, even though the pensioner has no other resources whatever.

Beveridge made it clear that the state pension was going to be worth more than any means-tested benefit. Anyone who had made full contributions to the state pension would have no need to be means-tested. That was what the British public was led to expect. They would not be paupers or, in modern language, 'welfare dependants'. They would have paid their dues and bought their own pension.

The British public endorsed this vision by voting for Labour in 1945. But actually both leading political parties agreed with it. The only difference was that the Conservatives were a little more cautious and concerned about the cost.

In the following years, the Labour Party remained very hostile to the idea of means-testing. The process was regarded as intrusive and demeaning. The Labour Party election manifesto of October 1974 declared: 'The Labour government will replace the unjust Tory pension scheme with our recently announced long term plan for adequate earnings-related pensions for everyone, fully protected against inflation. This will free future pensioners from the need for means-tested assistance.'

Labour won that election. People now had even more reason to believe that the state would provide. Moreover the state would provide an adequate pension received as of right because of contributions made. There would be no means-testing.

Labour in government immediately set about pursuing this aim, bumping up the state pension and setting about creating state earnings-related pensions. But the government spent freely in many other areas as well as pensions and soon got into financial difficulties. This ended with crisis negotiations with the International Monetary Fund and spending cutbacks. In 1979, when Margaret Thatcher came to power, the government's finances were still in a parlous state and the projections of the cost of state pensions were worrying. At the same time, the state pension was regarded as sacrosanct, so all Thatcher felt able to do was to link future rises in the state pension to the rate of inflation instead of average earnings. This signalled a long, slow decline in the value of the state pension compared to earnings and was accompanied by vigorous encouragement to people to save for themselves. But even then, the idea that the state pension would provide was not explicitly given up. Most people still had the impression that the state pension would be sufficient for their old age.

The Labour Party certainly kept that promise alive, saying throughout the period of Tory rule that it would restore the link of state pensions with average earnings. Whatever erosion the state pension had suffered under the Conservatives would be put right, it was suggested, when Labour got back into power. In 1993, the Labour shadow Chancellor, Gordon Brown, said, 'I want to achieve what in fifty years of the welfare state has never been achieved: the end of the means test for our elderly people.'[12] Nothing could have been clearer.

In 1997, the Labour Party finally won back power. This was the chance for Labour to do what it had been promising for the previous eighteen years. Did it do it? No. Not at all. Labour continued, like the Conservatives, to allow the state pension to dwindle compared with average earnings. The fine words of Gordon Brown about ending means-testing came to absolutely nothing. Below is the progression of how the basic state pension rose up until the late 1970s and has since fallen:

The rise and fall of the basic state pension

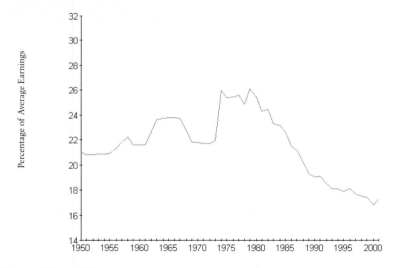

Source: Watson Wyatt

There is a clear difference between what people were led to expect and what they have actually got. The Wilson government, Brown and many others gave British people to understand that their contributions to national insurance and other schemes would give them an adequate pension. But when it came to the point, pensioners did not get that 'adequate' income. The promise of being lifted above means-testing has been comprehensively unfulfilled. People have been, without doubt, deceived.

One could say in mitigation that the deception by politicians was 'not intentional'. It is true that politicians and civil servants like Beveridge did not deliberately set out to trick people into a poor old age. But surely they had a responsibility to refrain from promising something which would not be delivered. Didn't they have a duty to their fellow human beings to be sure that they were not misleading them? I suggest they did, and that they failed in their duty. Politicians thought, above all, of appearing generous and of winning elections. They did not pause to think, as

GORDON BROWN, 1993:

'I want to achieve what in fifty years of the welfare state has never been achieved. The end of the means test for our elderly people.'

Ten years later, after he had been Chancellor of the Exchequer for seven years, more of the elderly than ever before were on means-tested benefits.

they should have done, that people would rely on their promises and that, as a result, would be poor in their old age. It is rare that the promises of politicians are so clearly shameful. In this case they helped cause people to be poor in old age. It is a terrible thing to have done.

It may be said that it was not really the politicians' fault, that they were innocent victims of demographics. Over the past sixty years, the proportion of people aged over sixty-five has increased dramatically. There are fewer young people to pay the pensions of the elderly and so there is a lack of money to pay state pensions. But the demographic trend has been clear for far longer than the past sixty years. It has been around for the past 160 at least. At no point in modern history has there been an excuse for any politician being unaware of it. In 1841, a mere 4 per cent of the population was over sixty-five. By 1951, the proportion had increased to 10.9 per cent, more than two and a half times as many. It really should come as no surprise that by 2041, the proportion is expected to rise to 21 per cent, nearly another doubling.

The politicians have long known there is a demographic 'time bomb' and any who did not know should have done. They deceived people and, with the exception, perhaps, of some ministers during the Thatcher administration, they did nothing to undeceive them. It has been 'pension misselling' on a scale which commercial insurance and pension companies have never approached.

If people had not been deceived, they might have led their lives differently. Which leads to Hill's third objection to state pensions: that she could not see how state pensions could possibly encourage 'thrift'. By this she meant that the state pension would in fact *dis*courage thrift. Has it?

How many people over sixty-five?	
1841	4.0%
1901	4.7%
1951	10.9%
1981	15.0%
2011	16.1%
2041	21.0%

Source: John Macnicol, *The Politics of Retirement in Britain 1878–1948*[13]

Does the state pension discourage thrift?

Mavis Wilson, a 66-year-old widow, is entitled to the basic state pension of £77.45 a week (in 2003/4). She has also always saved over the years to create a nest egg 'just in case'. She has never earned a lot, but she has nevertheless managed to accumulate £18,001. She has been prudent and sensible. Hasn't she?

She has put her savings in a Choice 2-year Individual Savings Account at Abbey Bank, which pays 4.5 per cent tax free, a pretty good rate by current standards. Her income from it is equivalent to £15.54 a week. She can also claim pension credit of £14.79, bringing her total weekly income to £107.78 a week.

What would her income be if she had saved nothing at all?

If Mavis had saved nothing, she would be entitled to the basic pension plus a much higher amount of pension credit – £24.65 – making a total of £102.10.

So her years of going without little luxuries, putting money aside, building up what is, to her, a good sum, have increased her weekly income by only £5.68 – equivalent to an interest rate on her savings of a mere 1.6 per cent, which is less than the rate of inflation. In fact, if she wants her nest egg to keep its real value, she needs to reinvest it all. Otherwise in eleven years' time, when she is seventy-seven – and perhaps wanting a heart operation or a hip replacement in a hurry – her nest egg will be worth a quarter less.

Her biggest mistake has been in saving anything more than £6,000. That is the level up to which savings are ignored for the purposes of the means-testing. All the sacrifices she made – the prudence she showed – in saving an extra £12,001 beyond that amount have brought her a trifling 50p a week – a return of only 0.2 per cent a year.

That is bad enough. But it gets worse. Mavis's savings also mean that she loses other means-tested benefits: council tax benefit and housing benefit. So as a result of her savings of £18,000, her income is actually lower than it would have been if she had stopped at £6,000. Her thrift and her saving is actually costing her money. The welfare state fines Mavis for having saved.

How Mavis's savings affect her weekly income

	If she had saved nothing	If she had saved only £6,000	With £18,001 saved
Basic state pension	£77.45	£77.45	£77.45
Interest on savings	0	£5.18	£15.54
Pension credit[14]	£24.65	£24.65	£14.79
Total weekly income	£102.10	£107.28	£107.78
Gain made by saving	–	£5.18	£5.68

Her gain made by saving £18,001 instead of £6,000 is only 50p per week even before the before the loss of council tax benefit and housing benefit, which causes her income to be lower as a result of saving more.

Of course each case is different. The wealthy, in particular, are not affected by loss of benefits when they save more. It is only the poorer half of society which is given the message by the state pension system 'Don't be a mug. Don't save.' Not for the first time, the welfare state damages the poor more than the rich.[15]

When saving can be punished like this, it is only logical that there are not many people like this imaginary Mavis. One might as well live for the day. There is no point saving unless you can get up to a much, much bigger sum. According to the Institute for Fiscal Studies, a man of sixty-five with no income other than the state pension and investment income would need to have saved £37,000 and then spend it all buying an annuity to make himself ineligible for pension credit.[16] But he actually needs to have saved more than that to make saving clearly worthwhile. He may also be losing housing and council tax benefits.

A couple retiring in 2003 would need to have saved £180,000, on the basis of current policies, to be keep themselves above qualifying for means-tested benefits in the future, according to Mercer Human Resources.[17] They would have to spend the whole sum on an annuity.

Some financial advisers are now concerned that they will be open to the charge of 'misselling' if they advise a low-income person to save.[18] Someone whom they advised to save might sue twenty or thirty years later because the savings had not been worthwhile, merely reducing the means-tested benefits they would otherwise have received.

The welfare state has made saving for retirement into an act of folly. Not for everyone, but just for the lower-paid. Those who should, in a sane world, be the most keen to spend thriftily, and conserve their resources, have been incentivised to spend, spend, spend.[19]

As the Institute for Fiscal Studies (IFS) has commented: 'The means-tested benefit system has long since dampened the incentive to save for those anticipating a low income in retirement.'[20] And again: 'The British means-tested benefit system has traditionally penalised those holding their savings in capital form especially harshly.'[21]

So the pension system discourages savings by the lower paid. Do they respond to this discouragement? Do they save or not?

A report by the IFS in 1999 showed that half of those coming up to retirement had savings of less than £1,750 – an astonishingly small amount. The *Financial Times* commented at the time that the figures 'cast doubt on how successful the current and previous governments have been in encouraging a culture of saving'.[22] That seems to be putting it mildly.

Yet it is not that people do not want to save. They have shown they are very keen to build up wealth in a different form. Millions of people, including those on low incomes, take on substantial debt – and the associated cost of paying interest and repaying capital – in order to buy a home. Over half of those described as the 'least wealthy' 10 per cent by measuring their financial assets own their home.[23]

One reason may be that they think a home is a good investment. But they have another reason for preferring to build up savings in the form of a home. The value of a home is completely ignored when means-tested benefits are assessed.[24] If a person owned £20,000 in stocks and shares, but was renting their home, their benefits would disappear in a puff of smoke. But another, much richer person with £80,000-worth of

> 'The welfare state has made saving for retirement into an act of folly.'

home would be entitled to means-tested benefits at the top rate. For low-income people, it makes sense never to keep financial assets but only to have wealth in a form that will not damage existing or potential benefits. And that is what they do.

Some people suggest that those on lower incomes do not save because 'they have not got enough money.' Clearly those living entirely on means-tested benefits are poor and have limited scope to save. But those in work, getting a median income, clearly could save. That is shown by the fact that they already do save by buying property as described above. It is also evident because their earnings are vastly higher than thirty years ago, let alone a hundred years ago, while the cost of the essentials – food and clothing – has fallen. These essentials of life take up far less of the family budget than before. In 1900 they accounted for nearly 38 per cent of all consumer expenditure.[25] After almost a century of growing prosperity, they now only amount to 16.6 per cent of it. Paying for food formerly used up three pounds out of ten. Now only one pound in ten buys far more food.

How the essentials became more affordable

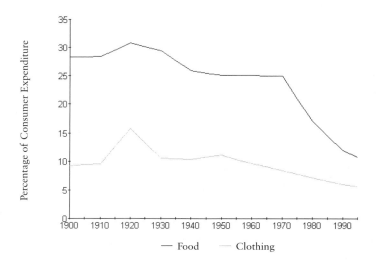

Source: Twentieth Century Social Trends[26]

There has been a considerable increase in what you could call 'surplus income' but it has not gone into financial assets. It has gone into servicing the purchase of property and into luxuries. For example, spending on food and non-alcoholic drink rose only 37 per cent in the three decades to 2001.[27] But spending on recreation and culture roared ahead by 471 per cent. Cash devoted to foreign holidays rocketed by 569 per cent.

Most families have cars

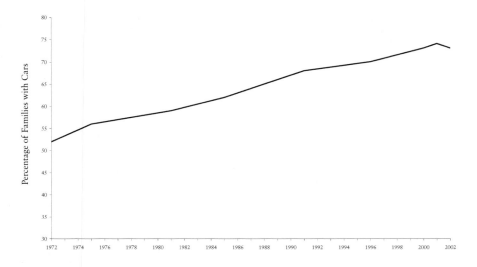

Source: Living in Britain 2002 (Office of National Statistics 2004)

In 2001, only 28 per cent of households did not possess a car – and that includes the homes of the elderly, many of whom can no longer drive or who never learnt. Cars, if bought new, cost £6,000 and upwards. Well over 70 per cent of households now own a mobile phone. The money goes on the phone, not on saving. Even among those who, according to official statistics, have incomes of between nothing and £150 a week, between 46 and 49 per cent have a mobile phone. Most of the consumer durables one can think of are owned by most households. They are things which previous generations managed without. However desirable they may be, they cannot be considered necessities of life. They are – or have been – expensive. Yet thousands of pounds are spent on buying them – by people who at the same time have not saved even as much as £750. Men spend £1,540 a year on drinking and eating out. They spend far less – £950 a year – on their pensions.[28]

The *Financial Times* commented that the government's attempts to create a savings culture may not have succeeded,[29] but this clearly does not go far enough. Successive governments have created an anti-saving culture. They have made saving into a mug's game for those on lower incomes. Octavia Hill was right. Her only mistake was to under-estimate just how anti-thrift the state pension system would become.

Children as pensions

Hill's fourth objection was that relatives would give up caring for their old. People today may regard that as the strangest of objections.

Very few expect people to look after their aged relatives nowadays. The expectation now is that younger people will continue to see their elderly parents and will very probably be outraged at the low level of the state pension and disgusted that their parents have to sell their homes in order to pay for care in a home. The selling of homes, as well as being sad for the pensioners, reduces the inheritances that the children can expect. But what middle-aged people do not generally expect is to take their elderly parents into their own homes, look after them or pay for them. It has come to be taken for granted that all this is the job of the state.

The welfare state has persuaded the poor to shop rather than save

Colour television	98%
Deep freeze/fridge-freezer	93%
Central heating	90%
Washing machine	88%
Microwave oven	82%
Video recorder	78%
CD player	62%
Mobile phone	49%
Tumble drier	39%
Home computer	22%

Ownership of consumer durables among those on incomes of £100 to £150 a week

Source: Living in Britain 2002 (Office of National Statistics 2004)

It was not always like that. Hill, in her evidence to the royal commission, reported something a poor old working woman, a widow, said to her: 'Of course, people need not talk to us about saving; we have worked for our children, and they work for us.' The woman had paid for her daughter to be educated to the point where she could become a schoolmistress, bringing in £4 or £5 a year. Now she expected to receive support, in return, from her daughter.

We can see this kind of expectation in other countries even today. Young adults who come to work in Britain from poorer countries often send money home to their parents. Such has been the culture in large parts of the world for much of human history.

There is a Brothers Grimm folk tale (the brothers researched their stories in the early nineteenth century) about a family of three generations living together.[30] The old grandfather's eyesight is failing and he trembles so much he sometimes spills soup on the tablecloth. The father and mother don't like this, so they give him an earthenware bowl and make him eat in a corner. One day he drops the bowl, which breaks. So he is given a wooden bowl instead.

A while later, the father sees his son working with some pieces of wood. 'What are you making?' asks the father.

'I am making a little trough for you and Mother to eat out of when I am big,' the boy replies.

The husband and wife look at each other and begin to cry. They lead the grandfather back to the family table and never complain again when he spills his food.

The story reflects and enforces the custom and morality of past times: that each generation was obliged to look after its parents.

None of this is to say it is not desirable that people should make provision so that they are not dependent on their relatives in old age. On the other hand, the welfare state has indeed reduced the extent to which families think of themselves as self-supporting units. This is a loss. People have less of the sense of belonging and responsibility which previously came from such a way of thinking. It is also a loss because contact between children and their parents can give each access to the other's friends and more distant family members. An extended community can provide emotional and sometimes material support, as described by Michael Young and Peter Willmott in their report on Bethnal Green in the 1950s (see Chapter 5). It is called 'social capital' these days. It appears to make people feel happier and more secure. It was routine before the welfare state. Young and Willmott reported that between two-thirds and three-quarters of married adults in Bethnal Green lived near their parents at that time.[31]

At any rate, Hill was right again. State provision – perhaps not just the state pension – has indeed 'done a great deal to destroy … the sense of responsibility of relatives'. However, she missed another problem that has resulted from state pensions. She failed to forecast that they would discourage work.

Should a working life end at sixty-five?

When Hill was speaking in 1893, most old people did not retire. Two-thirds of those over sixty-five were still working. Now the situation is quite different. Fewer than one over-65 in ten works. It is a massive social and economic change.

Of course, in one way it is a change for the better. Many people were working in 1893 because they had little choice. If people now retire instead because they are richer and able to choose, that is good. But is the end of work after sixty-five just a matter of wealth and choice?

Older people have stopped working

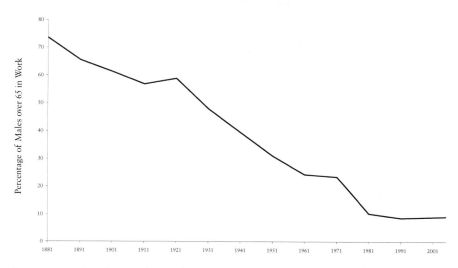

Proportion of males aged 65+ defined as 'economically active' according to census reports[32]

Would people – or some of them – actually be happier working when over sixty-five? The Department of Work and Pensions did some research and found that 'older workers ... have relatively high levels of job satisfaction and relatively few of the men wanted to stop working.'[33] The research also indicated that older people tend to favour part-time work.

Unfortunately, up until 1989, men aged 65–9 and women aged 60–64 had their state pension reduced if they earned above a certain threshold.[34] So for many years, the state penalised those who preferred to continue to work past a state-decided pensionable age. This helped create a culture in which it was considered abnormal to work beyond the state-decided ages: sixty-five for men and sixty for women.

Now, again, with pension credit, if a man over sixty-five does some part-time work, he may well find that his income

Who is 'living comfortably'?

Men 65–75 working	59%
Men 65–75 not working	40%

Proportion of men aged 65–75 reporting that they were 'living comfortably'

Source: Department of Work and Pensions[35]

wipes out the money he would have got in pension credit. The amount forgone could be up to £14.89 a week if he is single or £19.20 if he is married or has a partner. Since part-time work tends to be low paid, he could therefore be working for three or four hours a week just to make up for the loss of pension credit.

The discouragement of work after the state pension age reduces the contact that older people have with the rest of society. It makes them poorer – socially, as well as financially – than they would otherwise be.

The unplanned cost

Another thing which Hill did not foresee was the future cost of the state pension.

Despite attempts to contain the cost, payments to the old are now a major part of government spending. They are a significant part of the whole British economy. Around 6 per cent of total national income now consists of benefits paid to those over state pension age. Benefits for the old represent 57 per cent of total benefit expenditure.[36] The government therefore has to raise a great deal of money through taxation and national insurance contributions to pay for these benefits.

National insurance is levied on people currently in work. The tax is taken from virtually everybody. Six per cent of the national income was some £66.8 billion in 2003 – £2,288 for every working adult in the country.[37] When the money is raised in taxes on income, then according to many economists, economic growth is significantly reduced (see Chapter 8). In so far as the poor are taxed – which they are, through VAT and excise duties as well as income tax – the levy makes poor people poorer. Moreover the projections for the future are worse still. The proportion of over-65s will continue to rise, leading to a choice of evils:

1. Increasing the contributions demanded of the diminishing proportion of people of working age and/or
2. Raising the retirement age and/or
3. Cutting the real value of state pensions.

It must be doubted, given the past century of failure to face up to this reality, that the welfare state will make a clear and well-communicated choice. The record in the past has been one of promises broken and decisions deferred, eventually leading to lower pensions than people were led to expect. That, in a sentence, is the history of state pensions.

In passing, we may note that at least Britain is in less of a false position than many Continental countries. Continental state pensions have been bigger and, in some cases, payable younger than in Britain. As the proportion of old people has increased, governments have demanded higher contributions from the dwindling proportion of working people. Contributions have reached such a level now that they are probably one of the reasons why unemployment in Continental Europe is so high.

There are currently about three workers for each pensioner. On current trends, every three workers will have to provide for two pensioners within thirty years. This is unsustainable. In the words of *The Economist*, it is 'the most predictable economic and social time-bomb in Europe's history.'[38]

Continental countries will let down those who are currently relying on generous pensions when they retire. Whenever politicians attempt to bring some realism to the subject, they endanger their careers. In France in 1995, Alain Juppé, the then Prime Minister, was defeated over the issue. Gerhard Schröder, in Germany, was advised in August 2003 that pensions should be cut by 10 per cent and the retirement age increased from sixty-five to sixty-seven.[39] At the time of writing, he does not appear likely to bring about such a radical change.

Repeated delays, of course, mean that change, when it comes, will have to be all the more abrupt. The German bank Commerzbank says that, on current form, by 2040 the German government's unfunded pension liabilities will be three times the country's total annual output. This would be akin to government bankruptcy. France did eventually push through some reductions in the generosity of the state system in 2003.[40] The Prime Minister, Jean-Pierre Raffarin, trying to get the measure through, stated that it was 'about the survival of the republic'.[41] He warned, 'If we do nothing today, in less than 20 years our pensions will be reduced by half.'[42]

France took some action even though it may not be enough. Other countries, such as Italy, have still done far too little. In some countries, the adjustment will be late and vicious.

Nevertheless, people may say, 'Yes, but even a disappointingly bad state pension is better than nothing.' Is that right?

Is a bad state pension better than none?

For the whole of the nineteenth century there was no old-age pension. So how did the old get on? First, they saved – as never before in British history. One way in which they saved was through deposits at the Post Office Savings Bank. These rose from nothing in 1861 to £8.1 million in 1870. In the next five years they nearly doubled. Then they more than doubled again in the following five years. Then they quadrupled by the end of the century. It was fantastic growth – 1,500 per cent in the final thirty years of the nineteenth century.

Post Office Savings Bank deposits

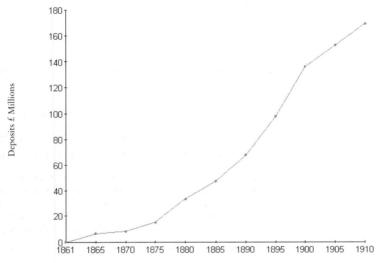

Source: *Abstract of British Historical Statistics*

It is true that cash deposits in Trustee Savings Banks grew less fast. But even when combining the two, there was a quadrupling of this kind of saving over thirty-five years.

Friendly societies were at the heart of welfare in the nineteenth century. About six million out of an industrial male population of seven million were members by 1892.[43] Friendly societies were not designed to provide old-age pensions – at least, not originally. But they coped as best they could. If members over sixty-five became incapable of work, they were given benefits. There was not much fraud because members of the friendly societies would regularly visit members who were ill. This provided succour to the genuinely ill and discouraged cheating.

Naturally, as people got older, there came to be an increasing number who were defined as being permanently incapacitated. This caused great financial difficulty for some friendly societies. Certain ones even went out of business. But the better-run ones survived and grew. The royal commission was told in 1895 that few members of friendly societies ever came to ask for Poor Law relief.

Of course some people who could no longer work had no family to care for them, and were not members of friendly societies. Were such people left on the streets?

The Aged Pilgrims' Friend Society was founded in 1807. The name may seem strange to most people now. But the origin of the name would have been crystal clear in 1807. 'Pilgrims' were people like Christian in John Bunyan's *A Pilgrim's Progress*, who sought the way to God. This was a charity created specifically to help elderly Christians, paying pensions to them, organising visits by members of the charity and, from 1834, admitting the elderly into a growing number of homes. Charities for the elderly grew prodigiously in the nineteenth century. Many have since

> '**The evidence on Friendly Societies, the Post Office Savings Bank, and other like agencies, has shown remarkably the great development of habits of thrift and providence among the working classes, and has satisfied us of the general ability of those who are in any regular employment to make direct or indirect provision for old age.**'
>
> **Majority report of the Royal Commission on the Aged Poor, 1895**

closed down – destroyed by the welfare state. But this particular one has survived to the present[44] with homes in Brighton, Chippenham, Great Finborough (Suffolk), Haslemere (Surrey), Leicester, Tunbridge Wells, Wantage and Wellsborough (Warwickshire). Charities assisted very large numbers of those who could not manage.

As a last resort, there was the Poor Law. The amount of help the Poor Law offered varied considerably at different times and in different parishes. At worst it provided sparse accommodation and food in the workhouse. At best it offered cash outside the workhouse (known as 'outdoor relief'). But as people grew richer, saved more and joined friendly societies, trade unions and other such mutual-help organisations, dependence of the

The Aged Pilgrim's Friend Society, founded in 1807 and, unlike many other charities, still operating to this day.

old on the Poor Law was diminishing. In 1861, 21.6 per cent of those over sixty claimed 'relief' (benefits). By 1905, the proportion was had fallen to 14.7 per cent.

There was every reason to believe that welfare dependency among the old would continue to fall in future. Membership of friendly societies had only recently reached the high level of that time, suggesting that an even bigger proportion of old people in the future would be members, and therefore probably not in need of benefits. The level of saving was also on a steep upward curve. This was a society increasingly well off, in which thrift and saving were part of the culture. The savings of this society were set to be very large indeed, paying for an even greater proportion of people to have an independent old age.

But after the state pension was introduced, more people were led to believe the state would provide. In 1905, less than 15 per cent of those aged sixty or over were drawing benefits. Now, 57 per cent of those over sixty-five are entitled to means-tested state benefits. Britain has become vastly wealthier but its old are much more welfare dependent than they were a century ago. The opportunity to have generations of independent old people with a lifetime of savings – savings which could be passed on free of tax to the next generation – was there. It was thrown away.

Welfare dependence of the old before the state pension

1861	21.6%
1871	21.7%
1881	15.2%
1891	14.0%
1901	13.8%
1905	14.7%

Percentage of those aged over sixty in receipt of Poor Law benefits

Source: C. S. Loch, *Statistics of Population and Pauperism in England and Wales*[45]

Some may say that the nineteenth century is irrelevant and that, for some reason, the growth in saving which started then would not have continued. It is hard to see any reasonable basis for such a view. But is there any country which has not fallen in with the worldwide trend towards state pensions? If so, what has happened there?

There is at least one such country or, at least, territory. For many years, Hong Kong had no specific old-age pension at all. The old, as with the Poor Law, were treated like everybody else. If poor, they could get some help but not by virtue of being old. By 1980, a old-age allowance had been introduced, payable to anyone over the age of seventy without means-testing. There was also a means-tested old-age supplement. But the key thing about these benefits has been the level. The amounts have been very low. The universal benefit for those over seventy recently amounted to HK$705 a month, which is £1.75 a day. The means-tested benefit is smaller. And the means-tested benefit is not payable to those with assets over £1,700. The assets counted for this means-testing include the home the person lives in, whereas in Britain the home is not counted, nor the first £6,000 of savings. In short, all provision for the old is low level and not granted to anyone who is not stony-broke. No one in their right mind in Hong Kong would deliberately plan a retirement dependent on the state.

This system, which is close to no pension at all, has helped to create a saving culture well known to anyone who has lived in Hong Kong. The saving takes the form of bank accounts, shares, gold kept in the many safe-deposit boxes in the banks, U.S. Treasury bills and so on and on. Hong Kong is known as a place where the taxi driver is ready to ask for – or offer – a share tip. Hong Kong is also a place where family connections remain strong. The modest level of all social-security payments surely contributes to this culture, including the low level of pension payments. When people can look to the state only for minimal help if they fall on hard times, they naturally save more and want to keep up family links which one day may sustain them in case of disaster.

In Britain, the overall savings rate is 17 per cent of all economic output.[46] In Hong Kong it is 34 per cent – twice as high.[47] It must be admitted that the overall savings rate is not a perfect guide to the amount of saving people do. It includes business and government saving. But all measures of saving have their faults and using the overall rate avoids some of the worst of them.[48]

All European countries with large state pensions have lower overall savings rates than Hong Kong. Germany, France and Italy have savings rates in the region of 20 to 22.5 per cent. In Germany and Italy, people have particularly low levels of savings compared to their incomes.

Detailed statistics on the incomes of the elderly in Hong Kong are not easily available. But the high savings rate suggests that the answer to the question 'Is a bad state pension better than none?' is 'no'.

It seems likely that if the state pension had not been created in 1908, British people would have saved a great deal more and, overall, would probably now be wealthier in their old age. The late-nineteenth-century trend for old people to become less benefit dependent would have continued and it would be normal for people to have very substantial savings. We would not be in the position, as we are now, where 57 per cent of old people, after a lifetime of work, need to fill in forms asking for financial help from the government. Old people would have more independence and dignity in retirement.

There would be massive savings on public expenditure, amounting to something close to 6 per cent of annual economic output. That would mean income tax could be lower, allowing faster economic growth. It would be easily affordable to abolish inheritance tax, thus allowing old people to hold wealth without worrying that 40 per cent of their savings above a certain level would disappear into the hands of the government on their death instead of going to their children.

Old people in particular, and society in general, would be better off today if the state pension had never been created.

CHAPTER 8
Tax and growth – Harold Wilson versus John Who?

It is 1961 and Walt Disney is bringing out *101 Dalmatians*. Audrey Hepburn is appearing in her little black dress and large dark glasses in *Breakfast at Tiffany's*. Elvis has plenty of number one hits, as usual, including 'Wooden Heart'. Harold Macmillan is the suave, patrician Prime Minister and urbane 'Rab' Butler, the Home Secretary, is his most prominent cabinet minister. John Profumo, who will later be disgraced because of his affair with Christine Keeler, is Minister of War. The Conservatives have been in power for a decade and are, perhaps, looking rather tired.

The Conservative Party has long since accepted the increase of the scope of the welfare state brought about by Labour after the war. The two political parties are so close in their views that people talk of 'Butskellism' – a political philosophy shared by both Butler and Hugh Gaitskell, the Labour leader. Butler himself introduced one of the biggest expansions of the welfare state in his Education Act and Macmillan established some of his reputation by building plenty of council housing when housing minister. In 1961, the Chancellor of the Exchequer, Selwyn Lloyd, brings in wage and salary controls. That is a measure of how much the Conservatives agree with Labour that big government is good government.

In this same year of 1961, six thousand miles away in Hong Kong, a tall, plump, balding, bespectacled civil servant has been promoted. John Cowperthwaite comes from a family prosperous enough to send him to Merchiston Castle, the leading independent boys' school in Edinburgh. The school has a grand main building of stone with a pillared portico resembling the front of a Greek temple. It boasts that it 'promotes the Scottish values of hard work, integrity and good manners'. Cowperthwaite is Scottish through and through. He is not Scottish like Rob Roy or Billy Connolly. But he is recognisably a Scot coming from a recognisable Scottish tradition. He knows Hong Kong well, having lived there since 1946, after the Japanese occupation ceased at the end of the Second World War.

Post-war Hong Kong – poor, ravaged and flooded with refugees.

What is Hong Kong? An oddity of history. A little bit of the Empire that has not yet been handed over to someone else. It is a strange place for a British outpost. Across the harbour, beyond the territories leased by Britain, is the vastness of China, now run by the communists. Chairman Mao Tse-tung dominates the country with fear. His 'little red book' is read by all who understand what is good for themselves and their families.

Cowperthwaite has seen the effect of Chinese communist rule all around Hong Kong. The small colony has been flooded with refugees, arriving with no more than they could carry, in their hundreds of thousands. The population has soared – from six hundred thousand or less in 1945 to 3,200,000. The refugees have built shanty towns or else live in boats on the water or in cramped government-provided units.

Cowperthwaite is forty-six years old and not famous at all. Few people outside Hong Kong have heard of him. He has been promoted to an important job in this outpost, but he has not become the top man, the Governor, or even the official number two. He has been made Financial Secretary, the number three in the official hierarchy. He goes to the government home provided for him, which is grand by Hong Kong standards. But he lives modestly during the next decade while he is there, doing little to improve it.

The Hong Kong press finds that he is not exactly media-friendly. He doesn't court newspaper attention, willingly give interviews, grin or show off his family. His manner is dry almost to the point of rudeness. One day he arrives back from meetings in London and climbs down the steps from his BOAC plane to be greeted by some local journalists.[2]

'What did you discuss at the meetings in London?' one asks.

'I really don't think that is the right sort of question to ask me.'

'Well, Financial Secretary, what should we be asking you?'

'It is not for me to tell you how to do your jobs.'

End of press conference.

It is a classic Cowperthwaite story. Perhaps it is not wholly accurate but it certainly conjures up the man.[3] He can be cussed and infuriating. He is only con-cerned to get on with his job and his duty. Over the next decade, he will frustrate the wishes of many more people than just that gaggle of reporters.

> 'I first visited Hong Kong in 1955, shortly after the initial inflow of refugees. It was a miserable place for most of its inhabitants. The temporary dwellings that the government had thrown up to house the refugees were one-room cells in a multi-storey building that was open in the front: one family, one room. The fact that people would accept such miserable living quarters testified to the intensity of their desire to leave Red China.'[1]
>
> **Milton Friedman, 'The Hong Kong Experiment'**

As Financial Secretary, he is urged to allow mortgage interest to be charged against salaries tax, as in Britain. He says 'no'. It would only benefit those with substantial incomes. He is urged to extend govern-ment housing to the middle class. He refuses again. He says that all public housing involves subsidy. The bigger the housing – which the middle classes would expect – the bigger the subsidy. It would be wrong to subsidise the middle classes, who should pay for their own housing.

Some businessmen want the government to build a tunnel across Hong Kong harbour. Cowperthwaite declines once more. He says that if they think the project would be so beneficial, they should build it themselves. (In due course, they do.) He is urged to tax people on all their incomes, as in Britain, instead of only on their salaries. Yet again, he says 'no'. Tax on all income is inevitably 'inquisitorial', he says, and would discourage investment and enterprise. Surely he should at least collect statistics on Hong Kong's balance of payments, he is asked. 'No,' he replies. 'If I let them compute those statistics, they'll want to use them for planning.'

As time passes, it gradually becomes clear which sort of Scot he is. He

is from the Adam Smith tradition, believing that entrepreneurial activity does good. He is also from the tradition of being careful with money. He is careful with not merely his own money but, more importantly, that of tax-payers. He has integrity – as demanded by his old school. (Perhaps his old school could also take credit for the fact that his knowledge was so extensive that he could playfully refer to the tax policies of Vespasian, the Roman emperor, in one of his budget speeches.) He resists the temptation to spend public money to make his mark or satisfy personal vanity. He is, as one person said of him, 'true to the ethics of Scottish Protestantism'.[4]

John Cowperthwaite, a little-known, tall, plump, balding, be-spectacled civil servant.

Cowperthwaite became the civil servant who liked to say 'no'. Although never in the top job, he dominated policy in Hong Kong. He held the line as best he could against all sorts of spending proposals. His bosses in London – Harold Macmillan and then Harold Wilson – both greatly expanded the welfare state. But Cowperthwaite held out against similar changes in Hong Kong. He did not always succeed. At the end of his period of office, he had to announce free primary education. He revealed what he disliked about it, saying, 'I hope that we shall be able to do something to limit free primary education … to the schools which do not cater for the affluent.' Towards the end of his time in Hong Kong, nearly half the children still went to private schools and most who went to government-subsidised schools attended ones which were privately run.

Cowperthwaite's most important reason for playing Scrooge was to keep down taxes. He thought high taxes slowed economic growth. Low taxes would eventually produce more revenue than higher ones, he argued, because of the growth they would encourage. Fast growth would also benefit the poor by boosting demand for labour and pushing up wages. Fast growth produced 'a rapid and substantial redistribution of income'. Successful capitalism benefited the poor.

Because he kept to his creed, at the end of his time in Hong Kong, the standard rate of tax was only 15 per cent. Even the richest were not asked for more than 15 per cent of their gross income. Profits tax was similarly low. There was no tax at all on dividends or foreign income. The poor were not liable for salaries tax at all.

Cowperthwaite was not the only Hong Kong official to believe in low spending, but he was the most influential. His legacy has gradually been eroded. But even now when China has resumed control, the top salary tax rate in Hong Kong is still only 15 per cent and as recently as 1997, a majority of the population was not liable to salary tax. The poor in Hong Kong are simply not taxed at all.

Back in Britain, meanwhile, a very different line was being followed.

Government spending seriously got going when Wilson became Prime Minister in 1964. Charges on NHS prescriptions were abolished in 1965.[5] New, extra salary-related benefits were paid to the unemployed or ill. Means-tested 'supplementary benefits' were introduced and paid as of right to those with low incomes. It was decided to raise the school-leaving age to sixteen.[6] Higher education was boosted, with the numbers of students almost doubling in a decade.[7] Government spending as a proportion of national income grew inexorably – from 36.5 per cent of national output in 1964 to 40.9 per cent in 1970.[8] Inevitably taxes had to rise, too.

Government spending seriously got going after Harold Wilson became Prime Minister in 1964.

So what was the effect of higher taxes? Who was hit and how? The politicians found that one of the politically easiest ways to raise tax was to let inflation do the job. Inflation and real wage increases raised incomes. So the government did not increase tax-free personal allowances by a similar amount, then more and more people would be automatically brought into the tax net. This way of raising tax went unnoticed by most newspapers and other commentators. It was controversy free. But who was caught in the ever more capacious net? The rich, of course, were already in it. The net was being widened to catch the less well off and then the poor.

In 1961 a married couple with two young children paid income tax if they brought in three-quarters of average earnings.[9] Ten years later, in 1971, couples in Britain with a mere 58 per cent of average earnings were paying income tax (see table on p. 257).[10] In Hong Kong such a couple would pay zero income tax.

Eventually Wilson lost office to the Conservatives in 1970 but they did little to cut back spending. He returned in 1974 and immediately increased unemployment benefits, among other things. His new administration took government expenditure to unprecedented heights, reaching 49 per cent of national income in 1975 (compared with only 34 per cent in 1950 and 12 per cent in 1913). Inevitably, taxes rose too. Excise duty on beer was increased by a third.[11] Relatively poor married couples on only half average earnings with two children started having to pay tax. The standard rate they had to pay reached 35 per cent – a world away from Hong Kong's 15 per cent. The top rate of tax reached 98 per cent under the Labour administration, including a 15 per cent surcharge on dividends.

In 1979, Margaret Thatcher came to power. She is thought by some to have taken a hatchet to public spending. But she got nowhere near reducing it to Hong Kong levels – normally about 17 per cent of the colony's income. The welfare state – particularly social security and the NHS – kept growing during the Thatcher years as if they had lives of their own, largely thwarting her ambitions to reduce spending and thus taxes. In 1986, in the middle of her time as Prime Minister, British government spending was still over two-fifths of national income.[12]

We might pause here to note that the huge and hard-to-control cost of the welfare state was not expected by its creators. Going back to Clement Attlee's postwar government, the cost was relatively modest. The bill for defence was more than those for housing, local government, the NHS, national insurance, national assistance and state pensions all put together. Now the cost of social security alone is four times that of defence. Government figures at present seem designed to obscure, rather than to reveal, the current overall cost of the welfare state. Nevertheless a minimum of £258.9 billion of welfare state spend-

The welfare state causes a massive rise in government spending

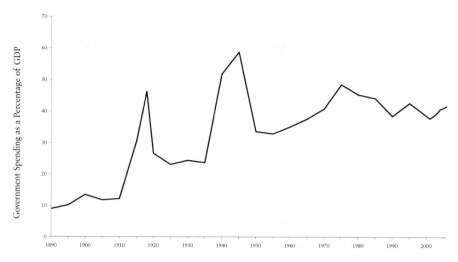

General government expenditure ('total managed expenditure' from 2000/01) as a percentage of GDP[13, 14]

ing can be identified in the 2003/4 Budget, accounting for 60 per cent of all government spending (excluding debt financing). The grand total of welfare state spending, including expenditure tucked away in such categories as 'Scotland', 'Wales' and 'Deputy Prime Minister's Office', is probably at least-two thirds of all government spending and it therefore accounts for about 30 per cent of all national output.

What government spends money on now

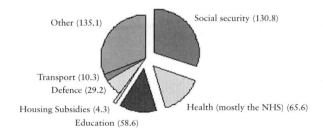

Expenditure in £billions
Source: Office of National Statistics website, planned figures for 2003/4

At the beginning of the twentieth century, government spending accounted for a tenth of economic activity. At the end, it accounted for 40 per cent of it (and that despite the reduction in defence spending). The welfare state is the reason.

So there is a big contrast in the policies followed by Britain and Hong Kong. Attlee, Macmillan, Wilson and others created a country with a highly developed welfare state and consequent heavy taxation. Meanwhile, the austere, little-known Scot, Sir John Cowperthwaite, and others in Hong Kong followed the opposite course of a minimal welfare state and low taxes. The effectiveness of Britain's state welfare is examined in the other chapters. Here, we consider how tax – necessitated by a big welfare state – affected our economic growth.

*

Britain in 1945 was one of the most advanced countries in the world. It had hospitals and doctors admired around the globe, and some of the finest engineers and scientists, who only recently had developed the Spitfire fighter and discovered penicillin among other achievements. Despite the ravages of war, it was far richer per capita than the vast majority of countries around the world. Hong Kong, in contrast, was a Third World country, like Kenya or India, only probably even poorer than either of those.

Hong Kong in 1945 was described as 'a barren rock'. It was poor. It had been occupied by the Japanese in the Second World War and then received a flood of refugees with hardly any money. To begin with, average incomes fell in Hong Kong because of this influx of penniless people, so that in 1960 the per capita output of Hong Kong was a mere 21.5 per cent of what advanced Britons produced. Britain was nearly five times more productive per capita and, broadly speaking, correspondingly wealthier.

Then, from 1961 – the year Cowperthwaite became Financial Secretary as it happens – output per person began to grow very fast. The rate in the 1960s was 6.0 per cent while Britain was growing at a snail's pace in comparison – only 2.3 per cent a year. Britain then had a currency crisis and devalued in 1967.

In the 1970s Hong Kong's output per person grew even faster – at 6.5 per cent a year. Meanwhile, Britain had to go cap in hand to the International Monetary Fund because its credit had run out. Its per capita growth slumped to a mere 1.5 per cent a year.

By 1992 Hong Kong's growth had been so outstanding – and so vastly better than Britain's – that its output per head actually overtook that of the 'mother country'.[16] Hong Kong, under the influence of Cowperthwaite, had transformed itself from being a poor relation – a poverty-stricken colony making cheap plastic toys – to Britain's equal. Hong Kong caught up with Britain in a mere three decades.

Britain and Hong Kong swap places

	Britain	Hong Kong
1870	2nd	
1913	4th	
1950	7th	20th
1973	12th	21st
1999	17th	11th

Level of GDP per capita compared to other countries in 1990 US$[15]

The prosperity of low-tax Hong Kong overtook that of high-tax Britain.

Average output of a person in Hong Kong as a proportion of one in Britain

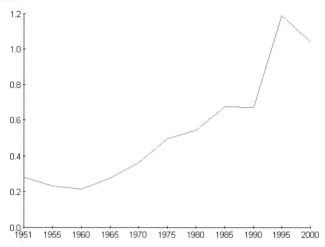

The movements are jerky because of exchange rate movements but the trend is clear. Source: various[17]

People can argue that Hong Kong benefited from a variety of factors which contributed to its extraordinary growth. It had light regulation and virtually no trade barriers. The colony developed a role as an entrepot for China's trade with the rest of the world. But Cowperthwaite would argue that low tax and small government were the key reasons why the barren rock developed spectacularly and became richer than the motherland.

Tax and growth around the world

The contrasting stories of Hong Kong and Britain are powerful evidence, but not proof, that 'tax matters'. Is there any other evidence in favour of such a view?

In 1960, one leading country had markedly lower government expenditure than all the others. In most advanced countries, spending was around thirty per cent of GDP.[18] But in Japan government expenditure was not much more than half that – only 17.5 per cent.

How did its growth compare? Other countries managed an average growth rate of 4.25 per cent between 1950 and 1973 but Japan did nearly twice as well, with an average annual growth rate of 8 per cent. No one could say it had an advantage, as Hong Kong did, in acting as an entrepot for China.

Let's take 1980 and a country at the other end of the spectrum of spending and taxing. By this time, most countries had significantly increased their government spending as their welfare states had expanded. One country, though, became well known for being particularly enthusiastic in its spending so that it soared above that of any other. Sweden's government, in 1980, accounted for 60.1 per cent of all the country's expenditure.

Over the period which most probably reflects such spending (and the correspondingly high taxes) between 1973 and 1999, what was the Swedish growth rate? A mere 1.4 per cent. When Swedish spending and taxing was at its peak, its growth was lower than that of any other leading country in the world.

We are gradually building up a string of associations: Hong Kong and Japan had low tax and high growth. Britain and, more recently, Sweden had higher spending and much lower growth. But in the end we have to look at studies based on lots of countries, which take into account all sorts of things that might affect growth. Nicholas Crafts, a leading British economic historian, has set about doing exactly this. He appears to have no obvious political bias and considers how things such as technology and capital investment may also affect growth. After considering the impact of these and other factors, he comes to taxation. He concludes that the 'econometric evidence' is that taxes on income are 'distortionary' and 'have an adverse impact on growth'.[19]

He adds that growth in 'transfer payments' (an economist's term for welfare payments and the tax-raising it makes necessary) in the 1960s and 1970s could be part of the reason why growth around the world slowed in the following years.[21]

> 'The great Maynard Keynes – no prophet of the Right – once told Professor Roy Harrod that he would be worried if public spending exceeded 25 per cent of the national product.'[20]
>
> Sir Geoffrey Howe

Crafts puts this claim in the most cautious, academic terms, perhaps not surprisingly considering that he is an academic at the London School of Economics – which has long been associated with the welfare state. But in the above, almost incidental, remark he puts forward a big idea: that the entire advanced world has been growing more slowly partly because of the expansion of welfare states.

The OECD similarly looked at many countries to establish the relationship between tax and growth. It came to the conclusion that for every 1 per cent of a country's economic output that is taken by tax, the output per person falls by 0.6 to 0.7 per cent. So, if a country has, like Britain, taxation of approaching 40 per cent of GDP (compared to well under 10 per cent in the late nineteenth century) it has reduced its GDP by about 20 per cent.[22] To put it another way, if we had not increased taxation, our output – and income – per capita would be a quarter higher.

What is wrong with tax?

Why should tax damage growth? Many will think, 'If someone is taxed at 60 or 70 per cent, surely they will go on working anyway? They will keep going to the office and trying to get promotion and so on. They get other things from work apart from cash.' That may be true for some people – notably those, such as civil servants, in jobs where there is little obvious opportunity to react to high taxes. But someone thinking of setting up a new business may be deterred if, after all the work and the risks, he or she will only be allowed to keep 60 per cent of any profit. Such a person might just take an office job instead. If so, the economy would lose someone who could have helped improve national productivity.

Someone on benefits may find that taxation means he or she may not be much better off in work. So he or she may not take a job. That would be a direct loss of output because of taxation.

A company thinking of investing in research would have less cash coming in, if the research is successful, if its profits are taxed at 40 per cent than a company in another country which is taxed at only 15 per cent. The heavily taxed company might decide the risk–reward ratio is not good enough – because of the tax on success – to invest in the research at all. The lightly taxed company in another country might meanwhile go ahead and make that investment.

Another company might like to expand quickly, hiring more people. But there is employer's national insurance to pay on everybody it hires. The company has only got a certain amount of money in the kitty. Therefore it hires fewer people and expands more slowly.

These are some of the many, varied ways in which tax discourages employment, investment and entrepreneurial activity. Part of the effect, over the long term, is psychological. In Britain in the high-tax 1970s, few people wanted to start businesses. There was little point. You would only get taxed for your enterprise. Many with ambition and talent left the country. It was referred to as 'the brain drain'. A culture of enterprise was lost.

In Hong Kong, at the same time, the attitude of get-up-and-go was electric. The colony buzzed with rags-to-riches stories. Hard work and full employment were normal parts of life. Expatriates and indigenous people alike were enthused by the entrepreneurial spirit. One of the greatest fortunes was made by Li Ka Shing, who started off in toy manufacturing and went on to become one of the richest men in the world with investments including Orange, the mobile phone company, and huge property holdings in Hong Kong, mainland China, Canada and the rest of the world.

Britain could have been a rich country

Let us imagine, for a moment, that Britain had not massively developed its welfare state in the twentieth century. Using the OECD estimate – that every one per cent of tax reduces output by 0.6 to 0.7 per cent – how wealthy might Britain have become?

Using the OECD estimate mentioned above, instead of having gross national income per capita of US$27,650 in 2003[23] as we did, it would have been US$34,562. We would have ranked as the third richest country in the world instead of the fifteenth. We would have had higher average incomes than the Swiss or the Japanese. The only countries with higher output per person than ourselves would have been America and Norway. And since we would not be as heavily taxed as them, our take-home pay would be a little higher even than theirs. It would be the highest in the world.

There seems no reason why British people would not easily have the highest average incomes in the whole world if we had stayed as a low-tax society. It is reasonable to suppose that there are cumulative effects in being a low-tax country that were not captured by the OECD analysis. An entrepreneurial culture develops over time. It does not respond instantly to changes in tax. If Britain had not created its welfare state but had kept taxation below 10 per cent of national output throughout the twentieth century, it seems likely that Britain would be decidedly more than a quarter richer than it is now. With such a spur to growth, it could easily have outpaced other countries in its productivity and success. It would now have a high rate of saving, and a high rate of investment and research (based on retaining virtually all profits made); it would consequently be a leader in technology and medicine. Instead of the top innovative companies in the world being predominantly American – IBM and Boeing in the 1970s and more recently Microsoft, Intel and Amgen – the world leaders would include a large number of British names, as used to be the case.

What about the poor?

The really important thing, many will think, is the wealth of people on average or below-average incomes. How would that have been affected if Britain had remained a low-tax society?

Cowperthwaite argued that a successful economy would drive up the wages of the average working person. He suggested, though he did not put it so grandly, that successful capitalism redistributes wealth to the less well off. Is there any evidence for this?

Not many British economists have even considered the idea – perhaps because most have been educated to think that only tax redistributes wealth. Meanwhile many non-economists probably adopt the saying 'The rich get richer and the poor get poorer.'

The statistics, though, suggest something different. In 1938/9, the top 1 per cent accounted for 17.1 per cent of all incomes in Britain.[24] Ten years later, their share had fallen to 10.6 per cent. Their share kept on falling so that by 1972/3 it was down to 6.4 per cent. So the richest certainly do not seem automatically to get relatively richer as an economy grows – rather the reverse. It is true that those coming between positions twenty and fifty out of every hundred people ranked by income were the biggest relative gainers over this period. These figures suggest a spreading out of income from the richest which does not immediately reach those of below-average incomes. But this may be because the least well off during this period became increasingly dependent on benefits. In any case, the poor did not get poorer. According to these figures, their income rose just slightly faster than the average rise in incomes.

If we take a longer period, with less distortion from benefits – from 1911 to 1960 – a greater redistribution of wealth appears. The share of the very richest was slashed from 69 to 42 per cent. Those outside the top 10 per cent more than doubled their assets – from an 8 per cent to a 17 per cent share. Looking at earnings of those in work is probably the best way of reducing the distorting effect of changing rates of welfare dependency. In 1913/14, 'higher professionals' earned 5.2 times the wages of unskilled workers. This great premium was slashed as the economy grew, falling to only 2.4 times the average by 1978.[25]

Certainly there are counter-arguments and conflicting data, but there is some reason to think that capitalism over time does spread wealth to the less well off disproportionately.[26] If this is true, it is reasonable to suggest that 'successful' capitalism – that is to say, the fast growth that low taxes encourage – should promote a correspondingly faster redistribution of income and wealth.

'It is logical that those defined as poor should not have their income reduced still further by income tax.'[27]

Frank Field, pictured, Molly Meacher and Chris Pond, *To Him Who Hath*

In 2002, the vast majority – eighty per cent – of all adults in full-time work were earning between £11,261 and £38,788. Considering that the total workforce includes manual and non-manual workers, some of whom have only just started work and some of whom are right at the top of their career, the difference is not so very great. The difference is surely a lot less than when, in the first half of the twentieth century, anyone who was upper middle class expected to be so much richer than the rest that he or she could employ several servants. That kind of marked disparity of income has disappeared, again suggesting that economic growth does indeed redistribute income to the less well off.

In the meantime, we know one thing for sure: there is one aspect of modern taxation that would have scandalised every one of the original creators of the welfare state, including David Lloyd George, Winston Churchill, William Beveridge, 'Rab' Butler and Aneurin Bevan. Modern politicians and observers have become accustomed to it but it was never in the worst nightmares of the pioneers. Poor people are now taxed.

The government's position is that anyone with less than 60 per cent of average earnings is in 'poverty'. This definition of poverty may be badly flawed but it is true that someone with only 60 per cent of average earnings can be described as 'relatively poor'.

How does the government treat someone in that position?

In April 2002, average earnings were £24,603,[28] so someone on 60 per cent of average earnings received £14,762. It could be, say, a widow aged sixty who still did some work or had a small pension. If her income was 60 per cent of average earnings, her tax position (using the personal allowances and tax rates of 2002/3[29]) was as follows:

Income	£14,762
Less Personal allowance	£4,615
Taxable income	£10,147
Tax on first £1,920 @10 per cent	£192
Tax on subsequent £8,227 @ 22 per cent	£1,809
Total tax due	£2,001

Calculation checked by accountants Grant Thornton.

In other words, the state took a woman it considered to be in poverty and forcibly removed £2,001 a year from her. In addition to that, she faced council tax, excise duty on alcohol and on petrol, VAT on most products and a variety of other indirect taxes. Lloyd George would have been astonished, Beveridge uncomprehending and Bevan disgusted.

In 1938/9, despite the state welfare which already existed,[30] there were still only 3.8 million individuals or couples who paid income tax. In the following decades, the numbers have steadily spread out to include virtually everybody in work. The projected number of people expected to pay income tax in 2003/4 was thirty-one million individuals.

How the tax net spread to the poor

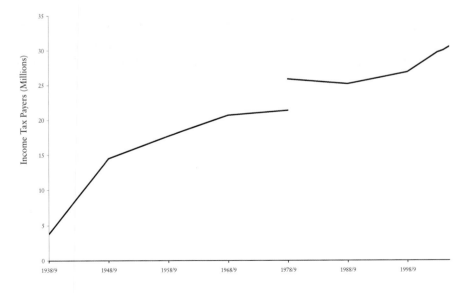

Millions of people paying income tax. In 1978/9 there was a change from married couples counting as one to counting all individual taxpayers. This increased numbers by about a fifth.
Source: Inland Revenue website

Modern politicians and the media accept it as simply normal that the relatively poor should be taxed. But it is quite contrary to the original intentions.

Of course it is easily possible for people, with hindsight, to come up with reasons why it is perfectly all right for the relatively poor to pay tax. They can say that the poor are taxed to pay for things they will themselves benefit from, such as a pensions and healthcare. In other words, the government takes money away to give it back later. But when the state takes money even from the poor, the question 'is the money well spent?' becomes all the more urgent and important. If it is not well spent, it is appalling to think that money is forcibly taken from the poor and then wasted. This is especially so bearing in mind that if the welfare state had not been created at all, the

> **'The principle that the poor should be exempt from tax no longer applies.'[31]**
>
> **Frank Field, Molly Meacher and Chris Pond, *To Him Who Hath***

relatively poor woman already mentioned would probably have a much higher income to start with, probably at least £18,452 (25 per cent more than what she has now), and she would also suffer no income tax whatever. Her take-home income might therefore have been nearly 50 per cent greater.

High taxation is a major part of what is wrong with the welfare state. It has made people – including those on average incomes and below – a great deal poorer than they would otherwise have been – the very opposite of what was intended.

CHAPTER 9
The reckoning

The proponents of the welfare state were ecstatically excited about what they were doing in 1945–50. Clement Attlee, at the climax of his speech to a Labour Party conference, quoted William Blake, saying:

I will not cease from Mental Fight,
Nor shall my Sword sleep in my hand,
Till we have built Jerusalem,
In England's green and pleasant Land.

Clement Attlee believed he was building 'a new Jerusalem'.

The welfare state would be the 'new Jerusalem'.

Michael Foot remembered how the election of the Labour Party in 1945 was greeted:

When the scale of the Labour Party's victory became known on the night of 26 July, bonfires were lit, people danced in the streets, and young and old crowded into halls all over the country to acclaim their elected standard bearers ... Eyes were fixed on the promise of a new society.[1]

Like faith in God, belief in the welfare state has since become less wide and deep. Nicholas Timmins in his account of the post-1945 welfare state, *The Five Giants*, declared himself a believer but almost in a defensive way.[2] He admitted that despite half a century of state education, one in five 21-year-olds had trouble with basic maths. He acknowledged the 'worrying' signs that although the country was three times richer than in 1950, in the very poorest areas death rates for men aged fifteen to forty-four were actually rising. When he wrote about how the country had got richer and life expectancy had increased, he admitted, 'the welfare state could not claim all the credit for these changes,' before quickly adding, 'but it could claim some.'

The most serious tarnishing of the reputation of the welfare state in recent years has taken place in the NHS, because of the waiting lists and because people have learnt that medical attention is quicker and better in other countries. This has sowed doubts in the public's mind – doubts which the political parties have attempted to quell by promising either more money or reform.

But the reduction of the public reputation of the welfare state is minor compared to the adverse conclusions about it reached in the previous chapters of this book. Many people may therefore react, 'Can it really be so bad? Can something meant to be so helpful have done so much harm?' But the evidence – adduced and discussed in previous chapters – has led to these judgements and it would be unworthy of the importance of the subject to understate them. In the following summary, the various damaging effects of the welfare state are brought together in one place.

We have seen that the welfare state began in 1563 when, under Elizabeth I, giving to the poor was made compulsory. The recognisably modern version was initiated in 1906 with the election of the Liberal Party. One of the welfare state's earliest damaging effects was to contribute heavily to mass unemployment over many decades, starting in the 1920s. Long-term mass unemployment only became normal after the modern welfare state was created. Although people talk about unemployment less frequently these days, it continues at a very high level up to the present because – in addition to the official jobless figure – there is mass hidden unemployment.

Few would dispute that the knock-on effects of this unemployment are serious. The jobless suffer depression; young men tend to experience 'diffused hostility' – a kind of aggressive alienation. There is plenty of reason to believe that joblessness has contributed to the rising crime and incivility which Britain has experienced over the past century. Unemployment has also wasted the economic contribution the jobless could otherwise have made.

> 'When there is an income tax, the just man will pay more and the unjust less on the same amount of income.'[3]
>
> **Plato (c.428–346 BC)**

State benefits have greatly discouraged the very large amount of self-provision and mutual provision which existed before the welfare state and was growing strongly. Such provision had the advantage that it did not create most of the serious ill effects of the welfare state. The welfare state has made it tempting and easy to cheat. This has undermined honesty. Tax cheating too has resulted from the welfare state, because the high level of tax, necessitated by the cost, has similarly offered too much temptation for too long. Welfare benefits have obliged millions of people to fill in forms detailing their personal circumstances – using up their time, making them feel dependent, reducing their self-respect and eroding their personal privacy.

The National Health Service has turned what was one of the leading medical services among advanced countries into one of the least successful – perhaps even the very worst. There is a serious and persistent shortage of doctors, who are therefore more difficult to see, have to give patients less time and offer less advice. Part of the shortage consists of a shortage of consultants, such as cancer specialists, so a patient has a serious risk of not being seen by such a specialist at all and consequently may get less than ideal treatment. There is a shortage of nurses too, but plenty of administrators – almost as many as there are nurses.

Since the NHS took over municipal and charitable hospitals in 1948, a great many have been closed. The NHS has sold off the family silver. Patients are therefore further away from help and, if admitted to hospital, are further from friends and relatives. The number of beds available has been cut down repeatedly and there is now a shortage.

There is a shortage of equipment too. Much of the equipment which the NHS does have is old and out of date. Some is dangerous.

The NHS has long waiting lists and waiting lists to get onto the waiting lists. Administrators are under pressure to mislead the public about the true extent of the problem and they sometimes do so. Waiting lists cause people to live in prolonged pain, fear and danger. A proportion of patients die while waiting to be seen. The old, the inarticulate and the poor are discriminated against by the NHS – the poor because they cannot afford to get off the waiting list by paying, the inarticulate because they cannot bully the system to provide the care they need and the old because their needs are reckoned against those of younger people and supply is limited.

A minimum number of 15,140 unnecessary deaths take place each year because we have the NHS instead of an average medical system.

Britain has also lost its position at the forefront of medical discovery and innovation, too. The very latest drugs, equipment and operating techniques are usually not available in the NHS.

Many people believe that if the NHS was not there, the poor would go untreated. This fear is unjustified. Even when the original arguments were offered in favour of the creation of the NHS in 1943, it was not claimed that the poor went untreated. On the contrary, it appears they received better care, relative to the rich, than they do now.

Meanwhile in education, after 130 years of increasing state control, it has become so ineffective that one in five adults is now 'functionally illiterate'. One in seven adults has no exam passes at all. Actual academic attainment – as opposed to exam results – is seriously down on what it used to be. Many state primary schools do not attempt to teach any language other than English. Many do poorly even at that basic task. The teaching of English grammar has been neglected – the teaching of foreign-language grammar even more so. Standards at universities have fallen too, to the point where Oxford and Cambridge are barely hanging on to world class status.

Waste in state education has been enormous with about one civil servant for every class. Teachers' time is extensively taken up in dealing with government initiatives rather than teaching. Morale is low and they take twice as much time off sick as teachers in the private sector.

Compulsorily keeping children at poor schools where they are disaffected and bored has caused a rise in youth crime. The crime has taken place within the schools too, with a great increase in bullying and victimisation. Fear of bullying has contributed to the amount of truancy.

In housing, the Rent and Mortgage Restriction Act of 1915 was meant to contain the cost of housing but took the profit out of private rented accommodation and thus led to a housing shortage, which was particularly damaging to the poor. The impact of this and subsequent rent Acts continued right until the 1980s, causing the creation of slums out of what had been good housing. The rent Acts gave an incentive to landlords such as Peter Rachman to terrorise tenants.

The provision of council housing reached its zenith after the Second World War. Though some very pleasant houses were created, production was slow and expensive. Fewer houses were built than after the First World War. The new housing also broke up existing communities and families. Places were created which often did not have a sense of shared community but rather made people feel they had no sense of possession – no stake. They felt alienated and, in some cases, frightened.

Many tower blocks and certain other estates built at great expense became so blighted by crime and vandalism that they had to be destroyed. Many people, including the old, have been trapped in estates where they are afraid to go out. The council housing idea rose, became extremely expensive and then collapsed in failure. The current Labour government has allowed it to continue to diminish in importance.

The welfare state has discouraged marriage – especially among the less well off. It has contributed significantly to a boom in divorce, separations and lone parenting. This in turn has caused women to be in greater danger of being hurt, since, on average, they are physically safer when married. But the worst damage has been done to the children, who have become dramatically more likely to be abused or hurt, or to die because many more are not brought up by their natural, married parents. The reduction of natural, married parenting, brought about by the welfare state, has caused more children to under-achieve in every way, to be less happy, to turn to delinquency and ultimately to crime. Such crime is the tip of an iceberg of alienation and incivility.

The state pension has caused the great majority of people to be poorer in old age than they would have been if it had never been created. The idea of saving was growing strongly in the nineteenth century. It has now been destroyed for all but the richest third of society. In 1905, only 14 per cent of those aged over sixty depended on the state for benefits. In 2003, it was expected to be 57 per cent. A massively richer society has been made vastly more benefit dependent by the welfare state. People have been deceived by the state about what they could expect. They have been strongly discouraged from saving by means-tested benefits both before and after retirement. The spirit of independence – and the self-respect it creates – have been undermined.

The cost of the welfare state has been enormous. State expenditure has risen to over 40 per cent of all economic activity. The burden of taxation has become so great that, grotesquely, people who – according to the government definition of the word – are in 'poverty' are obliged to pay income tax.

Heavy taxation caused by the welfare state has slowed British economic growth, turning Britain into an economically second-class country – a condition to which British people have now become accustomed, as if it were somehow natural. If the welfare state had not been created, Britain's superior economic performance would have continued and Britain would – at a minimum – have higher output per capita than Switzerland or Japan. In terms of take-home pay, British people would be richer than Americans – the most prosperous people in the world.

This catalogue of damage is long and the charges are serious. Yet even this list does not fully bring out one of the most important ways in which Britain has been damaged.

Gentle, courteous and orderly

We saw in the first chapter that Professor Geoffrey Gorer wrote in 1955 how the English were 'certainly among the most peaceful, gentle, courteous and orderly populations that the civilised world has ever seen'. George Orwell, in 1944, similarly wrote: 'An imaginary foreign observer would certainly be struck by our gentleness; by the orderly behaviour of English crowds, the lack of pushing and quarrelling ... And except for certain well-defined areas in half-a-dozen big towns, there is very little crime or violence.'[4]

> 'If I can help somebody as I pass along, then my living will not be in vain.'[6]
>
> **Popular post-Second World War song performed by Josef Locke at the Blackpool Opera House**

That decency, kindness and civility for which British people were once noted has been undermined. People previously gave heavily to charity and believed that kindness was a moral duty.[5] Now incivility, vandalism and law-breaking are routine.

Friendly societies used to encourage a sense of a mutual cause and shared responsibility. They were voluntary arrangements between people who usually knew each other. If one of them came to be in need, the friendly society would help. Members could take their turn at being one of the senior officers. They could also help each other in practical ways. There was natural peer pressure to lead good, decent lives. Such natural pressure was reinforced by explicit declarations that members should behave well. This has now been replaced by dependence on state benefits, which are doled out without anything like the same care or personal attention. People have changed from being team members in mutual support groups to being state dependants who feel no particular responsibility to act decently.

The welfare state has created persistent temptations to cheat and lie. Someone finds that he or she is no longer really entitled to a benefit which formerly was rightly received but does not get round to notifying the benefits office.

The lone-parenting epidemic has also contributed to the falling off of British decency. The state has encouraged men to feel that they can spawn children without taking responsibility for them. The responsibility which they formerly took on helped to make them more civil, responsible people – and not just in relation to their children. The damaged children meanwhile have been more likely to feel alienated and therefore unwilling to be kind or generous to others.

'Fuck you, Debbie, Debbie, fuck you!'[7]

Eminem, referring to his mother, Debbie Mathers, at Milton Keynes Bowl, 2003

Children are forced to stay until sixteen at unsatisfactory state schools with two damaging effects on character. The schools place disaffected children into groups where the main role models are other similar children. A gang-like atmosphere readily results in which power goes to the strongest. Such youthful gangs are likely to be amoral. The bored, alienated children are more likely to become delinquent, which is another form of incivility.

Council housing, by breaking up extended, mutually supporting

The welfare state has led to a falling off of decency and a rise in crime.

families, has left people more alone in the world and therefore more alienated. Such people are less able to compromise and to help each other – the sort of behaviour which enables a society to be civilised. The various ill effects have compounded each other – producing plenty of children, for example, brought up on welfare, living on a bad council estate, who have lone parents who were themselves badly educated and who enjoy little in the way of an extended family. Such children are tragic victims of the welfare state and have a high risk of turning out to be far from model citizens.

> 'We still get children who … come to school hungry and under-dressed. Some arrive here unable to speak. We try to civilise them. We teach them how to hold a knife and fork.'[8]
>
> **Mary Binns, head of a school in Sheffield, 2000**

In this wide variety of ways the honesty, kindness and civility of British people – once so noted – has been undermined by the welfare state. The former British culture of decency has persisted patchily into the latter part of the twentieth century and up to the present. It takes time to change a people from being outstandingly fine into being particularly unpleasant. But the islands of decency have become smaller – increasingly encircled by more aggressive, selfish behaviour. A transformation of the British people has taken place.

It is not going too far to say that all these conclusions together mean, in sum, that the welfare state has been a disaster for Britain. It is indeed 'as bad as that'. The welfare state has ruined lives and left people morally and culturally impoverished. It has left many depressed and alienated, too. It has caused some to become criminals – a waste of a life – and others to be the victims of criminals. It has spoiled trust between people and caused millions of patients to suffer and to worry. Tens of thousands have died prematurely. It has reduced the decency and happiness of the British people.

> 'There is no doubt that behaviour has deteriorated over the past twenty years.'[9]
>
> **Tony Blair**

The process can be expressed in diagrammatic form (see overleaf), which brings out the way causes lead to effects and then on to still other effects. It is not just one aspect of the welfare state that has caused the rise in crime, for example, but a combination of causes and secondary causes. Lone parenting, low-quality compulsory education, living on benefits, council estates and the widespread reduction of the sense that each of us must take responsibility for ourselves and our families; all of these – caused by the welfare state – have contributed to it.

This makes for a depressing story. But there is yet one more way in which the welfare state has damaged Britain which cannot be omitted. The welfare state has turned out to be a domineering state. It has circumscribed freedom, independence and innovation.

The welfare state versus personal freedom

As long ago as the 1890s, people bridled at the way the embryo modern welfare state was beginning to tell them what to do:

> *Truant officers who appeared to enforce school attendance were no more welcomed by the parents than by the children they were sent to chase. Nor were health visitors making domiciliary visits which could easily be seen to be patronising and uninvited intrusions on the privacy of the home and offering high-minded advice on nutrition and personal hygiene ... necessarily welcomed in working-class households.*[10]

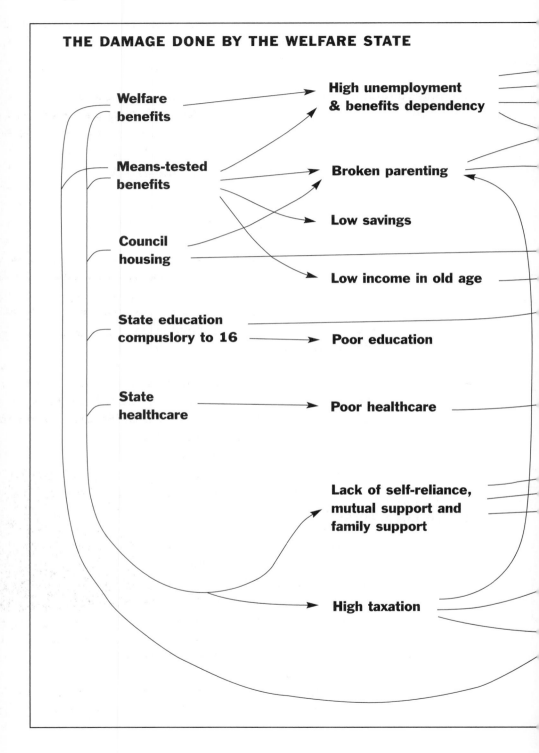

THE DAMAGE DONE BY THE WELFARE STATE

Welfare benefits

Means-tested benefits

Council housing

State education compuslory to 16

State healthcare

High unemployment & benefits dependency

Broken parenting

Low savings

Low income in old age

Poor education

Poor healthcare

Lack of self-reliance, mutual support and family support

High taxation

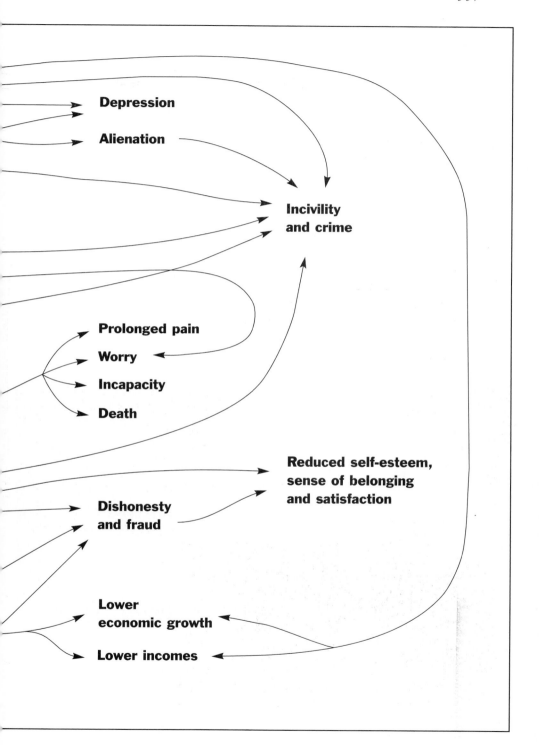

But such intervention was only a foretaste of the way the welfare state was going to infringe personal freedom and privacy.

Tax removes the freedom of an individual to keep the fruits of his or her labour. To obtain benefits, people must fill in forms and make promises, such as to seek work. In medical care, people's freedom to choose their doctor has been reduced. The health service administers only those drugs approved by the state. The training of doctors – the style and the numbers – is dictated by the state. The state determines the nature of the training of teachers. State schools are under great pressure to teach what is on the national curriculum. Even private schools are affected, being staffed by people trained by the state and accustomed to doing what the state variously recommends or demands. Removal of individual choice has been so widespread that the very spirit of independence has been damaged.

> 'The Collectivist State Is a Prig and a Bandit; It may be my Fate, But I'm damned if I'll stand it.'[11]
>
> **G. K. Chesterton**

'Blunkett's scheme is working, Sarge. I've fined someone for yobbish behaviour – he's getting the money now.' Mac cartoon, *Daily Mail*, 13 March 2003.

Through council housing, the state decides who may live where. Through means-tested benefits, the state has told low-paid people not to save. The welfare state pushes and pulls. Sometimes it does both at the same time – instructing people to save, for example, but making it not worth their while.

The state – finding that people are not doing as they are told or that its systems are not working – then tells people off. Failings of the NHS are blamed on 'selfish' consultants. Teachers are accused of being substandard. Parents are told to make sure their children miss not a single day of school – regardless of how bad or dangerous the school may be. The state insists that parents should give children the triple vaccine – for mumps, measles and rubella – refusing to allow people to opt for single vaccines. The government has even issued instructions on how people should wash their hands. The welfare state causes problems – such as increased crime – and then reduces freedom and privacy in an attempt to deal with those problems. The state gave rise to the increase in abuse of children by encouraging lone parenting. Then it proposed identity cards for every newborn child to improve protection against the abuse it had itself caused.[12]

The people are a great disappointment to their governors. They are forever needing to be upbraided. 'Task forces' are appointed to carry out 'strategies' to make the people behave better. But the reason the people have become less decent, civilised, law abiding and keen to save is precisely because of years in which government has taken responsibility out of their hands through

> 'The real problem for the government is the British people themselves. Whole sections of the population are regularly selected and denounced for their inadequacies. The government is displeased with merchants ("rip off Britain"), lawyers, doctors (unaccountable), parents, farmers (subsidised fraud) and many others ... It was, no doubt, a joke when Bertold Brecht, the German Marxist, responded to the 1953 riots in East Berlin by suggesting that the Government should dissolve the people and elect a new one, but it isn't a joke any more. The British are, to judge by the complaints of their rulers, under-educated, obese, uncultured, apathetic, uncitizenly, and cannot be trusted with guns, alcohol, punitive canes, sugary food or even children.'[13]
>
> **Professor Kenneth Minogue, *Civil Society and David Blunkett***

the welfare state. Trying to improve people by yet more government instruction and bullying does not address the fundamental problem.

People used to be proud of their independence. In the 1950s, when I was a child, people used to exclaim 'It's a free country!' if their choices were questioned. People don't use that phrase as much now, perhaps because they know in their hearts that Britain is not so free any more. A welfare state, by its nature, tells people what to do.

> 'Our opponents are driven by their vision, a messianic vision of the perfectibility of man. It may have been conceived with fine intentions; it may have been born of a passion, but it has become an engine of tyranny, impoverishment and unemployment.'[14]
>
> **Sir Keith Joseph**

The welfare state versus the poor

The poor have suffered the most. This will seem a bizarre assertion to many. The welfare state was created to look after the poor. But again and again, the truth of this has emerged in previous chapters.

The poor are the ones who have ended up with the worst schools and the worst healthcare. The poor now find it much more difficult to see a consultant than sixty years ago. There was no consultant shortage then. The poor, not the rich, have been induced by the welfare state not to save, not to marry and to divorce or separate if they have married. The poor have been similarly been led to unemployment. The children of the poor are consequently more likely to have suffered from broken parenting, more likely to have become alienated and to have turned to crime. Because the poor tend to live amongst each other, they are also more likely to be the victims of the vastly increased crime. The poorest tenth now often live in ghettos, leading lives without hope or dignity. Their character has tended to change in a way that causes unhappiness to others – generally other poor people – and no satisfaction to themselves.

Some people may feel 'surely there are *some* things that the welfare state has done well?' Certainly, it is true that a proportion of children have been well educated, many have been well treated by the NHS, thousands have been given pleasant homes and so on. But we are not comparing the welfare state with an imaginary world in which no other kind of welfare existed. We are not comparing state provision against zero provision. Any sensible judgement of the welfare state compares it against the welfare provision which would have existed if the state had not intervened. It is on that basis that the welfare state has failed so thoroughly.

We should not pretend that a Britain without the modern welfare state would have been perfect, of course. We are comparing two imperfect systems. But the welfare provided by the state has proved to be decidedly the inferior and more damaging of the two.

Some people cite cases of good provision by the welfare state to suggest that it is 'all right really'. But such cases of good provision should not be considered in isolation. In making a proper judgement on, say, council housing, one must count against the nice houses the estates that have become vile and dangerous. One must count the cost of providing the housing at the expense, to a large degree, of other working people. One must count the discouragement given to people to provide for themselves, which could have led ultimately to better housing provision for a larger number.

At the beginning of this book, the question was asked whether it was possible that the multi-faceted deterioration of Britain described there could possibly have anything to do with the welfare state. Through all the following chapters – and summarised in this one – we have seen how the welfare state has had damaging effects, causing precisely the things which have constituted this deterioration.

The welfare state credibly explains the decline of Britain from being the country of Stanley Matthews to that of Vinnie Jones. It makes sense of how Britain now has tourists with the worst reputation for bad behaviour in the world. It offers an explanation of why more than a quarter of children confess to having committed a crime in the past six months and why they are so ignorant about British culture and history. It helps explain, too, why Britons are even less happy than they used to be.

So the answer is 'yes', the welfare state has been the fundamental cause of the deterioration of Britain.

It would have been better if the modern welfare state had never been created.

CHAPTER 10

If the welfare state is so bad, why don't we get rid of it?

Anyone reading this book up to this point could object, 'Hang on a moment. If the welfare state has been so disastrous, why is there no rush to get rid of it? Why has this alleged "disaster" not even been noticed by most of those whom it is meant to have affected?'

Fair questions.

Part of the answer may lie in the story of Laura Touche. Mrs Touche was a young, attractive woman with everything to live for – a direct descendant of the American president Thomas Jefferson, who had married into a wealthy family. Her husband's great-grandfather had set up the chartered accountancy firm that became Deloitte and Touche. Laura Touche became pregnant in 1998 and in February the following year gave birth to twins at the Portland Hospital, a private hospital in north London. Celebrity couples such as Liam Gallagher and Patsy Kensit and the Duke and Duchess of York had also used it to bring their children into the world. Laura Touche's big day should have been a high point in a prosperous and happy life. But after the birth, which was by Caesarean, Mrs Touche experienced an agonising headache.

> 'One of the great puzzles of our time is why our voters support institutions which make them seriously worse off.'
>
> **Patrick Minford, Professor of Economics, Cardiff Business School**

Her blood pressure rose and was not checked as regularly as it should have been. The seriousness of the situation was not realised and acted upon as quickly as it should have been. Because of the delay, her condition got worse. She was transferred to another hospital and then another. But the doctors could not save her. She died, leaving behind Peter, her distraught husband, and Alexander and Charles, their two baby sons.

The coroner for Inner London, Dr Stephen Chan, ruled that Laura Touche had died from natural causes and that no inquest was necessary.

But Peter Touche went to the High Court and two senior judges ruled that an inquest should take place after all. At this inquest, the jury found that Mrs Touche had died from natural causes but neglect had contributed to her death. The coroner said, 'The principal and most catastrophic and at present inexplicable error was the failure by [midwife] Mrs Grace Bartholomew to carry out routine but vital post-operative monitoring.'

Laura Touche with her husband, Peter. Laura gave birth to twins at the Portland Hospital.

Many readers may remember this tragic story because it received considerable coverage in newspapers, on television and radio. Pictures of the good-looking young couple appeared. A search on BBC Online in the late 2003 revealed four articles on the subject with a combined length of eighty-six inches.[1] The *Guardian/Observer* website listed four articles devoted to the death of Laura Touche, another five which made substantial reference to it and a further four mentioning it – thirteen references in all. The combined length of those parts of the stories referring to Laura Touche amounted to seventy-two inches. The columns on the *Guardian/Observer* website were wider than those of the BBC, so the *Guardian/Observer* coverage was equivalent to about 115 BBC inches.

A number of points kept on being repeated in the many articles and broadcast reports: that it was a tragedy, of course, that it was the fault of the hospital, that the hospital was private and that Peter Touche was disgusted by the hospital's behaviour and believed it compared badly with NHS hospitals.

The coverage implicitly cast doubt on the safety of private hospitals. It highlighted the fact that private hospitals are generally not equipped to deal with as many situations as NHS hospitals. It was impossible to read or hear any of the coverage without gaining the impression that private hospitals may be more dangerous than NHS hospitals. That was the impression most people would have been left with.

Tracie Reynolds was another young mother-to-be. She, too, gave birth by Caesarean section, in her case at the New Cross Hospital,

Wolverhampton. In the words of the hospital's own spokesman, 'care was not of the highest standard.' There were communication failures, clinical staff were not there at key moments and the baby's condition was misdiagnosed for five hours. There was a string of warnings but they were missed. As a result, Tracie Reynolds' baby, later named Trinity, suffocated and died nine minutes before being delivered.

Was the death of Trinity Reynolds less important than that of Laura Touche? The question may seem unnecessary or frivolous but, in the circumstances which I will describe, I think it is worth establishing at the outset whether we think the loss of her life matters less. Her family was probably less well off than that of Laura Touche. Does that mean her death was less important? The death took place in an NHS hospital. Does that make the loss of life less tragic? Most people would surely respond 'no, of course not' when directly asked these questions.

Tracie and Simon Reynolds. Was the death of their daughter less important than that of Laura Touche?

But the death of Trinity Reynolds received very little coverage in national newspapers and on broadcast media. I only became aware of it myself because of a key word search on the BBC website.[2] I found reference to the tragic death of Trinity as part of a single story that was fifteen inches long – less than a fifth of the BBC Online coverage of Laura Touche's death. A search of the *Guardian/Observer* website also revealed a single article that was nine inches long – one-eighth of the coverage of Laura Touche's death. A search of the *Daily Telegraph* website revealed no coverage of the death of little Trinity Reynolds at all.

Of course journalists will immediately say there are good 'news value' reasons why Laura Touche got so much more attention than Trinity Reynolds. Editors believe, probably rightly, that the public is more interested in the rich or famous than everyone else. It is also true that Peter Touche had the money and confidence to defy a coroner, go to the High Court and sue the hospital. He also presumably supplied the photographs which were published and he apparently gave a press conference.

But the fact remains that one person died in a private hospital and it got a great deal of coverage. One person died in the NHS – also because of inadequate care – and it got hardly any coverage at all. And the contrast is actually even more extreme than so far described.

The story which mentioned Trinity's death was not mainly about her. The main news was that an inquiry had been started into a *series* of baby deaths at New Cross Hospital. According to the story, five babies had died. So the news coverage of Trinity's death was shared with the deaths of others, meaning that coverage of each death amounted to a mere one-twentieth of the coverage of the death in the private hospital on the BBC website. Even though five children had apparently died – as opposed to the single death of Laura Touche – all their deaths still only rated one relatively short article in the *Guardian/Observer* and no article at all in the *Daily Telegraph*.

Five deaths in an NHS hospital were worth a fraction of the coverage of one death in a private hospital. It seems that deaths in NHS hospitals are not 'news' unless they are on a truly spectacular and horrific scale, such as the deaths of well over thirty children in the Bristol heart surgery scandal of the late 1980s and early 1990s.[3] There is a double standard at work. A failure of private provision gets a huge amount of media attention. A failure of state provision gets far less.

	BBC	Guardian/ Observer	Daily Telegraph
Death of Laura Touche in a private hospital	86"	115"	192"
Death of Trinity Reynolds in an NHS hospital	15"	14.5"	0"

Column inches devoted to each story on *BBC Online* and the newspapers (*Guardian/Observer* and *Daily Telegraph* coverage measured in equivalent of BBC column inches)[4]

This double standard goes beyond the amount of coverage. Articles and broadcasts about the death of Laura Touche also raised doubts about whether private hospitals were safe.

But when the deaths of no fewer than five babies at an NHS hospital were reported, no suggestion whatever was made that NHS hospitals might be less safe than private hospitals. For some reason, private-sector provision was readily, even eagerly criticised whereas state provision – in this case NHS provision – was not.[5] Why is this?

Some may think that NHS hospitals are indeed safer. It is certainly true that private hospitals tend to have fewer facilities. But this is mainly for the simple reason that private and charitable hospitals in Britain are still relatively small. In the US, where they are big, they have more extensive facilities – and far more up-to-date equipment – than NHS hospitals. In many other ways, British private hospitals are far safer. For the details of how unsafe NHS hospitals are, see Chapter 3. Suffice to repeat here that NHS hospitals are far less determined and effective in preventing potentially fatal infection by MRSA; NHS patients are less likely to be treated by experienced consultants; there is a shortage of all frontline staff in NHS hospitals; NHS hospitals tend to have older equipment, which can be dangerous; and NHS patients have often waited so long to get into hospital for treatment that their condition has become more serious and more difficult to treat. Overall, NHS hospitals are considerably more dangerous than private hospitals. So the question remains: why is there a double standard by which private provision is judged harshly and state provision leniently?

One way to try to understand it is to consider a young nurse working in a busy NHS hospital. She is not paid well, she has great responsibility, she is battling with inadequate resources and sometimes she gets insulted by the very patients she is trying to help. She is perceived as heroic and she might well genuinely be so. Such a nurse rightly attracts respect and sympathy.

The image of that nurse affects the way people perceive the organisation she works for. The image is very different from, say, a consultant doing operations in the private sector. Such a consultant also works for the NHS but if he or she does plenty of private work, he or she is widely seen as 'being in it for the money'. The image of heroism melts away. The perception of brave self-sacrifice has been replaced by something more base.

Such images are, of course, far from being wholly accurate or fair. Some nurses in the NHS are time-servers who treat patients with barely disguised contempt. There are anyway eight managers and support staff for every ten nurses in the NHS and they would attract less sympathy. But the public and the media generally do not see them. Meanwhile, many of those in the private sector are conscientious and caring. They believe – surely with justification – that even better-off people deserve care and attention when they are ill. Popular perception disregards such things. Since the NHS nurses and others are thought to be acting philanthropically, anything that goes wrong is regarded in a forgiving way. The reaction is 'well, they're doing their best.' This may be one reason why a blind eye is turned to the failures of the NHS and other kinds of state provision.

What else might lie behind it?

One factor, possibly, may be that people expect state provision to fail so any instances of such failure are not 'news'. But if this were a factor, it makes it all the more puzzling that the public is not keen to give up state provision.

Are people frightened? Do they feel, perhaps, that the welfare state is their longstop? If they lose everything, the welfare state will help them somehow. The help may be miserable and inadequate but still better than nothing. Of course, as previous chapters have demonstrated, it is not actually true that the welfare state saves everyone in trouble. Far from it. Many people in desperate need of a heart operation, for example, do not get it and so die. Perhaps people are susceptible to the existence of this theoretical safety net and prefer not to think about its actual value and reliability.

> 'Every new administration, not excluding ourselves, arrives in power with bright and benevolent ideas of using public money to do good. The more frequent the changes of government, the more numerous are the bright ideas, and the more frequent the elections, the more benevolent they become.'[6]
>
> **Winston Churchill, 1927**

Fear of living without state welfare may well derive partly from ignorance. Most people have no idea that, prior to the modern welfare state, there was a variety of safety nets. Families helped each other. Friendly societies and trade unions supported their millions of members. There was a great multitude of charities as well as a basic, low level of state support. So a second reason why people may cling to the welfare state may be simple ignorance.

Another possible reason is that the richest third of society does not see the welfare state at its worst. Their children – like those of Tony Blair and of Harriet Harman, the former social security secretary – don't go to the worst state schools. They don't live in the most violent parts of Britain and, if need be, they can pay for that vital operation. The welfare state does not seem as bad to them as it really is. Without wishing to be cynical, it is possible that the existence of the welfare state also makes them feel that they are worthy people living in a good society. This may be such an attractive thought to them that they do not want to give it up, even if the facts don't fit.

Could the vanity and self-interest of politicians and welfare state workers also be a factor? Politicians naturally like to believe that they have the answer to various problems in the welfare state. They like to think they can make the schools teach effectively or make the hospitals overcome their waiting lists or 'abolish poverty'. Each succeeding government thinks it has a plan that will work or that simply more money will do the trick. They lack a sense – or more worryingly, a knowledge – of the history of the welfare state. If they could look back they would see a long procession of other politicians, just as clever as themselves, all thinking precisely the same.

Meanwhile those who work for the welfare state are also only human in wanting to believe that their work is productive and good. Even those who can see it is going badly tend to think 'we need to strive to make it better' in preference to 'we should abolish the organisation which employs me.'

There is, perhaps, one other explanation why people cling to the idea of the welfare state. The arguments in favour of a welfare state are simple: that the government should support those in need and offer free education and healthcare to all. The arguments against it are complex and sound negative. In the end, all the arguments against the welfare state come down to two: that it just doesn't work in what it tries to do and it causes a great deal of collateral damage. Neither of these statements is aspirational or inspiring. If one talks, to sound more positive, of self-reliance, mutual support and freedom it may sound, to an electorate, too much like hard work.

So there are many reasons why people may resist the idea that the welfare state has failed. Across the world, people have found the concept irresistibly attractive. It is a little-noticed fact that every single advanced, democratic country in the world has a welfare state. France, Germany, Italy, Belgium, Sweden, Canada, Australia and, yes, even the United States of America have welfare states. The United States is regarded by many as a bastion of free markets but it has government-funded healthcare, state schools and welfare benefits for the unemployed and the ill. All modern democracies have opted to have a welfare state.

Is there something about democracy which causes countries to create welfare states?

In Britain, the number of people with the vote rocketed from one million to twenty-one million between 1867 and 1918.

WHY PEOPLE DO NOT RECOGNISE THE FAILURE OF THE WELFARE STATE

1. Failure in state provision is viewed forgivingly because public-sector workers are perceived to have altruistic motives.
2. Fear that nothing else would be there to help those in difficulty if the welfare state did not exist.
3. Ignorance of the support systems which used to exist prior to the modern welfare state.
4. The ruling elite does not experience the welfare state at its worst, being able to buy or negotiate itself out of many of the problems.
5. The richest third of society may enjoy believing it is part of a 'good society' in having a welfare state without having to do anything personally and directly – which was normal before the welfare state.
6. Politicians perennially persuade themselves that they have a plan which will cure the ills of the welfare state.
7. Millions of employees of the welfare state do not wish to feel that they are working for a failed system.
8. The welfare state is a simple and attractive concept. The arguments against it are complex and perceived as negative or depressing.

When did the modern welfare state begin? Over the same period.

Education began its way to becoming a state monopoly in 1870. State pensions were introduced in 1908. National unemployment and health insurance were brought in three years later. Increases in the latter benefits – and less strict conditions – were introduced soon after 1918. In short, the modern welfare state began absolutely in parallel with democracy.

It looks like more than a coincidence, especially if one considers how politics was also transformed over the same time. According to one historian of the period, 'from 1884, a central assumption of British politics – which the Conservative Party did not dispute – was that finding an answer to the social question was bound to be an electoral imperative.'[7] The Liberal Party saw that if it was to keep its traditional working-class vote – a working-class vote that was being greatly increased – it had to offer something to attract them. It had to offer them something, in particular, to dissuade them from supporting the embryo Labour Party.

The growth of the power of the people – the *demos* – was key to the growth of the welfare state. In the early stages, of course, the working class thought that state welfare would be a one-way street: money would pass from the rich to themselves. As another historian wrote, 'the majority of voters could cheerfully support higher direct taxes of the sort imposed by Lloyd George without personal loss.'[8]

It appears that the British welfare state is indeed the product of British democracy. If that is true, it gives rise to the question: are democracies capable of giving up their welfare states? Are all democracies – Britain among them – bound to cling to their welfare states regardless of how badly they do?

There is certainly reason to think so. When politicians seek power by getting votes, the easy way to get votes is to say, 'Vote for me and I will give you something.' The something could be pensions, unemployment benefit, 'free' healthcare or 'free' education. Many voters, busy with other things in their lives, will have little understanding that such things are not really free and that they are letting a Trojan horse through the gates. The temptation to get something apparently for nothing is great. People tend to vote for the 'free lunch'.

> **WHO HAD THE VOTE?**
>
> **1832: The Great Reform Act – electorate increased from estimated 435,000 in England and Wales to 652,000 (4.7% of the population).**
>
> **1867: Disraeli's Reform Act – electorate increased from 1,056,000 to 1,994,000.**
>
> **1884–5: Gladstone's Reform and Redistribution Acts raised UK electorate from some three million to about five million.**
>
> **1918: Representation of the People Act gave vote to thirteen million men and 8.4 million women.**
>
> **1928: Equal Franchise Act increased the number of women voters by requiring the same age and residence qualifications as men.**
>
> **Major increases in the size of the electorate[9]**

Because of these simple facts, one can reasonably be pessimistic about the chances of Britain seriously reducing the size of its welfare state.

Is there anything, then, that can be done? Should those of us who believe the welfare state has been a tragic mistake just give up? Can the welfare state ever be reduced in size? Is there any guidance to be had from the ways in which the welfare state has, on occasion, been trimmed back?

There are three ways in which the welfare state has been reformed so far.

The first is grim: reform through failure. It has happened in dentistry. Dentists became increasingly disenchanted by the bureaucracy and low payments of the NHS. A shortage of dentists developed, as in virtually every aspect of the NHS. Eventually, an increasing proportion of the population gave up on NHS provision and simply paid. The welfare state got so bad in this area that millions of people gave up on it.

The same kind of thing has happened – to a more modest extent – in healthcare generally. When the NHS was first created, virtually everybody relied on it. Now between a fifth and a quarter of the population use some element of private healthcare. The failings of the state provision became bad enough for them simply to give up relying on it.

This reform through failure is surely not a good way since it tends to leave some people badly provided for by the state. It also means other people 'pay twice' – once, through taxes, they pay for state provision and then, through fees, they pay for private provision.

> **'Can we wonder if the uneducated are seduced into approving a system which aims its allurements at all the weakest parts of our nature – which offers marriage to the young, security to the anxious, ease to the lazy, and impunity to the profligate?'**[10]
>
> *Royal Commission on the Operation of the Poor Laws, 1834*

The second way in which welfare has been reformed is by stealth. Much of the shrinkage of the welfare state has taken place this way. Under Margaret Thatcher, the great majority of benefits became linked to consumer prices instead of being raised, from time to time, more or less in line with average earnings. A lot of attention was focussed on state pensions and the fact that they became linked to prices. But most people did not note that the same happened with other benefits. It was done without fanfare. Even the Labour Party made no great fuss about it and when it achieved power in 1997, it continued the same policy.

Labour got attention for new measures such as the minimum income guarantee and a variety of tax credits but it quietly allowed unemployment benefit and income support to rise only in line with prices, not earnings. In other words, it allowed the value of these major benefits to fall compared with earnings. The same kind of process has taken place with council housing, which now accounts for only 13 per cent of all households compared with 29 per cent at its peak in 1976.

The third kind of reform is the tough one: open, fully publicised reform. Peter Lilley, the former social security secretary, managed it to some extent in the 1990s. He said there was a great deal of fraud in the collection of welfare benefits and enacted measures to fight it. He was vilified for saying things his political opponents knew to be true. He was depicted by some of the media as being mean.[11] He managed to get some counter-fraud measures through, but it took political courage. He also managed to argue for and get through a rise in the age at which women become entitled to the state pension. The rise was to be phased in between 2010 and 2020.[12] Reform was put through by a mixture of direct argument and delay, to sweeten the pill.

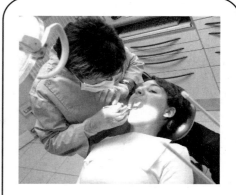

'A report published in *UK Dental Care* earlier this year found that, for the first time, dentists are receiving more than half their income treating private patients. It also found that the number of adults registered for NHS treatment is 1.5 million lower than when Labour took over, and five million lower than the Tory peak in 1994.'[13]

Private Eye, August 2003

Open cut-backs like these are not easy. They are sometimes possible. But it is a hard political slog.

It makes for a depressing picture. Reform through failure is hard on people who rely on the state and expensive for those who go outside it. Reform by stealth is necessarily slow and the fact it is unannounced also means that people may not arrange their affairs to adjust to the reduced provision. The third route – openly declared shrinkage of the welfare state – is very difficult for politicians to achieve.

That does not mean, of course, that reform should not be attempted. Voters and politicians who agree that the welfare state has been seriously damaging have a duty to argue the case and pursue it. But they must recognise that they will often be vilified for their attempt to do their country good.

There is, perhaps, one other way in which we may hope to achieve reform. Certain countries have been more cautious in introducing their welfare states. The same countries have also been more ready to reform them. These countries have something in common: a strong element of local democracy. In Switzerland, the cantons and even the towns have a powerful say in the laws. Switzerland also has referenda on particular issues. This local and single-issue democracy seems to concentrate minds. When something is local, people perhaps think, 'Gosh! I could be the one who ends up paying for this proposal. Do I really think it is a good idea? Are there potential side effects that I would not like?' But when democracy is national, people may be more likely to think, 'Oh well, the vast body of tax-payers will pay for this idea. I don't expect it will affect me very much at all.'

Which countries which have genuinely managed to roll back some of their welfare states? One is New Zealand – a small country in which everyone may feel 'local'. Another is the United States, where, again, there is a great deal of local democracy and, in some states, referenda can be called to decide the issues of the day.

If we want reform, we should, perhaps, encourage local democracy in welfare and referenda on the Swiss or American model. Unfortunately the European Union currently appears to be reducing both these kinds of democracy.

SOME WAYS IN WHICH THE WELFARE STATE HAS SHRUNK

1. A large minority of dental care is now paid for privately.
2. Virtually everybody relied entirely on the NHS in the early 1950s but now between a fifth and a quarter of people hold some form of private health insurance or pay directly for some of their medical care.
3. Building of council homes fell from 237,000 dwellings in the peak year of 1954 to fewer than 1,000 in the year 2000.
4. The basic state pension fell from 26 per cent of average earnings in 1974 to 17 per cent in 2001.
5. Other benefits such as unemployment benefit and income support also fell over that period in comparison to average earnings.

'A patriot must always be ready to defend his country against his government.'

Edward Abbey, American essayist

Is there anything else that can be done?

Yes. Individuals can act. They can, in their personal lives, try to take part in a revival of the charitable society which was so big and important before the welfare state. But charitable work and charitable giving need to be done with great care, as experts in philanthropy such as Thomas Chalmers, Octavia Hill and Lord Beveridge were well aware. First, one must think of the possible perverse effects. Second, those of us who have come to believe that the welfare state has been damaging should contribute to charity in ways which build up an alternative to the welfare state rather than shoring up the failed system. It is better to give to an independent charitable school or a charitable hospital than, say, contribute funds to a state school or a state hospital.

Those without any great wealth can help, too. They can assist the aged in their locality – as many people already do. There will be more and more of the old and infirm in future. They can join mutual-support organisations such as friendly societies. These still have the potential to give emotional and practical support that the state does not.

Individuals can help their family, friends and neighbours in need, for the welfare state will continue to fail people and, in some areas, the failure will become increasingly apparent. We need to prepare ourselves – and others – to deal with the widening cracks in the monolith as they appear.

> **'When meaningful reforms finally do occur, they will happen not because stingy people have won, but because generous people have stopped kidding themselves.'[14]**
>
> **Charles Murray**

Why do people talk more about 'poverty' now that there is less of it?

Here is a puzzle. In the Middle Ages there was terrible poverty. Britain was afflicted by at least ninety-five famines. In 1235, some twenty thousand Londoners died of starvation and many resorted to eating tree bark for survival.[1] Yet in the most famous piece of literature from that time – the *Canterbury Tales* by Geoffrey Chaucer – the word 'poverty' can be found only twenty-six times.[2]

A little later, during the time of the Tudor kings and queens, poverty was less common yet there were still famines. Peasants – the majority of the population – shared unheated hovels without toilets or baths. Yet in the entire works of Shakespeare, the word 'poverty' appears a mere twenty-four times.

'Poverty' used to mean lack of clothing and 'wasted hunger'.

Moving up to the nineteenth century, the condition of the poor had vastly improved. Clogs were routine at the beginning of the century and unusual by the end. The cost of food and clothing went down while average incomes went up. Yet curiously, Charles Dickens used the word 'poverty' vastly more than Chaucer and Shakespeare combined – a whopping 179 times.

In our own time, living standards have been transformed yet again. The cost of food has fallen through the twentieth and early twenty-first centuries while incomes have multiplied. The percentage of income spent on food has fallen dramatically. Clothes, too, have become cheaper. More than 99 per cent of households have a television. The major nutritional problem for the less well off in British society is now obesity.

Yet in the face of this, use of the word 'poverty' is vastly greater. In the House of Commons in 2002, the word was used in 1,307 speeches.[3] In many of those speeches it was used several times.

It seems back to front. As poverty has receded, the use of the word has soared. What can explain it?

To find the answer, we might listen in to two conferences. First, the Labour Party conference of 1959. It was the first conference after the Conservative Party had won three general elections in a row. Naturally, Labour Party members were depressed. Barbara Castle, the chairman of the conference, said in an aside, 'the poverty and unemployment which we came into existence to fight have been largely conquered.'[4] Her remark was a kind of explanation of why Labour had been in so much trouble for so long. It appeared to her that it had lost its *raison d'être*. Without poverty, what need was there for a Labour Party? It was a problem in need of a solution.

> **'96 per cent of 15- to 24-year-olds own a cellphone.'**
>
> *Daily Telegraph,*
> **27 November 2003**

Let us move forward in time three years to the second conference: the annual one of the British Sociological Association. Peter Townsend, a protégé of Richard Titmuss, Professor of Social Administration at the London School of Economics, presented some of his research findings and theories on poverty. Another of Titmuss' protégés was Brian Abel-Smith. The trio had been working on redefining poverty. Abel-Smith and Townsend had argued that the amount given in what was then called supplementary benefit should be considered as the 'poverty line'. Anybody with less income than that should be categorised as 'in poverty'. Anyone with less than that amount, plus 40 per cent, should be termed 'on the margins of poverty'.

This redefinition of poverty gained critical mass among left-wing academics at this conference in 1962. Harriet Wilson was there. She too had published research on related subjects: hardship among unmarried mothers, large families and the elderly. She said that in all the evidence about the poor at the conference and the redefinition of 'poverty', there was developing 'a mood of conspiratorial excitement'. Her words, not mine. So, one of those at the heart of the redefinition of 'poverty' used a word based on the idea of a 'conspiracy'.

BILL CULLEN is now a multi-millionaire but he was brought up in a slum in Dublin, living without a bathroom or 'electric light bulbs that go on with a switch'. In his fictionalised autobiography, *It's a Long Way from Penny Apples*,[5] he writes of how, when he was a child, he asked his mother one day why she gave money to the nuns.

'For to help the poor,' she replied.

'But aren't we poor?' he asked.

She gave him one of her twinkling smiles and said,

'Liam' (Bill Cullen) is second from the right.

'Not at all, son. You're not poor. Haven't you a roof over your head. Clothes on yar back. Kossicks [gumboots] on yar feet. Good food every day. As healthy and strong as a young bull, you are. With a mammy and daddy who minds ya and loves ya ... No, son, we're not poor. We're very rich.'

The historian of this change in the use of the word 'poverty', Keith Banting, refers to it as 'explicitly political'. There was a desire to shock – to use a word that, to most people, meant starvation, homelessness and lack of clothing.

In *The Parson's Tale* – one of the *Canterbury Tales*, in which the word was sparingly used – those condemned to hell were said to be going to suffer the misery of poverty which is defined, among other things, as lack of food and drink – 'they shall be wasted hunger' – and lack of clothing: 'they shall be naked of body save for the fire wherein they burn.' That idea of 'poverty' is vastly different from the government's current definition which, following the influence of the 1962 'conspiracy', now defines those with incomes 60 per cent of average or below as being in 'poverty'.

The word was redefined by politically motivated people. It was a clever piece of propaganda. The word still carries the emotive force of the old meaning but now only means people who are less wealthy than others.

One can only wonder what someone in 1235, chewing bark in a desperate attempt to stay alive, would have made of it.

Little stars of hope in education

In the midst of the gloomy picture of state education that I painted in this book, there are some little stars of hope. This is the story of two of them.

Grace Patterson came to realise that her son Miles was getting into 'the wrong crowd' at Westminster City School, a state school not very far from the Houses of Parliament in central London. She also knew he was not learning very much. But she did not know the full story.

Miles was about thirteen and big for his age. He was taking advantage of his size to threaten younger boys, aged eleven or so, demanding that they give him the lunch vouchers many had because they came from relatively poor families. When he had extorted about five of these vouchers, he would sell them to other boys. Then, after school, he would spend the profits in an amusement arcade.

Away from school, Miles had been involved in an incident with a knife. He had started shoplifting, too. As for academic work, he wasn't interested. He was unable to do long division or multiplication. His life was heading towards academic failure and crime.

The crunch came when Grace was called in by the school because Miles had got into trouble with the police. A £10 note had been stolen by a friend of his and Miles had looked after it for a while.

So what did Grace do?

She could easily have blamed other people or the school or the world we live in. Instead she took upon herself the responsibility of putting her son's life on a better track.

Grace knew of the Tabernacle School because she already worshipped at the church which had created it. But sending Miles to the Tabernacle was not an easy option. She was a single mother on a low income, living on a council estate in south

Grace Patterson made great sacrifices for her sons' education because she wasn't content with what the state provided.

London. The Tabernacle is in Notting Hill, west London. She had to send Miles across the city each day to go to it. Far harder, by sending her son to the Tabernacle she was giving up free education provided by the state and instead devoting a high proportion of her income to school fees. The Tabernacle's fees are small compared to those of big, well-established private schools such as Eton or Cheltenham Ladies' College. But they were massive for her.

After Grace made the move, it cost her £500 per month (in all twelve months of the year) for Miles and her younger son Michael to attend the school. This was out of her net income of £1,450 a month. So she was giving up more than a third of her taxed income for schooling. As if that was not enough, she also paid a tithe – ten per cent of her income – to the Tabernacle church. 'It was very difficult. I worked a full-time job and then also had a job at the weekend for three or four years.' She went without a foreign holiday for longer than that. New clothes were a rarity.

So what did her sacrifice achieve? Was it all worthwhile?

Miles Nanton was transformed from a troublemaker to a role model.

Well, six years on, I talked to Miles. He frankly admitted to me that if he had stayed at his state school, then by the time I met him he would have been in prison and would have fathered several children outside marriage. In other words, his life would have gone badly wrong and other people would have suffered, too.

And how is his life turning out after going to the Tabernacle School instead? He has become a particularly civilised and responsible young citizen – a gentle giant. His friend and classmate Kiaran told me that Miles was a role model on his council estate, to the point where other children came to him for advice. It was easy to believe. The pair of them are ambitious: they have made a short film together which was premiered at a cinema in Shaftesbury Avenue. Miles is currently trying to get into a film school. Meanwhile he is teaching part time at the Tabernacle.

How did the school succeed in turning round Miles's life? The answer is complex and difficult to define. Part of it is undoubtedly the dedication of Pastor Derrick Wilson, who founded the school, and his wife Paulette, the principal. Part of it is the very fact that the Tabernacle is independent and not a state school. This has all sorts of consequences, one of which is that the school can focus on making good, well-educated children rather than, for instance, achieving a series of government targets. It also only survives if it gets results.

Paulette and Derrick Wilson, respectively principal and founder of the Tabernacle School.

The Tabernacle – an independent, faith-based school – is one of a small but fast-increasing number of private schools for poor people. It is a remarkable phenomenon. There are state schools all over the country. They are free and government approved. But more and more people of limited means are giving up on them. They are paying high proportions of their incomes for schools with far more modest premises. Some observers assume it is all to do with the religious aspect of such schools, since nearly all of the new schools for poorer people are faith based. But according to the people I have talked to who are involved in Christian and Muslim schools, this is not the case. It is primarily a question of parents like Grace Patterson wanting their children to be well educated and well behaved. They have come to feel that the state schools available to them would take their children down a different, dangerous path.

I asked Grace how she felt about sacrificing so much to pay for the schooling of her two boys. She quietly said, 'I will have my reward when I see my children's success – walking in their success.' I found meeting her a moving experience. There is no doubt in my mind that she saved her son from a bad life – a wonderful achievement.

The number of independent, faith-based schools like the Tabernacle is growing pell-mell, jumping recently from 170 to 276 – a rise of over 60 per cent in a single year. Muslim schools are to the fore, followed by Evangelical Christian ones. Anecdotal evidence suggests the trend is continuing. Numbers at the existing schools are probably growing, too. It seems likely that more than 11 per cent of all independent schools in Britain are now Jewish, Muslim or Evangelical and they generally cater to parents who are not at all well off. The growth of these schools is a symptom of the failure of state education. But it is also a sign that a growing number of people are willing to do something about it and to make something better. That is one of the little stars of hope.

*

My second story comes from the other side of the Atlantic Ocean.

After attending a conference in Miami, Florida in 2005, I took a taxi ride twelve miles inland through one of those huge expanses of small detached homes with 'yards' that typically surround American cities. Eventually I was delivered to a long, low building in a nondescript street. It proudly bore the name 'Greater Miami Academy'.

I was taken to meet the headmaster – a kind, open man, clearly born for the position he held. There was a complete absence in his manner of the defensiveness you often meet in British state school heads. Perhaps it was because he didn't have to go along with government directives on what to teach, how to teach it and how to run the school. His school, like the Tabernacle in London, is independent. It is a fee-paying Seventh Day Adventist school.

Dr McKenzie, headmaster of the Greater Miami Academy, 'clearly born for the position'.

I asked if I could speak to some of the children there who were on a certain programme. Straightaway he arranged it and, before long, four girls aged fifteen or sixteen trooped into his office. Each one shyly shook my hand and then they went to sit together, happily squashed onto a sofa made for two.

I asked them why their parents had arranged for them to leave the government-run schools where they had been before in order to come to this school. They seemed shy and, at first, none of them spoke. So I looked at one girl in particular and tried again. Denise Balladares, perched on the left corner of the sofa, hesitantly said, 'They bring weapons ... drugs. I saw guns...'

She was reluctant to expand. I turned to another member of the quartet.

Yahaira Perlaza, squeezed onto the right-hand side of the sofa, with long, dark hair and looking more streetwise than the others, said that students at her previous school 'would get drugged'. Then she added that, academically, she was finding it 'more challenging' at the Greater Miami Academy.

One by one, all four told similar stories. All said that there had been drugs at their previous schools. 'A lot of drugs,' said Geniver Matamoro. 'I told my mom and she sent me here. My grades are a lot higher and I'm learning a lot more.' Most of them also told of seeing guns, knives or both.

It was clear, as with the Tabernacle, that the primary reason why parents had sent their children to this school was not religious at all. It was not even academic – though they had enjoyed a clear benefit from getting a better education. But first and foremost, the parents had wanted to save their children from present danger and also, very probably, to steer them away from an environment which could easily damage them for life.

I asked the four girls how their lives and expectations now compared with how they would have been if they had stayed at their previous, government-run schools. Denise said, 'If I had stayed where I was, I would be a completely different person. There were so many temptations.' She did not define the 'temptations', but this came straight after many references to drugs.

Elisabeth said that previously she would have expected to go to a 'medium college'. But now she might go somewhere like Columbia, one of the most celebrated universities in America. She said she now expected to have a good family and job when she grew up. Evidently that's not what she expected before.

Each one told a similar story. Their academic expectations had jumped. They were safe, whereas before they had been in danger. And the direction in which their lives were previously going had been transformed.

I can't resist mentioning one unusual feature of the school. It might seem irrelevant, at first. But perhaps it isn't. I visited a few classrooms and came across Yahaira, one of the girls I had interviewed, being taught aviation. I had never before heard of aviation being taught in a secondary school. The teacher was a lively, charming, middle-aged man – another natural teacher. He was obviously enjoying himself and inspiring his students. But why aviation?

Well, the school happens to be close to an airport. There the students can get practical instruction. They had managed to obtain a second-hand flight simulator. If you are going to try to inspire children – including ones from difficult backgrounds – to become interested in education, aviation is a good bet. For some boys in particular, the idea of getting to fly planes is likely to seem 'cool' in a way that history isn't.

The aviation class. Yahaira Perlaza is third from the right in the front row.

Getting airborne involves learning about weather patterns and aircraft engines. It means learning some geometry, geography and map-reading. The more I thought about it, the more aviation seemed an inspired idea for a subject. A few of the boys in the class planned to become airline pilots. They were getting leg-ups to good jobs. It is hard to resist the idea that it was the independent status of this school which allowed it the freedom, the imagination and, you might even say, the *joie de vivre* to go for it.

But why do I tell this story, which is similar in many ways to the one about Miles at the Tabernacle School in Notting Hill?

There is one key difference. In Britain, Grace Patterson got her son out of a state school by making positively heroic financial sacrifices. But in Florida, the parents of Yahaira, Elisabeth, Denise and Geniver – though they are required to make a financial contribution – have not had to pay anything like the full cost of their children's independent education.

First, the fees for all the children there are subsidised by the church which sponsors it. Second, these children are on a programme paid for by Florida Pride, an organisation funded by companies as an alternative to paying tax. This 'choice' programme is one of several in Florida. Another is called the Opportunity Scholarship programme, which is for children in demonstrably failing schools. The biggest scheme is the McKay Scholarships programme, for disabled pupils.

Many other states in America have 'choice' programmes. The movement is growing. As this is America, the supporters of the idea are determined and well organised. And yet it is clear that the numbers involved are still small in relation to the whole school age population.

It is important to understand why. It is because it has been an uphill political battle to get such programmes accepted. There has been equally determined opposition to these programmes from teachers' unions and some newspapers and politicians. These organisations and individuals have been against education paid for mainly by state governments but not run by them. These independent schools, of course, are not under the influence of teachers' unions to anything like the extent of government-run ones. The main difference between the Tabernacle School and the Greater Miami Academy is that one consists of a complete opting out from education supplied by the state, while the other is an attempt by government to channel tax dollars to private education.

Unfortunately, neither story leads towards an easy, uncontroversial answer to the problems of government education. In the British example, parents like Grace are paying twice for education and paying heavily. We must also remember that Grace Patterson's actions derived from the terrible failure of a state school. One can hardly plan a future for education based on widespread failure engulfing thousands of other children. Meanwhile, in Florida, the choice programmes are hemmed in by fierce opposition.

Such little stars of hope – even though they are growing in number – are still few. But they are certainly better than a completely dark sky.

The NHS: so did it 'get better'?

Since publication, one of the more common objections to this book has been 'yes, there have been problems with the welfare state in the past, but now things are getting better'.

The first answer to this is simple: people – especially politicians – have claimed this regularly ever since 1945 (and very probably before that too). But it is presumptuous and even absurd to try to persuade us to admire the welfare state on forecasts of what it will do sometime in the future. It should be judged on its actual performance. After all, it has been around long enough. To judge it by an uncertain future is like saying 'this is an old horse that has not won a single race in the past ten years but it is now about to win the Cheltenham Gold Cup'. Yet intelligent people are remarkably willing to believe that – by some amazing happenstance – this is the moment when the welfare state is about to pull off a remarkable improvement.

The belief that 'things must be getting better' has recently been so strong and so widespread that – despite my conviction that this should not be necessary – I will confront it. I will take the National Health Service because that is the sphere in which improvement has been most widely claimed and believed.

Niall Dixon, chief executive of the King's Fund, the healthcare think tank, has said that Britain has shown a dramatic improvement in its performance in treating cancer. He has mentioned breast cancer in particular. The government, of course, has loudly promoted the idea that the NHS is improving in every way. It has certainly had a major injection of funds. Spending on the NHS has increased from £40.2 billion in 1999/2000 to a projected £76.4 billion in 2005/6 – a rise of 90 per cent in

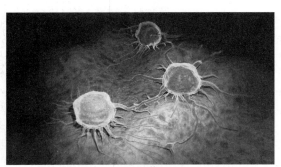

A model of breast cancer cells. Has treatment in England improved as the King's Fund claims?

nominal terms and about 65 per cent after adjusting for inflation. Has that cash boost brought the NHS up to standard?

I will look at one measure in particular: the treatment of cancer. Why cancer? Because claims about impressive progress have been made about it and it is one of the major causes of death in Britain. After that, I will also mention a few curious things about the much-vaunted reduction in waiting lists.

The latest authoritative cancer study is Eurocare III, a research effort funded by the European Union. I have covered the results in more detail in Chapter 3. In brief, out of eight major European countries – Austria, England, France, Germany, Italy, the Netherlands, Spain and Sweden – England had the worst survival rate for the major killers: lung, breast and prostate cancer. Yes, there certainly were some major improvements in the British performance compared to the previous study. But other countries also improved their survival rates. The outcomes in England were still the worst in this group and therefore almost certainly among the worst in the advanced world.

Those who claim the NHS is now much improved – maybe even up to the average – could object: 'But Eurocare III does not reflect recent improvements under the Labour administration.' That would be true, too. Eurocare III is a study of patients diagnosed between 1990 and 1994, and followed up until 1999. The biggest claims for improvement are made about the years after 2000. So how can we assess the recent record? It is not easy, because we won't know the five-year survival rates for people diagnosed, say, in 2005 until at least 2009 and probably – once the figures have been collected and analysed – not for some years after that. So is there any other way of getting a good idea of current performance?

Professor Karol Sikora.

According to a leading cancer specialist, Professor Karol Sikora, there is a proxy for the NHS's performance in cancer care which brings us more up to date. It is the extent to which Britain deploys the latest cancer drugs. New drugs are taken up because they offer improvements in outcomes compared to older drugs. In general, the take-up of important new drugs will result in saved lives. So how does Britain fare in this?

Dr Nils Wilking, a cancer specialist at Karolinska Institutet, Stockholm, and Professor Bengt Jönsson of the Stockholm School of Economics published a study in September 2005 of how quickly certain major cancer drugs have been taken up and prescribed by doctors across Europe. Among these drugs, four were introduced in Britain this decade or, in one case, just a few months before.

Oxaliplatin, for colorectal cancer, was launched in 1996 and introduced in Britain in September 1999. Britain, incidentally, is not particularly fast or slow in introducing cancer drugs compared to the European average. The difference arises in the speed with which the drugs come to be widely used. In Italy and Spain, after only three months, sales of Oxaliplatin reached 1,000 euros per person dying from colorectal cancer. After four and a half years, sales of Oxaliplatin reached over 3,700 euros in both these countries. After the same time in France, sales of the drug reached 2,400 euros and in Germany 1,700 euros.

Sales in euros of Oxaliplatin, four and a half years after introduction

Italy	3,800
Spain	3,700
France	2,400
Germany	1,700
United Kingdom	950

Sales per individual dying of colorectal cancer. Source: Nils Wilking and Bengt Jönsson, *A Pan-European Comparison Regarding Patient Access to Cancer Drugs*

How quickly was the drug taken up in Britain? Throughout the period for which there were figures available for all these countries (four and a half years), Britain's uptake rose very slowly indeed. Even at the end of the period, sales per person dying of colorectal cancer still had not quite reached 1,000 euros. It took over four and a half years for the NHS to deploy this important new drug as widely as Spain and Italy had done in only three months.

Of course, this is only one drug. It is conceivable that doctors in Britain took a different, less favourable view of this particular drug compared to their equivalents in other countries. It is only fair to look at other drugs, too.

The next cancer drug introduced in Britain in recent times and analysed by the researchers was Trastuzumab, described by Wilking and Jönsson as 'a cornerstone of treatment' for 'patients with advanced breast cancer overexpressing HER2'. It was launched in August 1999 and introduced in Britain in September 2000.

In Spain, again, it was widely used very quickly. Within a year, there were sales worth 3,000 euros per individual dying of breast cancer.

Sales in euros of Trastuzumab, four years after introduction

Spain	8,600
Italy	4,000
Germany	3,300
France	3,000
United Kingdom	2,000

Sales per individual dying of breast cancer. Source: Wilking and Jönsson, *A Pan-European Comparison Regarding Patient Access to Cancer Drugs*

After four years, this figure had reached 8,600 euros. The next fastest was Italy, where the latest figure available – after just under four years – was 4,000 euros. By that time, Germany had reached 3,300 euros and France had got to 3,000. And what about Britain? We had got to 2,000 euros. For most of the history of the adoption and deployment of this drug, Britain was clearly the slowest among this group of five major European countries.

The next drug to be introduced was Capecitabine – for both colorectal and breast cancer. In this case, deployment in Britain was not so markedly bad. Britain lagged for a couple of years but then moved up to approximately the middle of the rankings. This is one drug where the take-up rates were very similar across most countries. (At first glance, it appears that the rate in France was slow but the drug was introduced there more than two years before other countries.)

The final drug in this survey was Imatinib, used in the treatment of leukaemia. It was introduced in Britain in November 2001. Two and a half years after its introduction, treatments worth 13,000 euros were being sold in Britain for every individual dying of chronic myelogenous leukaemia. Italy spent about 14,000 euros, Germany some 17,000 and Spain about 24,000. France on this occasion introduced the drug a year and half later than Britain but then did so with great speed. By the same moment in time, two and half years after the introduction in Britain, sales in France – at 15,000 euros – had passed the British level. Six months later the figure had soared to 30,000 euros whereas usage in Britain had still only managed to get just above 15,000.

So, out of the four important cancer drugs introduced in this decade or just before and covered by this survey, Britain has badly lagged behind in the use of three. In the fourth, it lagged for a few years and was average for the rest. This slow take-up, incidentally, was a continuation of what had been happening over the previous decade. Overall, Britain undoubtedly had the worst performance of the five major European countries.

Living in Britain, therefore, is to be at greater risk of not getting the latest, most appropriate drug. And since, according to Professor Sikora, we may take the deployment of new cancer drugs as a proxy for the effective treatment of cancer, he continues to believe (as described in Chapter 3) that about 10,000 people a year die prematurely in Britain because our cancer treatment is so far below the average in Europe.

The NHS's relatively poor performance has cost many thousands of lives in the past. This continues to be the case.

I will add one further piece of evidence about the inadequate treatment of cancer patients in Britain. Another important treatment, in addition to drugs, is radiotherapy. Dr D. Dodwell and Dr A. Crellin, both consultants in clinical oncology at Cookridge Hospital, Leeds, wrote an assessment of British radiotherapy treatment in the *British Medical Journal* in January 2006, based on a variety of studies. Their conclusion? 'Radiotherapy services in the United Kingdom are inferior to those in most developed countries and indeed in many poorer countries.' That rider 'and indeed in many poorer countries' is particularly telling.

What about the waiting lists? This is an area of healthcare delivery in which the government has successfully persuaded many people that great strides have been made. I have already discussed how unreliable these figures are in the main text. But since publication, a few curious and disturbing additional facts about the claimed reduction in the waiting lists have come to light. Although the waiting list figures have indeed gone down, even if the statistics could be relied upon (which they can't), it would still not be such a wonderful thing. Why? Because the median waiting time has not fallen at all. It has gone up.

As the *Financial Times* reported on 4 January 2006, 'since March 2000, the median wait for an operation has risen from 6.1 weeks to 7.4, a 20 per cent increase'. This might seem bizarre. How could it be that the waiting list has got smaller while the median waiting time has increased? To the extent that the waiting list reduction may be true at all, it is because the government has concentrated on treating those relatively few people ('the relatively small tail', as the *Financial Times* put it) who had very long waiting times at the expense of those who previously waited a very short time. After this reprioritising, the median time it takes to be treated is longer than before. That is not such a great achievement.

Many people might nonetheless feel, 'It is still better that lots of people wait for a modest time rather than some being treated fast and others waiting ages.' The idea may seem attractive – although a wait of seven weeks is not so modest when you must add in the time spent waiting to see a specialist in the first place and time spent waiting for diagnostic tests. But in any case, is it really better for us all to have medium-length waits? There is another side to this that was angrily described to me by a consultant surgeon in Hampshire in September 2005. He was outraged by what had happened in his NHS hospital the previous weekend. He – and presumably his juniors – had had twelve patients there with fractures, or in other words, broken bones.

Elderly women are disproportionately likely to have broken bones because they are the most prone to osteoporosis, which causes bones to become brittle. So a large proportion of those lying in hospital beds with broken bones at that moment were probably elderly women. The consultant had been keen, like any other humane person, to treat these cases without delay. And yet, he fumed, 'the hospital was still bringing me elective cases'. In other words, he was being obliged by the hospital management to treat patients who were not emergencies at all ahead of genuinely urgent cases. Why? Because of the priority given to the waiting lists.

This, surely, is truly grotesque. The drawbacks of delaying such urgent operations are substantial. People with one of the most common fractures – a broken hip – are unable to walk. They frequently have to be heavily sedated to bear the pain. Elderly people are often set back quite substantially – physically and mentally – by long waits of this sort in hospital. They are susceptible to bed sores. Their muscles can become weak. Being on painkillers for a long time in such a condition is not good for them mentally or emotionally. It is horrible that during that weekend in Hampshire they were allowed to lie there with broken bones and suffer in this way. And unfortunately this was not an isolated case.

There are some other curious and even suspicious facts about the waiting lists that were described by the King's Fund, the think tank referred to above, which generally takes a pro-NHS line. The fund analysed the NHS's performance on waiting lists and, with regard to recent years, concluded:

> *The targets for eliminating long waits were met during this phase but the numbers of people treated on the waiting list actually fell during this phase. Seemingly at odds with this, so did the number waiting. There were a variety of possible reasons for this:*
> * *The number of some procedures carried out declined sharply*

in line with an evidence-based approach, which identified
some treatments, such as tonsillectomies, as being of low ther-
apeutic value.
- *Some procedures were reclassified as planned operations or*
  treated as diagnostic (neither planned operations nor diag-
  nostic procedures are included in waiting lists).
- *There was a significant reduction in the number of people put*
  onto the waiting lists, which pointed to some degree of
  'informal demand management'.

The measures introduced in this phase to improve capacity and
overall system performance had little impact.

Cutting through the jargon, the King's Fund is essentially offering two possible explanations for some very odd aspects of the waiting lists. One is that medical views on what should be treated has changed. The other is that the figures have been manipulated. Whichever explanation is correct, it is clear that the reduction in waiting lists is not a matter of major improvement in NHS performance. It is a classic case of 'lies, damned lies and statistics'. Of course, we should also not forget that waiting lists, even of the reduced size that the government now claims exist, are unknown in other advanced countries.

It would certainly be possible to catalogue a great deal of other evidence that the NHS continues to under-perform other healthcare systems. That is not to say that nothing has improved at all. More doctors have been trained and money has indeed been spent on hospital buildings and equipment. But we also know that the increases in the numbers of frontline staff have been overshadowed by bigger percentage increases in management and support staff. Wards have been closed. Some of the newly trained doctors have found a lack of hospital jobs for them to go to.

Given the amount of extra money that has been spent in the first half of this decade, the improvement is not at all in proportion to the extra money spent. And the fundamental point, as described above, is the fact that a patient with a serious, life-threatening illness such as cancer who goes to the NHS has a lower chance of being cured than if he or she was in virtually any other advanced country.

TEN THINGS WRONG WITH THE WELFARE STATE

1. It has made people poorer than they otherwise would have been.

2. It has created persistent mass unemployment.

3. It has depressed and alienated millions of people through unemployment and welfare dependency.

4. It has caused millions of children to suffer misery and to under-achieve by encouraging broken parenting.

5. It has increased crime by causing so much alienation through broken parenting, council housing, unemployment and welfare dependency.

6. It has caused a minimum of 15,000 deaths a year through the NHS, plus a great deal of unnecessarily prolonged pain and low-quality treatment.

7. It has left millions of people illiterate and innumerate.

8. It has created ghettos of vandalism, crime and fear on council estates.

9. Old people have been neglected.

10. British people have become less decent and civil.

TEN REASONS WHY THE WELFARE STATE HAS FAILED.

---

1. Welfare benefits have been set too high, disincentivising work and marriage.

2. Rigorous conditions have not been attached to benefits.

3. Means-tested benefits have become more important than insurance benefits – adding to the disincentives to work, saving and self-reliance.

4. 'Needs-based' benefits have encouraged broken parenting.

5. Patients have no power.

6. Parents of schoolchildren have very limited power.

7. Hospitals and schools have no independence, profits or competition.

8. State officials do not spend money as effectively as owners of businesses.

9. The state has responded to short-term crises (such as rising rents) without considering the worse, long-term crises its actions may cause (rent controls leading to a housing shortage and landlords like Rachman).

10. People who are allowed no responsibility become irresponsible.

FOUR REASONS WHY THE WELFARE STATE IS UNLIKELY EVER TO SUCCEED

1. **Not enough of the electorate will consistently understand that welfare benefits can be too high and generous.**

2. **The government is, in many ways, strong and capable of making a big difference. It is therefore difficult for people to think of government action as potentially dangerous and disruptive.**

3. **Government-owned organisations – such as schools and hospitals – are not strongly and automatically encouraged to think of what the consumer wants (whereas private companies have to concentrate on the consumer, otherwise they go bust).**

4. **All organisations tend to think of what suits them and their employees. In government organisations, there is no life-or-death competition to counter this. They therefore become self-indulgent and wasteful.**

Personal reflections on writing
The Welfare State We're In

Admirable, kind people (mostly) created the welfare state.

The great irony and paradox is that the admirable people who charac-terised Britain from the late nineteenth century up until the mid-twentieth century were the ones who made the mistake of creating the welfare state. They did it partly because they were so decent and kind. They wanted better lives not only for themselves but for others less fortunate. Our tragedy is that they made such a dreadful mistake in the means they chose. Perhaps it was their very decency which made them naïve about what would happen.

Schools 'n' hospitals are not the same

When I moved on from writing the chapter about the National Health Service on to writing about state education, I thought I was moving from one twin to the other. I thought, like most people, that they have a great deal in common: large staff, monopolies, many political supporters and so on. But when I looked at them up close, one key difference soon became apparent: in education, people don't die.

That is a shorthand way of saying several things. In medicine it is obvious what you are trying to achieve: to alleviate suffering, avoid incapacity and help people survive. People agree on the purpose, so it is quite simple to measure how successful they are. It is agreed, though you can argue over certain cases, that premature death constitutes failure. This important purpose of the NHS is clear and the failure is therefore equally clear.

Education, in contrast, is not clear at all. People do not agree on what is for. Some think its aim is to create a 'cultivated' person. Some think it should create 'equal opportunity' or break down class divi-sions. In the nineteenth century, education was seen as a means of reducing drunkenness and crime, primarily through religious instruc-tion. Recent governments have argued that the prime aim of education is to promote economic success. Some think that learning to read, write and do some basic mathematics is of fundamental importance. Others see these things as desirable but are far keener that no child should be regimented or made to feel a failure.

Since there are so many varied ideas about the purpose of education, it is very difficult to produce measures of success or failure which will convince everybody. In any case, measurement of success or failure in most of these areas is often highly debatable. Many people may feel that the dumbing down of exams which they perceive represents a kind of failure. But there are some people in education – highly intelligent ones too – who argue that it is not. There is no clear measure of success or failure which everyone agrees is significant and important. Nobody dies.

I am convinced that state education has been as disastrous as the NHS but because nobody dies, it is harder to prove.

> 'The one point of similarity which distinguishes all revolutions of a democratic tendency is this, that they are invariably started with the aid of sanguine and benevolent people, who have not the slightest thought of bringing about the confusion to which their efforts ultimately lead.'[1]
>
> **Lord Salisbury**

Are you sure you're a journalist?

I had far more contact with professors when writing this book than when I was an undergraduate at Oxford University. I talked to far more hospital consultants, too, than I would in the ordinary course of events. It was a great pleasure – even though it could be bracing – to interact with these extremely clever folk. Having never been highly rated by my tutors at University I was thrilled when one of these professors implied that I was not too far beneath him. He remarked in an e-mail: 'These are intelligent questions – are you sure you're a journalist?'

I used to think unmarried parenting was ideal

As recently as fourteen years ago I thought having children outside marriage was fine. I positively preferred the idea for myself. I had a little capital and I feared that if I got married and subsequently divorced, I could lose half of it and might have to provide further financial support to my ex-wife while any children were being brought up. As far as I could see, it was far less financially risky to make children without getting married. Such thoughts did me no credit but they were logical.

Only after I read research findings about children of unmarried parents, during the early 1990s, did I change my view. Only then did I come to believe that children born outside wedlock have far lower chances of success and happiness in life.

In view of my own history, I must readily concede that many people – probably still tens of millions – remain unaware of the facts. The evidence has become better known over the past fifteen years but it is still possible for those having children outside marriage not to realise that it is an unkind act. In a sense, therefore, it is not unkind. It is only 'uninformed'.

If more people became aware of the evidence, many might hold back from having children outside marriage. If such a change was to come over people – as it has in me – it would mark a change towards a new kind of sexual morality. The old one was based on the religious injunction not to commit adultery. The new morality would be based on social research.

Those silly people who lived in the past

We are educated to think that our ancestors got it all wrong. They were stuck in pre-democratic, relatively poor times without the benefit of our modern welfare state. Why on earth were they not sensible and democratic with a big welfare state, like us?

They must have been a bit short of intelligence, wisdom, decency or something.

This kind of attitude is never expressed openly. It is implicit. But reading a great deal that was written in the nineteenth century or before for the purposes of this book has made me realise, first, that I have taken part in this patronising attitude and, second, how absurd it is. If anything, I now have more respect for those who lived in the past that those who live now. They have often struck me as more perceptive, honest and clear in their writing.

It was a revelation to me when I first learned that Martin Luther and Thomas More had discussed the pros and cons of various welfare systems. It was even more of a surprise to see that the writers at that time were so open and explicit about the possible perverse effects of a welfare state. There is a whole gallery of people who have impressed me enormously on welfare state matters, including Edwin Chadwick,

Charles Loch, Octavia Hill, Edmund Burke, Thomas Chalmers, Aneurin Bevan, George Orwell and Lord Beveridge himself – who was far more clear thinking than the welfare state which resulted from the wholesale disregarding of his report. If anyone should be judging anyone, such people as these should be judging us. They would all – every one of them – be appalled by what has become of the welfare state and of the British people. In patronising the past, we reveal nothing but our vanity.

Acknowledgements

My greatest debt of gratitude is to my friend Jeremy Hosking, who, at a time when I was greatly concerned about the loss of income that researching and writing the book would mean, stepped in with substantial sponsorship. This helped me simply to get on with it. Alan Gibbs, who I did not know at all before, was remarkably generous in offering further sponsorship after he saw the proposal and quizzed me vigorously about it over a supper.

The publisher, Iain Dale at Politico's, went where many others were too appalled or terrified to tread. Neither of the two major publishing houses which had produced my previous (pretty successful) books would take this one on. A succession of other publishers considered the book and rejected it. This book expresses views far outside the mainstream and Iain Dale showed courage in taking it on.

Barendina Smedley did outstanding research on my behalf, specialising in anything before 1900. She also was generous with encouragement and reassurance at an early stage when I sorely needed them. Christian Wignall helped with research in a wide variety of areas – from education in Singapore to the story of Sir John Cowperthwaite in Hong Kong. My main help in education research came from James Stanfield of the E. G. West Centre. David Green was kind enough to offer advice on a variety of the aspects of the welfare state.

During the research, Phoebe Rudomino-Dusiacka helped me deal, week by week, with the many practical problems of obtaining publications from the OECD, from government departments and so on. My wife Anne kindly put up with living economically during the two years it took me to research and write the book. Her encouragement was vital. Anne's parents, Colonel Ethelwald and Mrs Beatrice Vella, generously let me stay several times with them in their home in Malta where I was able to work very peacefully and pleasantly – the only distraction being trying not to miss the daily visit to the village of the bread delivery van.

Various people were generous with their time in reading chapters in draft form: David Green of Civitas, Tom Burkard, Professor Philip

Booth of the Institute of Economic Affairs, the social historian David Gladstone, Rebecca O'Neill, Christian Wignall, John Wilden (retired consultant neurosurgeon) and Anne. They provided encouragement, extra material and, where necessary, correction. Of course all the remaining errors are my responsibility.

I attended many very useful talks at Civitas and the IEA and, in both cases, met people who went on to offer material assistance. Publications by other think tanks such as the Centre for Policy Studies were also useful. Eamonn Butler at the Adam Smith Institute was instrumental in helping to persuade Iain Dale that the book was worth doing and later in putting it before Milton Friedman, who – to my astonishment and delight – did me the honour of making some very complimentary comments about the book after reading it from cover to cover. Matthew Young, also of the Adam Smith Institute, was always ready to advise and give me the benefit of his awesome range of contacts.

I was encouraged by the support of many of the above people and also of Charles Moore, who, when editor of the *Daily Telegraph*, tried to persuade a publisher to take on the book and also indicated that he would take me back as a once-a-week leader writer after the book was finished. That was a comfort. John Blundell, director of the IEA, took an interest in the project from an early stage, offering encouragement and then substantial support.

The IEA made a bulk order of books prior to publication, which ensured there was the money to pay for the high production values. It also successfully recommended to the Earhart Foundation that I should be made the Earhart Foundation Senior Fellow in Social Policy at the IEA. The foundation provided me with a welcome monthly allowance which helped subsidise me in promoting the book after publication and in doing some further research. The IEA then awarded me the Arthur Seldon Prize, which is for the best book associated with the institute over the previous year. The institute further arranged for me to speak in Florida, for the Heritage Foundation, and at an educational colloquium in Potsdam – both of which were rewarding experiences. It is also intending to help in the promotion of this paperback edition.

Robert Boyd and Christian Wignall both offered further sponsorship for the book around the time of first publication.

Researching this book was a fascinating voyage of discovery. I did not know how ignorant I was until I learnt a little bit more. I thank all the above for their help in making the journey possible.

Select bibliography

I am keen to recommend some of the books I came across in my research. *Alexander Fleming* by Gwyn Macfarlane, despite its name, is an extended demand that Howard Florey, not Fleming, should get the main credit for bringing penicillin to the world.

Life without Father by David Popenoe is a persuasive account of the importance of fatherhood and marriage to children. The remarkable thing about *Family and Kinship in East London* by Michael Young and Peter Willmott is the honest responsiveness of the authors to what they found. They set out to research one thing and then when they discovered something else that was interesting, they changed the whole focus of their work.

Losing Ground by Charles Murray has been a seminal work in suggesting that a welfare state can damage a society, written in a dry, logical, compelling way by a first-class brain. *Aneurin Bevan* by Michael Foot is superbly written in a quite different style – with passion and even love. The only problem, of course, is the author's blindness to the disaster the NHS became.

I had difficulty for a while finding a long-run history of social security so I was glad to find *England's Road to Social Security* by Karl de Schweinitz. Despite its pro-welfare state bias, it describes very well those people who opposed state welfare over the centuries and the important, international dimension of the early history of welfare. I doff my cap, similarly, to *The Five Giants* by Nicholas Timmins. It explicitly starts from the belief that the welfare state is a good thing but is an excellent, highly readable account of the politics of welfare since the Second World War.

The Report from His Majesty's Commissioners for Inquiring into the Administration and Practical Operation of the Poor Laws (1834) is an extraordinary document, quite unlike any modern government report, bringing to life the welfare state of that time through real stories. I bought an original copy on the internet – the beginning of a small collection of welfare state memorabilia. Another treasured original document I have acquired is a copy of is the Labour Party pamphlet 'A National Service for Health' published in 1943 – a cleverly argued case but one which reveals, without intending to, just how little was wrong with the old system.

No single author has been more important to me than David Green. Again and again, his work has provided the vital evidence. *Reinventing Civil Society* showed how important friendly societies were before the welfare state hammered them. His essay in *Re-privatising Welfare* (edited by Arthur Seldon) on voluntary (or charitable) hospitals showed how significant they too were. Subsequently he did much to expose how the NHS compares badly with other countries in its results and how it discriminates against the old.

In *Re-privatising Welfare* is also an essay by the late, great E. G. West, who described how well education was developing without the state in the nineteenth century. His book *Education and the State* is a classic. His description of how politicians are tempted to do things that are unnecessary and meretricious is clinically devastating. In modern times, the work of James Tooley has been very important in showing that independent education can be for the poor as well as the rich.

Frank Field, Molly Meacher and Chris Pond wrote a very important book in *To Him Who Hath*. They described a problem which has become even worse subsequently: the poor are highly taxed. That, as they remind us, was not the original idea.

I rather dreaded reading *The Road to Wigan Pier* by George Orwell but the book surprised me by being brilliant and inspiring. Orwell was a socialist but his honesty and intelligence as a reporter meant that he sometimes revealed the failings of the welfare state in a particularly penetrating way. It would be wonderful if someone in modern times could get close to the lives of low-paid people as he did and report them so well.

Many other books and authors are mentioned in the endnotes. I have felt fortunate to read so many interesting works. It may sound sentimental but I have sometimes felt as if there were a loose community of researchers, authors and statisticians spanning the generations.

De Schweinitz, Karl, *England's Road to Social Security: From the Statue of Laborers in 1349 to the Beveridge Report of 1942* (University of Pennsylvania Press, Philadelphia, 1943)

Field, Frank et al., *To Him Who Hath: A Study of Poverty and Taxation* (Pelican, Harmondsworth, 1977)

Foot, Michael, *Aneurin Bevan* (MacGibbon and Kee, London, 1962; Paladin, St Albans, 1975)

Green, David, *Reinventing Civil Society* (Institute of Economic Affairs, London, 1993)

Macfarlane, Gwyn, *Alexander Fleming: The Man and the Myth* (Chatto and Windus, London, 1984)

Murray, Charles, *Losing Ground: American Social Policy 1950–1980* (Basic Books, New York, 1984)

Orwell, George, *The Road to Wigan Pier* (Victor Gollancz, London, 1937; Penguin, London, 2001)

Popenoe, David, *Life without Father: Compelling New Evidence That Fatherhood and Marriage Are Indispensable for the Good of Children and Society* (Martin Kessler, London and New York, c.1996)

Seldon, Arthur (ed.), *Re-privatising Welfare: After the Lost Century* (Institute of Economic Affairs, London, 1996)

Timmins, Nicholas, *The Five Giants: A Biography of the Welfare State* (HarperCollins, London, 1995)

West, E. G., *Education and the State: A Study in Political Economy* (Institute of Economic Affairs, London, 1965; 3rd ed., Liberty Fund, Indianapolis, 1994)

Young, Michael and Willmott, Peter, *Family and Kinship in East London* (Routledge and Kegan Paul, London, 1957; rev. ed., Pelican, Harmondsworth, 1962)

Illustrations

The Publisher would like to thank the following sources for their kind permission to reproduce the illustrations in this book:

Action Images /Tony O'Brien 14; The Aged Pilgrims' Friend Society 305; James Bartholomew 103, 127, 155, 170, 231, 361, 362, 363; Tom Burkard 166; Corbis 156, /BBC 96, /Bettmann 26 top, 100, 268, /Bradford T&A/Sygma 334, /Angelo Hornak 237, /Hulton-Deutsch Collection 6 top, 32, 43, 51, 56, 89, 94, 227, 310, 327, /John Heseltine 28, /Michael Nicholson 151, /Reuters19; Bill Cullen 359; Empics 12; Mary Evans Picture Library 26 bottom, 41, 92, 164, 229, 283, 357; Express and Star Syndication 83, 345; Courtesy of Dave Gaskill 120; Getty Images 368; Andrew Hasson 249; Hulton Archive 285; The Kobal Collection 68; Courtesy of Mac and the *Daily Mail* 174, 338; Courtesy of Ron McTrusty 22; Mirrorpix 233, 323; North News and Pictures 111, 190; Oxford University Press 369; Picture Partnership 206; Press Association 189, 273, 274; Rex Features 149, 204, 277, 280, 313 /Ashdown 317, /Matthew Butler 243, /Giovanni Canitano 333, /Everett Collection 7, 97, 259, 261, /Graham Jepson 8, /Phanie 353, /John Powell 6 bottom, /Roger-Viollet 2, /Mark St. George 344, /Snap 6, /Sutton-Hibbert 292, /Richard Young 133; Alexander Ruas 141; *South China Morning Post* 312; Mrs Anne Whittingham 95.

Picture Research: Emily Hedges

Notes

The Welfare State Quiz

1. 4,221 were recorded for 1898. In 1998/99 331,843 were recorded, a rise of 7,800 per cent. On the new method of recording, violent crime rose 63.7 per cent from 1998/9 to 2002/3. 7,800 x 1.637 = 12,800. Not a perfect method of calculation but the result is less dramatic than some others.

Chapter 1   From Stanley Matthews to Vinnie Jones

1. Halsey, A. H. and Webb, Josephine (eds), *Twentieth-century British Social Trends* (Macmillan, Basingstoke, 2000), p. 632.
2. Published by Cresset Press, London, 1955. Extract quoted in Davies, Christie, 'Crime, Bureaucracy and Equality', *Policy Review* 23, Winter 1983.
3. 'The English People' in *The Collected Essays, Journalism and Letters of George Orwell*, ed. Sonia Orwell and Ian Angus, (Secker and Warburg, London, 1968), vol. 3, quoted in Norman Dennis, *Rising Crime and the Dismembered Family: How Conformist Intellectuals Have Campaigned against Common Sense* (Institute of Economic Affairs, London, 1993).
4. *Soliloquies in England* (Constable, London, 1922), pp. 30, 32, 53, 54.
5. Himmelfarb, Gertrude, *The De-moralization of Society: From Victorian Virtues to Modern Values* (Knopf, New York, 1995).
6. Reissued by Egmont (2000), p. 58
7. Survey published 19 July 2002. Summary is shown in press release section of website.
8. *Daily Mail*, 22 September 2003.
9. *Daily Telegraph*, 5 July 1996.
10. *Daily Mail*, 17 July 2003.
11. Col. Morris Willoughby, letter to the *Daily Telegraph*, 1 April 2000.
12. Some will think that the fouling of today is due to the far greater sums of money now paid to footballers. They think it has corrupted a few otherwise decent people at the top of the game. But the figures show that the clubs with the most dismissals are not the leading ones at all. Between 1979 and 2001, only one of the ten worst clubs for sendings off – Wimbledon – was in the Premier League (or the First Division as it was before 1992/3) for more than four seasons. In contrast, four out of the five clubs with the best records enjoyed long periods in the premier league: Ipswich, Liverpool, Derby County and Tottenham Hotspur. The least violence was where the money was biggest. The overwhelming evidence is that foul play is more common in the lower divisions where the money is far less significant. Cynicism and deliberate unfairness in modern football is not merely a reaction to huge financial gain.
13. The figures come from *Red – Missed: Sendings-off in English Football 1979/80 to 2000/01* (Tony Brown, Beeston, 2001), supplemented by further figures kindly supplied by Tony Brown.
14. *Daily Mail*, 18 February 2000.
15. Ibid.

16. *Daily Express*, 6 January 1972.

17. Cutting dated 15 September 1954, newspaper not identified, supplied by Hayters.

18. BBC News online, 2 June 1998.

19. *Daily Telegraph*, 3 July 1998.

20. *Daily Telegraph*, 24 September 2002.

21. *Daily Mail*, 2 June 2003.

22. *Daily Telegraph*, 13 December 2003. Much of this paragraph is derived from this court report.

23. Ian Wooldridge, *Daily Mail*, 14 August 2002

24. *Daily Telegraph*, 16 November 2002.

25. Jimmy Greaves, *Sun*, 2 September 2002.

26. I have taken the population of thirty-two million shown for 1901 on page 72 of *Social Trends 30* (Office for National Statistics, 2000) and counted the population of fifty-two million for 1996/97 from the same source. The years are slightly but not significantly different from the years of the crime figures.

27. http://www.homeoffice.gov.uk/rds/pdfs/100years.xls

28. Some people might be surprised that, if crime is so much more widespread, they do not experience it themselves. But crime levels vary enormously according to where one lives. According to government figures, for every crime experienced by 'wealthy achievers' in the suburbs, nearly three are endured by residents of the poorest council estates. 'Affluent greys' experience less than one-seventh of the crime level of such estates. The relatively affluent – which includes the vast majority of media people, politicians and other opinion-formers – do not experience crime as it is suffered by millions of other people. The people who suffer most from crime are the poor. The wealthy are insulated, on the whole, from what is going on.

29. Harris, Jose, *Private Lives, Public Spirit: A Social History of Britain 1870–1914* (Oxford University Press, Oxford, 1993), quoted in Peter Hitchens, *A Brief History of Crime* (Atlantic, London, 2003).

30. Dennis, Norman et al., *The Failure of Britain's Police: London and New York Compared* (Civitas, London, 2003).

31. *Daily Mail*, 15 July 2002.

32. Kilsby, Peter, *Aspects of Crime: Children as Victims 1999,* Crime and Criminal Justice Unit, Home Office, July 2001. <http://www.homeoffice.gov.uk/rds/pdfs/aspects-children.pdf>

33. In case some may think this was a statistical aberration due, perhaps, to changes in the amount of abuse recorded by the police, the NSPCC recorded more than a doubling in the rate of physical abuse of children aged 0-14 between 1979 and 1989 (Robert Whelan, *Broken Homes and Battered Children: A Study of the Relationship between Child Abuse and Family Type*, Family Education Trust, London, 1994).

34. Office for National Statistics, 1999, p. 155.

35. *Guardian* Unlimited, 4 December 2000, 30 November 2000 and 29 November 2000.

36. *Guardian* Unlimited, 30 November 2000.

37. *Daily Mail*, 20 May 2002, interview by Helen Weathers.

38. *Financial Times*, 20 May 2002.

39. *Sunday Telegraph*, 28 April 2002.

40. Calculation made by Donal Shanahan, a surgeon at Homerton Hospital, quoted in the *Sunday Telegraph*, 14 April 2002.

41. *Daily Mail*, 23 August 2002 and *Guardian*, 24 August 2002.

42. Survey by Osprey, a book publisher, *Daily Mail*, 18 January 2001.

43. Stephen Glover, *Daily Mail*, 22 October 2002.

44. BBC Online, 22 October 2002 and *Daily Mail,* 10 October 02.

45. *Express*, 17 June 1997.
46. *Daily Mail*, 9 January 2003.
47. *Times Higher Education Supplement*, reporting a poll conducted for it by ICM, 23 May 2003.
48. *Times Educational Supplement*, 17 January 2003.
49. James, Oliver, *Britain on the Couch: Why Are We Unhappier Compared with 1950 despite Being Richer*, (Century. London, 1997), p. 345.
50. Ibid., p. 20.
51. *Daily Mail*, 17 October 2003. UK: 203 litres, Germany: 189, Netherlands: 107, Sweden: 82, Spain: 72, France: 70, Italy: 59, other Europe: 93, total Europe: 104.
52. *Britain on the Couch*.
53. Quoted in the *Daily Mail*, 21 March 2000.

Chapter 2   Social Security

1. I have referred to the 'expropriation' of the monasteries rather than, as is traditional, the 'dissolution' because the word more accurately describes what took place. Their land was taken by the King and that was the main reason for the whole event. 'Dissolution' may be regarded as a euphemism which, over many years, has suited those on the King's side of the argument.
2. Knowles, David, *Bare Ruined Choirs* (Cambridge University Press, Cambridge, 1976).
3. Cambridge University Press, Cambridge, 1976.
4. All three were executed in their time. Not a happy precedent for those who offer views on welfare reform.
5. The remarks about cheats were in his preface to Liber Vagatorum, cited in Karl de Schweinitz, *England's Road to Social Security* (Perpetua, New York, 1961).
6. Report from His Majesty's Commissioners for inquiring into the Administration and Practical Operations of the Poor Laws, 1834, p. 97.
7. Ibid., p. 89.
8. Ibid., pp. 87–8.
9. Ibid., p. 57.
10. Ibid., pp. 93–4.
11. Speenhamland was a village in Berkshire, which has since been subsumed into Newbury.
12. Ibid., p. 41.
13. Ibid., p. 15.
14. Ibid., p. 78.
15. Ibid., p. 46.
16. Ibid., p. 174.
17. Ibid., p. 171.
18. Ibid., p. 177.
19. Nicholls, Sir George, *A History of the English Poor Law*, quoted in de Schweinitz, *England's Road to Social Security*.
20. Royal Commission Report, 1834, p. 56.
21. De Schweinitz, *England's Road to Social Security*, p. 122.
22. Mitchell, B. R. and Deane, Phyllis, *Abstract of British Historical Statistics* (Cambridge University Press, Cambridge, 1962), p. 271.
23. Ibid., p. 344–5
24. Deane, Phyllis and Cole, William, *British Economic Growth 1688–1959* (Cambridge University Press, Cambridge, 1962).
25. See footnote in Chapter 1 for further detail.
26. The account of Chalmers is based on that in de Schweinitz, *England's Road to Social*

Security.

27. They are described vividly in *America's Social Revolution* (Civitas, London, 2001) by Melanie Phillips, the *Daily Mail* columnist.

28. Royal Commission, 1874, quoted in William Beveridge, *Voluntary Action* (George Allen & Unwin, London, 1948), p. 28.

29. Beveridge, *Voluntary Action*, pp. 59–60.

30. Green, David, *Reinventing Civil Society: The Discovery of Welfare without Politics* (Institute of Economic Affairs, London, 1993), p. 65.

31. Green, David, 'The Friendly Societies and Adam-Smith Liberalism', in David Gladstone (ed.), *Before Beveridge* (Institute of Economic Affairs, London, 1999), p. 23.

32. Spender, Harold, *The Prime Minister* (Hodder and Stoughton, London, 1920).

33. Some of the details of the trip come from articles by Harold Spender in the *Daily Chronicle* at the time.

34. De Schweinitz, *England's Road to Social Security*.

35. Matthews, Kent and Benjamin, Dan, *US and UK Unemployment between the Wars: A Doleful Story* (Institute of Economic Affairs, London, 1992).

36. Ibid., quoting from a 1930 essay, 'The Past and Present of Unemployment Insurance'.

37. Ibid., p. 58.

38. The biographical background on Beveridge comes mostly from Nicholas Timmins, *The Five Giants: A Biography of the Welfare State* (HarperCollins, London, 1995).

39. I myself have spent some seven or eight years as a part-time leader-writer for the *Daily Telegraph*. As a critic of the welfare state, I find it strange that Beveridge, a veritable symbol of it, played the same role. Churchill, who created the first national unemployment insurance in 1911, was also a journalist in his time, writing, among other things, opinion pieces for the *Daily Mail*, which I too have done. Of course I do not compare myself to either of these multi-talented and hugely important men. But it brings home to me how the people who most powerfully influence the way a country develops are among those few thousand at the centre of politics, the top of the civil service and on the comment side of journalism. Beveridge, in the course of his career, managed to be all three.

40. Timmins, *Five Giants*.

41. Fraser, Derek *The Welfare State* (Sutton, Stroud, 2000).

42. Collins *English Dictionary* (1984 edition).

43. Fraser, *Welfare State*.

44. Beveridge, William, *Social Insurance and Allied Services* (HMSO, London, 1942), section 231.

45. Cambridge University Press, Cambridge, 1950.

46. As the years go by, the average income which people are able to earn typically rises. During the war, real wages went down, but afterwards earnings growth resumed. So the attractiveness of benefits declined for two reasons: first because of inflation and second because wages were rising. Deflating the benefits to account for both these reveals that benefit was kept lower than in 1938 all the time from the end of the war until 1957. It was clearly and indubitably profitable for a low-earning man to work in 1957 whereas the advantage had been far less (if any) in 1938. Could that help explain why the unemployment of 1.8 million people in 1938 was reduced to a mere 285,000 in 1957?

47. SEK730 per day for the first hundred days for income-related insurance, for which premiums must be paid. Translated into sterling at SEK13.96 to the pound (rate in *Financial Times* on 24 January 2003).

48. Beatty, Christina et al., *The Real Level of Unemployment 2002* (Sheffield, 2002).

49. *Sunday Telegraph* 1999.

50. The number on housing benefit reached a peak of 4.8 million in 1996. The latest figure

available as at January 2003 was 3.8 million.

51. Beatty, *Real Level of Unemployment 2002*.

52. Words quoted are from the text of the novel by Wendy Holden (HarperCollins, London, 1998) based on the film.

53. Blanchflower, David and Oswald, Andrew, *Well-being over Time in Britain and the USA*, rev. ed. (University of Warwick, Coventry, 2002).

54. Allen, Sheila et al., 'Recent Trends in Parasuicide (Attempted Suicide) and Unemployment among Men in Edinburgh', cited in John Burnett, *Idle Hands: The Experience of Unemployment 1790–1990* (Routledge, London, 1994), p. 294.

55. Jahoda, Marie, *Employment and Unemployment – a Social-psychological Analysis* (Cambridge University Press, Cambridge, 1982).

56. Burnett, *Idle Hands*.

57. Quoted in Jahoda, *Employment and Unemployment*, p. 51.

58. Crow, Iain *et al.*, *Unemployment, Crime and Offenders* (Routledge, London, 1989), quoted in Burnett, *Idle Hands*, p. 295.

59. Heinemann, Klaus, *Arbeitslose Jugendliche*, quoted in Jahoda, *Employment and Unemployment*, p. 45.

60. *Daily Mail*, 6 August 1997.

61. Quoted in the *Daily Mail*, 6 August 1997.

62. *Daily Telegraph*, 2 February 1998.

63. *Daily Mail*, 9 May 2002.

64. Income tax allowance for persons aged 65–74 during 2002/3.

65. £4,615 in 2002/3.

66. *Financial Times*, 31 August 2002.

67. Department of Employment press release, 5 August 1992.

68. House of Commons library research, reported by Paul Goodman MP in House of Commons speech, 14 November 2002.

69. *Daily Telegraph*, 18 January 2003, quoting John Whiting, a partner of Pricewaterhouse Coopers.

Chapter 3 The NHS

1. Most of the biographical details of Bevan's life are taken from *Aneurin Bevan*, the superbly written biography by Michael Foot (MacGibbon & Kee, London, 1962 and subsequent editions).

2. Chapter 2, note 6 in the 1975 Paladin edition of *Aneurin Bevan*.

3. The story of Bart's comes from Victor Medvei and John Thornton (eds), *The Royal Hospital of Saint Bartholomew 1123–1973* (Royal Hospital of St Bartholomew, London, 1974) and Sir Norman Moore, *The History of St Bartholomew's Hospital* (C. A. Pearson, London, 1918).

4. Owen, David, *English Philanthropy 1660–1960* (Belknap Press, Cambridge, MA, 1964), from which the account of hospital development in the eighteenth century is derived.

5. Ibid.

6 Prochaska, F. K., *Philanthropy and the Hospitals of London* (Clarendon Press, Oxford, 1992).

7. Report on the British Health Services (London, 1937) quoted in David Green, 'Medical Care without the State', in Arthur Seldon (ed.), *Re-privatising Welfare: After the Lost Century* (Institute of Economic Affairs, London, 1996).

8. Beveridge, William, *Voluntary Action: A Report on Methods of Social Advance* (George Allen and Unwin, London, 1948), quoted in Green, 'Medical Care without the State', in Seldon, *Re-privatising Welfare*.

9. Robert Pinker of the London School of Economics, quoted in Green, 'Medical Care without the State', in Seldon, *Re-privatising Welfare*.

10. Green, 'Medical Care without the State', in Seldon, *Re-privatising Welfare*.

11. Muscular dystrophy is a genetic disease. Muscles deteriorate and cause walking difficulties.

12. Interview with the author, February 2003.

13. E-mail from David Green, 2 December 2003.

14. *Sidelights on the Life of a Wearside Surgeon 1859–1938* (Northumberland Press, Gateshead, 1939), p. 74.

15. In Seldon, *Re-privatising Welfare*.

16. Foot, *Aneurin Bevan* (Paladin, London, 1975), vol. II, p. 106.

17. Foot, *Aneurin Bevan*, quoted in Nicholas Timmins, *The Five Giants: A Biography of the Welfare State* (HarperCollins, London, 1995).

18. Foot, *Aneurin Bevan*, quoted in Timmins, *Five Giants*, p. 119.

19. For a fine account of Bevan's outwitting of the medical profession, see Timmins, *Five Giants*.

20. The planning starts at the top with the Department of Health itself. This employs 5,088 people, including those in its 'executive agencies'. That is before one gets to any staff who actually work for the NHS.

21. *Reform* bulletin, February 2003.

22 In 1964, a mere 48,016 people in the NHS were described as 'administration and clerical'. Ten years later, the figure had jumped by sixty-five per cent to 79,114. It had risen at a much faster rate than any other category of employee. House of Commons written answer, quoted in Heller, Tom, *Restructuring the Health Service* (Croom Helm, London, 1978).

23. I have personal experience of an elderly lady aged over 85, only receiving a flu jab once a year and no other attention from her GP. She was getting no annual check-up. Her family arranged for her to have a full check-up privately from a consultant physician. In the course of this, it was discovered that she needed a protein supplement drink and regular physiotherapy. Without the check-up none of this would have been discovered. Even once the need for physiotherapy was discovered, the NHS only offered a six-week burst, after which it would stop. This did not fulfil the need. It was not, in the words of the 1943 pamphlet, 'helping those who are fit to keep fit'.

24. *Daily Mail*, 2 June 2000.

25. Imperial Cancer Research Fund, quoted in the *Sun*, 17 May 2000.

26. Breast cancer five-year survival rates: Wales 69.5%, Scotland 72.3%, England 73.6%, Austria 75.4%, Germany 75.4%, Spain 78.0%, Netherlands 78.2%, Italy 80.6%, France 81.3%, Finland 81.4%, Sweden 82.6%. Source: Eurocare III.

27. Report by Professor Colin Pritchard of Southampton University, published in *Public Health*, the journal of the Royal Society of Health and Hygiene, quoted in the *Daily Mail*, 25 November 2000.

28. *Daily Mail*, 2 June 2000.

29. Figures taken from the British Heart Foundation Statistics website for 1998. <www.heartstats.org>

30. Source: European Society of Cardiology (2004), as cited by www.heartstats.org.

31. Quoted in *New Statesman*, 14 December 2003.

32. *British Medical Journal*.

33. The figure for 2001 was 30,525. <www.heartstats.org>

34. For me personally this is close to home. My aunt had a heart attack when she was on her way to stay with me. She was misdiagnosed by her GP. Did he use echocardiography? Were the best and most suitable drugs used? In view of all the evidence I have seen, I doubt it. My aunt died of a second heart attack within two years of the first. In Britain,

this is all too usual. To put it as I feel it, I suspect that my aunt died because we have the NHS rather than an average medical system.

35. *Laing's Healthcare Market Review 2003–2004* (Laing & Buisson, London, 2003) and conversation with William Laing, 5 December 2003.

36. According to *Laing's Healthcare Market Review 2003–2004,* 18.4 per cent of healthcare (including dentistry and nursing homes) was supplied by the independent sector in 2002. In elective surgery, the proportion paid for privately was 13.4 per cent (of which 1.2 per cent was supplied by the public sector, for example in the form of private beds in NHS hospitals).

37. *Daily Telegraph*, 1 February 2000.

38. *Daily Mail*, 21 May 2001.

39. Blendon, Robert et al., 'Inequities in Health Care: A Five-country Survey', *Health Affairs*, 2002, vol. 21, no. 3.The figures refer to 1998.

40. I would name the observer but I suspect that he would prefer to remain anonymous. Most people do not want to be quoted criticising the NHS, either because they work within it and it could cause them to be discriminated against or because they are private health suppliers who could lose their contracts. This bias against criticism from those who know makes the public announcements of those who dare speak all the more noteworthy.

41. *Daily Mail*, 30 August 2000.

42. Quoted in the *Daily Telegraph*, 5 March 2003.

43. *Daily Telegraph*, 5 March 2003.

44. Originally the King's Fund was a charity set up to provide money for hospitals (see earlier in chapter). But now the aims of the original contributors have been set aside and the organisation uses its considerable wealth for acting as a think tank instead.

45. Green, David and Irvine, Ben, Introduction, in John Grimley Evans et al., *They've Had a Good Innings! Can the NHS Cope with an Ageing Population?* (Civitas. London, 2003).

46. OECD Health Data 2001, quoted in Uwe Reinhardt *et al.*, 'Cross-national Comparisons of Health Systems Using OECD Data, 1999', *Health Affairs*, 2002, vol. 21, no.3.

47. Quoted in the *Daily Mail*, 22 July 2003.

48. OECD Health Data 2005, figures for 2003 or earlier.

49. *Daily Mail*, 18 August 2000.

50. Quicken Google website, 4 March 2003.

51. Dr Richard Taylor, *Guardian*, 22 May 2001.

52. Full title *Health in Danger: The Crisis in the National Health Service* (Macmillan, London, 1979).

53. *Guardian*, 8 June 2001.

54. *Prospect*, April 2002, quoting OECD and WHO sources. The figure given for the USA was even lower at 3.7 but I have not used it because I suspect it of being unreliable. Waiting times for treatment in the USA are very short and an analysis of hospital companies suggests that they have a problem with surplus beds rather than insufficient.

55. *Sunday Times,* 21 January 2001.

56. Quoted in Blendon et al., 'Inequities in Health Care'. The ratings referred to how many people in each country thought their treatment in these various respects was 'excellent' or 'very good'.

57. Quoted in Coulter, Angela and Cleary, Paul D., 'Patients' Experiences with Hospital Care in Five Countries', *Health Affairs*, 2001, vol. 20, no. 3, 2001.

58. *My Life in General Practice* (Christopher Johnson, London, 1948).

59. The figures relate to 2003. It is worth noting that the method of counting the number of physicians varies in different countries and some figures, for the USA and Japan for example, are for an earlier year.

60. *Daily Mail*, 4 July 2000, quoting the British Thoracic Society.

61. *British Medical Journal*, 1 February 2003.

62. *Daily Telegraph*, 22 April 2002.

63. *Guardian*, 21 January 2003.

64. My own wife went to St Mary's in London in 2003 – a hospital with a great history, the very place where Alexander Fleming discovered penicillin. She went as an outpatient with a broken wrist. When she went to the toilets, she found they evidently had not been cleaned in a long time and smelt like a sewer. She was disturbed enough to ring the Health and Safety Executive. She was told that they would write to the hospital but they could not just go and see for themselves – which they could do if the lack of hygiene was reported on, say, a building site. The irony is that one is far more likely to die of an infection caught in a hospital than die of anything at all on a building site.

65. *Daily Mail*, 16 October 2002 – a superb article by Rebecca Fowler.

66. A close relative of mine was admitted to the big county hospital in Winchester twice in 2003 and once each to two private hospitals also in Hampshire – Sarum Road and The Hampshire Clinic. In both the private hospitals, she was 'barrier nursed' for the first twenty-four hours until it could be established whether or not she had MRSA. That is to say, every member of medical staff who came into her room to carry out any procedure put on new gloves and an apron. On leaving the room, the gloves and the apron were thrown away into a bag which would be incinerated. Through this procedure, the hospitals were stopping anyone with MRSA spreading it through staff to other patients. On neither occasion that my relative was admitted to the county hospital in Winchester was this done.

67. *Daily Telegraph*, 2 March 2003.

68. *The Management and Control of Hospital Acquired Infection in Acute NHS Trusts in England* (National Audit Office, London, 2000), p. 15.

69. Quoted in the *Daily Telegraph*, 10 March 2002.

70. Quoted in the *Daily Mail*, 22 July 2003.

71. 'Outbreaks' were defined as occasions on which three or more patients were infected with the same strain in the same calendar month.

72. *Daily Mail*, 14 October 2003.

73. Interview with nurse who wishes to remain anonymous, 1 July 2002.

74. Quoted in Coulter and Cleary, 'Patients' Experiences With Hospital Care in Five Countries'.

75. 'Once the real devastation of the NHS is appreciated, the £5 billion medical indemnity bill now outstanding for the NHS might begin to look rather meagre.' Letter to the author, 16 April 2003, from John Wilden, retired consultant neurosurgeon.

76. I have not asserted that those in charge of policy – whether politicians or civil servants – knowingly or intentionally connive at avoidable deaths. I have nothing like enough evidence to believe that or assert it as a fact. However, there is evidence that there has, from time to time, been thinking along the lines that death saves money or avoids other problems. John Wilden wrote: 'When some of us went to the Department of Health in the 1980s suggesting new forms of surgical treatment for epilepsy, one of the reasons given for denying monies was on the basis that, even if we cured patients with epilepsy, it would only crease more unemployment or, at best, make somebody else unemployed.' (Letter to the author, 16 April 2003). I have myself heard one of the great and the good in health policy declare that it is a waste of money keeping old people alive because, on average, people use up a very high proportion of their lifetime medical costs in their last three months.

77. Hjertsqvist, Johan, 'Can the UK Learn Anything from the Stockholm Health Care Transition Programme?', in Edward Vaizey (ed.), *The Blue Book on Health* (Politico's, London, 2002).

78. Telephone interview with author, 11 October 2002.
79. William Robinson obtained all six scholarships obtainable at the time. He went on to become a surgeon. From *Sidelights on the Life of a Wearside Surgeon*.
80. *My Life in General Practice*.
81. Patel, H. R. H. et al., 'Outpatient Clinic: Where Is the Delay?', *Journal of the Royal Society of Medicine*, 2002, vol. 95, no. 12.
82. When one reads surveys about what happens in healthcare, one begins to notice how one's personal experiences fit into the pattern. My wife broke her wrist in January 2003. When she had X-rays taken at St Mary's she was advised to keep them with her because if they were kept at the hospital there would be only a 'slim chance' that they would be available when needed.
83. Conversation in 2002 with retired nurse who wishes to remain anonymous.
84. *Daily Mail*, 4 March 2002.
85. *Daily Telegraph*, 2 September 2002.
86. *Daily Mail*, 4 March 2002.
87. Letter to the *Daily Telegraph*, 22 August 2002.
88. Audit Commission report referred to on *Today* programme, Christopher Booker's Notebook, *Sunday Telegraph*, 8 September 2002.
89. The earliest report I have traced is that in the *Daily Express* on 20 November 2001. More detailed figures, however, appeared in the *Mail on Sunday* on 17 March 2002. I have used those figures with the exception of the fraud figure. This was shown as £1.3bn in the *Mail on Sunday* and £3bn in the earlier *Daily Express* article. I have preferred the *Daily Express* figure since it was closer to the date of the meeting and the figure makes the sum add up to approximately £9bn, which all newspapers refer to.
90. A *Daily Telegraph* leader, to which I contributed, made mention of these figures. A letter came from the ministry referring to 'back of the envelope' figures and boasting of targets created and duly met.
91. The secretary of state at the time was Alan Milburn.
92. John Appleby and Ray Robinson are among the others.
93. Le Grand, Julian, 'Further Tales from the British National Health Service', *Health Affairs*, 2002, vol. 21, no. 3.
94. The account of Joseph's 1974 reforms is taken from Timmins, *Five Giants*.
95. In Switzerland, the state does much of the paying. But consumers decide which insurance company to join and each insurance company decides which hospitals to employ. There is competition in two of the stages. In France, the state pays but the care is mostly provided by doctors and hospitals in competition. Sixty per cent of hospitals are privately owned and run.

Chapter 4 Education

1. Quoted in E. G. West, *Education and the State*, 3rd ed. (Liberty Fund, Indianapolis, 1994).
2. Ibid.
3. Ibid.
4. Ibid., p. 173.
5. Some historians have taken Forster's estimates in 1870 but these were based on a statistical error which was exposed in West, Education and the State, pp. 181–4 and again in James Tooley, *Education without the State* (Institute of Economic Affairs, London, 1996).
6. Just under six years.
7. Forster's civil servants assumed that children should be educated from five to thirteen. They estimated how many children there were in Manchester, for example, who were in that age bracket: eighty thousand. They then discovered how many children were actually

in school in Manchester and found that only sixty thousand were at school. They therefore concluded that twenty thousand children were not at school. The flaw in this analysis lay in the arbitrary assumption that children should be at school from five to thirteen – a total of eight years – when in fact, as the Newcastle Commission had discovered, children on average spent 5.7 years at their schooling. One may guess that by 1870, that average had reached six years. If that is right, then the number of children who should have been at school for 100 per cent attendance was not the total number of children aged between five and thirteen but only six-eighths of that number, i.e. sixty thousand pupils. That in fact is the number who were at school. So Forster wrongly informed the House of Commons that 25 per cent of children in Manchester were getting no schooling whereas his own raw data – without incorrect assumptions – suggested that 100 per cent of them were getting some schooling. This may have been an exaggeration. But it was nearer the truth than the wildly inaccurate scare story which he told other MPs. West, *Education and the State.*

8. All the material about King's Somborne comes from S. J. Curtis and M. E. A. Boultwood, *An Introductory History of English Education since 1800* (University Tutorial Press, London, 1960).

9. West, *Education and the State*, p. 175.

10. Gardner, Phil, *The Lost Elementary Schools of Victorian England: The People's Education* (Croom Helm, London, 1984).

11. Ibid.

12. Ibid., p. 171, quoting from Newcastle Commission Report, vol. 2, p. 227.

13. Smith, Frank, *A History of English Elementary Education 1760–1902* (University of London Press, London, 1931).

14. Quoted in Smith, *History of English Elementary Education*, p. 202. No date is given for Dickens's words.

15. Smith, *History of English Elementary Education.*

16. Quoted in Smith, *History of English Elementary Education*, p. 319.

17. West, *Education and the State.*

18. Webb, R. K., 'The Victorian Reading Public', in Boris Ford (ed.), *The New Pelican Guide to English Literature, vol. 6: From Dickens to Hardy* (Pelican, Harmondsworth, 1963), quoted in West, *Education and the State.*

19. Glass, David, 'Education and Social Change in Modern England', in A. H. Halsey et al. (eds), *Education, Economy, and Society: A Reader in the Sociology of Education* (Free Press of Glencoe, New York, 1961), quoted in West, *Education and the State.*

20. Samuel Bamford, 'the weaver poet', quoted by H. J. Perkins in *History Today*, July 1957, p. 426, quoted in turn in West, *Education and the State.*

21. Published by John Snow, Leeds, 1854, price sixpence.

22. This is a more complete list:

1. 'The duty of educating being assumed by the State, it is of course taken off from the parent, who thereby loses one of his most sacred responsibilities and with it loses ... influence [over his child]'.

2. The religious bodies and benevolent citizens who then sponsored education would also lose their 'happy social influence'.

3. Responsibility would move, instead, to a set of 'political officers' including some who do their work 'perfunctorily and heartlessly for the mere sake of the salary'. State enterprises were inefficient and 'nests of jobbing'.

4. The centre would not be able to keep real control of so many schools, so power would go to inspectors, who would become like 'little despots' dictating to school committees and headmasters.

5. One uniform system of tuition would dominate. Nothing could be more harmful to future improvements. There would be 'stereo-typed school-books' and 'invention of new methods

would cease.' It would be 'inflexible'.

6. Salaries for teachers would be reduced. The government felt generous towards education at that time, but the salaries of government servants in post offices, for example, were a warning.

7. Enormous bureaucracies would be created to direct education, 'resembling the bureaucracies of the Continent'. Such an increase in government activity and patronage 'is scarcely consistent with free institutions'.

8. The government would have the power to mould 'the religious and political opinions of the people – not a very fit thing for a great and free nation, nor compatible with its intellectual independence'.

9. Religion would be excluded altogether or only one sect would be taught or every sect would be taught. Each of these possibilities was objectionable.

10. If such things also extended to further and higher education, the objections listed above would be 'greatly aggravated and multiplied'.

23. Letter of 24 April 1876, quoted in West, *Education and the State*.

24. Inspector Fitch on the Lambeth district in 1878, quoted in West, *Education and the State*.

25. House of Commons, 10 August 1917, quoted in J. Stuart Maclure, *Educational Documents, England and Wales 1816–1967* (Chapman & Hall, London, 1968).

26. Grigg, John, *The Young Lloyd George* (Eyre Methuen, London, 1973).

27. Howard, Anthony, *Rab: The Life of R. A. Butler* (Papermac, London, 1988), p. 110. Churchill remarked at their interview, 'I should not object if you could introduce a note of patriotism into the schools. Tell the children that Wolfe won Quebec.'

28. White Paper on Educational Reconstruction, 1943, quoted in Maclure, *Educational Documents*.

29. See later in this chapter for a review of the reliability of this result. Without the private schools, Britain would have ranked two places lower.

30. *Daily Mail*, 18 December 2001, citing Department for Education and Skills figures.

31. *Improving Literacy and Numeracy: A Fresh Start*, report by the working group on post-school basic skills, chaired by Sir Claus Moser. <http://www.lifelonglearning.co.uk/mosergroup>

32. Quoted in the *Sunday Telegraph*, 8 February 1998.

33. Quoted in the *Daily Mail*, 17 January 2001.

34. Burkard, Tom, *The New Model School* (forthcoming), draft of book seen in March 2003.

35. 'Almost half of adults lack basic maths'.

36. 'Level of Highest Qualification Held by People of Working Age, England, Spring 1997–2005'. The figures quoted are for 2005. From DfES website Trends in Education and Skills. <http://www/dfes.gov.uk/trends/index.cfm>

37. 'The Level of Highest Qualification Held by Young People and Adults: England 2002', DfES First Release, 28 January 2003. <http://www.dfes.gov.uk/rsgateway/DB/SFR/s000379/index.shtml>

38. Some may think, 'Perhaps the figures for adults are distorted by the arrival of immigrants without qualifications.' But there are not enough of those to change the figures significantly.

39. 'Education and Training Statistics for the United Kingdom', 2005 edition, DfES website. The exact figure was 23.2%.

40. I can imagine many an academic harrumphing that two questions from old exam papers prove nothing. A whole academic industry has grown up to suggest that any number of exam papers, marking systems and passes prove nothing. Such is the ingenuity with which black, it is suggested, is actually white, that one learned person even argued that the introduction of microwave ovens was one of the reasons why it was just impossible to make fair comparisons between exams at different times.

41. 1955, University of Cambridge Local Examinations Syndicate, Paper II (Shakespeare). 1995, same syndicate, Paper 12, Shakespeare.

42. *Times Educational Supplement*, 21 March 2003.

43. Coe, Dr Robert, 'Changes in Examination Grades over Time: Is the Same Worth Less?' British Educational Research Association annual conference, Brighton, September 1999.

44. Confirming research comes from York University, where the Electronics Department has given new students the same maths tests each year for the past fifteen years. The average score for those who have achieved A and B grades at A-level has fallen from 78 per cent to only 54 per cent. Source: Campaign for Real Education, quoting *Daily Telegraph*, 31 October 2001.

45. Dr Coe, like a true academic, offers seven possible explanations for why this should have happened. But this is a ritual in which all the explanations are clearly without merit except the final one: that 'grade standards have slipped.'

46. This undergraduate told me about this on condition of anonymity.

47. But although the performance is below average, it is not right at the bottom of the table, as is the case so often in measurements of British medical treatment. Why should Britain's educational achievement appear less bad than its medical performance? One possibility is that the competition is less hot in education. In the vast majority of countries, the state is heavily dominant in providing education. So if there is anything wrong with state education, nearly all countries are likely to be suffering from it. In medicine, on the other hand, Britain is unique in having a system that is more state dominated than in any other advanced country. That could explain why it is so frequently at the bottom of league tables in medicine.

48. *Daily Telegraph*, 15 January 2003.

49. Quoted in John Marks, *Standards and Spending: Dispelling the Spending Orthodoxy* (Centre for Policy Studies, London, 2002).

50. *Sunday Telegraph*, 8 February 1998.

51. Quoted by Institute of Directors in publication about choice.

52. *Encounter*, July 1960.

53. John Clare, *Daily Telegraph*, 8 February 2003.

54. Routledge, London, 2003.

55. *Daily Mail*, 12 August 2002.

56. Bernard, G.W., *Studying at University: How to Adapt Successfully to College Life* (RoutledgeFalmer, London & New York, 2003).

57. July 1996.

58. Stevens, Robert, 'Barbarians at the Gates: A View from Oxford's City Wall', public lecture given at the George Washington University, Washington, DC, 24 March 1998.

59. Data from Oxford University information office.

60. *An Unfinished Autobiography* (Oxford University Press, London, 1941), p. 116.

61. *Financial Times*, 7 June 1999.

62. Quoted in Professor Antony Flew, 'Comprehensive Catastrophe' (2001), essay supplied by the E. G. West Centre, University of Newcastle, quoting Antony Flew, *Power to the Parents: Reversing Educational Decline* (Sherwood, London, 1987), p. 59.

63. Quoted in Flew, 'Comprehensive Catastrophe', quoting Susan Crosland, *Tony Crosland* (Jonathan Cape, London, 1982).

64. Interim report to the National Committee of Inquiry into Higher Education, 1997. Quoted in Report 6, *Widening Participation in Higher Education for Students from Lower Socio-economic Groups and Students with Disabilities*. <http://www.ncl.ac.uk/ncihe/r6_046.htm>

65. Ibid.

66 *Daily Mail*, 31 October 2003.

67. DfES website, performance tables for 2002.

68. Study by Professor Paul Cheshire at the London School of Economics, *Daily Mail* 5 September 2003.

69. *Times Educational Supplement*, 28 June 2002.

70. Quoted in *Explanations of under-representation...* op cit.

71. *Times Educational Supplement*, 11 April 2003.

72. A group of academics studied two groups of children. The first group was born in 1958, the second in 1970. The researchers looked at how much the children in the first group earned when they grew up, in their early thirties. They found that the children of the highest-earning parents (getting twice as much as other families) earned about 13 per cent more than other children in this group. Then the researchers looked at a group of children born in 1970 and looked again at how much the children of the richest parents earned. The premium for having rich parents had increased. The children earned 25 per cent more than others born in their year.

73. Quoted in E. G. West, 'Economic Analysis Positive and Normative', in William F. Rickenbacker (ed.), *The Twelve-year Sentence* (Open Court, LaSalle, IL, 1974).

74. Roberts, David, *Victorian Origins of the British Welfare State* (Yale University Press, New Haven, 1960), p. 58.

75. Quoted in Roberts, *Victorian Origins of the British Welfare State*, p. 53.

76. Speech at Abraham Moss High School, Manchester, 22 March 2002.

77. Ofsted report, quoted in the *Daily Telegraph*, 11 June 2003.

78. Quoted in 'Education and Crime: a Political Economy of Interdependence', *Character*, 1980, vol. 8, no. 4. Supplied by the E. G. West Centre.

79. Metropolitan Police figures quoted in speech by Estelle Morris, Secretary of State for Education, 29 April 2002.

80. BBC News online, 29 April 2002.

81. Ibid.

82. Quoted in 'Education and Crime'.

83. Sport in England survey, 25 February 2003. <www.sportengland.org>

84. *Sun*, 24 January 2003 and statement issued by Councillor Peter Hammond, deputy leader, Bristol City Council, 23 January 2003.

85. HMSO, London, 1993.

86. Speech at Abraham Moss High School, Manchester, 22 March 2002.

87. Interview, *Financial Times*, 9 July 2002.

88. *Daily Telegraph*, 18 January 2003.

89. Wolf, Alison, *Does Education Matter? Myths about Education and Economic Growth* (Penguin, London, 2002) examines this issue authoritatively.

90. From 9 to 17 per cent.

91. *Daily Mail*, 24 July 2002.

92. Singapore Ministry of Education website, www.moe.gov.sg, and interviews with Singaporeans by Christian Wignall.

93. www.sannet.ne.jp.

94. In America the private sector has come up with another technique for rescuing students from low standards in the government schools. It is called 'Saxon math'. There is a website, www.saxonpublishers.com.

95. *Korea Herald* survey, quoted in Casey Lartigue, 'You'll Never Guess What South Korea Frowns upon' (2000), Cato Institute website, www.cato.org/dailys/06-15-00.html.

96. Total state spending on education was £51 billion in 2001/2. Out of this the total cost of primary and secondary schools in England was £27 billion. There were 6.4 million pupils, so the average cost per pupil was £4,218. The average cost of secondary schooling was a bit higher at £4,768 per pupil (secondary schooling costs about 1.3 times as much per pupil as primary, according to the government). Adding in the higher cost for the one academic term which fell in 2002/3 brings the cost for that academic year to £4,855 per student. From 'Comparing State Education Costs and Private Education Costs', unpublished calculations by Maurice Fitzpatrick of the Tenon Group, supplied by the Adam Smith Institute, 2002.

97. Estimate according to Tenon Group, based on costs of independent day school education supplied by HaysMacIntyre.

98. Hillgrove quotes £1,000 a term and Tower College up to £1,310 a term, according to the Independent Schools Council Information Service website, 7 June 2003.

99. Letter to the *Daily Telegraph*, 17 September 2003.

100. *Times Educational Supplement*, 13 December 2002.

101. Full title *The Progress of the Nation in Its Various Social and Economic Relations from the Beginning of the Nineteenth Century to the Present Time* (Methuen, London, 1912), quoted in West, *Education and the State*.

102. This is the 'full-time equivalent'. There are '1,166 posts within the non-delegated budget of the Directorate'. Director of Education and Libraries statement – Staffing Structure, Newcastle City Council website, 4 June 2003.

103. Unfortunately I have not been able to obtain the details of the analysis on which the claim was based. There is a need for someone to do the same sort of work done by Maurice Slevin on the NHS and carefully divide up such staff into teachers and non-teachers, making sure that the ratio is authoritative.

104. PISA report, *Knowledge and Skills for Life* (OECD, Paris, 2000) p. 314. The meta-effect was minus 22.48 for those experiencing student/teacher ratios of over 30:1 and minus 10.01 for those experiencing ratios of between 25:1 and 30:1.

105. Three-quarters of pupils taught in the smaller classes completed school successfully compared with 64 per cent of those who had experienced the larger classes.

106. *Daily Telegraph*, 3 October 2001.

107. *Daily Telegraph*, 17 November 2001.

108. Summary of the Haydn Index from the *Daily Telegraph*, John Clare column.

109. Report of unfair dismissal hearing, *Daily Telegraph*, 19 March 2002.

110. Quoted by John Clare, *Daily Telegraph*, 9 October 2002.

111. *Sun*, 23 August 2002.

112. Your Shout, *Daily Telegraph*, 26 October 2002.

113. *Daily Mail*, 14 July 2003.

114. Speech at Abraham Moss High School, Manchester, 22 March 2002.

115. Phillips, Melanie, *All Must Have Prizes* (Little, Brown, London, 1996).

116. Ibid.

117. *Daily Mail*, 18 July 2002.

118. Part of the material on the teaching of English literature, geography and history is taken from Chris Woodhead, *Class War* (Little, Brown, London, 2002).

119. Full title *Civil Society and David Blunkett: Lawyers vs. Politicians* (Civitas, London, 2002).

120. In its press releases, the DfES stopped publishing the overall figure for appeals from 2003/4 because it 'could be misleading'. One reason given was that 'a place in an alternative school' could be accepted before the appeal reached a panel hearing. About 73 per cent of appeals reach a panel hearing.

121 Professors Joshua Angrist of MIT and Victor Lavy of the Hebrew University of Jerusalem, writing in the *Economic Journal*, October 2002.

122. Briefing note released 4 December 2001.

123. *Daily Mail*, 11 January 2003.

124. Research by Professor Alan Smithers and Dr Pamela Robinson of Liverpool University's Centre for Education and Employment Research for the National Union of Teachers. Quoted in BBC News online, 1 November 2001.

125. *Daily Telegraph*, 18 March 2002, quoting John Dunford, General Secretary of the Secondary Heads' Association.

126. This reason applies across public services generally. The Audit Commission surveyed former public-sector workers to find out why they had left. Nearly four out of five gave 'bureaucracy and paperwork' as a reason. It was the most common reason for leaving. *Recruitment and Retention* (London, 2002).

127. David Winkley in December 2002.

128. 21 June 2002.

129. *Times Educational Supplement*, 7 February 2003.

130. Page 177, margin. It is true that the negative correlation is not large or necessarily causal. But to justify the cost and personnel of central interference, there should be a powerful beneficial effect of state control and instruction.

131. Study by Tony Bowers and Malcolm McIver, quoted in the *Daily Mail*, 2 October 2000.

132. In 2001/2, 6.6 per cent of pupils aged eleven and 6.7 per cent of those aged twelve were at private schools. At ages fifteen, sixteen and seventeen, the proportion at private schools soars because many in the state system leave school and also perhaps because some parents send their children to private schools only for the later years of their education.

133. Page 307.

134. The World Bank reports I have used are: Jimenez, E. et al., *The Relative Effectiveness of Private and Public Schools: The Case of Thailand* (1988); Lockheed, M. and Jimenez, E., *Public and Private Secondary Schools in Developing Countries* (1994); *The Relative Effectiveness of Private and Public Schools: Evidence from Two Developing Countries* [Colombia and Tanzania] (1989); and 'Public Schools and Private: Which Are More Efficient', *World Bank Policy and Research Bulletin*, January/February 1992, vol. 3, no. 1.

135. Lockheed and Jimenez, *Public and Private Secondary Schools in Developing Countries*.

Chapter 5 Housing

1 Young, Michael and Willmott, Peter, *Family and Kinship in East London* (Routledge and Kegan Paul, London, 1957).

2 Victor Gollancz, London, 1937. This quote can be found on p. 65 of the 2001 Penguin edition.

3 Ibid. This quote can be found on pp. 64–5, of the 2001 Penguin edition.

4 Full title *Housing by People: Towards Autonomy in Building Environments* (Marion Boyars, London, 1976).

5 David and Charles, Newton Abbot, 1978.

6 Burnett, *Social History of Housing*, p 141.

7 Ibid.

8 Glendinning, Miles and Muthesius, Stefan, *Tower Block: Modern Public Housing in England, Scotland, Wales, and Northern Ireland* (Yale University Press, New Haven, 1994).

9 Burbridge, Michael et al., *An Investigation into Difficult to Let Housing* (HMSO, London, 1980), quoted in Alison Ravetz, *Council Housing and Culture: The History of a Social Experiment* (Routledge, London, 2001).

10 John Mogey in 1956 showed that the new Barton estate was a less happy place than the old part of St Ebbe's in Oxford from which people had been 'cleared'. In St Ebbe's, people still set store by a 'good funeral', children played in the street while doorsteps, knockers and even keyholes were scrupulously cleaned. St Ebbe's provided the 'cultural equipment' that enabled a majority 'to live happy and well-adjusted lives under conditions of work and housing that would daunt many people'. The key was the solidarity of the extended families with strong local loyalties. At the new Barton estate, children's play was confined to the boundaries of the home and there was a conflict-ridden community centre 'where officers resigned over various bungled projects' (Ravetz, *Council Housing and Culture*, pp. 159–60).

11 Joseph Rowntree Memorial Trust. Hilda Jennings' study of the redevelopment of Barton Hill in Bristol told a similar story. The so-called 'slum clearance' was strongly opposed by the residents, led by the vicar. 'The move separated more than half the new tenants from their parents or married children, and grandparents … were no longer able to help with child care. Some of the old who did undertake the move were said to have lost the will to live because of it.' (Ibid.).

12 *Daily Mail*, 30 August 1995. She was interviewed after a woman there was killed when concrete thrown from the roof fell on her.

Chapter 6 Parenting

1. *Daily Mail* 6 June 2002.
2. *Social Trends 2003* (The Stationery Office, London, 2003), p. 46; *Social Trends 2005* (The Stationery Office, London, 2005), p. 23.
3. Ermisch and Francesconi *Seven Years in the lives of British Families* (Policy Press 2000) cited in Jill Kirby, *Broken Hearts: Family Decline and the Consequences for Society* (Centre for Policy Studies, London, 2002).
4. No thoroughly researched figure appears to be available. But according to a calculation by Rebecca O'Neill, while at Civitas, using figures from Ermisch and Francesconi, the number having both parents until sixteen may be down to 51 per cent.
5. Published by the Stationery Office, London.
6. Hartley, Shirley Foster, *Illegitimacy* (University of California Press, Berkeley, 1975), pp. 36–9.
7. Social Trends 2002, quoted in Rebecca O'Neill, *Experiments in Living: The Fatherless Family* (Civitas, London, 2002), and Social Trends 2003.
8. Among various indicators of the way contraception, though easily available, is not widely used is an NOP poll done for the Family Planning Association which showed that 60 per cent of sixteen- to 24-year-olds use condoms 'sometimes' or 'never' (quoted in the *Daily Mail*, 4 August 2003).
9. Laslett, Peter: *Family Life and Illicit Love in Earlier Generations: Essays in Historical Sociology* (Cambridge University Press, Cambridge, 1980). pp. 102, 119, 123 & 125.
10. For those who don't remember pre-decimal days, there were twelve pence in a shilling, which was worth 5p.
11. Manual worker earnings supplied by what was called the Employment Department (in 1994), details of personal allowances from Inland Revenue website and kindly explained by Stuart Adam at the Institute of Fiscal Studies. Manual workers, of course, were paid somewhat less than the average of all employed people but figures for all employed people do not appear to go back that far. Also the proportion of manual workers in 1948–50 was far higher than now, probably accounting for the large majority. Table 6.5 previously incorporated some estimates of the average of all earnings. This shows that a family with the average of all earnings was not liable to tax in 1949/50 if there were two children.
12. Quoted in Frank Field et al., *To Him Who Hath: A Study of Poverty and Taxation* (Pelican, Harmondsworth, 1977), p. 32. This was – and remains – a very important book, showing how tax was extended to the poor in the decades after the war.
13. According to Rebecca O'Neill in 2003, a one-earner couple with earnings of £20,000 (not far from average earnings) would pay tax and national insurance of £4,800, of which they would get £1,400 back in child benefit. 'Final after-tax, after-tax credits, after-benefits household income is £16,570.'
14. The individuals and their stories are invented. The detailed financial calculations for people in their situation are derived from the Tax and Benefit Model Tables of June 2001 issued by the Department of Work and Pensions and quoted in *The Lone Parent Trap: How the Welfare System Discourages Marriage* (Civitas, London, 2002).
15. How the state discouraged the poor from having two-parent families.
    1950/51: Married couple on average earnings with two children became liable to income tax for the first time in British history
    1963–70: Doubling of tax burden on couples earning average income with children
    1967: Council rate (local tax) rebates introduced for those on low incomes (automatically included unemployed lone parents)

1967/8: Married couple with two children on two-thirds of average wage became liable to income tax

1972: Nationwide rent rebates introduced alongside increases in council rents. The rebates could also be claimed against rents in the private sector. Those not earning, such as unemployed lone parents, benefited. Those earning, such as married couples with children, had to pay more

1976: Standard rate of tax reached new high of 35 per cent. One-parent benefit introduced

1977–9: Child tax allowance phased out and replaced by child benefit

1980: Lone parents began to receive higher rate of welfare benefit (27 per cent higher than ordinary benefit)

1985: Local authorities became legally obliged to provide permanent housing even to the intentionally homeless if they were in a 'priority need category'. Lone parents generally qualified

1990/91: Married couples' allowance frozen.

This list is by no means comprehensive. The story is extremely complex and a full history of it is yet to be written.

16. Rowlingson, Karen, 'The Social, Economic and Demographic Profile of Lone Parents', in Jane Millar and Karen Rowlingson (eds), *Lone Parents, Employment and Social Policy: Cross-national Comparisons* (Policy Press, Bristol, 2001), p. 178.

17. Ibid., p. 179, quoting Karen Rowlingson and Stephen McKay, *Lone Parent Families: Gender, Class and State* (Prentice Hall, Harlow, 2001), based on government figures from the Family and Working Lives Survey conducted for the Department for Education and Employment in 1994–5.

18. 'Social Class and Socio-economic Differentials in Divorce in England and Wales', Population Studies, 1984, vol. 38, no. 3, pp. 419–38 (1984). It was written a while ago but the welfare state was in full swing and I know of no reason to think that similar findings would not be discovered if a similar analysis was made today.

19. Ibid.

20. Social Trends 2003, p. 46. The drastic decline in first marriages is shown in fig. 2.10.

21. Marriage, Divorce and Adoption Statistics (Series FM2), 1990, no. 16; Population Trends, 2002, no. 110; and Marriage and Divorces 1985-98.

22. Cato Policy Report, 2000, vol. 22, no.6.

23. Gonzalez, Libertad, 'The Determinants of the Prevalence of Single Mothers: A Cross-country Analysis', paper presented to the European Association of Labour Economists, September 2003.

24. Letter to the author, 16 August 1995.

25. Brown, George W. and Moran, Patricia M., 'Single Mothers, Poverty and Depression', *Psychological Medicine*, 1997, vol. 27, pp. 21–3.

26. Millar and Rowlingson (eds), *Lone Parents, Employment and Social Policy*, p. 26.

27. Stationery Office, London, 2001, p. 21.

28. James, Oliver, *Britain on the Couch: Why Are We Unhappier Compared with 1950 Despite Being Richer*, (Century, London, 1997), pp. 20–21.

29. Ibid.

30. The 2001 British Crime Survey (Home Office) p. 63. The figures are: married 0.2 per cent, cohabiting 1.1 per cent, single 1.4 per cent, divorced 1.9 per cent, separated 4.3 per cent.

31. Morgan, Patricia, *Marriage-lite: The Rise of Cohabitation and Its Consequences* (Civitas, London, 2000), p. 34.

32. Full title *The Case for Marriage: Why Married People are Happier, Healthier, and Better off Financially* (Doubleday, New York, 2000)

33. Jahme, Carole, *Beauty and the Beasts: Woman, Ape and Evolution* (Virago Press, London, 2000), pp. 286–91.

34. Diamond, Jared, *The Rise and Fall of the Third Chimpanzee* (Vintage, London, 1992).

35. The television programme was an edition of *Newsnight* shown in 2000. The author saw the programme and has also drawn on a report of it in the *Sun* of 22 November 2000. Stanley Claridge was convicted on nineteen charges including rape, buggery and indecent assault in April 2002 at Liverpool Crown Court (BBC News online and *Liverpool Echo* online, 1 March 2002).

36. Whelan, Robert, *Broken Homes and Battered Children* (Family Education Trust, London, 1994).

37. Ibid.

38. Daly, Martin and Wilson, Margo, *The Truth about Cinderella: A Darwinian View of Parental Love* (Weidenfeld and Nicolson, London, 1998) and Whelan, *Broken Homes and Battered Children*.

39. Daly and Wilson, *Truth about Cinderella*, p. 35. Study conducted in 1996.

40. Page, David, *Communities in the Balance: The Reality of Social Exclusion on Housing Estates* (Joseph Rowntree Foundation/York Publishing Services, York, 2000).

41. *Daily Mail*, 11 April 2003.

42. Whelan, *Broken Homes and Battered Children*. These were cases about which various government departments collected the family details. This sample of cases is even smaller than the ones where death did not result. But again I include it because it differentiates family types more precisely than other studies.

43. Daly and Wilson, *Truth About Cinderella*, p. 28.

44. Ibid., pp. 31–3.

45. Roy, Penny et al., 'Institutional Care: Risk from Family Background or Pattern of Rearing?', *Journal of Child Psychology and Psychiatry*, 2000, vol. 41, no. 2, pp. 139–49.

46. A government report into 650 allegations of child abuse in forty council care homes in north Wales said abuse had been systematic amidst a climate of violence and that a culture of secrecy existed in dozens of homes over two decades. BBC News online, 29 June 2000, citing the Waterhouse report.

47. Interview with Paul Burrell, *Daily Mirror*, 7 November 2002 and interview with Charles Spencer, *Sun*, 26 June 2002.

48. *Daily Telegraph*, 14 September 2002.

49. *Mail on Sunday*, 29 December 2002.

50. *Daily Mail*, 21 June 2002.

51. *Daily Mail*, 9 October 2002.

52. www.crimelibrary.com

53. *Sun*, 18 December 2003.

54. *Daily Mail*, 18 December 2003.

55. Albert, Robert S., 'Family Positions and Attainment of Eminence', in Robert S. Albert, *Genius and Eminence: The Social Psychology of Creativity and Exceptional Achievement* (Pergamon, Oxford, 1983), quoted in Oliver James, *They F*** You Up: How to Survive Family Life* (Bloomsbury, London, 2002).

56 Singleton, Nicola *et al*, *Psychiatric Morbidity Among Prisoners in England and Wales* (Stationery Office, London, 1998), quoted in James, *They F*** You Up*.

57. Popenoe, David, *Disturbing the Nest: Family Change and Decline in Modern Societies* (Aldine de Gruyter, New York, 1988).

58. Letter to the *Daily Telegraph*, 7 November 2002.

Chapter 7 Pensions

1. This work will culminate in *Life and Labour of the People in London*, which will be published in 1902–3 in seventeen volumes.

2. Halsey, A. H. and Webb, Josephine (eds), *Twentieth-century British Social Trends*

(Macmillan, Basingstoke, 2000), p. 328. GDP per capita £2,449 in 1900 and £10,901 in 1995 at 1997 prices.

3. Abel-Smith, Brian, 'The Beveridge Report: Its Origins and Outcomes', York Papers, vol. A, quoted in Nicholas Timmins, *The Five Giants: A Biography of the Welfare State* (Harper-Collins, London, 1995) Means-tested benefits were better in the sense that they could include rent, whereas national insurance benefits did not.

4. *A New Contract for Welfare: Partnership in Pensions*, Cm. 4179, (Department of Social Security, 1998), p. 8, para. 41, cited in Mike Brewer and Carl Emmerson, 'Two Cheers for Pension Credit?' (Institute for Fiscal Studies, Briefing Note 39, 2003).

5. Average full-time employee earnings in April 2003 were £25,170 according to Joanna Bulman, 'Patterns of Pay: Results of the 2003 New Earnings Survey', *Labour Market Trends*, 2003, vol. 111, no. 12.

6. BBC News Vote 2001, quoting Conservative manifesto report about House of Commons library research. In April 2003, Watson Wyatt, the actuaries, quoted the Institute for Fiscal Studies estimate that 52 per cent of adults over sixty-five would be eligible to receive pension credit. Since there are other means-tested benefits apart from pension credit, this does not contradict the House of Commons library estimate.

7. A Guide to Pension Credit (Department of Work and Pensions, 2003) gave the minimum amount as £102.10 a week for a single person and £155.80 for a couple (p. 14). These figures are multiplied by 52.142857, being the number of weeks in a year.

8. The definition has been used by the government to define child poverty, but the principle appears to be capable of being extended to cover poverty for adults. In 2002, the government appeared to be interested in creating a new definition of poverty after failing to meet its 1997 manifesto claim about how it would reduce poverty (*Guardian*, 19 April 2002). Strictly speaking, the definition is a household with below 60 per cent of median household income after housing costs.

9. Households Below Average Income 1994/5–2001/02 (Department of Work and Pensions, 2003) shows median income of £311 per week. Multiplying by 52.142857 results in a yearly figures of £16,216.43. This is likely to have risen by at least seven per cent by the year 2003/4, using the earning index as a guide. Adding seven per cent results in a average income of £17,351.58. Sixty per cent of this is £10,410.95. This is income 'before housing costs'. But we are comparing like with like in that the minimum payment under the pension credit also excludes consideration of housing costs.

10. Brewer and Emmerson, 'Two Cheers for Pension Credit?'. Between 24 and 32 per cent did not claim the minimum income guarantee in 2000/01, between 32 and 38 per cent of pensioners entitled to council tax benefit did not claim it and one in ten did not claim their housing benefit. The target for the take-up of pension credit is 73 per cent by 2006. In that case 950,000 lower-income households will still not be receiving the benefit to which they are entitled. The non-take-up of pensions may not be part of a deliberate plan, but the result is that the government saves money and is therefore able to appear to be more 'generous'. It is generosity based on knowing that nearly a million people will be poorer.

11. Quoted by David Willetts in a speech made on 27 February 2002, viewed on the Conservative Party website

12. Ibid.

13. Cambridge University Press, Cambridge, 1998.

14. With £18,001 of savings, Mavis is 'deemed' to have an income of £25 a week (far above actual returns on capital). Therefore her 'net income' is £25 plus £77.45 (her basic state pension), making £102.45. This is just above the 'appropriate amount' of £102.10 for a single person. She is therefore not eligible for the 'guarantee credit' element of pension credit. However, she is eligible for the 'savings credit' element. Her 'qualifying income' of £102.45 (state pension plus 'deemed' interest) is £25 above the 'savings credit starting point' of £77.45.

She gets 60 per cent of this £25 up to a maximum of £14.79. Her real income is therefore her state pension of £77.45 plus her actual interest on £18,001 of £15.54 plus her pension credit of £14.79, making a total of £107.78. If she had no savings or £6,000 of savings, she would be eligible simply for the 'guarantee credit' element of the pension credit, namely the difference between the state pension and the 'appropriate amount' (£102.10 minus £77.45 = £24.65).

15. Some would say that Mavis would get a higher income if she bought an annuity. But why should she buy an annuity? She wants a nest egg. Is that not reasonable? In a rational system, would it not be a sensible thing that was encouraged or, at least, not discouraged?

16. According to my own calculations, a single person would cease to qualify for pension credit when he or she had about £39,000 of financial assets. But that does not mean that such a person would have an income which the government considers the minimum acceptable – the 'appropriate amount'. That person would be deemed to be getting an income of £1 a week for every £500 of capital above £6000. That rate of interest is far above what is available commercially. To get the amount of income which would be above the minimum considered acceptable by the government (£102.10), the capital would need to amount to £71,406.67 (using an interest rate of 4.5 per cent and assuming no tax charge – which may be difficult on such a relatively large sum). This still does not allow for the person to reinvest interest to maintain the real value of the capital after inflation.

17. Letter to David Willetts, 13 October 2003, released to the press.

18. Telephone conversation with Alison O'Connell, Director of the Pensions Policy Institute, October 2003.

19. This means that statistics about wealth inequality being extreme in modern times are a completely unreliable guide to the realities of life. The lower paid have every reason not to save. Therefore their lack of savings does not necessarily – or probably – reflect inability to save, let alone 'poverty'. It reflects, at least partially, the incentives put in their way by government to avoid saving.

20. Clark, Tom and Emmerson, Carl, 'The Tax and Benefit System and the Decision to Invest in a Stakeholder Pension' (Institute for Fiscal Studies, Briefing Note 28, 2002)

21. Ibid.

22. Nicholas Timmins, *Financial Times*, 22 October 1999.

23. It is a powerful illustration of how statistics on wealth can be misleading. Banks, James et al., 'The Distribution of Financial Wealth in the UK: Evidence from 2000 BHPS Data' (Institute of Fiscal Studies, Working Paper WP02/21, 2002).

24. The exception is the means test for long-term care for the elderly.

25. Halsey and Webb, *Twentieth-century British Social Trends*, p. 342.

26. Ibid.

27. Social Trends 2003 (The Stationery Office, London, 2003), p. 118.

28. Women spend £685 a year on drink and eating out compared to £530 on pensions. Figures from Axa, *Daily Telegraph*, 19 December 2003.

29. Nicholas Timmins, *Financial Times*, 22 October 1999.

30. 'The Old Man and His Grandson' in *The Fairy Tales of the Brothers Grimm* (Constable, London, 1909).

31. Young, Michael and Willmott, Peter, *Family and Kinship in East London* (Pelican, Harmondsworth, 1962).

32. John Macnicol, *The Politics of Retirement in Britain 1878–1948* (Cambridge University Press, Cambridge, 1998); Department for Work and Pensions for latest figure.

33. Smeaton, Deborah and McKay, Stephen, *Working after State Pension Age: Quantitative Analysis* (Department for Work and Pensions, Research Report 182, 2003)

34. Disney, Richard and Tanner, Sarah, 'The Abolition of the Earnings Rule for UK Pensioners' (Institute of Fiscal Studies, Working Paper WP00/13, 2000)

35. Smeaton and McKay, *Working after State Pension Age*.

36. Banks, James et al., 'Retirement, Pensions and the Adequacy of Saving: A Guide to the Debate' (Institute for Fiscal Studies, Briefing Note 29, 2002).

37. £1,113 billion is the estimated national income for 2003, using the figure of £1,063 billion for 2002 in the National Statistics Online Time Series Data and increasing it by the GDP growth forecast to be 2.0 per cent and the RPI increase 2.7 per cent in 2003 according to outside forecasters as shown on the HM Treasury website in October 2003. The number of economically active people was 29.2 million in 2002 according to Social Trends 2003.

38. 27 September 2003.

39. *The Economist*, 27 September 2003.

40. Public-sector workers currently have to work 37.5 years to qualify for full benefits. By 2020 they will have to work 4.25 more years. 'Pension Reform 2003', Global News Briefs, Watson Wyatt website, August 2003.

41. *The Economist*, 27 September 2003.

42. Quoted in National Center for Policy Analysis daily policy digest 28 May 2003, from website.

43. For more details on the growth of friendly societies, see Chapter 2.

44. Nowadays it is called Pilgrim Homes.

45. Quoted in Macnicol, *Politics of Retirement in Britain*.

46. Serres, Alain de and Pelgrin, Florian, 'The Decline in Private Saving Rates in the 1990s in OECD Countries: How Much Can Be Explained by Non-wealth Determinants?' (OECD, Economics Working Paper 344, 2002), p. 35.

47. *Hong Kong Yearbook 2003* (Hong Kong Special Administrative Region Government, Hong Kong, 2003).

48. The overall savings rate includes, for example, savings made by investing in a private business, which may not be included in figures for purely household saving.

Chapter 8 Tax and Growth

1. *Hoover Digest*, 1998, no. 3.

2. BOAC was a British long-distance airline, which was later nationalised and subsumed into British Airways.

3. I tried to check it and much else besides. As part of my research he was telephoned at his home in St Andrews – where he remains a member of the Royal and Ancient Golf Club. But he declined to be interviewed.

4. Much of the research on Sir John Cowperthwaite was done for me by Christian Wignall, to whom I am most grateful. The reference to Vespasian is from a talk which Christian gave in San Francisco in November 2003. The remark about Scottish Protestantism was made by Professor Alvin Rabushka.

5. Butler, David and Butler, Gareth, *British Political Facts 1900–1994* (Macmillan, Basingstoke, 1994), p. 335. Prescription charges were reintroduced in 1968 with certain exemptions.

6. Ibid. But the start date was delayed until 1973.

7. Ibid., p. 343.

8. General government expenditure as a percentage of gross domestic product, 1901 to 1998, *Social Trends 30* (Office for National Statistics, 2000), accessed on Office for National Statistics website.

9. Field, Frank et al., *To Him that Hath: A Study of Poverty and Taxation* (Pelican, Harmondsworth, 1977), p. 32.

10. Ibid.

11. Butler and Butler, *British Political Facts 1900–1994*, p. 394.

12. General government expenditure was 42.2 per cent of GDP in 1986. Source: Social Trends 30, viewed on National Statistics website.

13. Social Trends 30. For 1890,1895,1900 figures from *Economic Trends*, October 1987.

14. Total Managed Expenditure from HM Treasury website, 19 September 2003 and 29 November 2005 (Public Expenditure Statistical Analyses). Forecast figures for 2004/5 and 2005/6. It is a pity that the government has stopped making the long-established series of figures for general government expenditure readily available. That is why it has been necessary to convert to total managed expenditure for the final figures. The new measure rarely differs from the old by a large margin.

15. Crafts, Nicholas, *Britain's Relative Economic Performance 1870–1999* (Institute of Economic Affairs, London, 2002) p. 41.

16. The growth of Hong Kong's income compared to Britain's has been jerky because of exchange rate movements but, whichever way you measure it, the outperformance by Hong Kong was astonishing.

17. Many thanks for the research and calculations by Christian Wignall which form the basis of this chart. He used per capita GDP figures from the Office of National Statistics in Britain and from Henry C.Y.Ho, 'Growth of Government Expenditure in Hong Kong', *Hong Kong Economic Papers*, 1974, no. 8, together with various Hong Kong government publications including the Hong Kong Census and Statistics website for figures from 1980 to 2001.

18. Britain was on 32 per cent, the USA on 27 per cent and Germany 32.4 per cent.

19. He suggests that indirect taxes such as VAT are not a problem. Even if this is entirely true, how many leading countries rely exclusively on indirect taxation? Precisely none. As soon as countries need to finance a welfare state, they inevitably tax income and damage growth.

20. Quoted in Edward Leigh, *Right Thinking: A Personal Collection of Quotations Dating from 3000 BC to the Present Day Which Might Be Said to Cast Some Light on the Workings of the Tory Mind* (Hutchinson, London, 1979).

21. 'Throughout the OECD, government spending is now vastly higher than before World War II, and the surge in transfer payments financed by distortionary taxation during the 1960s and 1970s emerges as a candidate to explain part of the subsequent growth slowdown.' Crafts, *Britain's Relative Economic Performance 1870–1999*.

22. Unfortunately the government's figures on tax as a proportion of GDP are not necessarily calculated in a way that is universally considered sound. In 2003, net taxes and social security contributions were projected to be 36.3 per cent of GDP. However, this figure was stated to be net of personal tax credits. Some observers believe such credits should be considered as part of social-security spending, not as negative tax. Amidst the obscurity in which public finances are now draped, it is not clear – except perhaps after more extensive investigation – what the level of taxation is, on a basis that might receive wider acceptance. In 2000/01, which may be before credits became such an important part of government tax policy, tax was stated to be 37.4 per cent of GDP.

23. World Bank figures adjusted for purchasing power parity.

24. Royal Commission on the Distribution of Income and Wealth, date uncertain, supplied by Inland Revenue press office to author in January 1994.

25. Routh, Guy, *Occupation and Pay in Great Britain 1906–79* (Macmillan, London, 1980), cited in A. H. Halsey and Josephine Webb (eds), *Twentieth-century British Social Trends* (Macmillan, Basingstoke, 2000).

26. One can argue that the lower premium for top jobs in the late 1970s was due to the very high taxation of the time, which encouraged employers to use every possible means to remunerate higher-paid employees in ways other than their salaries. Meanwhile the Low Pay Unit has offered conflicting data for relative earnings.

27. Pelican, Harmondsworth,1977.

28. Office of National Statistics, telephone conversation with press office, 18 September 2003. Figure is for male and female, manual and non-manual.

29. To make her tax bill as low as possible.

30. This included pensions, unemployment benefits, state-subsidised education, national assistance and council housing.

31. Op. cit.

Chapter 9 The Reckoning

1. Foot, Michael, *Aneurin Bevan* (Paladin, St Albans, 1975).

2. Full title *The Five Giants: A Biography of the Welfare State* (HarperCollins, London, 1995), pp. 498–9 in particular.

3. Republic, quoted in Edward Leigh, *Right Thinking: A Personal Collection of Quotations Dating from 3000 BC to the Present Day Which Might Be Said to Cast Some Light on the Workings of the Tory Mind* (Hutchinson, London, 1979).

4. 'The English People' (1944), in Sonia Orwell and Ian Angus (eds), *The Collected Essays, Journalism and Letters of George Orwell* (Secker and Warburg, London 1968), vol. 3, quoted in Norman Dennis, *Rising Crime and the Dismembered Family* (Institute of Economic Affairs, London, 1993).

5. The average of 10 per cent of income given by middle-class families, according to a *Times* survey in 1895, has now been replaced by average donations by British people generally of not much more than one per cent (£5.76 billion in 2000 in Great Britain, according to the National Council for Voluntary Organisations, compared to compensation of employees of £553 billion in 2000, according to Economic Trends Annual Supplement 2003. It is not clear whether this figure includes self-employed income. It certainly does not include investment income).

6. 'A major tear-jerker for Josef Locke at the Blackpool Opera House', according to the text accompanying the audio tape of the film *Hear My Song*, about the life and songs of Josef Locke.

7. Quoted in the *Daily Mail*, 23 June 2003. The audience was encouraged to join in this refrain.

8. *Express*, 24 January 2000.

9. Speech at Abraham Moss High School, Manchester, 22 March 2002.

10. Thompson, F. M. L., *The Rise of Respectable Society: A Social History of Victorian Britain 1830–1900* (Fontana, London, 1988), cited in David Gladstone, 'Laying the Foundations of the Welfare State: the Growth of Government c1880–1914' (Libertarian Alliance, *Historical Notes* 36, 2000.)

11. Quoted in Gladstone, 'Laying the Foundations of the Welfare State'

12. Launch of Green Paper and announcement of a 'Children's Commissioner', *Daily Mail*, 9 September 2003.

13. Civitas, London, 2002.

14. He said this in 1976. It was quoted in Leigh, *Right Thinking*.

Chapter 10 If the Welfare State is So Bad, Why Don't We get Rid of It?

1. Searches of the BBC, *Guardian/Observer* and *Daily Telegraph* websites made on 7 and 10 November 2003.

2. I think the key words used were 'baby' and 'death'.

3. Between thirty and thirty-five 'excess deaths' took place compared to other such centres in England between 1991 and 1995. This is from www.bristol-inquiry.org.uk/final_report. But the scandal began before that date, so the number of 'excess deaths' is likely to have been higher. There were also at least thirty children left permanently brain-damaged according to Dr Phil Hammond and Michael Mosley in Trust Me, I'm a Doctor (*Metro*, London, 2002).

4. The coverage of the Laura Touche case shown for the *Daily Telegraph* would be even longer but it seemed fair not to include coverage by the legal correspondent primarily concerned

with whether the legal system with regard to coroners should be changed.

5. It applies in a great variety of spheres – not only ones to do with the welfare state. When the Paddington rail crash resulted in the death of thirty-one people, it paved the way for the effective renationalisation of rail track building and maintenance. The crash had brought into question the privatisation of the railways. But when in 1988 the Clapham Junction crash killed slightly more people, thirty-five, it did not similarly lead to widespread suggestions that the state should not own the railways. The idea was not contemplated, as far as I remember, when even more people, forty-three, died when a train hit a cul-de-sac tunnel at Moorgate Underground station in 1975. Nor was the subject raised, so far as I can recall, when a derailment at Hither Green killed forty-nine people in 1967.

6. Quoted in Edward Leigh, *Right Thinking: A Personal Collection of Quotations Dating from 3000 BC to the Present Day Which Might Be Said to Cast Some Light on the Workings of the Tory Mind* (Hutchinson, London, 1979).

7. Green, E. H. H., 'The Conservative Party, the State and Social Policy, 1880–1914', quoted in David Gladstone, 'Laying the Foundations of the Welfare State: The Growth of Government c1880–1914' (Libertarian Alliance, *Historical Notes* 36, 2000).

8. Roger Middleton, *Government versus The Market* (Edward Elgar, Cheltenham, 1996), quoted in Gladstone, 'Laying the Foundations of the Welfare State'

9. This listing is based on a summary by Barendina Smedley of information in John Hostettler and Brian P. Block, *Voting In Britain: A History of the Parliamentary Franchise* (Barry Rose, Chichester, 2001).

10. Page 59.

11. I should, however, add the comments of Peter Lilley himself: 'Although politicians usually remain terribly sensitive to any criticisms they receive I simply do not remember ever being particularly wounded by being labelled mean. Indeed, my recollection is that the general public (and I often travelled by bus through the People's Republics of Islington and Lambeth) invariably greeted me with the words "keep it up, Lilley" or words to that effect. Moreover our opinion research showed that while the last Tory government's standing fell on every issue, the only exception was "welfare reform" where it rose. That was why Labour had to drop their initial opposition and promise that they, too, would tackle the welfare budget.' E-mail to the author, 11 November 2003. My own memory of the time – and I was covering social security in particular – was that he was being attacked quite regularly on the BBC and elsewhere and that he was, for example, treated as though he were 'persecuting' lone mothers. However it is certainly true that objections to welfare scroungers are far more angry and passionate among the honest poor than among members of the relatively prosperous media.

12. His White Paper on the subject came out in 1993.

13. John Major promised everyone access to an NHS dentist, and Tony Blair did the same at the 1999 Labour Party conference. 'His deadline of September 2001 failed so pitifully that Downing Street pretended he just meant everyone could phone up NHS Direct and find out where their nearest dentist is.' Doing the Rounds, *Private Eye*, 22 August 2003.

14 *Sunday Times*, 11 July 1993.

Afterword

1. Encyclopaedia Britannica 1998 CD-ROM.

2. www.concordance.com. The modern English translation of Chaucer is used.

4. Hansard website search.

5 Quoted in Nicholas Timmins, *The Five Giants: A Biography of the Welfare State* (Harper-Collins, London, 1995), p. 255. The material on Townsend, Titmuss, Abel-Smith and Wilson also comes from this book, pp. 255–8.

5. Mercier Press, Dublin, 2001.

Personal reflections on writing The Welfare State We're In

1. Lord Salisbury lived from 1830 to 1903. Quoted in Edward Leigh, *Right Thinking: A Personal Collection of Quotations Dating from 3000 BC to the Present Day Which Might Be Said to Cast Some Light on the Workings of the Tory Mind* (Hutchinson, London, 1979).

Index